Essays on Spanish: Words and Grammar

Juan de la Cuesta
Hispanic Monographs

Series: *Estudios lingüísticos*, N° 3

Essays on Spanish: Words and Grammar

by

DWIGHT BOLINGER

Harvard and Stanford Universities
Emeritus

Edited by

JOSEPH H. SILVERMAN

Late of The University of California, Santa Cruz

Juan de la Cuesta
Newark, Delaware

270 Indian Road
Newark, Delaware 19711
(302) 453-8695
Fax: (302) 453-8601

MANUFACTURED IN THE UNITED STATES OF AMERICA

ISBN: 0-936388-44-7

Table of Contents

Part IV Word Order

Part V Modality

Part VI Postscript

Preface

WITH CHARACTERISTIC MODESTY Dwight Bolinger introduces this collection of his papers on Spanish as an "empirical study with a minimum of theoretical apparatus," but for those who have been reading and enjoying his work throughout these decades of turbulence in linguistic theory, there is more to it than that. To be sure, one quality that will impress readers of these pages is Bolinger's sharp eye for linguistic detail, the sheer accuracy of his observations and subtlety with which he grasps and interprets nuance.

But Bolinger's kind of observation of linguistic facts reminds us of Goethe's remark, that with every attentive look at the world we are already theorizing; for what controls and gives significance to this "empirical" work is a lucid and brilliant theoretical intelligence. Over the years during which these papers were written the prevailing linguistic theory has changed many times, but Bolinger's has remained a steady and always distinctive voice.

While the touchstone of theoretical good standing at any one moment during these years has been the use of the favored theoretical apparatus of the day, Bolinger has always maintained his independence, and he has often been among the first to point to the logical difficulties of the currently fashionable model. I think od his memorable remark in *Aspects of Language* (1968) that "To think of the surface as superficial is a self-deceiving metaphor," a notion fully developed in his later paper "Meaning and Form." At the time, anyone who objected to the use being made within linguistic theory of the opposition of deep structure was seen by the theoretical establishment as hopelessly untheoretical. But sure enough (*en efecto!*) by 1976 Chomsky was forced to say that his usage here was not as natural as it might seem, and that he had been misunderstood because his readers had not grasped the fact that there were purely technical terms within the theory; and even this stop-gap argument could not prevent the entire notion from continuing to unravel. Dwight Bolinger had been right after all.

Bolinger's independence also has given him a unique advantage as an observer of the pattern of historical events; his dispassionate judgment of the twists and turns of linguistics makes him an astute guide to the history of these times, and there are many acute remarks on the progress of linguistic theory spread over these pages. My own view is that he is unsurpassed as a historical analyst of the field; the historical surveys in successive editions of *Aspects of Language* still seem unique in their ability to convey in few words the essential strengths and weaknesses of each stage in linguistics, and while these demonstrate Bolinger's penetrating logical mind, they also show his fair-mindedness and humanity.

I was to have collaborated with Joseph Silverman in the writing of this foreword, but that was not to be. It was Joe who first introduced me to Dwight Bolinger and his work; this was just one of the many blessings of a friendship with Joe.

JOHN ELLIS
Crown College
UCSC

Author's Foreword

TEACHING SPANISH was my apprenticeship in linguistics. Of my generation, not many who came to call themselves linguists (I would have preferred George Trager's term *linguicist* here, but it never caught on) had the benefit of regular instruction in linguistics, and mine was limited to a course or two in "historical grammar," that small corner of the field dominated by sound change and etymology. The real challenge came when I faced my beginning Spanish students. How could I persuade them not to be put off by the seeming strangeness of a language that was new to them? One way was to exploit what they already knew—often without knowing that they knew—about their own language. The trick was to find the parallels. I had the flicker of a hypothesis—that any phenomenon in any language will have, somewhere in its meaning or structure, a matching phenomenon in any other. We would see this as a rash form of "universalism" nowadays, but my vision was not quite so grand; I merely believed that I ought to be able, when a student resisted something because of its oddity, to say, "Look: you do this yourself every day; you just haven't recognized it," and proceed to peel off the disguise.

Any teacher faced with a "why?" is compelled to test this hypothesis or fall back on the rapturous Whorfian copout that reads, "Every language is a world to itself; accept it for what it is." The sink-or-swim method. Of course we all must sink or swim eventually, and not every attempt to help someone across will succeed. But I think one is entitled to say, "I offer you a bridge; just don't expect me to carry you over it." So there were some modest successes, and they are the main sources for this book, and putting them in one place is the main excuse for it. For instance, why does Spanish sometimes use *de*, a preposition that is plain enough as 'of' or 'from', with the meaning of 'than', as in *más de diez,* 'more than ten'? Think of a scale, and think of the English expression *upwards of*. Upwards on the scale is up from ten, *más de diez,* and downwards is down from ten, *menos de,* 'less than'. The use

of a preposition meaning 'from' is perfectly sensible, and young children learning their native English often overextend *from* to cover 'source' in general.
Or where, in English, is there anything that compels the speaker to rely on the same intuition as for the Spanish subjunctive in noun clauses? There is, indeed, a pattern in English that involves the same choices as the one governed by cognitive versus affective main verbs, 'I suppose he wants it' *Supongo que lo quiere*, 'I doubt he wants it' *Dudo que lo quiera*. In English we are allowed to parenthesize these main verbs when they are cognitive, *He wants it I suppose*, but not when they are affective, **He wants it I doubt*. Having this link makes it unnecessary to try to define the verb classes; the distinction already exists for us in English, even for such a verb as *fear*, which can go either way: 'I'm afraid he already knows (He already knows, I'm afraid)' *Temo que ya lo sabe*; 'I dread his already knowing (*He already knows, I dread)' *Temo que ya lo sepa*. (*I fear lest* embodies just the affective meaning of *fear*.)

Not all students benefit equally from such analogies, and that is why a teacher must be a model as well as an instructor. But aside from their pedagogical value they have an intrinsic interest: we do well, as foreign language teachers, to give our students some appreciation of the nature of language. Like a satellite, the language we teach is a platform from which to view the world we inhabit but rarely see objectively and almost never question, the world of our native language, whose norms surround us and whose rightness in all things is self-evident.

Though what follows was written over a period of almost half a century, I have arranged the chapters not chronologically but in order of approximately increasing complexity, starting with problems of word usage, the easiest ones first, and continuing through word classes, word order, governance, and modality. The collection is in no way a complete grammar of Spanish. All the matters raised have been inspired in the classroom. Most, I hope, hold some theoretical interest; none stray far from the questions that students have asked day by day, and I suspect that few have been, or ever will be, so completely settled as to make these pages obsolete.

* * *

I CAN'T REMEMBER WHEN Professor Joseph Silverman first suggested that there might be a reader here and there who would welcome a collection of my writings on Spanish, whether because they were not sufficiently noticed on first appearance or because it would make for a certain continuity to bed them together between just two covers. I procrastinated because of an ambition that turned out to be unattainable, to write a comparative grammar of English and Spanish, toward which I had collected grammatical and lexical material over many years. The previously published stuff was to have been incorporated in that loftier design. Unfortunately, keeping faith with other promises interfered, and the project never came off.

Meanwhile, my friend and mentor again brought up the question of the collection. Thanks to his generous and timely help in assembling the material, minding the editing, and finding a publisher, the work was done, and I hope it will fulfil its more modest aim: to preserve and focus a body of material that I think still useful. Though the horizons of linguistics today are scarcely what they were in 1950 or even 1975, a reasonably sound empirical study with a minimum of theoretical apparatus should still command an audience, especially if the topic remains an invitation to debate. The last word has yet to be said about *ser* and *estar*, *por* and *para*, the passivization of indirect objects, preterit and imperfect, and other distinctions that conspire against the native speakers of a language that ignores them, who need to communicate in a language that enshrines them. The debates on precisely these topics continue in the pages of *Hispania* and elsewhere, and all too often the debaters proceed as if the question were being posed for the first time—generational amnesia is a prerequisite for discovery, it seems. (For my own confession and expiation, see Chapter 14.)

The most signal honor I could have enjoyed in seeing these pages to print was to have Joseph Silverman's authorship of this FOREWORD. Alas, it could not be. But in a less conspicuous way, his hand is evident here to anyone who knows him. With pride at having been associated with him during two periods of his richly productive life, I dedicate this work to JOSEPH SILVERMAN, my one-time student, my all-time teacher, Professor of Spanish at the University of California, Santa Cruz and lately Provost of Stevenson College, whose contribution to Hispanic studies puts him in the foremost rank of American Hispanists.

DWIGHT BOLINGER

March 15, 1989

Essays on Spanish:
Words and Grammar

Part I

Words and Phrases

En efecto Does not Mean *In Fact*

[*Author's Note:* When this note was first written, nobody was talking about discourse particles, those small additaments that are not part of the message but whose function is to situate audience or speaker in some desired way TOWARD the message, things like *well, all things considered, oh, pues bien, por si acaso, desde luego. En efecto* and *in fact* are discourse particles. They are also false friends, and dictionaries have equated them in spite of their difference in function: *en efecto* gives you your money's worth, *in fact* gives you more. I had the distinction right, but it took the genius of Gerald Sullivan to come up with the exact English equivalent for *en efecto.* It is *sure enough,* as in *I said it was going to rain, and sure enough it rained* (compare *I said it was going to rain—in fact, it poured*).

The Williams dictionary of 1963 picked this up and gave *sure enough* as the translation of *en efecto.* The Collins of 1971 and the Heritage-Larousse of 1986 have gone back to the old mistake. Habits die hard.

Discourse particles are a maze of delicacy. Is there one, unlike *in fact,* that looks down instead of up? My feeling is that *in actual fact* or *the fact is that* would tend in that direction: *I thought he was just moderately well off but in fact he was a millionaire, I thought he was a millionaire but the fact was that he was just moderately well off.* I leave it to the reader's amusement to ascertain whether *en realidad* or *el hecho es que* embodies some such form of downplaying.]

* * *

AS WRITERS OF BOOKS for teaching Spanish, we have vast resources of imitativeness.[1] Anyone who wishes to prove this may do so by citing the apparently indestructible error of coupling *en efecto* and its synonym *efectivamente* with *in fact* and its synonyms *actually, really, in truth,* and *as a matter of fact*. Of the twenty-odd readers and grammars that I have close at hand, the majority contain *en efecto* or *efectivamente* in their vocabularies (which testifies to its importance), and except for a couple of instances of the ambiguous *indeed,* the only equivalents offered are the ones that I have listed. One of those volumes, I humbly confess, is mine.

The dictionaries are equally at fault. Velázquez and Cuyás make the false equation in both directions. The Chicago dictionary and the War Department technical manual give a better account of themselves from English to Spanish (with *en realidad*), but in the opposite direction they revert to the old formula.

En efecto and *in fact* are among those peculiar expressions which, though near-synonyms, are not interchangeable. This is because they are used not with the force of their literal content, but to show an attitude on the part of the speaker. *En efecto* and *efectivamente* are for 'confirmation.' *In fact* is for 'enhancement.'

To appreciate the contrast, take the example under *efecto* in the War Department dictionary: "*en efecto,* in fact *¡En efecto, no sabe nada!* In fact, he doesn't know anything." Both the Spanish and the English are valid, but they would not be used in the same context. An appropriate setting for the Spanish would be: "Me habían intimado que era un ignorante, y para averiguarlo le hice varias preguntas. En efecto, no sabe nada." What was assumed is confirmed. In English we might have: "I'm satisfied that he knows very little about the business. In fact, he doesn't know anything." Here is more than confirmation, for *in fact* has the trait of always swallowing a larger mouthful than is fed to it, or a smaller one if the enhancement is negative.

Only when *in fact* is weakened by a preceding *and* does it approach close in mood to *en efecto*: "He promised to come early, and in fact he showed up (*or* he did show up) around six." Even this is perhaps enhancement in that it shows an upward revision of the

[1] This article was first published in *Hispania* 33 (1950): 349-50.

speaker's doubt of the promise (note that *in fact* is somehow grudging, while *en efecto* suggests that the promiser was as good as his word); but the parallel is close enough to allow of equating the two.

Actually embraces *in fact*, but includes downward revision as well as upward. Thus we may say "Ten were supposed to come; actually twenty put in an appearance." Here *in fact* may replace *actually* (though properly *in fact* telescopes two events while *actually* overlays a hypothesis with an event). Or we may say "Ten were supposed to come; actually only five put in an appearance." Here *in fact* will not do. *But in fact*, however, will, which suggests that when combined with a conjunction *in fact* becomes more nearly synonymous with *actually*—this effect we saw with *and in fact*. The Spanish equivalent of *actually* is *en realidad*, and this is probably the closest equivalent to *in fact* when introduced by a conjunction; but it is not entirely satisfactory for the independent *in fact*, as it is too inclusive.

As a matter of fact is still broader than *actually*, embracing not only upward and downward revision but implying 'any added information' (often verging on *to tell the truth*, as if to reveal information previously withheld). Since it implies so much more than mere confirmation, it is not equivalent to *en efecto*.

Really is so comprehensive that we can hardly assign one precise meaning to it unless it be that of alerting the hearer to what the speaker wishes to insinuate is the truth. *Really* is too broad for *en efecto*, and *in truth* is both too broad and too bookish.

This leaves us with no satisfactory equivalent, and I am inclined to believe that there is none, except what can be supplied to fit individual contexts. In " 'Usted lo odia' 'Efectivamente" ' or " 'Usted lo odia' 'En efecto lo odio" ' we might translate "You're right, I do." In "En efecto, no sabe nada" we might translate, depending on whose judgment is confirmed, "Just as they (he, you, etc.) said" or "Just as I thought (was told)." The words must be chosen to suit the particular brand of confirmation, and may now be *just so*, now *that's right*, or again *precisely*. If I am right, *en efecto* is like *¿verdad?*, which is seldom the same in two successive contexts, being *is he?*, *do they?*, *has she?*, *could you?*, *etc.*, depending on the environment.

I concoct the following mongrel sentence to show *in fact* and *en efecto* with their relative values: "The preacher expected them to make a donation. En efecto, they handed him a check for a generous amount. In fact, they took the lead in soliciting other contributions from their friends." Here *en efecto* would probably be translated *as expected*.

Neuter *todo,* Substantive

[*Author's Note*: Among the numerous ad hoc rules with which students have been confronted is the one prescribing the neuter pronoun *lo* alongside the word *todo* when used as an object, whether it translates *all* as in *She knows all and sees all Lo sabe todo y lo ve todo,* or *everything* as in *He lost everything Lo perdió todo* (with the alternative choices *Todo lo sabe y todo lo ve, Todo lo perdió*). This extra pronoun is not unfamiliar to English, as we see in the epithet *Mr. Know-It-All,* but it is used a lot more in Spanish, so students must be taught to put it in. It helps to know that the conceptual distinction is the same, and that in Spanish a *todo* without a *lo* simply takes a bigger bite out of the universe of discourse. Dropping the *lo* has the same broadening effect as in dropping the article in *Todo hombre es así* and *por todas partes.*]

* * *

SAYS ANDRÉS BELLO[1], speaking of *todo,* substantive, "cuando sirve de complemento acusativo le agregamos *lo,* que es otro neutro en complemento acusativo." Salvá[2] is equally positive: "*Estos cuerpos lo tenían, ó, teníanlo todo bajo su inspección,* y de ningún modo, *Estos cuerpos tenían todo bajo su inspección,* francesismo que hallo en Viera." Hanssen[3] even cites an instance where the *todo* is not accusative and still takes *lo,* from Blasco: "La riqueza lo es todo."

---

[1] *Gramática de la lengua castellana,* Paris, Andrés Blot, 1936, §354 (*b*). This article was first printed in *Hispania* 28 (1945): 78-80.

[2] *Gramática de la lengua castellana,* Paris, Garnier, 1854, p. 144.

[3] *Gramática histórica de la lengua española,* Halle v. S., 1913, §557.

Lenz[4] essays a historical explanation: "En cuanto a la construcción particular del español *'Dios lo sabe todo,'* creo que se habrá formado según el modelo de frases con complemento determinado, como 'el pan que estaba en la mesa lo he comido todo.' *Todo* indica sólo la extensión de un objeto, pero no el objeto mismo; por esto se prefiere añadir un neutro vago *lo* como una especie de atributo." We might add that analogical support would come from all those constructions in which an accusative standing before the verb is repeated by a pronoun: "Esta máquina la voy a comprar"; "Eso no lo dije yo"; "Todo lo perdió." But *todo* extends this to virtually insisting upon the redundant pronoun whether *todo* itself stands before or after the verb: "Todo lo perdió" and "Lo perdió todo." Note, as a point to be developed further on, that the neuters not admitting of any *lo* at all are the really indeterminate ones, *algo* and *nada*: "Algo hizo," but "Eso lo hizo."

But analogy, while it suffices to explain the origin, hardly suffices to explain the vitality of *todo . . . lo* and *lo . . . todo*. It also leaves us in the dark as to why the pronoun was not extended to other substantive positions: "Todo está bien" might be expected to give "Todo ello está bien" and "Está listo para todo" to give "Está listo para ello todo" as required constructions. Ramsey[5] rationalizes the *lo* as having been added in the accusative construction in order to show that *todo* is accusative, to clear up, for example, the doubt that would attach to "Una diversión que todo me lo hace olvidar" if no *lo* were present. But this can hardly be so, since in other constructions the *lo* may have the opposite effect—making them ambiguous instead of clearing them up; thus "Todo me lo dice" makes sense as 'Everything tells me so' or as 'He tells it all to me.'

The survival of the *lo*, if not its origin, is, I think, to be explained on other grounds. The greatest survival value in any tool attaches to usefulness. Is the *lo* useful? Yes, if it is meaningful. In order to test its usefulness we may inquire what difference in meaning is to be found between using and not using a redundant pronoun. It is somewhat difficult to compare "Está listo para todo," which does not use the

[4] *La oración y sus partes*, Madrid, 1920, §101.
[5] *Text Book of Modern Spanish*, New York, Holt, §611.

redundant pronoun, with "Lo sabemos todo," which does, since the constructions are not parallel. This leaves us at the disadvantage of seeking accusative constructions without the *lo,* which are so few that the comparison will seem unbalanced. We may make it, however, and then inquire whether on the basis of the comparison itself, some explanation of the fewness may be found.

Such constructions without *lo* do exist, despite the assertions of Bello and Salvá. Hanssen[6] cites Blest as saying "Sabemos todo." Other possibilities are "Yo haría todo por él," "Es muy desgraciado, porque ha perdido todo," and "Êl río ha desbordado por los campos e inundado todo."

The semantic difference between "Lo sabemos todo" and "Sabemos todo," or between "Lo haría todo por él" and "Haría todo por él," is evident: *lo . . . todo* refers to a DEFINED 'all' or 'everything,' whereas *todo* alone refers to an UNDEFINED 'all' or 'everything': "Haría todo por él" takes in not only the definite 'everything' that is before our eyes, but includes things unseen and as yet unimagined; it is 'everything' in the sense of 'anything' or 'everything whatever.' "Lo haría todo por el," on the other hand, refers to a previously defined 'everything,' such as 'everything we have discussed' or 'everything that we can see has to be done.' It is the English *it all* (although *it all* is even more definite than *lo. . . todo,* as may be seen when we try to use it to translate "Lo compro todo").

Returning to Lenz's remark about the *lo* as the true complement, with the *todo* as a sort of "attribute," we see that he might have gone farther and considered *todo* to be here what it is most of the time in other positions: an adjective. The error in analysis on the part of the other grammarians resulted, no doubt, from wanting to regard neuter *todo* as always a substantive. It is probably more consistent to regard the *todo* of undefined 'all' as the substantive, and the *todo* of defined 'all' as an adjective. With *lo* thus fixed as a sort of determinant, we now see why it does not fit with the expressions cited above, the absolutely indeterminate "Algo hizo" or "Nada hizo."

---

[6] *Op. cit., ibid.*

This raises the question of what to do with *todo* in subject position, in sentences like "Todo me interesa," where the *todo* may be interpreted as defined ('Todo lo que acabamos de describir me interesa') or as undefined ('Todo—cualquier cosa—me interesa'). This can still be accommodated to my analysis, however, by doing exactly as we do when we parse a sentence like "Todos somos así." Just as *todos* here is an adjective modifying an unexpressed *nosotros,* so in "Todo me interesa," when we give it the defined interpretation, *todo* modifies an unexpressed *ello.* In the undefined interpretation, *todo* is again a substantive in its own right.

Since *ello* as a subject is practically never expressed in Spanish, it follows that instances of *todo,* adjective, standing alone in subject position will be numerous. But since the OBJECT pronoun MUST be expressed, *todo,* adjective, will always carry *lo* with it when in verb-object position. We now see why it was thought necessary to make a rule about supposedly redundant pronouns as objects but not as subjects.

We have remarked the rarity of examples of *todo* in verb-object position without *lo.* Is there anything in the meaning of undefined 'all' which would make it rare as the object of a verb?

Transitive verbs have a DEFINING function, i.e., tend to be incompatible with an undefined object. Most transitive verbs indicate an action performed on something, a physical affecting of the thing in such a way that it shows marks of it. The majority of transitive verbs are on the order of "I eat candy," or "I put the candy in the bag," where something happens to the candy. We do not operate on things in general, as a rule, but on things in particular. We move object *A,* taste object *B,* break object *C,* etc. A broad and inclusive concept such as *todo* substantive is thus far more likely to be the subject of a verb than the object of it; this is attested by the fact that general—collective and abstract—nouns (which we identify for our students by pointing out that the definite article is required with them in Spanish) are oftener subjects of verbs than objects of them. ("Bebo café," not "el café," because I drink the coffee I drink, not coffee in general; "el café" here would mean 'the particular coffee'. Verbs which do freely admit general nouns as objects are the non-operational, verbal, conceptual verbs: *to discuss, like, evaluate, appreciate, understand, etc.*) *Todo,* substantive (undefined 'all'), therefore, is not often used as object of a verb, and when so used is probably not, as a rule, literally true: "Yo haría todo por él" is an exaggeration. "Ha perdido todo" is a greater loss than "Lo ha perdido todo."

By the same token, having an *all* as the object of such a doing-something-to-it verb tends to make us think of the *all* as defined. The all-inclusive is as definite as the particular (hence the definite article in both *el hombre* 'the man' and *el hombre* 'mankind'), so that one gets sentences like "Dios lo ha creado todo" and "Ese hombre cree que lo sabe todo"—everything there is to be known, the whole universe of discourse.

Prepositions, however, do not for the most part involve operations, and instances of *todo,* substantive, are frequent after them: "Se opone a todo"; "Discutimos de todo" (this partitive construction is particularly common); "Estamos de acuerdo en todo"; "Es un remedio para todo"; "Con todo, hemos salido bien." The prepositions involving more specific relationships, on the other hand, where a defined 'all' would be expected, are less usual with *todo,* substantive: *entre todo, sin todo, debajo de todo, delante de todo* (contrast the high frequency of non-spatial *ante todo*) are less usual if the preposition has its literal sense and is not hyperbolic.

The verbal identity of "Todo está muy bien" and "Todo [ello] está muy bien" probably results in a semantic wavering. Many utterances having *todo* (substantive or adjective) in subject position can doubtless be taken either way. In this case the speaker would not commit himself on the inclusiveness of his *todo,* just as the English speaker does not commit himself on the should-would of "*I'd* do it if I were you."

Por and *para*

Purpose with *Por* and *Para*

[*Author's Note*: The English preposition *for* covers meanings that Spanish encodes largely in the two cognate prepositions *por* and *para*. Its ambiguity (or perhaps *vagueness* is a better word) can be seen in expressions like *I did it for you* (because of you, motivated by you) and *I made it for you* (you are to receive it), which translate, usually, as *Lo hice por usted* and *Lo hice para usted*. The distinction is hard to develop a feeling for.

This article involves two pieces, one involving *por* and *para* with infinitives and clauses of purpose. The next one deals with a particularly troublesome connection with the verb *trabajar*: How do you work for someone? Is the person you work for the cause of your working, or its goal?]

* * *

POR WITH INFINITIVES to denote purpose is one of the "fine points" ignored by most elementary grammars. Although other distinctions of lesser frequency are taught, the average textbook is content to offer *para* in this construction and omit *por*, doubtless justifying itself on the ground that one way of expressing the idea is enough, but probably moved as well by the fact that the difference is a psychological, subjective one, depending on the intent and attitude of the speaker, which makes it too difficult to teach.[1]

---

[1] This article was first printed in *Modern Language Journal* 18 (1944) 15-21. Thanks go herewith to several of my friends, especially J. M. Osma, W. E. Bull, E. Neale-Silva, and Lloyd Kasten, who allowed themselves to be interrogated

Actually we have been too prone to ignore subjective distinctions. It is possible to analyze *por* and *para* with infinitives and arrive at a clear statement of the difference, one that is readily teachable. Without attempting to make a historical study of how the present usage grew up, let us take the phenomenon as given and see whether the choice of one or the other preposition may be hinged to a single principle.

It might seem that *a* ought to be considered alongside of *por* and *para,* since "Vengo a verlo," "Vengo para verlo," and "Vengo por verlo" are all acceptable translations of "I come in order to see it." For a historical analysis this would be fitting; but in usage *a* is so simple to teach that it may be left aside. We have only to point out to the student that *a* may be used before an infinitive after any verb which may govern it before an ordinary noun (if "Corrió a la estación" is correct, "Corrió a verme" is also correct), apply this to verbs of motion and add that the construction with *a* shows a purposive connection but reveals nothing of the KIND of purpose, and *a* is disposed of. *Por* and *para,* however, cannot be handled mechanically.

The use of both prepositions with infinitives is of long standing. In the thirteenth stanza of the *Poema de Fernán González* appears the verse:

> *Pora* ir buscar un puerco, metiós por las montañas;

and the eighteenth stanza reads as follows:

> A ti me manifiesto, Virgen Santa María,
> que de esta santidat, Señora, yo non sabía;
> *por* í fazer enojo yo aquí non entraría,
> si non *por* dar ofrenda o *por* fazer romería.

This is spoken in apology for having unintentionally broken into the sanctuary of a hermitage.

---

unmercifully on this subject. They are not, of course, responsible for any errors in my text.

One other historical point concerns us: the disappearance of *porque* as a purposive conjunction. Although not entirely obsolete,[2] *porque* has been absorbed by *para que, de modo que, de manera que, a fin de que, de suerte que,* and other conjunctions of this type, and rarely appears nowadays—in fact, it is small wonder that it should have been lost among such a variety of ways of expressing pretty much the same idea. But where it was used, and on the infrequent occasions when it is still used, *porque* versus *para que* with clauses is identical with *por* versus *para* before infinitives. This is easy to demonstrate from Cervantes. *El Celoso Extremeño* is of convenient length for a simple count, and offers, besides, examples of all the purposive uses of *por* as they are usually classified. The examples chosen for consideration here include all instances of *para, por, para que,* and *porque* denoting purpose and modifying a verb or verbal idea. Expressions like "un aparato para matar moscas" are omitted, since a mere noun is modified; but "sus esfuerzos por conseguir su objeto" would be included, since *esfuerzos,* though a noun, names an action. Actually instances of *por* with nouns are comparatively few, *por* with infinitive usually being employed to modify a verb or verbal phrase. The reason for eliminating noun modifiers is that of keeping *por* and *para* to those instances where they might be confused. A good test is to see whether the English *in order to* or *in order that* may be supplied.

The first fact that emerges is the high proportion of examples of *por*. One can read many pages of modern fiction without coming across any examples of *por* with infinitives; yet here there are eleven of *por* to fourteen of *para* and five of *porque* to nine of *para que*. Furthermore, of the total of twenty three of *para* and *para que,* six are ambiguous and might be taken to modify nouns[3]:

---

[2] The *Revista de los Archivos Nacionales de Costa Rica,* May-June 1943, p. 299, gives this in a speech of D. Francisco Calvo, delivered in 1870: "Cartago . . . ha promovido la enseñanza, sus autoridades han velado porque no faltase." D. Antonio Heras said, in a casual conversation Mar. 1, 1945, "porque tenga clases ese buen señor."

[3] The pages as given refer to the *Clásicos Castellanos* edition of the *Novelas Ejemplares,* II, Madrid, 1917.

Ex. 1. "Ellos le pidieron tiempo *para* informarase de lo que decía, y que él también le tendría *para* enterarse ser verdad lo que de su nobleza le habían dicho." Page 95.

Ex. 2. "Compró un rico menaje *para* adornar la casa." Page 98.

Ex. 3. "Dificultaban el modo que se tendría *para* intentar tan dificultosa hazaña." Page 107.

Ex. 4. "Propuso en sí de ponerla por anzuelo *para* pescar a su señora." Page 153.

Ex. 5. "Tomara la venganza que aquella grande maldad requería, si se hallara con armas *para* poder tomarla." Page 159.

If all six are thrown out, *por* becomes almost equal to *para*. Later we shall attempt an explanation of this great frequency, from the modern point of view, of *por*. For the present it is evident that *para* has been the more aggressive of the two prepositions, partially superseding *por* and, in the form *para que* along with other purposive conjunctions, almost completely ousting *porque*. It would also nowadays replace *por* in this example:

Ex. 6. "Diera un brazo por poder abrir la puerta." Page 110.

The modern rejection of por before *poder* seems to be partly stylistic, due to the unpleasant similarity of the sounds, but may also have to do with meaning, in that the *poder* is somewhat redundant.

Following are the unambiguous examples of *para* and *para que*:

Ex. 7. "Y a quien más encargó la guarda y regalo de Leonora fué a una dueña de mucha prudencia y gravedad, que recibió como para aya de Leonora y *para que* fuese superintendente de todo lo que en la casa se hiciese, y *para que* mandase a las esclavas y a otras dos doncellas de la misma edad de Leonora, que *para que* se entretuviese con las de sus mismos años asimismo había recebido." Page 100.

Ex. 8. "Mirad que no dejéis de venir a cantar aquí las noches que tardáredes en traer lo que habéis de hacer *para* entrar acá dentro." Page 120.

Ex. 9. "A lo demás dijo que *para* poderle ver hiciesen un agujero pequeño en el torno." Page 129.

Ex. 10. "Traer a su señora *para que* le viese y oyese." Page 131.

Ex. 11. "Pidiéndoles encarecidamente buscasen alguna cosa que provocase a sueño, *para* dárselo a Carrizales." Page 131.
Ex. 12. "Lo primero que hicieron fué barrenar el torno *para* ver al músico." Page 132.
Ex. 13. "Poníase una al agujero *para* verle, y luego otra." Page 132.
Ex. 14. "Todas rogaron a Luis diese orden y traza como el señor su maestro entrase allá dentro, *para* oírle y verle de más cerca." Page 133.
Ex. 15. "¿Qué medio se dará *para que* entre acá dentro el señor maeso?" Page 135.
Ex. 16. "Les pidió si traían los polvos, o otra cosa, como se la había pedido, *para que* Carrizales durmiese." Page 137.
Ex. 17. "Mas *para que* todas estén seguras de mi buen deseo, determino de jurar como católico y buen varón." Page 146.
Ex. 18. "Hizo muestras de arrojársele a los pies *para* besarle las manos." Page 147.
Ex. 19. "Decían era menester *para que* en sí volviese." Page 161.
Ex. 20. "No será menester traeros testigos *para que* me creáis una verdad que quiero deciros." Page 164.
Ex. 21. "Quiero que se traiga luego aquí un escribano, *para* hacer de nuevo mi testamento." Page 167.

Though not explicitly present in all these examples, there is a common suggestion of "taking steps"; in five (examples 8, 14, 15, 20, and 21) this suggestion is verbally present in such phrases as "lo que habéis de hacer," "dar orden y traza," etc. It might be said that *para* represents *planning*.

The explanations of *por* with infinitive to denote purpose, as commonly given, are the following, extracted from sixteen elementary and review textbooks: (1) *por* expresses 'uncertain result'; (2) *por* expresses 'effort' or 'striving'; (3) *por* expresses 'desire' or 'feeling'; and (4) *por* translates the English 'for the sake of.'

Since these four explanations deal with a common phenomenon, they overlap somewhat; nevertheless, the examples from Cervantes fall under them with a fair degree of clarity. Since they are functionally the same, *por* and *porque* are given together, as were *para* and *para que* above.

(1) Uncertain result:

Ex. 22. "Mudando la voz *por* no ser conocido." Page 109.
Ex. 23. "No se atrevió a tocar de día, *porque* su amo no le oyese." Page 126.
Ex. 24. "*Porque* le pudiesen ver mejor, andaba el negro paseándole el cuerpo de arriba abajo." Page 133.
Ex. 25. "Y anda, no te detengas más, *porque* no se nos pase la noche en pláticas." Page 142.
Ex. 26. "Andando pie ante pie *por* no ser sentido." Page 159.
Ex. 27. "Le volvió de un lado a otro, *por* ver sin despertaba si ponerles en necesidad de lavarle con vinagre." Page 160.

(2) Effort or striving:

Ex. 28. "Vuesas mercedes pugnen *por* sacar en cera la llave." Page 135.
Ex. 29. "Su señora les había dicho que en durmiéndose el viejo, haría *por* tomarle la llave maestra." Page 138.

(3) Desire or feeling:

Ex. 30. "Ya me comen los dedos *por* verlos puestos en la guitarra." Page 120.
Ex. 31. "Me muero *por* oír una buena voz." Page 125.
Ex. 32. "Había pedido con muchos ruegos a su maestro fuese contento de cantar y tañer aquella noche al torno, *porque* él pudiese cumplir la palabra que había dado de hacer oír a las criadas una voz extremada." Page 126.
Ex. 33. "Esperando Loaysa con gran deseo la venidera [noche] *por* ver si se le cumplía la palabra prometida de la llave." Page 138.
Ex. 34. "Mas *porque* todo el mundo vea el valor de los quilates de la voluntad y fe con que te quise, en este último trance de mi vida quiero mostrarlo de modo, que quede en el mundo por ejemplo." Page 167.

Example 6, above, also belongs in this class.

(4) 'For the sake of':

Ex. 35. "Y así pasaba el tiempo con su dueña, doncellas y esclavas, y ellas, *por* pasarle mejor, dieron en ser golosas." Page 101.

Ex. 36. "Dijo que haría lo que su buen discípulo pedía, sólo *por* darle gusto, sin otro interés alguno." Page 126.

But such a four-way classification, besides missing the common principle that binds all four together, is not sufficiently definite to rule out *para*. The student can readily find or invent examples with *para* that appear to show the same traits: thus in "He reservado este dinero *para* comprar la casa" the result is uncertain, since the owner may refuse to sell (only by carefully explaining that the certainty or uncertainty is subjective, in the mind of the speaker, can this be obviated—but most textbooks leave it undefined); in "Está trabajando de firme *para* graduarse el año que viene" there is as much effort or striving as in any instance of *por*; in "Quiere demostrar su inocencia, *para* salvarse" there is plenty of desire or feeling. And 'for the sake of' could translate any of these instances of *para*. To add to the confusion, no textbook that I have found treats all four explanations; most of them are content with one or two.

Before attempting a synthesis, let us glean a few more examples. First, those used by the textbooks to illustrate *por*:

Ex. 37. Hace lo posible *por* conseguirlo.
Ex. 38. Yo daría mis riquezas *por* salvarla.
Ex. 39. Luchando *por* entrar.
Ex. 40. Hacía esfuerzos *por* mostrarse disgustado.
Ex. 41. Luchó con furia *por* desasirse.
Ex. 42. Pasó veinte años esforzándose *por* aclarar el misterio.
Ex. 43. Se desviven *por* aventajar a sus vecinas.
Ex. 44. Me volví *por* verlo.

Now from miscellaneous sources:

Ex. 45. "Fué tanto lo que el pastor la aborreció . . . que, *por* no verla, se quiso ausentar de aquella tierra." Cervantes, *Don Quixote*, Part 1, Chapter 20.

Ex. 46. "Algún mal encantador de estos que él dice que le quieren mal la habrá mudado la figura, *por* hacerle mal y daño." *Ibid.*, Part 2, Chapter 10.

Ex. 47. "Si sabes que estoy muriendo *Por* / dar la mano a don Mendo." Ruiz de Alarcón, *Las Paredes Oyen*, Line 432.

Ex. 48. "Yo, que siempre oí decir: 'Dime con quién andas y diréte quién eres,' *por* ir con buena compañía puse el pie en el umbral del camino." Quevedo, *Las Zahuradas de Plutón.*

Ex. 49. "Lleguéme más cerca *por* oírlos." *Ibid.*

Ex. 50. "No te interrogué *por* saber tu intención . . . , sino *por* oírte las bonitas promesas con que la encubres." Galdós, *Electra,* Act 3, Scene 10.

Ex. 51. "Pugnaba *por* arrastrarme consigo." Bécquer, *La Cruz del Diablo.*

Let us now unravel certain common elements from among all the foregoing examples of *por,* considering the four rules given above as the first four:

(5) The action introduced by *por* is of more than usual importance.
(6) The governing verb or phrase oftener than not indicates a broad and general action rather than a single, specific one.
(7) Instances of *por no* are especially frequent.
(8) The notion of "satisfaction" is present with *por,* absent with *para.*
(9) The governing action is personal; such a construction as "Es necesario para demostrarlo" (the English here would admit 'for the sake of'!) would not call for *por.*

One more factor that must be taken into account is the fundamental use of *por* to show causation, as in "*Por* ser tan viejo no quería acompañar a los jóvenes," or in this from Valdés,[4] "Ni *por* sacurdirle fuertemente por el brazo ni *por* dirigirle los insultos más groseros fué posible que cerrase la boca."

This use of *por* as a sign of causation supplies, I believe, the key to the problem. When do actions constitute causes, in the individual, of other actions that seem to precede them in time? When they operate as UNDERLYING MOTIVES or INCENTIVES. In saying "Vengo *para* verlo" I imply that I AIM to see him; but with "Vengo *por* verlo" I imply that I AM MOVED to see him. With *para* one makes a conscious and deliberate choice, plans, takes steps; with *por* one acts to satisfy some

[4] "Impresiones Musicales" in *La Novela de un Novelista.*

felt need, very often some need of the organism as a whole. Hence the implication, with "Vengo por verlo," that 'I need to see him.'

An analysis of purposes always reveals a point beyond which one cannot go, a point where "you do it just because you do it," where the question "why?" ceases to elicit information but elicits instead a rationalization or just irritation. I refer to introspective analysis, of course, the kind on which a subjective distinction such as this would have to be based; objective psychological analysis might go on indefinitely. At this stopping point stands *por*. For example: "I took the cab in order to catch the train in order to arrive on time in order to, etc., etc.," can be carried out to the place where one encounters a purpose that is held just for its own sake, as, for example, "in order not to disappoint my mother." This rock-bottom purpose is shown by *por*; it is the incentive, that which makes the chain of actions worth while. To show the contrast in Spanish:

> "¿Por qué le diste el regalo?"
> "Se lo di *para* complacerle."
> "¿Y por qué quieres complacerle?"
> "Lo hago *por* heredar su dinero."

The intent of *por* to designate underlying motive or incentive also explains its relative infrequency as compared with *para*. Modern writing in general, and especially modern fiction, is far more objective than that of any preceding epoch. Where Cervantes was not averse to revealing the underlying motives and inner feelings of his characters, a modern writer would feel that he had no right to act the part of omniscience, and would prefer to let his readers guess at those internal secrets. The temper of our conversations has changed, too; we fancy ourselves intellectual and hard boiled, and consequently tend away from revealing underlying motives.

Examining the theory in the light of the nine foregoing "rules" we find that: (1) Underlying motives or incentives impel one to act even when the outcome may be doubtful; hence one frequently has 'uncertain result.' (2) Great physical effort is most frequently indulged in to accomplish a strongly motivated end; hence 'effort' or 'striving.' (3) Strong feelings and desires are underlying motives (though not all underlying motives and incentives need be feelings or desires). (4) 'For the sake of' is useful in many cases where an incentive is expressed, though not good as a criterion, unless specially defined, since *para* may also be so translated. (5) Underlying motives and incentives always loom with particular urgency or importance. (6) They impel to more than one individual act; hence the frequency of broad and general action. (7) *Por no;* 'in order not to,' is the verbal formula that we use to express the many inhibitions that living with fellow human beings imposes upon us, and which operate as negative incentives—'in order not to create a wrong impression,' 'in order not to give cause for gossip,' 'in order not to wake you.' More generally, it is used for those actions which, if they are not avoided, will bring unpleasant results; avoidance thus becomes a strong incentive. But if the negative is really but a substitute for an affirmative verb, *para* is called for: "Me di prisa para no perder (=para coger) el tren"; "Hurté el cuerpo para no ser cogido (=para escaparme)"; "Se abrazó al cuello del alcalde para no caerse (=para sostenerse)."[5] (8) Underlying motives and incentives, being felt needs, impel to the satisfaction of those needs. (9) The personal reference obviously has to be specific, since the attitude of the individual psyche is what determines the choice of *por.*

So the theory appears to stand the test, and represents, I believe, a true synthesis.

If called upon to set up a textbook rule, one might say: "*Por* and *para* are both used with infinitives to designate purpose. *Para,* in keeping with its fundamental notion of *direction,* shows the *aim* of an action and is always conscious and deliberate. *Por,* in keeping with its fundamental notion of *cause,* shows the *underlying motive* which is felt as an incentive or need that must be satisfied. Depending on the attitude of the speaker, either may be used in most expressions; but *para* is more frequent than *por,* since we reveal our aims more often than our underlying motives."

---

[5] Escrich, *Fortuna,* Chapter 4.

Trabajar para

VENTURING A DISPUTE with a native speaker on a question of usage is treading on quicksand.[1] The danger is less if native speakers themselves disagree and one can assume the guise of arbitrator. If some practical translation problem is involved, the risk may have to be run. There is such a problem in the translation of *to work for*, about which Gerardo Sáenz comments interestingly in *Hispania* (September 1963, pp. 616-617). According to Mr. Sáenz, *trabajar para* suggests a menial or sacrificial status on the part of the worker. A check with native speakers of Spanish suggests that this is often true, and the following citations seem to bear it out:

"...su decisíon irrevocable de seguirla a dondequiera que fuese, trabajando y viviendo para ella"—Antonio Heras, *El laberinto de los espejos*, p. 117 (Madrid 1928).

"...indios que trabajaran para ellos"—Américo Castro, *Iberoamérica*, p. 83 (New York 1946).

"Rafael Díaz Balart (ex-cuñado de Castro)... trabajó para Batista hasta el final"—*Cuadernos* No. 49, p. 23.

"Están dispuestos a trabajar para usted"—Mexican film "Qué Lindo Es Michoacán."

Funangué, the Prime Minister of Uganga, lays down the law to Paradox and his expeditionaries: "Ya sabéis, pues, viles gusanos, cuáles son vuestras obligaciones. Trabajaréis para nosotros, para el rey, para su respetable familia, para los magos, para los nobles y para los soldados. Nosotros os daremos lo bastante para que no os muráis de

[1] This article was originally printed in *Hispania* 48 (1965): 884-86. This article was prepared with Robert Jackson, who generously connsented to its reproduction here.

hambre." Paradox replies: "Eres magnánimo, gran señor. Te obedeceremos, trabajaremos con gusto por tu rey, por su señora madre, por su familia, por ti y por toda la demás tropa que honra este bello país de Uganga."—Pío Baroja, *Paradox, Rey*, p. 73 (New York 1937).

Yet there seems to be nothing slavish about the following, since it is reflexive: "Son los escritores solitarios que trabajan para sí mismos, porque sus ideas no llegan a ningún corrillo"—*El Tiempo*, Bogotá, 11 de julio de 1949.

The question can be approached in two ways. First, how do the variants in Spanish match related variants in English? Perhaps it is as wrong to ascribe to *for* any more of a universal employee-employer relationshp than to ascribe it to *para*. Second, what is the best compromise for a beginning textbook, assuming that beginners have to be given the gross features and that fine detail is to be filled in later?

Mr. Sáenz does not attempt to answer the first question. His rule for the second is "because in Spanish a self-respecting person does not say that he works 'for' but 'with' his fellowmen, when translating 'I work for Mr. Smith' we should say *Yo trabajo con el Sr. Smith*. And in other sentences where the English preposition 'for' appears in the same sense, one should translate it into Spanish as *con* instead of *para*." In other words, *con* should be generalized, rather than *para*. But is this really safer? Not all native speakers agree. For some, *trabajar con* should be used only for collaboration, not for the usual relationship between employee and employer. It appears that we must look for an answer to the first question before trying to answer the second.

The observations we submit are based on informal discussions with several native speakers from various parts of the Spanish-speaking world[2] in addition to responses (see the end of this article) from six other speakers from six different countries of Spanish America to a set of questions designed to elicit *para* or other prepositions. Besides *trabajar* we included a few other verbs denoting particular kinds of action that can be done for a reward (*jugar, correr, cantar*). The problem is too narrow if confined to one verb.

---

[2] Three from Colombia, one each from Spain, Uruguay, and Puerto Rico, plus earlier conversations.

1. Is "servility" the correct characterization of *para*? Two of the most clear-cut instances are No. X, "Yo trabajo _______ el que me paga más. No tengo el menor sentido de lealtad en estos asuntos" and "Les pago 3.000 por cantar ______ el Presidente," in both of which *para* was favored. Three other native speakers[3] accepted *¿Quiere usted cantar para nosotros?* as normal—one observed that *para* implied a paid performance. A similar example is "si es que las funciones de las bailarinas es [sic] solamente bailar para el público o para los millonarios que tienen yates"—*Ecos de Nueva York*, 19 Oct. 1957 p. 7. These contexts suggest that "venality" would be a better characterization than "servility." There is certainly no devotion in No. X, which is a counterpoise to No. XII, "El más alto deber del cura es trabajar _______ su iglesia y el cristianismo," where *para* was favored in the same degree. An Argentinian speaker[4] offered the example *Trabaja en esa compañía*, which he preferred unless the employment were temporary, in which case he would say *trabaja para*. A Colombian speaker preferred *trabajar con* in general, but would use *trabajar para* if the meaning were to sustain oneself or one's family. A Uruguayan speaker, who also preferred *con*, felt that *trabajar para una compañía* implied being "demasiado absorbido en la compañía."

There you have it: servility, venality, temporariness, self support, and absorption. One is inclined to agree with one Spanish informant, who said that *para* is simply neutral—we would say expresses its normal goal relationships (compare No. IV)—and that other meanings are read in from the context. This does not, of course, rule out the desirability of using *con* for some POSITIVE reason, say to express status.

2. Is there a difference among the objects of the preposition? What about working for a person and working for a company? Or a difference between working for a company that is viewed as an employer and one that is viewed as a place? Or between piecework

---

[3] Prof. Laudelino Moreno, Prof. J. M. Osma, Srta. Carmen Roldán, two Spaniards and one Costa Rican respectively.

[4] Prof. Marcos A. Morínigo, who went on with an anecdote of a dispute in Argentina over whether to say *jugar por ese equipo* or *jugar para ese equipo*. Apparently *jugar por* won the decision, though there was the handy compromise of *jugar en*.

and teamwork? Spanish seems to parallel English with "play *on* a team," "play *with* the Dodgers," "work *at* a factory," etc.

Where the employer is a person rather than a firm, Spanish does indeed seem to prefer *trabajar con* to *trabajar para*. All of Mr. Sáenz's examples are of persons. And here, English has the same preferences. "I've Got My Captain Working For Me Now" was the title of an old Post-World-War-I song that carried as strong a hint of subordination as *trabajar para* could possibly carry. A *with* in this context would produce the same effect as *con* in Spanish.

3. What about giving oneself airs? If *para* is neutral, and hence applicable to low as well as high, do the high require some other word as a mark of status? Among junior executives in this country one hears expressions like *I'm in advertising* (a recent television show twitted this with the remark "If he's in banking, I'm in steel") or *I'm with Ford.* Differing degrees of status-consciousness may well account for the unequal preferences for *para* and *con*. Speakers would be especially sensitive to this if the relationship is person-to-person rather than person-to-company. But the sensitivity can be shown as readily in English as in Spanish.

In short, the best generalization still seems to be the one that is easiest for the student: if English says *work for*, translate *trabajar para;* if *work with*, *trabajar con;* and if *work at* or *in*, *trabajar en*. *Trabajar por* should be relegated to the special treatment of *por*. But Mr. Sáenz's caution about the possibility of suggesting menial status certainly deserves a note, if for no other reason than to call attention to the existence of a distinction in both languages, which perhaps assumes more importance in Spanish than in English.

Questionnaire and Responses

Following are the countries represented by the six informants:
1. Mexico, 2. Chile, 3. Venezuela, 4. Guatemala, 5. Cuba, 6. Peru.

I. Francamente me despidieron. Pero la verdad es que no me importa. Hace tiempo que no me ha gustado trabajar _________ ellos, y la otra compañía me ha ofrecido un mejor puesto.

1. por. 2. con. 3. con. 4. con. 5. para. 6. con.

II. ¿Y cómo no le va a gustar trabajar _________ esa compañía, si lo han ascendido a presidente?

1. con. 2. en. 3. con. 4. en. 5. para. 6. con.

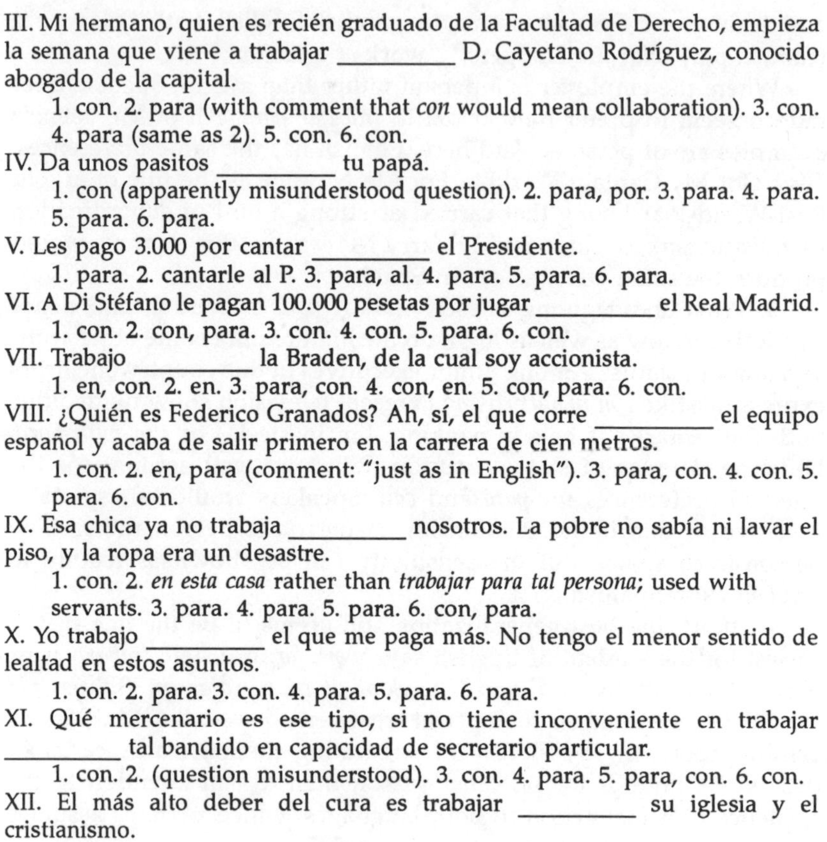

III. Mi hermano, quien es recién graduado de la Facultad de Derecho, empieza la semana que viene a trabajar _________ D. Cayetano Rodríguez, conocido abogado de la capital.

1. con. 2. para (with comment that *con* would mean collaboration). 3. con. 4. para (same as 2). 5. con. 6. con.

IV. Da unos pasitos _________ tu papá.

1. con (apparently misunderstood question). 2. para, por. 3. para. 4. para. 5. para. 6. para.

V. Les pago 3.000 por cantar _________ el Presidente.

1. para. 2. cantarle al P. 3. para, al. 4. para. 5. para. 6. para.

VI. A Di Stéfano le pagan 100.000 pesetas por jugar _________ el Real Madrid.

1. con. 2. con, para. 3. con. 4. con. 5. para. 6. con.

VII. Trabajo _________ la Braden, de la cual soy accionista.

1. en, con. 2. en. 3. para, con. 4. con, en. 5. con, para. 6. con.

VIII. ¿Quién es Federico Granados? Ah, sí, el que corre _________ el equipo español y acaba de salir primero en la carrera de cien metros.

1. con. 2. en, para (comment: "just as in English"). 3. para, con. 4. con. 5. para. 6. con.

IX. Esa chica ya no trabaja _________ nosotros. La pobre no sabía ni lavar el piso, y la ropa era un desastre.

1. con. 2. *en esta casa* rather than *trabajar para tal persona*; used with servants. 3. para. 4. para. 5. para. 6. con, para.

X. Yo trabajo _________ el que me paga más. No tengo el menor sentido de lealtad en estos asuntos.

1. con. 2. para. 3. con. 4. para. 5. para. 6. para.

XI. Qué mercenario es ese tipo, si no tiene inconveniente en trabajar _________ tal bandido en capacidad de secretario particular.

1. con. 2. (question misunderstood). 3. con. 4. para. 5. para, con. 6. con.

XII. El más alto deber del cura es trabajar _________ su iglesia y el cristianismo.

1. con (*por* if it means "sacrifice"). 2. por. 3. para. 4. para. 5. para. 6. para.

Parecer

The Syntax of *Parecer*

[*Author's Note*: Some time before generativists began talking about "tough movement," "raising," and "subject hopping" in cases like

> It is tough to convince John.
> John is tough to convince.

where the second is supposed to be a transformation of the first, I had noted the same phenomenon and labeled it "absorption," using the metaphor of a subject in the lower clause being absorbed into the higher clause. (What determines the success of a label?)

It was clear that absorption, or whatever you want to call it, was no stranger to Spanish, and the most obvious parallel is that of *seem* and *parecer*:

> It seems that John is tired.
> John seems to be tired.
> Parece que Juan está cansado.
> Juan parece estar cansado.

The parallel with English *look* is also noteworthy, and is etymologically closer than *seem*. *Look*, like *parecer*, implies 'by the look of things':

> John looks to be tired.
> It looks like (as if) John is (were) tired.
> *It looks that John is tired.

The starred example shows that *look* has not evolved as far as *seem* and *parecer* in an abstract sense. But *parecer* too has its limits. This first article on *parecer* is an attempt to identify them, historically and semantically. The one following is a postscript to an early (1946) discussion of subject raising with *parecer que* (referred to as "exposed subject").]

* * *

ONE OF THE HAPPIER results of recent turns in linguistics is the search for universals and the emphasis on parallel developments in various languages.[1] How does one explain the creation of a progressive in Italian and Spanish that virtually duplicates the progressive in English,

---

[1] From Albert Valdman (ed.), Papers in linguistics and phonetics to the memory of Pierre Delattre, 65-76. The Hague: Mouton, 1972. An earlier draft of this paper was read at the December 1967 meeting of the American Association of Teachers of Spanish and Portuguese.

Thanks go herewith to the Seminary of Medieval Spanish Studies at the University of Wisconsin, and in particular to Professor Lloyd A. Kasten, for assistance and for making the Alfonsine vocabulary files available for copying. Following are the abbreviations used for citations from those files:

A: Corrected version of *Libros del saber de astronomía del rey D. Alfonso X de Castilla, anotados y comentados por don Manuel Rico y Sinobas* (Madrid, 1863-67).

Cruz: Alfonso el Sabio, *Libro de las cruzes*. Edición de Lloyd A. Kasten y Lawrence B. Kiddle (Madrid y Madison, Wisconsin, 1961).

GE I: Alfonso el Sabio, *General estoria*, Parte I. Edición de Antonio G. Solalinde (Madrid, 1930).

GE II: Alfonso el Sabio, *General estoria*, Segunda Parte, Tomo I. Edición de Antonio G. Solalinde, Lloyd A. Kasten y Victor R. B. Oelschläger (Madrid, 1957).

GE IV: Alfonso el Sabio, *General estoria*, Cuarta Parte. (Vatican MS U).

Jud: *Judizios*, MS.

Lap: Photostatic copies in general corresponding to *Lapidario del rey don Alfonso X*. Códice original (Madrid, 1881).

PC: *Primera crónica general. Estoria de España que mandó componer Alfonso el Sabio y se continuaba bajo Sancho IV en 1289.* Publicada por Ramón Menédez Pidal (Madrid, 1906).

Pic: *Picatrix*. (Escorial MS).

Set: Alfonso el Sabio, *Setenario*. Edición e introducción de Kenneth H. Vanderford. (Buenos Aires, 1945).

when neither French nor German, both more closely related to English, has anything of the sort? It is as if given certain elements from a common heritage, plus a need to communicate the same ideas, common solutions are going to be hit upon sometimes though the element of chance still plays its part.

The verb *parecer* in Spanish and the verb *seem* in English reveal just such a convergence. The etymological sources are quite different. Yet once set on the path toward the common meaning of that which is evident to the senses, their developing grammars grow more and more alike. Though *parecer* and not *seem* is the topic of this paper, some examples in English will help to set the stage:

1. It seems to me (meseems) that they ought to wait.
2. It grieves me that you are not well.
3. I grieve that you are not well.
4. It seems that he is tired.
5. He seems (to be) tired.
6. He seems like he's tired, as if he were tired.
7. I seem to hear a noise.
8. I can't seem to get this right.

The English examples show a gradual personalization of *seem,* starting with constructions like (1) in which the subject is a clause, never quite making the complete personalization that one finds with such a verb as *grieve* in (3) (Mustanoja, 1960: 435), but accomplishing something of the sort in (5) and extending to the point of picking up the auxiliary *can* in (8). All of these possibilities except the last two are shared by Spanish. (The reason why *can't seem* is not shared is probably that Spanish accords the full conjugation to *poder*: it is not a defective verb, and there is no need to move it before the main verb:

9. Parece no poder hacerlo.

is perfectly manageable, whereas

10. *He seems to can't do it.

is impossible.)

As a starting point we need not go behind medieval Spanish except to consider the Vulgar Latin etymon, *parescere,* replacing *parere,* 'to come forth, be visible, put in an appearance', hence 'be evident, be apparent'. The later shift from the meaning 'obviously' to the meaning 'apparently' seems to be common in verbs of this type. These two principal meanings, Number 1, 'to appear' (that is, 'to be visible, put in an appearance'), and Number 2, 'to be evident', both inherited from Latin, account for the bulk of the uses in Old Spanish, with the great majority—probably three-fourths of all cases—still representing Number 1:

11. son cuemo las flores de las yeruas, que parescen e a poco de tiempo se secan (*GE* II 172*b*).
12. et parescio ell en uision a unos buenos omnes (*PC* 450*b*)

Since the affirmative can mean 'to appear' in a physical sense, it is rather common to find the negative in the sense 'to disappear':

13. ua menguando fasta que non parece, assi ira menguando assi como omne (*Pic* 14*r*)

Though nearly all examples are in third person, this is not a restriction:

14. et paresçremos todos en la batalla con armas blancas (*PC* 401*a*)

It is in Meaning Number 1, the primitive 'to put in an appearance', that one must look for the first glimmerings of *parecer* used as a copula. The line of development is exactly the same as has been followed subsequently by a number of other verbs. Clearly, 'to put in an appearance', 'to come on the scene', like the kindred verb *nacer*, which is similar in its syntax, is a kind of verb of motion. In Old Spanish, *parecer* could appear coupled with a verb of motion, e.g.,

15. nin uiene nin paresce (*GE* I 468*b*)

and furthermore, it formed its resultant state ('perfect tense') in the old manner, with *ser*, like other verbs of motion:

16. las que son hy parecidas siempre hy parecen (*A* I 196)

Consequently, just as today we would have the analogy

17. Apareció cansado Llegó cansado

this is how the examples of *parecer* plus adjective are to be interpreted. As with such verbs as *llegar, venir,* and *seguir* in Modern Spanish, one may find the literal meaning of the verb uppermost, as in

18. dizen unos que non parescio mas uiuo nin muerto (*PC* 648*b*)
19. e parescio Maria malata duna malatez blanca como nief (*GE* I 629*b*)

or only a suggestion of the literal meaning, as in

20. los dannos le paresçen y manifiestos (*GE* II 115*b*)
21. quandol tuellen una tela que tiene de suso paresce de dentro amariello (*Lap* 43*a*)

or as virtually a pure copula; this is the usual case:

22. de fuera parece uermeia (*Lap* 54*b*)
23. a cabo de los diez dias uio como parescien las caras daquellos moços mas gruessas (*GE* IV 60*c*)
24. el so uestido parescie blanco como nief (*GE* IV 65*d*)

But the copulative use, then as now, still reflected the active origins of the verb in permitting adverbial complements. *Parecer bien* was the usual combination, but others appeared, as they would today also with *estar, seguir,* and with the other linking verbs except *ser*:

25. todas paresçen bien a los que las ueen (*Lap* 7*c*)
26. parescioles muy bien la tierra dalent et pagaron se della (*PC* 217*a*)
27. e pintan y estorias por quelas fagan mas fermosas e parescan meior a los omnes (*GE* I 450*a*)
28. que parescie muy a abte (*GE* I 186*a*)

The most productive adverbial combination, however, is with *como*. Here we see it as a correlative of the adverb *así*:

29. assi como oy en dia paresce (*PC* 478*a*)

and again as a parallel of the simple adverb *bien*:

30. E bien paresce e como con razon (*GE* I 259*b*)

These *como* phrases rather startlingly resemble the English *to look like,* serving both to introduce subordinate clauses, as in

31. et paresçia como era uermeia (*PC* 698*a*)
32. Acabo de tres meses paresciesse le a Thamar como era prennada (*GE* I 207*a*)

and to introduce adjectives and nouns:

33. parecien dessa part los oteros como unados (*PC* 72*a*)
34. diz que parescien como los cuernos de la luna ante que sea mediada (*GE* II 181*b*)
35. Et a en ella un luzimiento que paresce como relampago o brasa de fuego ardiente (*Lap* 6*c*)

([31] reminds us of the rival comparisons in English,

36. It looked like it was red.
37. It looked as if it were red.

and in fact,

38. Parecía como si fuera bermeja.

would be the standard form today.)

When we try to analyze these expressions with *como,* we are pulled in two directions. It seems easiest to regard them as adverbial modifiers of *parecer,* so that (31) answers the question *How did it look?* with *like it was red* responding to *how* just as (25) answers *How do they look?* with the adverb *well.* Going at it that way, the answer to *How did they look?* in (34) would be *like the horns of the moon look* or *like they were the horns of the moon,* with a *ser* or a *parecer* deleted.[2] But in the other direction there is the pull of the well-known use of *como* in Spanish with the meaning 'a sort of', 'something like'. Here I have to appeal to Modern Spanish for lack of a clear-cut Old Spanish example:

39. Pronto vieron como una nubecita de humo a lo lejos.[3]

---

[2] Example 33 would require a *ser* or *estar* expansion.

[3] From a thesis by Rosa Choplin (University of Southern California).

I have heard the same in English:

40. A little boy could have like a sweater.[4]

Consequently it is impossible to tell whether *como* + noun is to be viewed as having *como* as a sort of indefinite determiner, hence as part of a noun phrase, or whether it still retains its adverbial status. In some cases, context rules out one of the interpretations: in (34), the full text reveals that *como* has to be part of an elliptical adverb clause. But in (35), both interpretations are possible and this brings us full circle back to the use of *parecer* as a copula. In other words, (35) is a link-up between *parecer* as a copula and *parecer* with adverbial modifiers: 'It seems something like a lightning bolt' and 'It seems somewhat like a lightning bolt (seems)' (*something* vs. *somewhat* is this same interchange between indefinite and adverb). We can now compare it with regular noun complements of *parecer*:

41. diz que assaz parescie la gaffez (*GE* I 532*b*)
42. varon paresçio el (*PC* 616*b*)
43. bien paresces tu buen maestro e sabio (*GE* II 25*a*)
44. lo que parecie omne yazie muerto (*GE* IV 231*d*)

To summarize, for the first of the two main branches of the meanings of *parecer*: the fundamental meaning of 'to put in an appearance' is extended, by way of adverb complements as well as adjective and noun complements, toward that of a mere linking verb. The process is already so well advanced in Old Spanish that it must have been under way long before. The modern senses of *parecer* are clearly established, and overlap those of *ser* and *estar*:

45. Parece hombre de bien	Es hombre de bien
46. Parece mal	Está mal
47. Parece viejo	Es (está) viejo

Witness this example of coupling with *ser*:

48. muy mester es que el sabio, pora parescer e ser sabio, que sea muy bien razonado (*GE* II 57*b*)

[4] Overheard Feb. 23, 1960.

We turn now to the second meaning inherited from Latin, that of 'to be evident, apparent'—or even 'to be set forth': the meaning could be as strong as this, especially in the phrase *según parece,* and in references to an authority:

49. segund paresce en estas palabras que uienen en la estoria dela Biblia adelant (*GE* I 627*b*)
50. e paresce por Moysen que fue en ellas e las conquisto con los ebreos (*GE* I 664*b*)
51. pareçe de sus dichos et de sus judizios que a este signo de Gemini dan el regnado dEspanna (*Cruz* 162*a*)

But much of the time the meaning was less positive, though how much less is hard to say:

52. Et quando uino el tiempo del parto parescie que traye dos (*GE* I 207*a*)

That it is less positive is suggested by the frequency with which some reinforcing adverb is added. About half of my thirty-odd examples of *parecer* plus clause have an addition of this kind; *bien* is the most frequently used adverb, but there are others:

53. bien paresce que Moysen part ouiesse en aquellas malautias (*GE* I 534*b*)
54. manifiestamientre paresçio que assy fue commo el judio dixo (*PC* 643*a*)

The meaning of mere seeming is shared with the use of *parecer* as a copula and testifies to the semantic cohesiveness of the verb. Compare

55. los ques abiuan despues que parecen muertos (*Jud* 397*a*)

This fundamental unity of the verb can be seen even more convincingly in the syntax, which is what concerns us more closely, since it shows that the amalgamation of *parecer* and *que* into a depersonalized adverb with the meaning 'apparently' was still in process. In other words, the modern sense of

56. Parece que han llegado = Por lo visto han llegado

which can be compared to the English

57. Seems like they've arrived,
58. They've arrived, seems like (it seems)

(the postposition is a pretty sure sign of adverbialization), had not yet completely jelled. The best evidence is in examples of the 'to be apparent' meaning not tied to *que*:

59. e paresce por las palabras dont es este nombre conpuesto (*GE* II 204*b*)

'one can tell (it is apparent) by the words what this name is composed of'. Realizing this, we have to take a second look at some of those reinforcing adverbs that were mentioned earlier. It is significant that they may go either before or after *parecer*. When they go before, they suggest sentence adverbs in the modern manner:

60. Ciertamente parece que dijo la verdad.
 'It certainly seems that he told the truth'.

But postposition in Modern Spanish is not good:

61. *Parece ciertamente que dijo la verdad.
 '*It seems certainly that he told the truth'.

Instead, we expect an adjective:

62. Parece cierto que dijo la verdad.
 'It seems certain that he told the truth'.

So, when we encounter examples like the following,

63. nos finca agora que paresce assaz de llano que propheto Sophonias en tiempo de Josias (*GE* IV 75*a*)
64. e parescie ya assaz que era el tiempo enderesçado (*GE* I 245*a*)
65. e esto diz que paresce mucho en que por aquellos mismos nombres usan dellas los texedores en Persia que en Francia (*GE* I 568*a*)

it is to be assumed that the construction is not that of modern *parecer*, but that of modern *constar*:

66. Consta claramente que ha mentido.

Though I have no evidence for it, most likely an inversion would have been possible that today is most unlikely:

67. Que profetara Sofonias parece assaz de llano.

in view of the possibility of this with *constar*, though the effect is somewhat *rebuscado*:

68. Que haya mentido consta bien ciertamente.
'That he lied stands out quite definitely'.

To sum up: *Parece* + adverb + *que* suggests that *parecer* was still felt as an active verb. An expression on the order of *It seems quite definite that he did it* was rather to be interpreted as *It shows up quite definitely that he did it.*

We come now to the most complex step in the evolution of *parecer*, the one that has led to personal subjects and infinitive complements like the modern

69. Ellos parecen haber perdido el dinero.
'They seem to have lost the money'.

Infinitive complements of *parecer* must have been rare in Old Spanish. In the upwards of 700 examples of *parecer* that I have examined, there were only the following three:

70. paresçie grieue de guerrear Calatraua a aquellos que la uinien combater (*PC* 695*b*)
71. quiero y dexar cient moros et cient moras, ca paresçrie mal de leuar moros nin moras en nuestro rastro (*PC* 525*b*)
72. Nin paresce bien de apartar se una de tantas (*GE* II 141*a*)

I have referred to these as complements, but of course they were not that really; instead, they were infinitive phrases introduced by *de* and used, here, as subjects. A similar instance as an object is the following:

73. et por que era Mars so hermano, no tenie el por guisado de trabaiar se de matar le..., touo por meior de callar se (*GE* II 202*b*)

This usage with *de* persisted through the sixteenth century. Keniston (1937: 513) comments, 'the infinitive with a preposition, particularly *de*, can serve in the sentence any purpose which might be served by the simple infinitive." A few relics survive today; Seco (1962: 188) cites *Me pesa de haberos ofendido. Haber de,* of course, preserves the object infinitive with *de,* now stereotyped.

How might the personalization have come about? Eventually the *de* had to be lost, to bring *parecer* in line with *soler, poder, deber,* which of course already had thing-or-person subjects:

74. cuemo suelen fazer las cozinas (*GE* II 257*b*)

But personalization with some other constructions could have begun at an earlier period even with a *de* present. It probably happened in the *difícil de hacer* type of phrase through a semantic reinterpretation that assigns the same adjective to a person or thing as to the action that it performs or that is performed on it: if a man who does a bad action is a bad man, then if it is tough to convince a man, the man is tough to convince (it is nice to see the man, the man is nice to see, etc.). This would have been helped along in Spanish by the relatively free word order. If we take

75. Es difícil de hacer el trabajo.
'It is difficult to do the work'.

and begin to think of *trabajo* as a postposed subject, which of course it is free to be, then nothing prevents it from being moved 'back' to the front of the sentence:

76. El trabajo es difícil de hacer.
'The work is difficult to do'.

Meanwhile, the loss of the *de* enabled the infinitive to pick up the original meaning and this differentiated the two senses:

77. Es difícil hacer el trabajo.
'It is difficult to do the work'.

To avoid the problem of *de,* the personalization of *parecer* plus infinitive must have leaned on some kind of prior personalization of *parecer* with *que.* One other obstacle, that almost required that this route be taken, was—and is—the impossibility in Spanish of having a truly complementary infinitive that carries its own explicit subject in nominative form. We can have this in prepositional phrases, e.g.,

78. para yo hacerlo
'for me to do it'

but not in complements of verbs—and it makes no difference whether the verb taking the complement is transitive or intransitive, i.e., whether the infinitive is a grammatical subject or a grammatical object:

79. *Sería imposible hacerlo él.
'It would be impossible for him to do it.'
80. *Odio hacerlo tú.
'I hate for you to do it.'

So even with the loss of *de* before infinitives, there was no way for *parecer* to be personalized directly, since one could not get complement structures like

81. *Parece creerlo él.
'It seems likely for him to believe it.'

from which to derive

82. Él parece creerlo.
'He seems to believe it.'

But the personalization of *parecer* with *que* could readily occur by way of a blend between the two main uses already described for Old Spanish. Thus, we find

83. departe maestre Johan el ingles que fizo Baco por sos encantamientos a Pentheo parescer que era puerco montes (*GE* II 192*b*)

which combines these two:

84. Hizo parecer que Penteo era puerco montés.
85. Hizo a Penteo parecer puerco montés.

There is a similar blending in

86. el cuerpo paresçe que es ffecho de cosas conpuestas (*Set* 60*rb*)
87. el Monte Etna parece que arde siempre (*GE* IV 180*d*)
88. por quales ellos parescien de mas que se razonaron bien (*GE* IV 202*a*)

One can even find a blend where *parecer* carries an adjective complement:

89. esto assaz paresçe manifiesto quelo dixo Jacob (*GE* I 250*a*)
    'it appears manifest that Jacob said it (this)' +
    'this appears manifest that Jacob said it'.

We find just such a blending today in an example such as

90. El conquistador español no es posible que pudiera asimilar el caudal sortílego del vocabulario extraño.

which José Joaquín Montes (1965: 138) declares must have been felt by its author to have *conquistador* as the subject of *es posible.*

The stage is now set for a switching of the noun clause and the infinitive phrase. Since these two constructions fill the same slot much of the time, e.g.,

91. Creo saber la verdad.
92. Creo que sé la verdad.

the crossover must have occurred with *parecer* as it has occurred with other verbs. A good independent example is *poder*. In answer to the question *¿Quién es*? one can have the following:

93. Puede que sea Juan.
    'That it be John is possible.'
94. Puede ser Juan.
    'It (the person in question) can be John.'
95. Parece que es (sea) Juan.
    'That it is John appears true.'
96. Parece ser Juan.
    'It (the person in question) seems to be John.'

The personalization of *parecer* with infinitive had already been accomplished by the sixteenth century, though Keniston (1937: 505) gives only one example, with *estar,*

97. donde pareció estar el señor de aquel valle

and that in itself is a point worth investigating: were *ser* and *estar* the first infinitives to make their way in, being copulas themselves—a kind of redundant reinforcement of the linking use of parecer?—i.e.,

98. Parece bueno → Parece ser bueno.

I have no answers to this.

A similar personalization with the passive, now defunct, gives evidence of the same incorporation of *ser*, and the same early link-up of infinitive and clause. Martínez Amador (1954: 759) cites examples from Bello and the Academy, e.g., this, from Fray Luis de León:

99. los justos son dichos ser generosos y liberales (= es dicho ser generosos y liberales los justos, = se dice que . . .)

Now for the situation in Modern Spanish. Here, the acceptability ordering of constructions with *parecer* seems to reflect their eccentric origins. After years of desultory questioning of native speakers, directly and through my students, I find it impossible to draw any firm lines. The dilemma is posed by the following two examples, the first universally accepted, the second almost universally condemned:

100. Juan parece haber perdido el dinero.
101. *Yo parezco haber perdido el dinero.

The rejection of 101 I think is to be explained partly on historical and partly on semantic grounds. Historically speaking, if we start with the understanding that infinitive constructions with *parecer* made their way in through the accidental resemblance between an impersonal third singular and a personal third singular, that is, that

102. Etna parece que arde siempre.

has only to displace its thing-person subject in order to accomplish the shift, whereas

103. Parece que yo no soy así.

cannot put *yo* in front without giving a seemingly ungrammatical *yo parece,* we can see why very conservative speakers are apt to dislike any form except a third singular. This appears to be the case. One finds complete agreement among native speakers on third singular, less agreement on third plural and second singular, and pretty general condemnation of first singular. First plural is about fifty-fifty. How the impersonal third singular can still ring in the ear of a speaker today is exemplified again by the verb *poder*. Thus,

104. Juan puede no venir.

is ambiguous—it may mean 'Perhaps John won't come' (Puede que Juan no venga) or it may mean 'John is able not to come, John can choose not to come.' But,

105. Tú puedes no venir

for some speakers is unambiguously 'You are able not to come.' So, with *parecer* the persistence of the impersonal third singular still trammels the free exercise of this verb, both with *que* clauses and with infinitives. In constructions such as

106. Ellos parece que han perdido el dinero.
107. Ellos parecen que han perdido el dinero.

both generally but not universally accepted, the reluctance to accept an apparent disagreement in (106) is just about counterbalanced by the reluctance to accept anything but third singular in (107). But in

108. Juan parece que está enfermo.
109. *Yo parezco que estoy enfermo.

the first singular is rejected by a majority of native speakers.

An example in English, similar to *parecer* in that it too is an auxiliary in the making, is the verb *go*, where, as with *parecer*, not all the persons of the verb have yielded. We can say

110. Go get the paper.

This, the imperative, is the entering wedge, and *go* under whatever guise is now acceptable:

111. I'll go get the paper.
112. Why don't you go get the paper?
113. He won't go get the paper.

But other forms of the verb are not acceptable:

114. "Did he go get the paper?"
115. *"Yes, he went get the paper."
116. *"No, but he's going get the paper."
117. *"I think he has just gone get the paper."[5]

I have suggested that there are also semantic reasons for rejecting the form *parezco*. These evidently have to do with the implied person whose views are presumably reflected. If I say *He seems to be tired,* it is rather clearly implied that 'He seems *TO ME* to be tired', though I might want to suggest that others ought to share my view. So, to say *yo parezco* in most contexts is a little odd, because I don't have to rely on opinions where my own states and sensations are concerned; I experience them directly. This I think partly explains the rejection of (101), *Yo parezco haber perdido el dinero*—I simply would not say that I seem to myself to have lost the money. In this we see how much farther English has gone in the liberalization of *seem,* since *I seem to have lost the money* is normal. But if we compare *parecer* with the English verb *look,* we discover very similar restrictions. As between

118. John looks to have lost his last dollar.
119. *I look to have lost my last dollar.

the first person is less acceptable than the third. If in Spanish we can rig a context so that the person whose views are reflected is clearly someone other than the first, then a *parezco* gets by more easily. Suppose someone wants to put on an air of humility. He might well say

120. Yo parezco vivir bien.

I only seem, in your eyes, to live well; actually my taxes are eating up practically all my income.

The infinitive constructions, once they made their way in, were able to personalize more fully than the *que* constructions. The same conservative speaker who rejected

121. *Tú pareces que no quieres.

[5] Pointed out by Professor Celia Millward in a private communication.

accepted both

122. Tú parece que no quieres.
123. Tú pareces no querer.

A daily newspaper carries

124. Los colombianos parecemos perder los estribos con morbosa facilidad.[6]

There remains one further curious complication. When the speaker actually expresses the person whose views are reflected, there are restrictions that are absent when that person is only implied. Thus

125. Juan parece creerlo.
126. *Juan me parece creerlo.

John can give me the impression of believing it, but—for some speakers at least—I mustn't say 'me'. It seems that the indirect object with *parecer* retains a function which without it *parecer* has not been able fully to assume in Spanish, at least in first person, but one which English has adopted:

127. I seem to hear a slight noise.
128. *Yo parezco percibir un leve ruido.
129. Me parece percibir un leve ruido.[7]

This use of the indirect object appears in Old Spanish (we note the *de* infinitive again):

---

[6] *El Tiempo* (Bogotá, 17 de febrero de 1965) p. 4.

[7] Third person has a choice: *Le parece percibir* 'He seems to hear' ('It seems to him that he hears'), *Él parece percibir* 'He seems (to me, etc.,) to hear'. Actually the 129 type does not for all speakers interfere with the 126 type; some regard 126 as perfectly normal.

130. et semeiaua me estonces que oya yo cerca mi gemidos cuemo de omnes que se muriessen; et maguer que digo yo que me parescia en semeiança de oyr lo, digo que lo oy (*GE* II 139*b*).[8]

When the indirect object is given, there is a strong inclination to take the following infinitive as having the same subject:

131. Me parece estar (yo) a su lado.
132. Nos parece escuchar (nosotros) su voz como si viviese todavía.

and if another subject is given, some speakers at least will reject:

133. ?Me parece existir una duda acerca de ese relato.

The grammar of *parecer* reveals two specializations. The first, probably not yet accomplished in the Middle Ages much beyond the same stage exhibited by *nacer* and other verbs of motion, is that of a copula (though probably it took noun complements more freely than other verbs of its type, as in [41-44]). Today this is complete, with *parecer* admitting the same kind of complementation, or lack of it, as *ser* or *estar*:

134. ¿Está enfermo?—Sí, lo parece (~ lo está.).
135. ¿Está enfermo?—Sí parece (~ sí está).

which cannot be done with, e.g., *seguir*:

136. ¿Está enfermo?—Sí, sigue enfermo.
137. ¿Está enfermo?—*Sí, (lo) sigue.

The second is the gradual conversion to an auxiliary, perhaps by way of *parece ser (estar)*,[9] with a personalization still incomplete today. This

---

[8] This citation points to the rival verb *semejar* for mere seeming (cf. *semeia que non ama ella a ellos, GE* II 208a). The situation was probably the same as for Modern French *sembler* and *paraître*. Apparently the translator wrote *parecer en semejanza* here to make sure that *parecer* received its weaker meaning.

[9] A similar incorporation of *ser* occurs in other constructions. **Ser Juan hombre de bien se cree* 'John's being an honest man is believed' is personalized to *Juan se cree ser hombre de bien* 'John is believed to be an honest man', 'John believes himself to be an honest man', the latter meaning having picked up a

development can be viewed as a grammatical accident, in which certain elements amenable to being attached in more than one place have got shifted about. Or it can be pictured as a tendency in language for speakers not to want merely to suffer an action but to assume the role of actor.[10] It probably is a bit of each.

References

Davis, J. Cary,
1955 "*Resultar* 'seem'," *Hispania* 38: 81-82.

Keniston, Hayward,
1937 *The Syntax of Castilian Prose* (Chicago, University of Chicago Press).

Lakoff, George,
1970 *Irregularities in Syntax* (New York, Holt, Rinehart, and Winston).

---

ser from *Juan se cree hombre de bien* 'John believes himself an honest man'. Note also *Nos suponemos (ser) dignos de este honor,* and especially *Resulta (ser) bueno.* On *resultar* and its analogy to *parecer,* see J. Cary Davis (1955).

[10] For the speaker to assume this role fully, not only must the verb be personalized but the action must be capable of being intended; that is, the verb must pass from "stative" to "non-stative." For these terms see Lakoff (1970, Appendix A). The English set *seem, look, appear, act, play* shows this transition in ascending order of strength. *Seem* is virtually always stative, as can be shown by testing with the imperative: in answer to *How can I avoid the draft?* one would not normally get **Seem crazy. Look crazy* is possible, especially if *just* is added: *Just look crazy* (but we cannot be sure to what extent this may be an elliptical sentence using a *to*-less infinitive subject: *Just look crazy is how, How you do it is [to] look crazy*). *Appear crazy* is a shade more likely. *Act crazy* is normal; *act* is freely used for both intended and unintended action (for the latter, *He acts crazy but he can't help it*). *He plays crazy, He plays dead,* etc., is fully intentional. For at least one native speaker of Spanish, *parecer* has already made the transition; for him, *Parece estar trabajando* means 'He is pretending to work.' *Parecer* thus becomes a synonym of *aparentar* and *fingir.* The English analog, as far as incorporating a 'be' verb is concerned, is of course *pretend: Parece estar, He pretends to be.*

Martínez Amador, Emilio M.,
1954 *Diccionario gramatical* (Barcelona).
Montes, José Joaquin,
1965 "Dos observaciones sintácticas," *Boletín del Instituto Caro y Cuervo* 20: 138.
Mustanoja, Tauno F.,
1960 *A Middle English Syntax* (Helsinki).
Seco, Rafael,
1962 *Manual de gramática española* (Madrid).

Spanish *parece que* Again

EPHRAIM CROSS, in his analysis of Spanish *parece que* (Lang. 21.265-7), gives the phrase as an apparent instance of anacoluthon which has become naturalized in Spanish idiom to the extent of being "equivalent to an adverb meaning 'apparently', 'seemingly'." He recognizes that in *El lugar parece que es Salamanca* one may have merely an instance of an exposed subject[1], an inversion from *Parece que el lugar es Salamanca.* But the plainly unanalyzable *Un oficial y un criado suyo, que parece que se van a Zaragoza* furnishes what seems to be proof that something more than an exposed subject is involved, with the result that Cross prefers to analyze the construction *parece que* as an adverbial element in all cases.

Given the frequency of exposed subjects in Spanish, however, I wonder whether that explanation should be abandoned so readily. There is no end of examples on the order of *Juan supongo que se va conmigo, Esos hombres sabemos que son enemigos nuestros, Los otros está claro que no se conformarán, Las naranjas dicen que van a sufrir una alza de precio.* So characteristic is the exposed subject in Spanish syntax that *Las naranjas dicen* does not appear at all absurd.

But the really weak point of the argument lies in the fact that even the crucial example *Un oficial y un criado suyo, que parece que se van* is not unique. In fact, it can be duplicated with any impersonal verb whose meaning lends itself to this kind of construction. The following is judged correct by a Castilian and by a Costa Rican whom I have consulted: *Los hombres que consta que son de nuestro partido son aceptables; Los hombres que se sabe que son,* etc. Instead of *se sabe* one may substitute *se cree, se piensa, se nota, se espera,* etc. So common is the doubling of *que* clauses that Keniston (Sp. Syntax List §42.51) lists as exceptional

[1] This article was first printed in *Language* 22 (1946): 359-60. The "exposed subject" is "topicalization" in today's terminology.

the omission of *que* in the examples *Llama al criado que se supone está en la pieza inmediata* and *Tengo un presentimiento que creo se va a complir.*

As with *parece que,* the appearance of a subject which seems to agree with the verb is no bar to the construction where other verbs are concerned: *Esa gente consta que es de nuestro partido.*

It is even to be questioned whether the use of a superfluous *que* is to be regarded as an instance of anacoluthon, in view of the liberality with which Spanish subordinates many constructions by means of it: *Digo que ¿Como es que está allí?—¿Que no?—Que se va a recalentar el motor* (Keniston, op.cit.).

Perhaps *parece que* is used oftener than other verbs in this way. The proof of Cross's point of view would lie, then, in the frequency of the construction, not in its uniqueness.

More on *Ser* and *estar*

[*Author's Note*: In 1942 William Bull presented his "norm versus change-from-norm" theory of the distinction between *ser* and *estar*, provoking a good deal of discussion at a time when teachers were still talking about "permanence" for *ser* and "temporariness" for *estar*, and grammarians were resorting to some version of the philosophers' "essence" and "accident." Bull held that the choice depends not on what the thing is but on how it is viewed, and was thus able to accommodate a variety of conflicts whereby "permanent" things might be expressed by *estar* and "temporary" things by *ser*. *Ser* was the "speaker's norm" for a given entity: *Juan es calvo* represents our norm for Juan, he is a baldie (William Moellering made a good point about *baldie* being a noun here); *Juan está calvo* would contain an element of surprise.

In my response accepting Bull's argument I simplified norm versus change to norm versus non-norm, or, as we would say nowadays, [+Norm] versus [-Norm], and I brought forward some ancillary ideas including "nature of the subject" and "action versus state," the latter exemplified in the possibility of translating *He was rude to me* with either *Estuvo descortés conmigo* or *Fue descortés conmigo*. Though not touched upon here, *ser* and *estar* with past participles also fit the mold, with their references to action and state.

In the last of the three papers here I come back to essence and accident. As we realize the expressive nature of language we see its overriding subjectivity everywhere, and need not insist on it in particular cases. Even when we strive for objectivity our humors rise and overwhelm it: *I literally sank through the floor*. So if we say that something expresses essence we are understood to mean not necessarily essence in the natural world but essence as we view it. (Needless to say, the natural world is an indispensable source of easy-to-understand examples.) The history of *ser* is too suggestive to pass up the opportunity to make the philosophical connection. It comes from two Latin sources, *esse* (itself the source of *essence*) and *sedere* ('to be seated'), whereas *estar* was originally 'to stand'. The imagery of being seated, added to that of "really being" (*esse*), shows which way *ser* and *estar* had to go. The English metaphor of *deep-seated* paints the same picture, contrasting with the poised-for-flight, up-and-away verb for 'standing'.

The last piece was also intended to make a broad linguistic point: that attitudinal contrasts like the one embodied in *ser* and *estar*, even when not coded directly as in Spanish, are too fundamental not to show up somewhere.And this is handy in the classroom: "You don't have to LEARN this distinction; you already DO it in English."]

* * *

THIS IS IN PART an extension of W. E. Bull's "New Principles for Some Spanish Equivalents of 'To Be,'"[1] in part a criticism, and in part a reply to other criticisms that have been brought forward since Professor Bull advanced his theory. It stays within the framework of the theory, and tries only to expand one or two points which at the first writing, because of the newness of the principle, may have seemed unacceptable to some readers. A theorem that has been long taught develops many approaches to it as different teachers view it in different lights; a new theorem will not lose, therefore, if it is sighted at a slightly different angle from the original one.

First, however, a word in support of Professor Bull's general position of subjectivity, which transcends the remarks on *ser* and *estar*. It is hard to overemphasize the importance of this view, for it touches upon nearly all the moot questions in grammar instruction. Language students are like most other people in wanting a positive basis of choice which their teacher can point out to them in the world beyond their own sensations. What they require, and what too few teachers have given them, is to be made to realize that language, being a tool, is used like other tools—to satisfy the needs of the moment, do what the speaker wants it to do. In tackling the subtle problems of adjective

[1] This article was first printed in *Modern Language Journal* 28 (1944): 233-38. *Hispania*, December, 1942, pp. 433-443.

position, *ser* and *estar, sino* and *pero,* etc., the only fruitful approach is not what the thing is, but what the speaker wants it to appear to be. The fact that speakers tend to have the same intentions gives an appearance of objectivity that inevitably tricks the student into error when he attempts to set up, on the basis of the ninety per cent, rules which break down whenever a native speaker feels like changing his intentions. Objectivity must be thrown out as a final test for *ser* and *estar,* as Professor Bull has shown, as well as for many other distinctions.

And second, in support of the change in terminology. Professor Bull's adoption of norm-change instead of the traditional inherent-accidental is of course more than a terminological shift, but even if it were only that, if norm were precisely the same as inherent and change precisely the same as accidental, the substitution would be valuable from the student's point of view. *Norm* and *normal,* and of course *change,* are a part of the student's vocabulary; *inherent* and *accidental* (as the latter term is used in connection with grammar) are not, and pinning them down to something is another burden in addition to the already heavy load of learning *ser* and *estar.* We have overencumbered our language with professional jargon. Instead of *object-taking* verbs we have *transitive* verbs; instead of *commanding* verbs we have *imperatives.* This is not the least of the vices which have made grammar the most unpopular of academic subjects.

The real value of norm-versus-change is shown, indirectly, in Mr. Moellering's criticism[2] of the principle. Mr. Moellering is right in pointing out the philosophical background of essence and accident and combating the idea that *accident* here signifies "mishap"; but Professor Bull is, I am sure, aware of the distinction too. The trouble is that even after one has said to one's students, as a number of us have done, that "if anybody here is interested in philosophy, he will find that the Spaniards are native philosophers in making an everyday distinction between essence and accident," the class, excepting perhaps one student once in five years, still misses the point. Essence-inherence and accident are objective concepts; they have to do with the *being* of the thing. If then one may choose between "Juan es calvo" and "Juan está

[2] *Hispania,* February, 1943.

calvo," both in reference to the same immutable fact, or between "La madre es ciega" and "La madre está ciega,"[3] one is either contradicting oneself or there must be some factor present which is neither essence nor accident. That factor is the individual's subjective concept. And if in order to reconcile the contradiction one speak of subjective essence and subjective accident, one goes so far from the intention of the philosophers that the terms are no longer useful even for grammarians, to say nothing of students. A further trouble with the term *accident* is that even objectively regarded it has connotations which a modern scientist or logician would reject as invalid for practical use. As language teachers we had better forget about essence-inherence and accident. I do not mention *permanent* and *temporary*, for Professor Bull's article disposed of them, and their meaning is simple and clear enough to need no discussion.

I have said that objectivity will have to go as a final test for *ser* and *estar*. Does it then not enter at any point into the distinction between the two verbs? This might easily be the text for a sermon on realism and subjective idealism, which a language teacher should avoid at all costs. Without going too deeply into the clockwork of the thing, I believe that this much can be said for objectivity:

First, that objective permanence influences the average human being to form a subjective concept that will call for *ser*. Obviously if John is repeatedly observed to be bald, and my exteroceptors are working properly, I can hardly avoid the conclusion, in my mind, that "Juan *es* calvo," But note that the objective fact always works through the concept—the latter is what immediately underlies the choice of verb; if this were not so, people would be infallible in their statements. Given our fallibility, the most that one can say of the statement "Juan es calvo" is that baldness constitutes the norm about Juan for whoever made the statement.

Second—and this is a point that Professor Bull might have added—objectivity may itself be something that we at times wish to verbalize. *Ser* would be, then, to this extent expressive of inherence-

[3] "La princesa suspiró: –¡Yo no sabía que estuviese ciega!" Valle-Inclán, *Sonata de Primavera*.

essence: that when the speaker wants to imply that Juan is "really" bald, he uses this verb rather than *estar*. It becomes a deliberate objectification of a subjective concept. Ordinarily we are not so self-conscious as this in our choice of *ser*—the choice is determined automatically by our inward feelings about the subject; but it is true often enough to lend credibility to the essence-accident view. Note that even here, however, the notion of essence depends upon a subjective intent. Back of the deliberate use of *ser* to show the "real being" of a thing lies the fact that the folk, the makers of language, are by and large naive realists and think themselves capable of getting at the real nature of objects. The linguist, however, is concerned directly only with verbalizations—somebody's verbalizations, that is, he cannot escape the somebody, and it need make no difference to him whether the somebody's verbalizations are accurate and truthful or false and mendacious; he has explained enough by showing that the intent behind the choice of *ser* is that of expressing, for that somebody, a normal concept. The normal concept may purposely be a symbolization of a feeling of "real nature" or essence; it may be a recognition of a relatively persistent trait, as in "Era flaco"; or it may be some other fact which causes the attribute to be regarded as normal for a given period of time. Essence-inherence is only one of many things that may be subsumed under *norm*.

Two other of Mr. Moellering's statements deserve attention. "The concept of inherence," he says, "can not be divorced from the meaning of *ser* by insisting on a necessary dependence of inherence on permanence. Temporary or unstable entities may . . . have qualities involved in their constitution or essential character, hence inalienable or inherent." I believe that this criticism reads something into the theory that was never intended to be there. One may conceive of permanence in two ways: as between the subject and the universe, or as between the subject and its attribute. Of course there are many things impermanent from the point of view of history which nevertheless are permanently hitched in our minds to certain qualities. Thus in "Su vuelo fué un poco triste" the flight is of small duration, but whenever the person who expressed this view summons *flight* back to mind he will find *triste* "permanently" hitched to it. It was not, I am certain, Professor Bull's intent to insist upon permanence from the historical point of view, wherein inherence does depend upon permanence.

The second is Mr. Moellering's own "foundation rule" for *ser:* "A sign of equality, linking two nouns or pronouns which refer to the same thing." The validity of this depends upon regarding the predicate of *ser* as a noun, in support of which Mr. Moellering says that constructions such as "Es viejo" may be interpreted as readily one way as the other, implying that when an attribute has reached the point where it may be dignified into nounhood, at that point enters *ser*. While I would agree that in the case of those adjectives which have acquired dictionary status as nouns there's no point in arguing about the part of speech, I would say that the criterion is inaccurate and that even if it were accurate it would have little value for teaching. The inaccuracy is revealed at once in the clear difference of function between "Es mío" and "Es el mío." *Mío* is not indifferently an adjective or a pronoun in the first of these two expressions, since there, as an adjective, it is used to show an attribute of one object, whereas in the second expression the pronoun is used to single out one object from among more than one. The same is true of "Fue de los primeros don Alonso," a type of sentence which Raúl Moglia and Amado Alonso justly criticize Keniston's classifying as an instance of the omission of *uno*[4]—classifying it, in other words, as pronominal when it is really adjectival; by implication these critics reject the notion that what comes after *ser* is substantive. Since the function is purely descriptive, and parts of speech in scientific grammar can be determined only by functions, it is putting the cart before the horse to call them nouns just in order to rationalize a question about *ser* and *estar*.

Professor Bull appeals to the nature of attributes as a means of determining whether *ser* or *estar* would be used before a predicate adjective. "Limiting adjectives and those the negative of which cannot be expressed by the positive of another adjective are used only with *ser;* the other group of adjectives may be used either with *ser* or *estar*." I propose as an alternative to this method an appeal to the nature of the subject. The two methods are corollary to each other, inasmuch as

---

[4] Review of Keniston's *The Syntax of Castilian Prose, Revista de Filología Hispánica*, v. 4, no. 1, Jan.-Mar. 1942, p. 78.

the nature of the subject to a certain extent determines the kind of attributes that it may have; and the only value that I claim for using subject rather than attribute is that doing so may perhaps be more teachable, or that it may be worth while to get at the question from both directions. Let me emphasize that when I say "Nature of the subject" I mean that nature as subjectively conceived. Subjectivity is as basic to this approach as to the other.

There are three types of subject as I shall classify them: infinite, infinitesimal, and evolutionary. As an example of the infinite we have metaphysical entities such as *Dios, amor, fortuna, santidad,* and other concepts when taken abstractly. As long as these are thought of as metaphysical entities, they always call for *ser*. Thus to say "Dios está" and follow it with an adjective is absurd almost on the face of it. Only when these general terms are referred to everyday experience may they take *estar* with a predicate adjective, as in "La santidad está decadente hoy en día." But when so referred they cease to be abstractions; *santidad* in this case is no longer a transcendent thing, but a type of human behavior. So we may say that abstract entities, as such, require *ser* before a predicate adjective. Since they are, to begin with, pure concepts, nothing interferes with our attributing to them some quality as of their essence. Here, in the purely mental sphere, the criterion of essence-inherence may apply.

I use "infinitesimal" in a relative sense, to describe events of very limited duration. "Su vuelo fué un poco triste" is an instance—*vuelo* is too brief, as we would ordinarily conceive it, to be capable of undergoing any change of concept. To quote Professor Bull, "*Ser* is used to indicate a first impression or a normal or average concept." With the infinitestimal, or what Mr. Moellering calls "unstable entities," the first impression is the only impression that we usually get. We grasp the whole in a flash. *Ser* is consequently called for, unless, as with the infinite, we twist the meaning somewhat. Thus "El casamiento fué muy bonito" would be the regular manner of conceiving *casamiento;* but we might warp it into a symbol of marriages in a wider sense, which would permit us to say, "Los casamientos ahora están menos lujosos a causa de la guerra." Our rule, however, stands: that when conceived as infinitesimal, the subject calls for *ser* before a predicate adjective.

Now observe that verbal nouns and noun clauses will almost invariably fall into the category of the infinitesimal. "Es difícil trabajar aquí," "Es imposible comprenderlo," "Fue necesario que lo prendieran," etc., being actions, are ordinarily too limited in duration to admit of a change of concept regarding their attributes. And such being the nature of most infinitives and noun clauses, they have imposed a verbal habit upon even those instances where *estar* might be used before a predicate adjective according to the principle. We therefore have an explanation for that class of adjectives which Professor Bull was unable to fit into his scheme of antonyms admitting shift of range: adjectives such as *posible, probable, necesario, preciso,* etc. Such adjectives are almost always used with verbal nouns, noun clauses, or nouns symbolizing events of relatively brief duration: in short, the infinitesimal.

Note that the infinitesimal has broad metaphorical uses. In "He was very discourteous with me" we would ordinarily regard *discourteous* as a change from the normal concept, hence calling for "Estuvo muy descortés conmigo." But by taking it figuratively, shrinking the person to the dimensions of his one act, so to speak, we may say, "Fue muy descortés conmigo." In this interpretation we have deliberately blinded ourselves to everything about the person except his discourtesy; if there has been a change we refuse to see it. So with "No sea usted tan presumido" or "Perdóneme el ser tan breve en esta carta."

Finally there are those subjects which we conceive in an evolutionary sense. They are not timeless entities, for they are facts of our daily experience; and they are not mere points or nearly points in that experience, but have duration, a "life history." It is here that *estar* enters in—practically by definition, since only of things conceived as changing do we have attributes assumed to change.

There remains a class of adjectives, including those of nationality (which typify the class), which Professor Bull accounted for by showing that they do not share the range with an antonym having gradations between[5]. According to this rule, one may not say "Ya estoy americano," even though coming fresh from the naturalization

---

[5] For gradability in general, see Bolinger *Degree Words* (The Hague: Mouton, 1972)

chamber, because *americano* has no antonym of the type described. One is either conceived as an American or one is not; the division is absolute. This would be true of all adjectives used as mere labels. Like infinite concepts, labels are purely mental; they do not represent an attempt to form a picture of phenomena of the external world independent of our natures. The change from A to B is one that we make ourselves, like a man's changing his name, not one that we conceive as being forced upon us from outside, with attendant periods of uncertainty. Here it must be admitted that Mr. Moellering might argue that such words are nouns when in the predicate.

To summarize: A subject conceived as infinite or infinitesimal will call for *ser* before a predicate adjective; one conceived as evolutionary will call for either *ser* or *estar*, depending on whether the attribute is regarded as normal or as a change from the norm. No part of Professor Bull's principle is abrogated by this restatement, since the infinite, being "all norm," so to speak, would call for *ser* by the rule, and the infinitesimal, being "all first impression," would likewise call for *ser*.

Still More on *ser* and *estar*

IN THIS REPLY to Luis Crespo's amusing and in many ways illuminating article "Los verbos *ser* y *estar* explicados por un nativo,"[1] I shall try to demonstrate that the differences between Crespo's point of view and that of W. E. Bull[2] (at which Crespo's article is largely directed) are, save in one important detail (see 5, below) merely terminological. I believe that it is important to reconcile the arguments rather than to treat them as rival theories, one of which must be rejected if the other is accepted. This is the scientific thing to do. The scientist builds upon the solid part of his predecessor's work rather than drawing attention only to its deficiencies. In this way syntax can progress to the point where it is the joint product of many minds rather than the particular effort of this or that individual. Bull's theory offers that solid basis. His study is the only one on the subject which manages to be more than a *causerie*.

1. Sr. Crespo's article makes one assumption which reveals a misconception about language in general. His preamble is based on the fallacy that because a linguistic habit is simple in operation, it is therefore simple in structure. This fallacy is apparent in the beginning in references to the ease with which a native can tell when to use one or the other verb, and in the body of the article in the frequent allusions to a native's not having to "solve a problem of philosophy"—implying that if a function is simple, the explanation of the function is also simple. Actually the reverse is often true. The lexicographer finds the simple words—*and, but, the, whatever*—hardest to define without making the definition harder to understand than the

---

[1] This article was first printed in *Hispania* 30 (1947): 361-67. Crespo's article is in *Hispania* 29 (1946): 45-55.

[2] "New Principles for Some Spanish Equivalents of 'To be'." *Hispania* 25 (1942) 433-443. See also Wm. Moellering's criticism, *Hispania* 26 (1943) 82-85.

word itself. There is no function simpler than the act of seeing, and no physiological structure more complex than the eye. The easier a car is to operate, the more complex is the engineering job that must be done on it. Easy as it may be, therefore, for the native to handle *ser* and *estar* correctly, this in no way signifies ease in explaining the difference.

2. Sr. Crespo analogizes *ser-estar* with *shall-will* and *who-whom* to demonstrate the extreme simplicity of *ser-estar*. The parallel is a false one. The two English pairs are RENDERED difficult for the speaker of English because of the anti-popular complications introduced by purists. *Shall-will* is difficult because the speaker of English cannot rely upon his own linguistic habits in order to use them "correctly"; *ser-estar* is easy—for the native—because he CAN rely on his own lingusitic habits. Draw the comparison rather with something in English that has not been corrupted by purism—with, for example, the difference between *make* and *do*, or *of* and *from*, or between the single possessive and the double possessive, distinctions which the native speaker of English finds perfectly natural and easy, but which, since Spanish does not make them, offer complex problems to one who teaches English to Spanish-speaking natives.

3. Too much is made of the supposedly "normal" locutions which admit of *estar* and which therefore seem to contradict Bull's principles. It is not fair to insist upon a too-literal interpretation of any semantic principle; languages are flexible, are constantly being twisted by their users, and, where metaphor enters in, can hardly be subjected to any rule. When Sr. Crespo uses "Vamos a Casa Juan, allí las sopas están rebuenas" to controvert Bull's principle of the norm, he ignores the possibility of metaphor. Of course it may be true that "Las sopas están rebuenas" refers to soup which is normally good. But is it the intent of the speaker to refer to it as a norm? What is the very adjective that Sr. Crespo uses?—*re*buenas: *ab*normally good. The phrase "están rebuenas" is simply an example of hyperbole. The fact that *estar* here is a nonce-usage, to enhance something here and now, is borne out by the readiness with which one may say "Hoy el servicio *está* bueno," by contrast with the much less usual "Démosle una buena propina y mañana el servicio *estará* mejor." If *estar* fundamentally signifies non-norm, then naturally when we wish to picture something as *extra*ordinarily good, or bad, we may use it even though the resulting expression may not be literally true. Bull emphasized the extreme necessity

of construing his rule as a SUBJECTIVE concept. Far from falling down in these examples, it actually deepens our understanding of such uses of *estar*.Whatever the objective facts about the particular soup may have been, the speaker subjectively regarded it as EXCEPTIONALLY good, i.e., as non-norm.

4. While the agreement among natives as to the choice of *ser* or *estar* is highly consistent, it would be wrong to assume that it is perfect. The following *era* from Larra's "El Castellano Viejo" elicited a protest from two natives, one a Spaniard, the other a Costa Rican:

—¿Sabes que mañana serán mis días? *Estás* convidado a comer conmigo. Te espero a las dos....

Llegaron las dos, y como yo conocía a mi Braulio, me vestí muy despacio. *Era* citado a las dos, y entré en la sala a las dos y media.

5. Sr. Crespo's explanation following the example "Este árbol está torcido," to the effect that "En estos casos y en otros similares, creo que no se expresa cambio de ningún concepto normal, porque en la forma en que crecen los árboles no hay norma," is a valid and important criticism of Bull's theory. The theory assumes "norm" and "change from norm" as its two opposite poles; but the polarity would be simpler and more defensible as just "norm" and "non-norm." In this form I have taught Bull's principles. Obviously when one says "El agua está caliente" one does not refer to a change from a norm, since no particular temperature is a norm for water (except in the unusual aspect of water *versus* ice or steam), but one does have a non-norm. Sr. Crespo's example "María está rubia... hasta que le dé por teñirse" is instructive because it shows how the speaker may imply, by choosing *estar*, that for him no particular color is a norm for Mary's hair.

6. Whether a quality will be pictured as norm or non-norm depends not only upon the quality, but also upon the object (noun) to which the quality is referred. It is important to recognize two disparate uses of nouns: (1) as singulars; (2) as collectives, often implicit. When the collective is implicit, it is often deceptive. An example of both singular and implicit collective in a single sentence would be a customer's remark on leaving a meat market: "La carne está buena hoy, porque este pedazo de carne que compré es bueno." The first *carne* is an implicit collective: it refers not just to a piece or pieces of meat, but to the meat-sold-from-day-to-day-at-this-store. The *está* then

comes along and cuts a cross section out of this day-to-day meat. In other words, when *meat* is pictured as a continuing phenomenon, and the speaker has at the back of his mind something like "The meat sold at this store is generally indifferent (or poor, or variable) as to quality," he may then express today's sale as a non-norm (departure from norm "poor" or one of many non-norm variables). In the second part of our sentence, however, *meat* becomes a singular; we refer not to a continuing phenomenon of day-to-day meat, but to one piece of meat. We may picture that single piece of meat as normally good, as we have here, and use *es* (remember that Bull's examples reveal the tendency to treat first impressions as norms). If the piece of meat begins to spoil tomorrow, we may use *está* for this non-norm; or if it turns out to be extraordinarily good we may also use *estar*, if only to enhance our appreciation for the benefit of our hearer.

Another illustration of the singular *versus* the implicit collective is afforded by the remark of a native colleague, who, referring to the circumstances under which a certain thing might be done, said that it might be done by a child "si el niño *está* muy pequeño." Here the concept *Niño* embraces a broad field, in which no particular size is a norm; it embraces either all the changing phases of the life history of one child, or the stages or growth of *childhood* in general, or both. In any case, "*Niño* (collective) está pequeño" = "*niño* (singular) es pequeño." In the aspect of the collective, *pequeño* is non-norm; in the aspect of the singular, it is norm—and both statements may be used of the same OBJECTIVE fact.

Overlooking these implicit collectives enables Sr. Crespo to cite examples of apparent norms which are used with *estar*. In all of them the ostensible anomaly results from seeing double: picturing the noun as collective and as singular at the same time. In "Las arenas del Sahara están siempre calientes" there is an overall concept of *sands* for which no given temperature is a norm; it is as if we had said, "En el caso del Sahara, vemos arenas que están siempre calientes." The speaker is picturing the sands of the Sahara against the background of other sands. In "Usemos este acero porque está más sólido," we have an overall concept of *steel* of which the steel in question is a species or variant. If it were not *steel* versus *steel*, but *steel* versus *wood*, could we use *estar*?: "Usemos este acero en lugar de la madera, pues está más sólido." In the remote chance that such a statement would be made, it would probably be by mentally referring both *wood* and *steel* to some archetype such as *building materials*.

Of course, the reader will object that this is Sr. Crespo's main point—that what I have referred to as *steel* versus *steel*, i.e., as something particular versus something inclusive, is simply the "comparison" which constitutes Sr. Crespo's rule. Granted. And it is right here that we see that what divides Crespo's rule from Bull's is merely words. If we adhere to the principle of "norm" *versus* "non-norm," we accept the inevitability of "comparison," for how is one to tell that a quality is non-norm except by comparing—either with the norm of the thing or with other non-norms if the thing has no norm?

The weakness of the term "comparison" is twofold. First, it does not relate *estar* to *ser* in the neat way in which norm (*ser*) and non-norm (*estar*) relate the two words; for obviously one cannot use "non-comparison" to describe *ser*, in the light of explicit comparisons such as "La carne *es* más nutritiva que el pan" and "El agua de nuestro barrio *es* más saludable desde que nos deshicimos de las moscas." Since both verbs can be used in comparisons, we are back where we started. There is an implied comparison in "Las manzanas que se comen crudas *son* maduras," but since the speaker here is emphasizing "norm," he may use *ser*. Second, "comparison" would, to be accurate, have to be modified to "SELF comparison," for *estar* is used for comparisons WITHIN a given genus: comparisons of a thing with its archetype or with previous or succeeding states of itself. When we say "Comeré la manzana, pues está más madura que la pera," we do not use *estar* because of the comparison of apple with pear, but because of the mental picture of successive states of ripeness of *apple* (collective) or of the genus *fruit*. Sr. Crespo's footnote (p. 55) confirms this, for he says *"esta piedra está más dura que el acero*, equivale a: *esta piedra está más dura que lo que esperaba"*—in other words, the *estar* comes not by way of the comparison of *stone* with *steel*, but by way of the self comparison of *stone* (actual hardness) with *stone* (expected hardness). But how much neater Bull's principle is! What we expect of a thing is our norm for it; a departure from the expectation is a non-norm. In "Estos zapatos me están grandes" the speaker has a size in mind which is his norm, and the size in question violates it.

7. Sr. Crespo's return to the term "state" for *estar* is hardly worth discussing, for the ambiguities of "state" were clearly exposed by Bull.

His return to "characteristic" to describe *ser* is another merely terminological change. "Characteristic of the subject" is no improvement on "norm of the subject," and *norm* has sharper outlines for the student when we are put to the task of selecting a term whose general intention is closest to the special import that we wish to read into it.[3]

8. Bull's whole purpose was to get a unifying concept. The return, therefore, to *ten* rules such as Sr. Crespo enumerates at the end of his article, is of no practical gain unless it adds to the information that was summarized in Bull's principles. Rules 1, 2, and 3 are simply variants of Bull's "subjective norm"; rules 4 to 10 are variants of a "subjective non-norm," which, as I have indicated, is an improvement over Bull's "change from norm." It goes without saying that the examples are excellent, and should be embodied in corollaries to Bull's principles; for, though "norm" and "non-norm" may stand for the fundamental differences, they are by definition subjective and we still need illustrations that will help us predict when the native is likely to picture a quality one way or the other. When all our toil with "comparisons," "norms," "subjective attitudes," and "characteristics" is done, students must still cope with the low frequency of *está pobre* versus the high frequency of *está enfermo*, and other instances which do not involve principles *per se* but rather involve the problem of getting idiomatic Spanish by predicting which way, given this or that setting with its cultural backgrounds, the native speaker of Spanish will be MORE LIKELY to express himself. "Las manzanas que se comen crudas son maduras" is acceptable to the native speaker, who is willing to picture this as a norm; but the parallel "Somos muy orgullosos de nuestra democracia" will probably be rejected in favor of *estamos*, however patriotic the speaker may be. These are adversaries that simply have to be vanquished in single combat. The fact that, regardless of theory, we must still teach such matters piecemeal accounts for the success of even erroneous principles in the hands of

[3] "Norm" has this practical weakness: students often try to use it in the idealistic sense of 'what would be normal if conditions were perfect,' and so to quarrel with *está bueno* since *health* "ought" to be the norm for all living creatures. No term that we could select, however, would be perfectly univocal.

an energetic teacher who plies his students with a great many individually correct examples.

9. Sr. Crespo points out the persistence of *ser* in its older meanings of 'existir' and 'verificarse,' It is probably wrong, however, to include the example "¿Sabe usted dónde *es* el Teatro Bolívar?" as one of these vestiges; rather it is similar to "Aquí *es* donde vivo," where expressions of location occur on both sides of *ser* and *ser* is therefore a mere copula or sign of equivalence. This is demonstrated by the fact that while "Allí es la casa que usted busca" is acceptable (since *casa* can be thought of as 'place'), "Allí es el libro que usted busca" is impossible. "Mi trabajo es aquí" is acceptable because *trabajo* may be conceived as a process (whence *es* = 'se verifica') or as locale of process (whence *es* is a mere copula). The distinction of process *versus* place is illustrated by the example "El discurso es (está) en inglés." With *es* we should most likely take this to refer to the speech as delivered, with *estar* to the speech in written form (metaphorical location). A good deal remains to be done in working out the use of the two verbs with prepositional phrases.

10. Apropos of process, there is a wide pattern of examples that Sr. Crespo might have drawn upon in order to put the "norm" theory to a more severe test. It is a pattern which resembles the formal distinction in English of "You *are being* very rude" *versus* "You *are* very rude," where in the progressive *be* refers to 'action' and the adjective is one of 'behavior.' In such cases Spanish admits of *ser* regardless of comparisons or previous or successive states; in fact, the speaker may explicitly refer to a state, and yet use *ser*:

> *Fué* muy exigente conmigo, aunque después cambió por completo.
> Conmigo *es* muy cortés, aunque con mi padre no.
> ¿Por qué *fué* usted tan amable ayer, si nunca lo ha sido?
> Usted *fué* ayer muy cruel conmigo.
> *Es* muy consecuente cuando califica sus exámenes, aunque en lo demás no lo es.
> Usted debe *ser* más enérgico con los alumnos.

About the only discernible difference between "Estuvo muy descortés conmigo" and "Fué muy descortés conmigo" is that the one suggests something external while the other, coupled with the suggestion of 'portarse,' implies that the person was that way through-

and-through. *Ser* would be unlikely with adjectives that denote mere appearance rather than behavior; thus "¿Por qué es usted tan pensativo (alegre, despierto, etc.) hoy?" is hardly to be considered possible.

Unless we can stretch "norm" to include *to be* = 'to behave,' instances of this kind seem to constitute an exception.

Essence and Accident: English Analogs of Hispanic *Ser-estar*

THE *SER-ESTAR* CONTRAST—conceptually the one between essence and accident—is the most notorious peculiarity of Spanish for English-speaking learners of that language.[1] To the best of my knowledge no systematic parallel has ever been pointed out in English, though various rules of thumb are offered in teaching manuals, such as the association of one or the other of the two verbs with noun complements, adverb complements, and the like. Yet if recent thinking about linguistic universals is valid, we should suspect that something so fundamental might at least show up as a covert category somewhere, not necessarily embodied in a polar opposition of two words but betraying itself by what Benjamin Lee Whorf termed 'reactance'.

It happens that essence-accident does crop up at a number of points. There is nothing quite so striking in the standard language as what Stewart (1968:15) reports for one dialect of English: "In Gullah, observable characteristics are usually indicated by means of the verb *stan'* (or *'tan'*) which can be translated roughly as 'look', 'seem' or 'appear"'—a striking coincidence in that *stand* and *estar* are etymologically related. But there are other subtle ways in which the contrast makes its presence felt.

---

[1] From Braj B. Kachru, Robert B. Lees, Yakov Malkiel, Angelina Pietrangeli, and Sol Saporta (eds.), Issues in linguistics: Papers in honor of Henry and Renée Kahane, 58-69. Urbana: University of Illinois Press, 1973.

I begin with some imperfect parallels. These involve conceptualizations that have a partial congruence with essence-accident. The first is zeugma. We do not ordinarily conjoin complements that in Spanish would call for different verbs. The following are odd:

*He's wicked and afflicted.
*He's home wise.
*What and where is the theater?

We are most comfortable when both complements would take the same verb:

He's sick and afflicted.
He's home free.
Who and what are these people?
It's safe and reliable
They're here working.
She's well and happy.

But the distinction is unclear in cases like

He's mendacious but contrite.
The writing is correct but messy.

And zeugma depends on so many forms of incongruity that one can never be quite sure that the mismatch between essence and accident is at the bottom of it:

*He's here and wet.
*She's American and clever.

Second is the use of terminal prepositions. Ordinarily we feel especially uncomfortable in trying to apply the puristic rule that puts prepositions ahead of interrogatives and relatives when the Spanish verb would be *estar*:

?In what condition is he?
?I don't know in what town they were.
?The place at which they were was a little beach spot.

But if the construction is one that would call for *ser,* we feel somewhat less discomfort:

Of what does it treat?
From what city is he?

Nevertheless, the difference is relative, and a sentence like

What's it about?

which is a case of *ser*, would be as unlikely with an initial preposition as any sentence using a *be* equivalent to *estar*.

Third is postmodifiers. It often happens that a modifier which in Spanish would require *estar* if in a clause, in English must follow its head noun. This is a rule with adverbs:

The people here are friends of mine.
*The here people are friends of mine.

It also is found with adjectives, so that a premodifier if expanded to a clause calls for *ser*, and a postmodifier for *estar*:

The only visible stars (estrellas que son visibles) are Aldebaran and Sirius.
The only stars visible (estrellas que están visibles) are Aldebaran and Sirius.

But the actual distinction in English has to do with 'characterization' and its opposite. Ordinarily only essential qualities characterize, but the language permits accidental ones to do so also, though less frequently:

The sick man (el hombre que estaba enfermo) got up.
The away games are more fun becaue you get a trip thrown in.

The remaining parallels strike me as true examples of an essence-accident contrast in English.

Disjunction of be and complement

Though the effect is not particularly graceful either way, it is detectably easier to insert a parenthesized higher sentence after *be-ser* than after *be-estar*:

The squadron is, admittedly, from England.
?The squadron is, admittedly, in England.

John is, admittedly, quite clever.
?John is, admittedly, quite sick.
The place he lives is, admittedly, at home.
?John and Mary are, admittedly, at home.
The chairs are, admittedly, rather uncomfortable.
?The guests are, admittedly, rather uncomfortable.
He was not, apparently, hired; at least not right then.
?He was not, apparently, tired; at least not right then.
The day was, for that time of year, unusually hot.
?The air was, for that time of day, unusually hot.
The stranger was, as all observed, dirty-minded.
?The stranger was, as all observed, dirty-faced.
Her manner is, as you can see, cutting.
?The mowers are, as you can see, cutting.
The attack was, admittedly, in the park.
?The attacker was, admittedly, in the park.

Be-ser, it seems, is more independent of its complement than *be-estar.*

All

All is one of a large group of modifiers that have changed their function through reinterpretation, becoming intensifiers. The pre-intensifying meaning, which does not affect the essence-accident contrast, nevertheless impinges on it at two points. Both relate to 'totality' in the literal sense. The first is with plurals and mass nouns, e.g. *all the sugar* and *all the men,* and also with count nouns having the feature of Divisibility as in *all that heap, all morning.* When postposed, *all* in this sense creates an ambiguity with the intensifier (and is, no doubt, its etymological source). The first example is ambiguous, the second not, since *all* is not used for 'totality' with a dual:

Fine, children, your hands are all clean; you may come in to dinner now ('all your hands are clean', 'your hands are quite clean').

Fine, George, your hands are all clean; you may come in to dinner now (only 'quite clean').

The second point of contact shows *all* clearly as a modifier of the complement, not the subject; but the meaning is still literally '100%':

This product is all British.
The suit is all wool.
George is all boy.

The intensifier is a figurative extension of 'totality' but is not commutable with totality:

George is all boy = George is 100% boy.
I'm all tuckered out ≠ *I'm 100% tuckered out.
Your face is all wet ≠ *Your face is 100% wet.

—the starred examples would be understood but would be accepted, if at all, only as freshly coined and rather strained figures of speech.

It is, in fact, the *be-estar* meaning that permits *all* to become an intensifier, for essentially it refers to 'arrival at a state', which can be viewed as figuratively complete or not. The comparison between English and Spanish is secure as far as it goes: all instances of the intensifier occur, I believe, with *be-estar*. But at least two cases are not covered in their own right: the locational and the progressive. Figurative locational, referring to a state, is found, but not literal locational:

He is all in a dither.
*He is all in New York.

Similarly with the progressive. If it describes a state of the subject or a state of the object, the result is acceptable; but pure process is not:

She's all bubbling with enthusiasm.
I'm all smarting from what she said.
Don't press so hard; you're all crushing it ('getting it all crushed').
*She's all singing.
*It's not my fault; why is he all blaming me?
*He's all punishing them.

The virtue of *all* is that it discriminates the uses of *be* which are most difficult: with past participles and adjectives. There is, after all, no problem with the locational and the progressive: one can make a good case for distinguishing the *be* of *John is here* from the *be* of *John is a lawyer*, and as for the progressive we customarily regard the *be* as an auxiliary. But with *The house is painted* and particularly with *Mary is beautiful,* that solution is not so easy. Nevertheless, *all* does the trick. With past participles we find:

The house is all painted. (state)
*The house was all painted by the workman. (process)
Goliath was all overcome by (with) the bad news. (state)
*Goliath was all overcome by David. (process)

and with adjectives:

The air is all hot. I can hardly bear it.
*The weather is all hot. I can hardly bear it.
As soon as the blanket is all dry, bring it in.
*His wit is all dry.
She's all beautiful in her new dress! Mama, just look at her!
*I like to look at Miss America because she is all beautiful.
But look, it's all hard; I can't dent it anywhere.
*The problem is all hard.
This is all nasty and old; throw it away.
*The man is all old.
My glass is all empty; fill it up.
*That idea is all empty.
He's all wrong about that.
*He's all intelligent.
He's all ready.
*He's all clever.
I'm all afraid.
*I'm all cowardly.
Poor thing, she's all toothless!
*The snake is all toothless by nature.

Other examples typical of *estar*:

Are you all awake now?
The bud isn't all open yet.
I'm all sick about it.
We're all through now.
They were all agog with the scandal.

The synonym *completely* can be used with *be-ser*:

The snake is completely toothless by nature.
I'm completely cowardly.
That idea is completely empty.

To think x (to be) y, to feel

The contrast shows consistently—again as far as it goes—with the verb *to think* plus a predicative complement. It is exclusive to *be-ser.* I classify the situations in the traditional way:

1. Adjective complements:

I thought him (to be) clever.
*I thought him (to be) ready; it's time to go.
I thought him (to be) sickly. I thought him chronically ill.
I thought him (to be) ill and was wondering why no one came forward to help.
I thought him (to be) tiresome.
*I thought him (to be) tired.
I thought the climate (to be) cold.
*I thought the milk (to be) cold.
I thought him (to be) weak in character.
*I thought him (to be) weak from loss of blood.
I thought him (to be) very philosophical in those matters.
*I thought him (to be) very philosophical on saying that.
Do you think her attractive?
*Do you think her eye-catching?
She thought the meat expensive (the price of *x* piece).
*She thought your meat expensive today ('meat' as a perduring subject).

If the adjective complement refers to behavior, we expect *ser,* and consequently *think (to be)* should be normal—and it is:

I thought him (to be) very rude, acting like that toward you.

2. Adverb complements. If the hypothesis is correct, these should be excluded, since they occur normally only with *estar*:

*I thought him (to be) here.
*I thought them (to be) with their parents.

But where the adverb phrase denotes an essential trait, it is not excluded:

I thought the facts (to be) beyond doubt (to be indubitable).

3. Noun complements. These should all be normal, since *ser* is acceptable and *estar* not:

I thought him (to be) a man of honor.
I thought it (to be) a good example.
Do you think that animal (to be) a gorilla?

4. The progressive. This should be excluded, since it requires *estar*:

*I thought Juanita (to be) singing.
*Did you think him (to be) waiting?

(For the possibility of *I thought him to be telling the truth* = *I thought him to be being truthful, I thought him to be misbehaving terribly* = *I thought him to be being terribly rude, etc.*, see below.)

Two uses of *ser* are not matched by *think (to be)*. The first is equational, typically in the form of cleft sentences:

*I thought it (to be) John who did it.
*I thought who did it to be John.
*I thought it (to be) in London that he lived.

The second is for events, whether passive voice as in

*I thought the portrait (to have been) finished at six o'clock.
*I thought the composition (to have been) written quickly.

or with *be* = 'happen', 'take place':

*I thought the concert (to be) in the park.

Since neither of these situations describes a thing in terms of its essence, we can put the divergence down as due to a specialized use of the verb *ser* in Spanish.

Other verbs with deletable *to be* with complements do not display the *be-ser* restrictions of *think*:

I consider him (to be) ready.
I consider her (to be) singing.

I consider it to be John who did it.
I consider the composition to have been written quickly.
I supposed (assumed) him to be weak from loss of blood, but he wasn't.
I guessed him to be afraid.
I knew it to have been accomplished easily.
I knew them to be alarmed about it.
I imagined it to be in London that he lived.
I found them to be ready.
I found it to be you who did it.
I believed it to be someone else.
I judge them to be ready.
I judge them to be talking.
I judged it to be someone else.[2]

The only other verb of this infinitive-taking class that so far as I am aware shares the range with *think* is *hold*:[3]

I hold him to be intelligent.
*I hold him to be sick.
I hold him to be pretty impertinent, talking like that.
*I hold him to be here.
I hold him to be a man of honor.
*I hold him to be singing.
*I hold it to be John who did it.
*I hold it to have been done yesterday.

The synonymy with *hold* gives the clue to the meaning of *think*, which distinguishes it from the other verbs that take discourse complements:

---

[2] I am not attempting to make any point here except that these verbs differ in more than one way from *think*. To describe them as a class it would be necessary to account for which ones require *to be* and which do not, which ones may take cleft sentences as their complements, which ones may take progressives, how they are affected by the passive, etc.

[3] Possibly also *see*, but not *sense*:

I saw him to be timid (*afraid).
I sensed him to be timid (afraid).

it signifies not a mental picking up and laying down, but a holding in the mind. The view thus expressed does not expect to be controverted. In this respect, *think* has curiously diverged from *think that;* in the first of the following examples we sense no incongruity, but the second is a virtual nonsequitur:

I thought that he was unfriendly, but I was wrong.
?I thought him unfriendly, but I was wrong.

The reverse incongruity occurs in the imperative:

?Don't think that he is unfriendly.
Don't think him unfriendly.

and shows up again in the difference between a judgment and an opinion:

We both stood there looking at the house—Mary thought it red and I thought it a shade of brown.

*Mary wanted to know why I didn't want to buy the house, and I said it was because I thought it red (OK I thought it was red).

If we are tempted to assign the difference here to the contrast between an infinitive and a finite complement, comparing the verb *to feel* shows that it lies elsewhere; for *feel that* matches the *be-ser* aspect of *think* and *hold*:

I feel that he is insane (feel him to be insane).
*I feel that he is queasy (*feel him to be queasy).
I feel that he is pretty impertinent, talking like that (feel him to be impertinent).
*I feel that he is here (*feel him to be here).[4]
I feel that he is a man of honor (feel him to be a man of honor).
*I feel that he is chopping the wood (*feel him to be chopping the wood).

Where *feel* + infinitive and *feel that* diverge is with cleft sentences:

[4] This could be used with a different meaning for *feel*: 'I can practically feel his presence'. **I feel that he is outdoors* is a better example.

*I feel it to be John who did it.
I feel that it was John who did it.

—but this is a side issue.

Although in principle the progressive is excluded from infinitive constructions with *think, hold, feel,* and certain other verbs, there is one sense in which it is allowable. Compare the following:

I knew her to be faking.
I thought (imagined) him to be telling the truth.
I believe her to be doing her best.
I found him to be winning their confidence.
*I knew her to be drinking the chocolate.
*I thought (imagined) him to be telling a story.
*I believe her to be waving at us.
*I found him to be scratching his head.[5]

---

[5] The restrictions in the passive are not identical with those in the active. The acceptable examples are all acceptable in the passive, but some unacceptable actives become acceptable in the passive:

*I found him to have been scratching his head.
He was found to have been scratching his head.
*I believe her to have been waving at us.
She is believed to have been waving at us.

The unacceptable actives require a shift to perfect to be acceptable in the passive; no such shift is required of the acceptable actives:

*He was found to be scratching his head.
*She is believed to be waving at us.
He was found to be winning their confidence.
She was known to be faking.

The acceptable examples–those not requiring perfect–still answer to the *be-ser* principle, in view of

She was known to be taking hashish.

which means 'She was known to be a hashish-taker'–the progressive refers to a custom. Some other principle I think must be invoked to account for the cases that are rendered acceptable by a shift to perfect passive.

All the examples are acceptable with *that* clauses: *I knew that she was drinking the chocolate.* In addition, *feel* once more falls into place, in being the one verb which shows the same restriction with *that* clauses as with infinitives, provided the infinitive can be used at all (some will reject the infinitive construction in the following):

> *I feel that he is eating his breakfast (him to be eating his breakfast).
> I feel that he is eating too much (him to be eating too much).
> I feel that he is speaking his mind (him to be speaking his mind).
> I feel that he is behaving like an ass (him to be behaving like an ass).

The acceptable examples comprise actions which characterize the subject: 'She is a faker', 'He is truthful', 'She is diligent', 'He is persuasive', and, for the *feel* examples, 'He is gluttonous', 'He is frank', and 'He is asinine'; actions in the unacceptable group tell nothing about the subject. Acceptability answers to the *be-ser* criterion: cf. *Hay que ser franco.* This is not true of verbs such as *consider* and *judge.*[6]

Specifying "in" phrases

When two things are compared, the sense in which they are comparable may be specified by an *in* phrase, e.g.,

> You resemble me in demonstrativeness.

The property referred to is one which the things compared 'have' in the essence sense. Often it has a semantically cognate adjective, which in Spanish would occur with *ser.* In the following pairs the nouns are

---

[6] *Find* of course can appear in *I found him drinking the chocolate,* but this is *find* in the literal sense of 'run across'. The story of *feel* too is a bit more complex. It is closer to passing judgments (expressing what is essentially true) than to transmitting data. I will not inform you that the oranges are ripe by saying *I feel that they are ripe (think* here would do quite well), but I may share my wisdom by saying *I feel that they are ripe enough to ship.* Needless to say, *estar* would appear in both.

more or less synonymous, but contrast in terms of essence and accident:

He is like his brother in irritability.
*He is like his brother in anger (in indignation).
He is like his brother in cowardice.
*He is like his brother in fear.
She resembles you in appreciativeness.
*She resembles you in gratitude.

Where a noun may refer either to an essential quality or to an accidental one (the latter including 'location'), only the essential quality is acceptable in the *in* phrase:

Our two families are alike in closeness; there never is any disunity in yours or in mine.
(I live in Madison, Wisconsin.) *Chicago and Milwaukee are alike in closeness.
This weave is like that one in looseness.
*This knot is like that one in looseness.
(This house is comfortable and so is that one.) This house resembles that one in comfort.
(John is comfortable and so is Jerry.) *John resembles Jerry in comfort.
This wine is like that one in dryness.
*This glass is like that one in dryness; I wiped them both carefully.

For reasons that cannot be gone into here, the contrast is unclear with action nominals, nominals with definite determiners, and nominals transposed to initial position.

Get

It is well known that the verb of becoming in Spanish which correlates with *estar* is *ponerse*. The verb means 'to put on', and the qualities or states to which it refers are viewed as put on and taken off—they are no more part of the nature of the entity than the hat and gloves are part of the man. The corresponding verb in English is *get*, and if Jespersen is right in assuming a reflexive basis, e.g. *get wet* < *get oneself wet* (*MEG* III 16.28), we can appeal to a similar imagery: an entity capable of getting itself this way or that (with *be-ser* qualities inherent in it), plus the states that it gets itself into (expressible by *be-estar)*. In any case there is no mistaking the correspondence, and *get* goes *ponerse* one better by covering 'location':

> Get over here quick.
> We got home before six.
> Get off that ladder.

With the passive, a *get* yields an *estar* result.[7] This is true whether the construction is basically reflexive, as in the first example below, or passive with an external agent, or a mere expression of transition:

> He got dressed in a hurry.
> The infant got dressed by its mother.
> She got tired.

Elsewhere the parallel continues to hold; *get* is not used with complements that call for *be-ser*:

> The coffee got cold.
> *The climate got cold.
> Mary got sick.
> *Mary got intelligent.
> He got free by a strategem, and came to America.
> *He got American by a strategem, pretending to know the Constitution and fooling the judge into naturalizing him.
> Water gets hard as it freezes.
> *Water gets ice as it freezes.
> Mary got all beautiful for the party.
> *As she grew up, Mary got beautiful.

The use of *get* as a progressive auxiliary is limited, but it is at least possible:

> After a while we got talking and found we had mutual friends.
> Better get going before they catch you.

---

[7] The same is true of the *be* passive, but we do not have the apparent anomaly of *be-ser* yielding a *be-estar*.

If you don't get moving I'll have to arrest you.

The parallel between *get* and *estar* with adjectives is striking, but not perfect. We can perhaps explain expressions like

He got rich.
Get wise.

in terms that do not affect the argument: our culture views wealth as transitory (we note that

?He got poor.

is much less likely), and *wise* is being used in a slang sense, 'Get with it'. But *get* takes a somewhat longer view than *estar,* as can be seen with long-range 'becoming', where *ponerse* would be unlikely but *get* can nevertheless be used:

People do get old.
As Mary grew up, she got more and more beautiful.

But this deviation, it seems safe to say, is no more than one should expect in the details of what is essentially the same conceptualization in any two languages one might choose.

To summarize: If a phenomenon is an accident, it can overtake its host entity with greater or lesser force, i.e. be intensified; hence *all.* The entity itself can be held in the mind; hence *think.* And what is essentially unchanging can submit to changes that do not transmute what underlies them into something else; hence *get.* This is not intended as a scientific explanation of the contrasts, but as a verbalization of the metaphor. A good deal of what passes for meaning in language is pictorial, and can be described better than it can be defined.

Reference

Stewart, William A. 1968. Continuity and change in American Negro dialects. Florida FL Reporter 6.15.

Part II

Governance

One Each in English and Spanish

[*Author's Note*: Does *They ate their lunch* mean that they shared a lunch, or that they each had one? (Notice the clever take-your-pick of combining *they* with *each* in that sentence.) Does *They ate their lunches* mean that each had one, or each had several? There is no way of getting completely out of this confusion of grammatical number, and English and Spanish have floundered equally throughout their history.

Given the similarity between the languages, the point is not hard to teach.]

* * *

SOMETIMES IT IS HARD to steer a middle course between polygamy and polyandry[1]:

(1) Tom and Jerry seduced each other's wives.
(2) *Tom and Jerry seduced each other's wife.

I have starred (2) because the situation is so bizarre—with its suggestion that the two men share a wife but each views her as belonging to the other for purposes of seduction—that we would reject it out of hand; and yet the sentence is the same structurally as

(3) Tom and Jerry guaranteed each other's signature.

in which the absurdity of sharing a signature steers us straight to the only reasonable interpretation, one signature each. And the high unlikelihood of either person being a forger makes (4) a good substitute for (3):

---

[1] From Joseph V. Ricapito (ed.), *Hispanic studies in honor of Joseph H. Silverman*, 361-69. Newark, Delaware: Juan de la Cuesta, 1988.

(4) Tom and Jerry guaranteed each other's signatures.

The substitute is the rub. Do we universally have a choice beween singular-for-one-each and plural-for-one-each when the situation is truly one-each and not more-than-one-each? (More-than-one-each would be a good interpretation of [1] if Talha and al-Zubayr replaced Tom and Jerry.)

English and Spanish share both the problem of ambiguity and the problem of what to do about it. Bosque (80) describes the ambiguity of *Hay silla para todos*—which of course applies to English *There's a chair for everyone* as well: "puede describir una situación en la que a cada persona le corresponde una silla distinta... o aludir a una única silla que han de compartir varios." The *one each* meaning is the one that concerns us in what follows.

Salvador Fernández states the situation for Spanish (147-48): "Cuando el enunciado es descriptivo y la descripción se descompone en diversos momentos, suele aislarse, por lo menos, un *singular distributivo*.... Cuando se atenúa la descripción o se reducen los momentos de la descripción, suele producirse la asimilación al plural dominante." Some of his examples:

(5) venía una escolta de *soldados* con *la* bayoneta calada en los negros fusiles (Valle-Inclán)
(6) aparecían *enfermos* con *el* gorro de dormir en *la* cabeza (Baroja)
(7) media docena de *jóvenes,* con *los* abrigos desabrochados (I. Agustí)
(8) se metían en los portales cerrando *sus* paraguas (Baroja)

Quirk *et al.* state it for English (768): "The distributive plural is used in a plural noun phrase to refer to a set of entities matched individually with individual entities in another set....While the distributive plural is the norm, the distributive singular may also be used to focus on individual instances. We therefore often have a number choice...." Among the examples are

(9) We all have good appetites (a good appetite).
(10) Pronouns agree with their antecedent(s).

There is clearly a wide range of choice, with—as both Quirk and Fernández point out—a difference in focus, or what Talmy (25-26) calls "level of exemplarity": with the singular, "a single *exemplar* out of the multiplexity is placed in the foreground of attention."

Though this conceptual distinction underlies the choices, both languages seem to have undergone shifts of fashion at various times, and many factors, pragmatic, grammatical, idiomatic, and stylistic, influence which form will be used. On the stylistic side, for example, Middle English poetry used "the singular and plural almost indiscriminately, to meet the exigencies of rhyme and metre" (Mustanoja 56).

Broadly speaking, it appears that the plural has been favored throughout the history of both languages. Chaucer used it more than the singular and in his translation of Boethius often replaced Latin singulars with English plurals (e.g. *youwre dignytes* for *dignitatem vestram,* Mustanoja 56-57). The plural is overwhelmingly favored in the *Cantar de Mío Cid.* In (11a) we see seven plurals, three of which the modern translation (Bolaño e Isla 46) converts to singular:

(11*a*) Enbraçan *los escudos* delant *los coraçones,* abaxan *las lanças* abueltas de *los pendones,* enclinaron *las caras* de suso de *los arzones,* ívanlos ferir de fuertes *coraçones.*

(11*b*) Embrazan todos *su escudo* delante *del pecho,* enristran *las lanzas* unidas a *sus pendones,* inclinan todos *sus caras* sobre *los arzones,* y atacan, para herir moros, con valiente *corazón.*

An instance of the comparatively rare singular (Bolaño 146):

(12) que todos prisiessen *so derecho* contado.

for all to get their due—significantly, an abstraction. If this meager sample tells us anything, it is that a popular style probably favors the relative looseness of the plural. Similarly in English, if Chaucer is an indication. A hint also comes from a count of the use of *heart* by Bunyan in this construction: plurals are seven times as frequent as singulars (Mustanoja 57). A cultivated literary style is more apt to favor the singular. In sixteenth-century Spanish the plural is still in front (Keniston, *Syntax* 38), but now it only "predominates slightly," e.g.

(13) los moços cortesanos aun no tienen en el cuerpo dolores, ni cargan sobre sus coraçones cuydados.

In the modern period the balance has continued to shift, if Keniston's conclusions from his idiom count can be trusted: "Spanish usually uses the singular, especially if the notion involved is a part of the body. With notions more remotely associated with a person, such as articles of clothing or other personal attributes, the plural is sometimes used" (*Idiom* 42). As our older sources are all in written form, there is a bias here, but it is not hard to imagine a literary influence on speech stemming from the cultivation of a literary style detached from the popular culture that formed the basis of the earliest vernacular writing. As careful an observer as Luis Flórez would not have put down as "vulgarismos" the following expressions if some kind of norm were not in effect, at least for parts of the body (Flórez 215):

(14) cierren las bocas
no muevan las cabezas
saquen los pechos (gym teacher to students)

The strength of the norm can perhaps be gauged by (15), provided by Col. Gordon T. Fish:

(15) ¿Caretas? No tengo. Se *la* han quitado a todo el mundo.

Here, in spite of the antecedent *caretas*, the pronoun is singular in referring to *one each*.

I am unable to say whether the "vulgarismo" is gaining ground in Spanish, but my observations of spoken English—mostly from emcees, callers, and guests on radio talk shows—definitely suggest a shift toward the plural. I believe that this is part of a broader tendency to pick the plural noun in any doubtful case. For many speakers, "contact agreement" has all but supplanted agreement between verb and subject, especially in plural:

(16) One of two *men were* involved in the robbery (KCBS 9 Feb. 1979, 7:13 A.M.).[2]

(17) The status of *women are* always lower (KGO 8 May 1978, 11:13 P.M.).

[2] Station signatures are for the San Francisco area unless otherwise noted.

(18) Report on what the medfly fight *people* say *are* going on (KGO 17 Aug. 1981, 5:46 P.M.).

Similarly something that has long been common in Spanish, making the verb agree with a plural predicate noun:

(19) Mi infancia *son recuerdos* de un patio de Sevilla (Antonio Machado).
(20) El eje de la vida política *han sido los "caudillos"* (Américo Castro).
(21) It turned out that one of the things it was being applied to *were* Soviet *tests* of a particle beam.[3]
(22) What she owns *are leopards.*[4]

Nevertheless, the *one-each* phenomenon defines some of its own conditions, and to discover how the change is progressing it will help to look at the forces influencing the choice. In some situations the language itself may compel the choice or at least constrain it. The clearest instance of restriction, as Quirk points out (768), is idioms and metaphors. No one is apt to pluralize

(23) They vented their spleen on him.

Similarly

(24) He keeps everyone at each other's throat and then casts himself as the soother.[5]

Yet this barrier has been widely breached:

(25) They sit back and mutter under their breaths (Jim Eason, KGO 9 Sep. 1976).
(26)... women should... stop getting out of men's ways in public[6]
(27)... the opportunity the [Civil] War gave for women to enter public lives (personal letter).

[3] *Columbia Journalism Review* May/June 1979: 40.
[4] *Los Angeles Times* 1 Jan. 1979: I, 3.
[5] *In These Times* 5-11 Nov. 1986: 9.
[6] *UCLA Monthly* Jan./Feb. 1981: 3.

(28) We thank you from the bottoms of our hearts.[7]

(29) Some of the contenders for the White House had great senses of humor (KNBR 11 Nov. 1984, 8:58 A.M.)

Similar to idioms are semantic bifurcations between singular and plural. The plural of *honor* normally refers to tokens of honor, so that the plural is unlikely in

(30) They pledged their honor.

Nevertheless we find the following—in spite of the fact that *facilities* tends to refer to some form of public convenience, *conditions* to ambient phenomena (such as weather) or stipulations, and *attentions* to amorous approaches:

(31)... there were 30 Puerto Rican teachers studying to improve their facilities as teachers.[8]

(32) The conditions of those injured were not immediately known.[9]

(33) Today many copier companies focus their attentions on ... (KCBS 17 Sep. 1986, 12:35 P.M.).

(*Attentions* and *conditions* are frequent in my data.)

There are also grammatical restrictions. *Together*, as in

(34) They put their heads together.

requires the plural. In both English and Spanish there is a contrast between the definite article and the possessive (although the range of the article is narrower in English):

(35) They suffered irritation to their noses and throats (KCBS 30 Sep. 1986, 6:56 A.M.). (Cf. to the nose and throat.)

(36) Multitud de frailes misioneros perdieron sus vidas (Américo Castro). (Cf. perdieron la vida.)

[7] Speech by President Fred D. Fagg, Jr., University of Southern California, 11 May 1953.

[8] Indiana University report, 5 Jan. 1959.

[9] *San Francisco Examiner* 3 July 1977: A, 2.

The reason is not purely grammatical: the possessive individualizes and hence favors the plural. The situation is similar to that of *house-hunting* (no individualization) versus *hunting for a house (houses)*. But the restriction on pre-adjunct possessors seems to be purely grammatical:

(37) Those boys' minds (*mind).
(38) The mind(s) of those boys.

The area most affected by the plural drift is that of abstractions that are not subject to the restraining influence of idiom, metaphor, bifurcation, or grammar. The speaker seems to be thinking, "Let the hearer figure it out"—the plural is the unmarked line of least resistance:

(39) With government... and private agencies exerting increasing influences on... (KCBS 18 Sep. 1983, 7:22 A.M.).
(40) Scotland Yard is looking for clues to their identities (KCBS 21 Jan. 1984, 7:12 A.M.).
(41) I really and truly value their friendships (KGO 3 Oct. 1983, 10:58 P.M.).
(42) Both [accident victims] are in comas (KGO 29 Sep. 1986, 12:14 P.M.).
(43) Officials released accused spies in the custodies of their respective embassies (KPFA 11 Sep. 1986, 6:02 P.M.).
(44)... hire people with bad reputations (KGO 26 May 1976, 11:15 P.M.)
(45)... he may have been involved in the murders of his parents (KCBS 19 Sep. 1983, 7:12 A.M.)
(46) People won't have to pay their rents (KPFA 5 July 1983, 6:15 P.M.).
(47)... forced the evacuations of hundreds of people (KGO 18 Apr. 1983, 8:05 P.M.).
(48)... including the killings of several prominent leaders (KCBS 25 Feb. 1980, 7:09 A.M.).
(49) These include the resignations of the warden and one assistant warden (Boston WEEI 1 Jan. 1973, 7:35 A.M.).

(50) Comparative studies have established a breath-taking degree of independence in the evolutions of individual Munda and Mon-Khmer languages.[10]

(51) The three policemen had five days to appeal their firings (KCBS 25 Apr. 1976, 2:07 P.M.).

(52) All speakers consulted have university educations.[11]

Educations is frequent in my data.

Instances of the singular of course continue to show up (and are probably underrepresented in my data because they are less surprising to me and I do not notice them):

(53) Too many athletes are overpampered individuals who have been told all their life that they are special.[12]

(54) Hotel guests use it [the elevator] after they have left their car in the garage.[13]

(55) A huge jet crashed into Jamaica Bay, carrying 95 people to their death.[14]

(56) [The ideas that] made them a millionaire (KCBS 12 May 1983, 5:22 P.M.).

It may be significant that (53)-(55) are from written sources.

In other cases one can see a deeper reason for the choice:

(57) Deaths of Eugene J. Thomas and Juergen Schaefer.

This headline (1985) if in the singular would have suggested that the circumstances of death were shared.

(58) The names of the suspects... were withheld because of their ages.[15]

Because of their age might suggest "because they were too old," whereas the opposite meaning applies here.

---

[10] Chicago Linguistic Society 1983.

[11] *Language* 61 (1985): 219.

[12] *The Nation* 27 Sep. 1986: 279.

[13] Johannes Mario Simmel, translation.

[14] *Saturday Evening Post* 19 Jan. 1963: 68.

[15] *Palo Alto Times* 25 May 1976: 2.

(59) I tell her I want her hand to drop so that there is no life in it at all. It is extraordinary how many people cannot drop their hand; they let their hand slowly fall, and then ....[16]

The pairing of hands creates an ambiguity that calls for singular.

(60) Each of us has to put our principles and consciences on the line.[17]

The preceding plural motivates a parallel plural. The same is true of Keniston's example (*Idiom* 43)

(61) Creo notar una agitación de cosas blancas, como si me saludaran con los pañuelos.

"Having a reason for the choice" of course leads back to the idioms, metaphors, and bifurcations outlined earlier:

(63) Al pasar D. Julián, todos se quitaron el sombrero.
(64) Hacía tanto calor que todos se quitaron los sombreros.[18]

Here we have the symbolic act of "doffing the hat" contrasting with a more practical motive. Flórez's *cierren la boca* "shut up" also belongs here, contrasting with *cierren las bocas* (*por si las moscas*). A cleansing ritual might encourage singular in

(65) Wash your face all of you and get in here fast—supper's ready.

but the material side would probably take over in

(66) And after they had washed their faces ....

To sum up: What we have in both languages is a distinction that "doesn't matter" a great part of the time, and this leaves room for chance and, accordingly, changing fashion, with the plural tending to be the unmarked construction. In English this has been coupled with what seems to be a much greater readiness to pluralize abstractions,

---

[16] *Reader's Digest* May 1947: 93.
[17] Nancy Reagan, 14 Sep. 1986.
[18] Preferences as indicated by Prof. Laudelino Moreno.

a tendency that has been rather more true of Spanish all along. My Spanish data are too slight for me to say whether the plural there too is, colloquially, the unmarked form, but it seems likely.

All the same, wherever there is a potential semantic distinction we have to allow for speakers being swayed by something other than chance and fashion. Peter Erades (§110) offers a prime example from Erskine's *Private Life of Helen of Troy*:

(67) "If we all lived on your plan," said Hermione, "I don't see what would become of people. We haven't the right to live our own lives."— "We don't live our own life," said Helen, "we are in danger of trying to lead someone else's."

As one of Erades's correspondents points out, the first *we* is people collectively, hence the plural *lives*, whereas the second *we* is "you and I," each separately, hence the singular.

And yet—the same correspondent declares a sentence like (68) to be impossible:

(68) Three pupils in this class write with their left hands.

I am sure that the pluralizing trend would sweep this in along with all the rest.

Works Cited

Bolaño e Isla, Amancio. *Poema de mío Cid*. México: Porrua, 1968.

Bosque, Ignacio. "Clases de nombres comunes." *Serta Philologica F. Lázaro Carreter*. Madrid: Ediciones Cátedra, 1983, 75-88.

Erades, P. A. "Points of Modern English Syntax." *English Studies* 39 (1958): §110.

Fernández Ramírez, Salvador. *Gramática española, 3.1, El nombre*. Ed. José Polo. Madrid: Arco/Libros S.A., 1986.

Flórez, Luis. *Temas de castellano: notas de divulgación, segunda edición*. Bogotá: Instituto Caro y Cuervo, 1967.

Keniston, Hayward. *The Syntax of Castilian Prose: The Sixteenth Century*. Chicago: U of Chicago P, 1937.

———. *Spanish Idiom List*. New York: Macmillan, 1931.

Mustanoja, Tauno F. *A Middle English Syntax: Part I, Parts of Speech*. Helsinki: Société Néophilologique, 1960.

Quirk, Randolph, Sidney Greenbaum, Geoffrey Leech, and Jan Svartvik. *A Comprehensive Grammar of the English Language*. London: Longman, 1985.

Talmy, Leonard. "The Relation of Grammar to Cognition." *Topics in Cognitive Linguistics*. Ed. Brygida Rudzka-Ostyn. Amsterdam: Benjamins, 1987, 1-36.

Retained Objects in Spanish

[*Author's Note*: There is just enough similarity between the passive in English and the passive in Spanish to make learners assume there ought to be more. What's wrong with *fuimos dichos que* when *we were told that* is a legitimate passive in English? The safest way to ward off oddities is to condemn outright any attempt to passivize a noun that is not the DIRECT object of a verb.

And yet the non-accusative oblique cases—dative-object and preposition-object—are not so sharply distinguished from the accusative in Spanish as never to passivize. The form taken by this passive is the same as it would be if the verb were transitive—that is, though the English keeps the preposition (*She was alluded to*), Spanish drops it (*Ella fue aludida*).

The study mentioned in Note 11 is Dorothy Hurst Mills's "Spanish case: influence of subject and connotation of force" (*Hispania* 34 [1951] 74-78). It illustrates the fluctuation between dative and accusative that enables some non-accusatives to passivize.]

* * *

MOST SIMPLE DATIVES in English[1] admit of a passive construction in which the dative object becomes the grammatical subject: *He gave me the book* becomes *I was given the book by him*. Not all datives are amenable—*The work took me an hour* cannot be converted to *I was taken an hour by the work*; in fact, not even some apparently accusative forms allow it: *The suit becomes him* is unacceptable as *He is become by the suit*.

[1] This article was first published in *Hispania* 33 (1950): 237-39. I define the English dative by position. In American English the first of two objects is the dative: *Give John the book, Show him these.*

The phenomenon is general enough to be productive in English, however, and even extends to the majority of stereotypes with prepositional objects: *The car ran over him* gives *He was run over by the car; They spoke of me* gives *I was spoken of by them.*

The rule in English is the exception in Spanish, though Bello seems to be the only grammarian who recognizes that it even exists[2]. He gives, as an example of dative-to-subject, *Les lisonjea la popularidad de que gozan: Lisonjeados por la popularidad*[3], and of prepositional object-to-subject, *El reo apeló de la sentencia: Sentencia apelada*[4]. It almost goes without saying that in the latter there will never be a retained preposition—*Sentencia apelada de* is impossible. Even Bello has no interest in the phenomenon, which he calls "uno de los caprichos de la lengua,"[5] beyond using it to prove that the existence of a passive construction does not necessarily imply that there was an accusative to begin with.

It is only natural that confusion between dative and accusative should be paralleled by retaining datives as subjects. In the active voice a sizable number of verbs may take either dative or accusative, or even alternate between an accusative and a prepositional object,

---

[2] Gili Gaya (*Curso superior de sintaxis española,* Mexico, 1943), Kany (*American Spanish Syntax,* Chicago, 1945), Ramsey (*A Textbook of Modern Spanish,* New York, 1894), and Keniston (*The Syntax of Castilian Prose, The Sixteenth Century,* Chicago, 1937) say nothing on this score. Lenz (*La Oración y sus partes,* Santiago, 1944) mentions the English construction and similar constructions in other languages, but draws no parallel with Spanish. The Academy (*Gramática de la lengua española,* Madrid, 1931) does not recognize the possibility of a passive with *ser* in this case, but theorizes–on doubtful logic, I suspect–that examples of the type *Torcuato está comido* have developed from the reflexive dative in *Torcuato se comió media pierna de carnero* (§461c). Benot (*Arquitectura de las lenguas,* Buenos Aires, n.d.) makes the unequivocal statement, echoed in most grammars, that "if a sentence in the active voice does not have an accusative, it cannot be converted to the passive voice by means of the verb *ser* and a participle" (II,50); he does, however, set down as a possibility, apparently without realizing its significance, the sentence *El ministro hubo de ser hablado oportunamente* (II,212).

[3] *Gramática Castellana,* Paris, 1936, §739.

[4] *Op. cit.,* §735.

[5] *Op. cit.,* §897.

with the result that a passive may exist apparently tied to a dative but actually tied to an accusative. An erstwhile accusative may become entirely dative in some dialects without destroying the passive construction that corresponded to the original accusative. But confusion between the cases accounts for only part of the examples of conversion that I have come upon; others were undoubtedly helped into existence by the freedom with which past participles can detach themselves from their verbs and live an independent existence with traits of their own, as, for instance, the intransitive participles do when they behave like transitives: *La gente venida a la fiesta* paralleling *La gente traída a la fiesta* or *El árbol caído* paralleling *El árbol cortado.*

Accordingly we may divide the verbs that admit of retained datives or retained prepositional objects into two classes: those which take, in the active voice, either an accusative or a non-accusative (dative or prepositional) object, with or without some change in meaning, and those which have no alternative, but which, as it turns out, usually have some close synonym that sanctions the other type of object.

A. *Verbs with alternate dative and accusative*

(1) Verbs of order: *preceder, anteceder,* and *seguir.* Navarro Tomás exhibits the confusion: *El descenso comprende hasta la última sílaba fuerte o hasta la que inmediatamente* LE *precede*[6] and *Al principio de la frase la sílaba débil inicial resulta siete semitonos más baja que la primera acentuada que* LA *sigue*[7]. Dr. Ricardo J. Alfaro (no *leísta* in the feminine) writes *Las generaciones de su tiempo y las que* LES *siguieron*[8]. Other speakers whom I have consulted are for the most part indifferent to the case used with these verbs. So when Bello cites *La filosofía debe ser precedida de la gramática*[9] as the conversion of a dative, he probably should have regarded it as the conversion of an evolving accusative.

---

[6] *Manual de entonación española,* New York, 1944, 141, n. 14.
[7] *Op. cit.,* 143, n. 15.
[8] *Boletín del Instituto Caro y Cuervo,* 4.105, 1948.
[9] *Op. cit.,* §897.

(2) Verbs of emotion. *Gustar* is named by Benot[10], along with *agradar, faltar, quedar,* and *sobrar,* as impossible to make passive. But the analogy of *gustar* seems to be reflected in certain synonyms such as *fascinar* and *encantar,* enabling many speakers to demand the dative with them when the verb is used in its figurative sense and not in its primitive sense: *El mago la encantó* but *Le encantan (a ella) los nuevos vestidos.* These same speakers, however, accept the conversion in either sense: *Ella es fascinada (encantada) por los nuevos vestidos. Temer* gives both *Todos le temen a ella* and *Todos la temen a ella* (with dialectal preferences), both convertible to *Ella es temida de todos.* The type *Le (la) inquietó (preocupó) la noticia* gives *Ella fué inquietada por la noticia*[11].

(3) Factitive verbs. *Llamar* and its synonyms for many speakers demand the dative for the person or thing *to* which the name is applied, thus *A ella le* (instead of *la*) *llamamos traidora.* The conversion *Ella es llamada traidora* is nevertheless acceptable. With an infinitive complement, where *hacer* and *dejar* take dative and accusative indiscriminately (*Le [la] hicieron [dejaron] salir*), I have found grudging acceptance of *La casa fué dejada caer,* but this is highly doubtful.

(4) Miscellaneous. The Mexican speaker who preferred *le* to *la* in *No le ruegue usted tanto* and *Esos vestidos no le favorecen en nada* admitted the passive in *Ella fue rogada* and *Ella se ve favorecida llevando tales vestidos.*

B. *Verbs with dative only*

Combining the reactions of several speakers of different nationalities, I find that (for them at least) the verbs *avisar, participar,* and *comunicar* require dative in the type *Le [a ella] voy a avisar del asunto.* For these same speakers the synonymous set *informar, advertir,* and *notificar* may take either dative or accusative, while *enterar* may take only accusative. So closely knit in meaning are all these verbs, however, that even the first three allow of a passive: *Ella fué avisada del*

[10] *Op. cit.,* II, 208.

[11] The dative with verbs of this type, denoting psychological effects upon persons, is being investigated by Miss Dorothy Hurst. She reports that there is a fairly clear semantic pattern.

asunto. Other dialects or idiolects would undoubtedly show variation in cases here; but the fact remains that even those who demand the dative accept a passive without hesitation.

C. *Verbs with alternate prepositional object and accusative*

Cumple con su deber is virtually synonymous with *Cumple su deber,* and we have the conversion *Un deber cumplido por él.* Since we have practically no basis for supposing a confusion between pairs of this type such as we find all along the frontier between dative and accusative, however, it is better just to match the conversion with the regular accusative and not imagine a retained prepositional object. I include the example only for symmetry.

D. *Verbs with prepositional object only*

Besides the instance of *apelar de,* cited by Bello, I have encountered three others: *influir en, contribuir con,* and, for some speakers, *habitar en* in the sense of 'to inhabit (a place)'—for these speakers *habitar* alone is unacceptable in this sense. We may convert *Su regionalismo influye en lo que piensa* to *Lo que piensa es influido por su regionalismo; Contribuye con dinero* to *Lo contribuido;* and *Habitan en el país* to *El país es habitado por ellos,* acceptable even to those for whom *habitar* is not transitive in the active voice. The case of *tirar* is somewhat different. We have, according to one informant, the possibility of *El carro fue tirado por el buey* corresponding to *El buey tira del carro,* and this is supported by transitive uses of *tirar*—but the meanings are not the same.

E. *Mixed verbs*

At least one verb, *aludir,* straddles all three constructions. A Chilean writer[12] says *La había aludido por grosero modo,* and is seconded by a Chilean and by a Nicaraguan speaker. Though the Mexican speakers consulted preferred a directional *a, Había aludido a ella,* and

[12] Rafael Maluenda, *Algunos cuentos chilenos,* Buenos Aires, 1943, 63.

recognized the dative, *Le había aludido a ella,* they as well as the others were equally willing to accept the passive *Ella fué aludida por Juan.*

Conclusions

Retained dative and prepositional objects are found with verbs whose constructions analogize closely with accusative constructions. Though rare, they are found with relative frequency where dialectal or individual preferences obscure the line between dative and accusative, or where the dative has suspended its usual function merely to set off two different uses of a verb (as when we say *Les creemos* for persons and *Los creemos* for things, both giving *Son creídos*). The most typical use of the dative, *Le dieron el libro,* is not susceptible of conversion (as in English *He was given the book*) by the passive voice except by keeping the dative as dative with *Le fué dado el libro* or *Se le dió el libro.* The latter, both with dative and with prepositional object (*Se llegó a un acuerdo, Se habló de mí*), is the only fully productive pattern in Spanish.

Of Undetermined Nouns and Indeterminate Reflexives

[*Author's Note*: The issue of the passive in the last chapter is esoteric by comparison with that of the "middle voice"—the "impersonal reflexive" or "reflexive-for-passive" as it is usually referred to. Speakers who favor the singular in *Se alquila casas* charge the advocates of *Se alquilan casas* with gross ungrammaticality, and the latter just as energetically reverse the charge. Here I try to arbitrate.

The term *deep grammar* sounds quaint today, but for a time it rivaled *deep structure* (it was introduced, I believe, by Charles Hockett in his *Course in modern linguistics*, 1958). The triumph of the latter term was a curious switch because it was precisely American structuralism that the proponents of "deep structure" were out to get. Given later developments, *grammar* was the better descriptive term for what lies "below the surface" in the organon of language.]

* * *

C. P. OTERO SCORES a number of points in his penetrating review of the works of Ángel Rosenblat (*RPh* 20 [1966] 53-68), and what follows is in no sense a rejoinder nor a defense of the faults that Otero singles out.[1] Rather it is a development of one topic along lines that establish a position between Rosenblat's and Otero's; a problem of dialectal variation is involved, and a little more flexibility on either hand will help to understand the shifts that are taking place.

Otero objects (56) to Rosenblat's having thought it necessary to gloss *Se vende naranjas* and *Se alquila casas* as 'Se venden naranjas' and

[1] This article was first printed in *Romance Philology* 22 (1969): 484-89.

'Se alquilan casas'. About such an "uso irreprochable" there need be no reservations, he feels, and Rosenblat should have realized that:

1. The noun cannot be the subject of the verb because Spanish requires a determiner under these conditions and there is none; consequently it is wrong to expect agreement between *casas* and *alquila(n)*.

2. *Naranjas venden a sí mismas* is ungrammatical and *Las buenas naranjas en el arca se venden* or *Las casas se alquilan por sí solas* are entirely different in meaning from the impersonal use of *se*. Therefore it is wrong to appeal to true reflexives for an analogy.

3. The proportion *Las señoras se sientan: Se sienta a las señoras::Las buenas naranjas en el arca se venden por sí solas: Se vende naranjas* suggests that *Se sienta a las señoras* and *Se vende naranjas* are syntactically the same except for the human vs. non-human victim. (I hope that this interpretation is correct.)

Taken at face value, the FIRST POINT is open to question because one often finds undetermined common nouns acting as grammatical subjects, e.g.,

1. Propósito de este libro, es, pues, "llenar el vacío . . . ."[2]
2. El oficio del artista no es otro que tomar un breve trozo de la realidad . . . y hacer que nos sirva para expresar el resto del mundo . . . .Arte es simbolización.[3]

But Otero hardly intends it to be taken quite at face value. He cites Anna Hatcher's example *Casos se han dado* (fn. 6), accepting it as normal but explaining it as an ellipsis: "*Casos se ha* [sic] *dado* no es, desde luego, una oración simple, sino elidida: '(Algunos o varios) casos se han [sic] dado'. Esto lo había señalado ya Alonso . . . "[4] Elsewhere—not in this review article—he admits the possibility of an undetermined subject when the construction is passive: *Altares fueron levantados a los ídolos*.[5] The interpretation that these arguments seem

[2] L. Flórez, in *BICC*, XVI (1961), 220.
[3] J. Ortega y Gasset, quoted *PMLA*, LXVII (1952), 620.
[4] In *Estudios lingüísticos, temas españoles* (M., 1954), pp. 168*f*.
[5] *RPh*, XXI (1967-68), 49.

to lead to is some such rule as: "The only common nouns which can serve as grammatical subjects without determiners are those which are not subjects without determiners in deep grammar." In deep grammar they may be objects, later converted to subjects by a passive transformation, or they may be subjects with determiners, converted to subjects without determiners by a deletion transformation.

It is curious that Alonso should have been cited in support of this position, for Alonso, so far as I can ascertain, said the opposite. Alonso cites the long series of undetermined nouns from the "Jura de Gadea," beginning "Villanos te maten, rey, / Villanos, que non hidalgos . . . ." and explains as follows: "Tan persistente oposición bilateral no quiere decir 'que unos villanos (algunos de los villanos) te maten y que los hidalgos no te maten' etc., sino 'que los que te maten SEAN villanos, no sean hidalgos . . .' "—an explicit denial of any ellipsis of determiners. What appears to have made Otero think that Alonso was on his side was the fact that Alonso, too, insists that undetermined common nouns cannot be subjects in Spanish, but the impression is false, for Alonso is talking about PSYCHOLOGICAL subjects.[6] For Alonso, the passive example *Altares fueron levantados a los ídolos* would not differ from the active *No bastarían altares para los dioses*—both lack the article because the meaning refers not just to extant altars but to altars in their essence.[7] (I find no example of a passive construction in his article, but in several the noun is a grammatical object, e.g., pp. 174*f*.) In order to accommodate Alonso to his view, Otero would need to set up a transformation that derives *Villanos te maten* from an underlying sentence containing an embedded clause in which *villanos* is in the

---

[6] Otero, though aware that Alonso is not speaking in strictly grammatical terms, gives no indication of realizing that his ellipsis and Alonso's are quite different. Also, it is not clear from Alonso's article that he would defend the notion of ellipsis in any but a figurative sense. To justify it in grammatical terms calls for a transformation (the *quienes sean* one, noted below) that may be quite *ad hoc*.

[7] My former colleague L. Moreno and I reached the same conclusion independently of Alonso. Our best example was *Hombres no se portan así* vs. *Los hombres no se portan así*. The first implies the way a man must behave in order to merit the name: 'Quienes sean hombres no se portan así'. The second states that men as an extant reality do not behave that way.

predicate: *Quienes sean villanos te maten*. But if he does this, there is no need to resort to the passive transformation. *Quienes sean traidores deben ser matados* and *Quienes sean traidores deben morir* would yield the same result as far as undetermined nouns are concerned.

Altogether, the whole matter of undetermined subjects seems rather wide of the mark. Clearly, undetermined nouns can be subjects in surface grammar, and if they are, the verb normally agrees—which is enough to give Rosenblat the impulse to gloss *Se vende naranjas* as 'Se venden naranjas', if he views *naranjas* as a grammatical subject. He could do this and agree in principle with Otero.

On Otero's SECOND POINT—that *Se alquilan casas* is not a true reflexive construction—one is left to understand (though he does not assert it) that *se* is a kind of subject pronoun: "Si *Pepe vende naranjas* es una oración castellana, ¿por qué no ha de serlo *se vende naranjas*? ¿No son las naranjas las cosas vendidas en ambos casos?" For native speakers who feel this analogy the argument is sound. The question is whether all of them do. Assuming some do not, then it becomes a matter of terminology whether *Se vende(n) naranjas* is reflexive or something else. If the historical ties of the impersonal with the personal use of *se* are now so loose that it makes better sense to call the former, say, a middle voice, we can call it that, just as we are free to call *Won't you sit down?* an invitation rather than a question, though it has all the earmarks of the latter. (*Se alquilan casas* and *Se suicidan cobardes* are likewise the same in form.)

It is in the THIRD POINT, where *Se sienta a las señoras* as a parallel to *Se vende naranjas* enters the picture, that one glimpses the complexity of the dialectal situation. A valuable tenet of the linguistics of the past decade is that a grammarian should, before committing himself to a given analysis, consider whether it is "motivated"—i.e., whether there are repercussions elsewhere in the system. Otero implies by his analogy that *a las señoras* is a direct object. Do other parts of the grammar confirm this?

A noteworthy difference between American and Peninsular Spanish is the readiness with which most Spaniards accept a construction such as *Doy el libro a Juan*, and the reluctance of most Spanish Americans to accept anything but *Le doy el libro a Juan*. This seems to be generalized to other dative constructions besides those containing both a dative and an accusative. So, for *temer*, my Venezuelan informant rejects *Él teme a las chicas* in favor of *Él les teme a las chicas,* though he accepts *Él ama a las chicas;* and so for other verbs that govern dative, such as *dar* and *pegar* in the sense of 'strike', *ganar* 'beat' (in a game), etc.; likewise for verbs of the *gustar* class—*Le encantan a María las flores.*

There are speakers who require *Se les sienta a las señoras* or at least accept it on a par with *Se sienta a las señoras,* while rejecting *Yo les siento a las señoras* (except with *les* referring to a third party). Taken with the fact that Spanish Americans are normally *loístas,* this usage adds up to pretty strong evidence for *Se (les) sienta a las mujeres* as a dative construction, not an accusative one. For these speakers, at least, *Él sienta a las mujeres* and *Se sienta a las mujeres* are not true parallels.

The dativeness of this construction was discussed by Cuervo in a long note (No. 106) to Bello's intuition (*Gramática de la lengua castellana,* §791) that sequences like *Se colocó a las damas en un magnífico estrado* should be regarded as containing a dative, not an accusative. Cuervo agreed, citing historical antecedents and the preference for *le, les* in both masculine and feminine in Spanish America and of *les* over *los* in Spain; "el instinto común de los que hablan castellano," he said, "tiende a emplear el dativo en estas frases." It seems that popular usage in Spain still favors *le, les* for both genders (which proves Cuervo right in attributing the preference for accusative pronouns here to hyperurbanism). The following paradigm, judged by a Castilian,[8] illustrates both this and the dative-sign *a* required when the complement is a noun:

1. *El verbo *hacer* se lo usa como subordinado.
2. Al verbo *hacer* se lo usa como subordinado.
3. Al verbo *hacer* se le usa como subordinado.
4. *El verbo *hacer* se le usa como subordinado.
5. El verbo *hacer* se usa como subordinado.

My informant preferred 3 to 2, but note that even with *lo* he required the *a,* which of course would be unnecessary, even unlikely, with this non-person object if it were accusative. (Another informant rejected 3 and 4.) A similar example from a (presumably) Colombian source:

[8] L. Moreno, Burgalés.

Como vocativo afectivo de padres a hijos es muy usado *m'hijito/a*, AL CUAL se lo siente como una unidad.[9]

The following, from T. Navarro, is typical of his style:

A unas [lenguas] se les admira y elogia y a otras se les considera faltas de belleza y atractivo.[10]

Reactions to this last example were instructive: A fellow-Spaniard wanted *las* but two Mexican speakers, an Argentinian, and a Costa Rican agreed on *les*. If *lenguas* were replaced with *idiomas*, the Spaniard said he would use *los*, adding that in his younger days he might have said *les*.

Before one can state with assurance that a given dialect has fully accepted the paradigm:

Se alquila casas.
Pedro alquila casas.
Se sienta a las señoras.
Pedro sienta a las señoras.

the following questions need to be answered affirmatively:

1. Is the speaker consistent in using *Se alquila casas* rather than *Se alquilan casas*?
2. Is *Se alquila casas* paralleled by *Se alquila las casas*, as *Pedro alquila casas* is by *Pedro alquila las casas?*
3. Can a preposed noun object omit *a*, as in *Las casas se las alquila fácilmente* rather than *A las casas se las (les) a.f.?*
4. If the speaker requires a redundant *le* or *les* in the ordinary dative constructions, is he happy without it here?
5. If *Se alquila las casas* is the norm, does it produce *Se las alquila* as its pronominal counterpart?
6. Does *se* exhibit other characteristics of a subject pronoun? E.g., can one witness, paralleling *Si uno vende naranjas, recibe dinero,*

[9] M. B. Fontanella in *BICC*, XVII (1962), 560.
[10] *Fonologia española* (Syracuse, 1946), p. 108.

> omission of a second *se* in *Si se vende naranjas, recibe dinero?*[11] Can *se* be detached from the verb, as other pronoun subjects can be (e.g., would the normal question form be **¿Alquílase casas?* and the normal negation **Se no alquila casas*[12])?

The dispute between Otero and Rosenblat is a replay of that between J. Aristigueta, a feature writer for the *Diario de la Marina* (Havana), and the Cuban grammarian Alonso F. Padrón, in 1933. Aristigueta in his column had complained about "los letreros que tanto abundan por ahí: *Se alquilan casas, Se componen zapatos, Se zurcen medias*" which he felt were ungrammatical, "pues si el verbo se coloca en plural, resulta que se alquilan las casas a sí o entre sí. . . ." (The "tanto abundan" suggests a POPULAR use of the plural, and a hyperurban insistence on the singular.) Padrón replied that grammatical agreement between the victim and the verb is no more surprising here than in the passive, citing constructions like *Se alquilan casas por los inquilinos* to show the parallel.[13] Many speakers are chary of such *por*-agent phrases with impersonal *se*, but there is copious evidence for them in the dialects. This leads to a seventh question to add to the list: Does the speaker either reject altogether such passive-like constructions as *Se alquilan casas por los inquilinos,* or accept them in the form *Se alquila casas por los inquilinos*? (In the latter case, the grammar will be

---

[11] I believe that historically refl. *se,* whatever its use now, is the least likely of the conjunctive pronouns to be omitted. A Peruvian who accepted *Los vimos y saludamos* as perfectly normal was willing to grant only that he had heard *Se levantó y lavó,* not that he would use it. One condition that seems to ease the way to omitting a repeated *se* is the relationship between the two verbs: If the second is a kind of complement to the first, the two may act as a unit, e.g., *La intensidad se atenúa y ablanda* (T. Navarro, *Manual de entonación española* [Syracuse, 1944], p. 196), or, with impersonal *se, El derecho de asilo diplomático se solicita y concede en circunstancias excepcionales* (example invented by Moreno). One would look, then, for something slightly less close-knit than *Se compra y vende casas.*

[12] The issue of the position of *se* in the negative is raised by S. Saporta in *RPh,* XX (1966-67), 234. He credits it to a paper read by L. Contreras.

[13] A. F. Padrón, *Cuestiones lingüísticas y gramaticales* (Havana, 1947), pp. 88-92.

complicated by having to set up *por los inquilinos* as an expansion of *se,* if *se* ranks as a subject pronoun.)

Some dialects have taken one or more of the seven steps, perhaps enough to grant *se* a borderline status as a subject pronoun—the example *El verbo* HACER *se lo usa como subordinado,* though starred above, was actually used, and the same construction with other words occurred several times, in a written report by an Ecuadorian. In others, however, the development has not gone far enough to justify that, or to vindicate Otero's surprise at Rosenblat's gloss. It still makes good sense for some if not most dialects to regard (*Este salón es donde) se examina* as a middle voice using a reflexive pronoun (or call it something else) with emphasis on the action, in contrast with the active, where the emphasis is on the actor, and with the passive, where it is on the victim.[14] When a victim is optionally added, it takes, in these dialects, the dative case: *Se (les) examina a los heridos.* A passable analytical translation is 'Examining goes on with reference to the injured'. The grammatical contrast between this object, which would pass as accusative in the ordinary active voice (*Examinan a los heridos*), and the object in, say, *Se les habla,* which would already be dative in the active *Les hablan,* is lost: 'Talking goes on with reference to them'.

How general is the *Se alquila casas* construction? Lacking a survey, it would be hard to decide. After defending it ("*Se* ¿puede ser alguna vez sujeto gramatical o lógico?" pregunta un corresponsal. —Sí, puede ser...."), Flórez opines: "En Colombia es más bien poco usual, pero se da...."[15] The type *Se alquilan piezas,* he says, involves "el uso tradicional, literario y más general."

---

[14] This follows from the elements that are obligatory, besides the verb, in each construction. In *Examinamos (a los heridos)* the *-mos,* i.e., the reference to the actor, is mandatory, while the victim can be disregarded. In *Los heridos son examinados (por los médicos)* the mention of the victim is obligatory, if only in the person and number of *son,* while the actor, expressed by a *por* phrase, is optional. In *Se examina* neither actor nor victim need be identified.

[15] *Temas de castellano, notas de divulgación,* 2ed. (Bogotá, 1967), pp. 76*f.*

The Comparison of Inequality in Spanish

[*Author's Note*: Probably no other learning problem has been beset with more trumped-up "rules" than the comparison of inequality, where the great obstacle is the distinction between *que* and *de* for English *than*: "*De* is used before numerals"; "*Que* is used before numerals after a negative"; "*Del que* is preferred to *que el que* to avoid repeating *que*"; "*Del que* is used when the second member of the comparison is a clause." It seemed to me that there had to be some underlying semantic principle rather than scraps of mixed-up grammar, and I undertook a corpus-based study to see if it might be possible to identify some simple mechanism driving the choice that native speakers make so effortlessly.

It turned out, unsurprisingly, that *de* is behaving like its normal self, as a preposition: She has more than ten = She has upwards *of* ten, *Tiene más de diez*. *De* is used when amounts are scaled and the compared amounts are explicitly given: *more* and *ten* are two amounts of the same thing. But in *She has more than John, John* is not an amount, and we say *Ella tiene más que Juan.*

There are complications owing to Spanish syntax, not bearing directly on the choice of *de* or *que*. The chief one is the requirement of a complement in a subordinate clause after *than*, which is optional in English. We may say either *John has more than he needs* or *John has more than what he needs.* Spanish requires the *what—lo que, el que, la que, los que, las que,* according to the gender and number of the referent of *what*:

John has more (stuff) than he needs = Juan tiene más de *lo que* necesita.

John has more oranges than he needs = Juan tiene más naranjas de *las que* necesita.

Since the *what* names the amount—amount of stuff compared with amount of stuff, number of oranges compared with number of oranges—*de* is triggered: John has upwards *of* what he needs. The rule for *que* may also apply:

We have taller athletes than (what) you have on your team = Tenemos atletas más altos que *los que* tienes en tu equipo.

Más altos gives an amount of tallness, but *los que* is not a comparable amount of tallness—*what* here is 'the ones (athletes) who', i.e., *We have athletes who are taller than the ones that you have (are tall).* To get a comparable amount of tallness we need a sentence like

Their athletes are taller than I thought = Sus atletas son más altos de lo que yo creía.

'más altos de lo altos que yo creía que eran'.

The problem is the elliptical nature of comparison, as much as the semantics of *de* and *que*.]

* * *

1. Introduction

THIS STUDY OF unequal comparison was undertaken in order to establish with greater precision the distinction between the uses of *que* and *de* to connect the elements of the comparison.[1] The problem is neatly stated from the English standpoint as '*que* and *de* as translations of *than*'. The material covered—approximately a million running words of Spanish and Spanish American authors, in addition to responses from a number of native speakers—was broad enough to enable some other conclusions to be reached besides those

[1] This article was first printed in *Language* 26 (1950): 28-62, reprinted here with permission.

embraced by the original problem. The written sources[2] include a wide variety of modern literary, scientific, and journalistic prose.

1.1 Nature of the Problem

While grouping *que* and *de* together under the single heading of 'comparison' seems axiomatic to the speaker of English, actually it calls for justification. Often a matter assumed to be problematical WITHIN a given language turns out to be merely a translation problem—this is true of *tomar* and *llevar,* which cause no trouble until they are matched with English *take.* So we must inquire whether it is right to take *que* and *de* as two facets of one phenomenon within Spanish, or as a specious unity induced by English *than.*

Actually it is both. Most of the time, as we shall see, the modern Hispano distinguishes *que* and *de* sharply—here the confusion is from

[2] These are as follows, with the initials used to identify them here: AME = *América* 24: 1, 2, 3, enero, febrero, marzo (Habana, 1945). B = Benito Lynch, Los Caranchos de la Florida (Buenos Aires, Espasa Calpe, 1938). BRL = G. A. Becquer, Rimas y Leyendas, 7ª ed. (Buenos Aires, Espasa Calpe, 1943). C = Memoria, IV Congreso Panamericano de Carreteras (México, D. F., 1942). CA = Ciro Alegría, La Serpiente de Oro, 2ª ed. (Santiago de Chile, Nacimiento, 1936). CM = Ciro Alegría, El Mundo es Ancho y Ajeno, 7ª ed. (Santiago de Chile, Ercilla, 1944). GDB = Rómulo Gallegos, Doña Bárbara (Barcelona, Araluce, n.d.). H = Antonio Heras, Vorágine sin Fondo (Madrid, Espasa-Calpe, 1936). JA = B. Pérez Galdós, Marianela (Boston, Heath, 1910. JM = B. Pérez Galdós, El Abuelo (Boston, Heath, 1910). M = V. Blasco Ibáñez, La Barraca (Madrid, Sempere, n.d.). MA = *Mañana* (México, D. F., 1946). OO = Daniel Samper Ortega, La Obsesión (Bogotá, Minerva, 1935). P = *La Prensa* (Buenos Aires, enero 1946). R = Carlos P. Rómulo, Yo Ví la Caída de Filipinas (Madrid, 1945). RA = *Revista de América* (México, D. F., 23 de marzo 1946). RM = *Revista Mexicana de Sociología* (México, D. F., Instituto de Investigaciones Sociales de la Universidad Nacional Autónoma, 27 de febrero 1946). XY = *Todo* núm 656 (México D. F., 4 de abril 1946). YZ = *México Cinema* núm 42 (México, D. F., marzo 1946). ZZ = *Fotofilm Cinemagazine* núm. 3 (México, D. F., mayo 1946).

Grateful acknowledgement is due to the readers who collected the citations from the written sources: A. E. Conway, Fidel J. González Jr., Murel Harris, Madeline Kaplan, Raymond V. López, Carmen Masino, Alonzo Montes, Lorenzo Sandoval, Clark Tardy, Angelo Villa, Ruth Volz, and Margaret Ziegler.

the point of view of English. But some of the time the Hispano is uncertain, choosing now *que* and now *de*, just as speakers of English may hesitate (since the notions of 'contrast' and 'separation' are easily confused) between *different from* and *different than* or between *another... than* and *another... from*. Furthermore, a large part of the modern clarity of the distinction between *que* and *de* has grown up since the sixteenth century. On this account, the coupling of *que* and *de* is properly a matter of Spanish syntax, not merely one of correlating two languages.

1.2 What Material is Included

A. EXPLICIT COMPARISONS ONLY. No comparisons were collected unless they contained *que* or *de*. Implicit comparisons of the type *John's is good but mine is better* are not recorded. There appear 623 examples of explicit comparisons, of which 489 use *que* and 134 use *de*.

B. COMPARISONS MUST CONTAIN AN EXPRESSION IN THE 'COMPARATIVE DEGREE'. On the whole this criterion is not hard to apply, since regular comparisons contain *más* or *menos* and are easy to recognize, and the irregular comparatives (*mejor, peor, mayor, menor*) are only four in number. To these must be added the etymologically comparative *otro*, which like English *other* is regularly encountered in comparisons identical with those of other comparatives.

As has happened with English *different*, certain other expressions have by their close similarity in meaning been made similar to comparisons in form as well.[3] The similarity in meaning between 'I'd *rather* do this', 'I'd *sooner* do this', and 'I'd do this *first*' is obvious. So it is not surprising that *antes*, which matches with *sooner*, and *primero*, which translates *first*, should be construed with *que*, in the sense of 'rather'. Four examples of *antes*, e.g.

> H 18 Casi hubieran preferido morirse *antes que* llamar al endiablado y hereje Foncerrada

[3] Keniston, The Syntax of Castilian Prose: The Sixteenth Century (Chicago, 1937), records (42.773) examples of *al revés, ante, antes, contrario, diferencia, diferente,* and *primero* construed with *que* in the sixteenth century.

and one of *primero*

CM 41 *Primero* muerto *que* cansado

so used were recorded. *Antes* and *primero* are not included in the statistics.[4]

As with English *prefer,*[5] *preferir* may govern *que*. Sr. Julio Jiménez Rueda was heard to say (September 1946),

Prefería crear con la imaginación *que* [copiar de la historia].

It may be partially the analogy of *antes* and *después* with the comparatives that has kept the simplification of *antes de que* and *después de que* as *antes que* and *después que* when followed by a substantive or substantive phrase:

Llegó *antes que* yo = Llegó *más pronto que* yo.

This analogy goes even farther, as witness

R 26 Y me hicieron presentir el horror que se acercaba por momentos y que llegaría a mi propio país *antes de lo que* yo mismo pensaba,

and may be worked out as follows:

Llegó antes que yo matches with *Tenía más que yo*
Llegó antes de las diez matches with *Tenía más de diez*

---

[4] Real Academia Española, Gramática de la Lengua Española (Madrid, 1931) records (§428 *j*) instances of *diferente, distinto, diverso,* and *primero* construed with *que*. It attempts to explain them on the basis of ellipsis–*Acaban de comer con costumbres diferentes que empezaron* being presumably from *Acaban de comer con costumbres* DIFERENTES *de las costumbres con* QUE *empezaron.* Analogy, however, is probably a better premise, especially as it works both ways–*En cuanto al desempleo, el problema de Puerto Rico no es peor al de ningún otro país* (*Ecos de Nueva York,* 19 octubre 1947 page 10)–here a true comparative is used with *a,* the preposition which, alternating with *de,* is normal with *diferente.* See Bolinger. Analogical Correlatives of *Than, American Speech* 21.199-202 (1946).

[5] See Bolinger, op.cit.

Llegó antes de lo que yo pensaba matches with *Tenía más de lo que yo pensaba*

A similar parallel is found in *además,* etymologically a comparative. It may behave like a comparative in *además que,* although as a preposition in *además de*:

Además que yo, estuvieron allí Juan y María ('besides the fact that I was there')
Además de mí, estuvieron allí Juan y María ('in addition to me')

C. COMPARISONS MUST BE RECOGNIZED AS SUCH FROM CONTEXT. The formal clue of a comparative plus *que* or *de* is not sufficient, as witness *Tengo más de eso* = I have more OF that' or 'I have more THAN that'. Contextual clues supply the distinction; in the two examples

GDB 145 No tenía más sangre que pudiera afluirle al rostro
P 76 De este encuentro resultó un motivo más de cólera para toda la huerta

the context shows that the comparisons are not explicit. The presence of a definite article often marks the phrase as superlative, as in

ZZ 35/1 La maquinaria más moderna que se construye en los Estados Unidos.

D. SOME STEROTYPES EXCLUDED. The fossilized *además de, a más de, más allá de* and *por más que* are not counted. Those with *de* analogize better with compound prepositions (*fuera de, dentro de,* etc.), and the one with *que* is an offshoot of *por mucho que*. We must recognize, however, that *de* even in comparisons is essentially a preposition, and that the resemblance between the *de* of comparisons and the *de* of *más allá de* is a family one—note the kinship of *He went farther than Boston* and *He went beyond Boston* or between

RA 39/1 Es cierto que esta cifra está *muy por debajo de* la que tienen otros países

and the same sentence with *mucho menos de*. In fact, we shall find that a simple test for most uses of *de* 'than' is that it shall be translatable by the English prepositions *over* and *under* (*He has more than ten* = *He has over ten*).

2. *Que* in Expressions of 'Exclusion' and 'Ratherness'

Semantically there are three main uses of full comparison in Spanish: (1) in expressions of 'exclusion' and 'ratherness', employing *que*; (2) in expressions of 'degree', employing *que* or *de*; (3) in expressions of 'quantity', employing *de*. Despite some overlapping, it is possible to describe formal differences, as well as semantic ones, with a fair degree of accuracy.

More frequent than in English is the Spanish use of comparison to show not a greater-lesser relationship between alternatives, but a yes-no relationship between them. When we say

M 205 No se oía más que el ruido lejano de carros

we do not compare a *ruido* which is 'more' with a something else which is 'less'; rather, we affirm one particular *ruido* and deny every other sound. Such expressions of 'exclusion' fall into five general types: (1) negative or question ... *más... que*; (2) negative... *menos... que*; (3) *otro que*; (4) *más bien... que*; and (5) simple *más... que* under certain conditions. In order to abbreviate I shall use *N* to stand for a generalized negative (i.e., for *no, nada, sin,* etc.), *M* for *más*-or-*menos,* and *Q* for *que,* though the full words will be retained when it is necessary to distinguish.

2.1 *N* or question... *más... Q*

The frequency of this combination is high—115 in the compilation, or 18%.[6] The examples enable us to formulate with assurance the suspicion set forth by Cuervo[7] (and confirmed by

---

[6] Though less used than in Spanish, the construction is no stranger to English, as witness *It was no more than right that she should come, He undertook no more than to accept the challenge.*

[7] A. Bello and R. J. Cuervo, Gramática de la Lengua Castellana nota 126 (París, Andrés Blot, 1936).

Hilario Sáenz[8]): 'Se percibe diferencia entre *No se gastaron más de cien pesos* y *No se gastaron más que cien pesos*: lo último me parece significar que se gastaron sólo cien pesos; lo primero, que pudo gastarse hasta cien pesos.' This distinction is modern. Keniston shows[9] that in the sixteenth century *N... M... Q* and *N... M... de* were interchangeable in the sense of 'only'. The present compilation contains a few ambiguous examples of *... M... de* (admitting either 'only' or 'not more than'), but none that REQUIRE the interpretation 'only'; some confusion is natural, since one speaking vaguely about 'only ten' and 'not more than ten' would be indifferent to the distinction. The cleavage in modern Spanish seems to be practically if not entirely complete. Since probative examples to the contrary are lacking, the few ambiguous examples of *N... M... de* are counted as conforming to the distinction.

While it is sometimes difficult to paraphrase the construction by the actual word *sólo*, the meaning is always precisely that of *sólo*. I quote here a few of the more difficult passages—the vast majority show the kinship with *sólo* even more clearly:

ZZ 14/1 No vieron más que una solución ('Vieron sólo una solución')

YZ 30/1 Las misteriosas actividades del invisible "Socio" a quien nadie más que Hugo conoce ('a quien sólo Hugo conoce')

M 22 Los adobes de barro, sin más que algunas ligerísimas manchas ('con sólo algunas ligerísimas manchas')

XY 23/4 No hago más que cumplir con un deber de humanidad ('sólo cumplo con un deber de humanidad')

P, 6 enero 4.2 Pero la diferencia esencial, si existe, parece ser muy poco importante, apenas más que una diferencia verbal ('parece ser... sólo una diferencia verbal')

YZ 36/1 No hay más que poner unas barras entre un hombre y una mujer, para que el uno parezca más atractivo al otro ('sólo hay que poner' etc.)

---

[8] Hilario Sáenz, The Spanish Translations of *Than*, Hispania 23.327 (1940).

[9] Syn. Cast. Prose 40.72.

YZ 40/3 Hay nada más que ver las estrellas—insistió Cornel.—Y también la luna cuando se asoma por sobre las colinas (here used for enhancement, i.e. 'the one thing, the only thing you simply must see is' etc.)

It is obvious that Cuervo's criticism is correct, and that *más que* here has lost the notion of QUANTITY or DEGREE and assumed that of IDENTITY: *no más que* = 'nothing OTHER than', hence 'only'.

The rule as usually stated, to the effect that while numerals call for the correlative *de*, negatively *que* may be used, must therefore be changed to take into account the difference in meaning that we find in

YZ 40/4 No habían transcurrido más de tres semanas (perhaps two weeks had passed, or two and a half)

MA 6 abril, 61 La población no tiene más que quince mil habitantes (it has only fifteen thousand, but it does have those fifteen thousand)

and also the fact that *N* ... *más* ... *Q* with numerals is but a special case of *N* ... *más* ... *Q* with anything in the sense of 'only'.[10]

But not all examples of *N* ... *más* ... *Q* signify 'only'. How are we to distinguish those that do from those that do not?

The compilation furnishes an ostensible answer: that *N* ... *más* . *Q* will signify 'only' if the *más Q* is unsplit, e.g.

M 187 No sacó más que tres raspaduras

or if *más* ... *Q* is split by a substantive, e.g.

M 154 Sin más luz que la de la puerta

but not if split by an adjective or adverb, e.g.

RA 55/1 Nada hay más emotivo que el triunfo de lo nuevo.

[10] After observing soundly that *no más que* = 'sino', the Academy grammar reverts (§429 *e*) to 'Si la oración principal es negativa, puede ponerse *que* en vez de *de*' for numerals–as if there were no semantic difference, adding that either *más de* or *más que* may be replaced by *sino*. This relapse may be due to the fact that the Academy does not distinguish epochs of usage, but tries to give a composite picture of all but medieval Spanish.

But while this answer fits all the material of the compilation, it is not accurate, and its faultiness reveals how dangerous it can be to rely solely upon written sources, without inventing crucial examples to be judged by a native speaker. The following invented examples fit the description but do not signify 'only':

> El no trabaja más que yo
> Es joven, pero no lo es más que María
> 'Es más animal que hombre.' —'No, señor, *no es más animal que hombre.*'

Actually the syntax of *N... más... Q* is identical with that of English *no other than,* a compound coordinating conjunction equivalent to 'but' ('sino'). This being the case, we may say that the *más* must (1) modify a negative word or phrase which is parallel[11] in construction with the word or phrase introduced by *que*:

> GDB 302 Poniéndole el revólver en el pecho nada más que para asustarlo (*nada,* adverb, parallels *para asustarlo*)
> No van a ninguna parte más que allí (same)

[11] A good example to show the significance of the parallel is MA 23 marzo, 81 *No tuvo calidad más que en su principio.* Here the *más* is adverbial, signifying (since it has to parallel *en su principio*) 'at any time other'. If the order were changed to *No tuvo más calidad que en su principio, más* would be an adjective, its parallel with *en su principio* would be destroyed, and *no más que* would not signify 'only'. Similarly in AME 57/2 *Su táctica no ha tenido más éxito que la del falangismo español,* the gender of *la* shows the parallel to be with *táctica* rather than with *éxito,* whence again the *no más que* does not signify 'only'.

Though ordinarily close, the parallelism is extended to the matching of nouns and adjectives when predicate complements, as in JA 112 *Yo no soy nada ni nadie más que para uno solo.*

The remarkable flexibility of *nada* as regards part of speech is illustrated by the examples, proposed by one native speaker: *Salió del accidente con nada menos que un ojo negro,* and *Salió del accidente nada menos que con un ojo negro,* both correct.

In the formulas to follow, the symbol ~ indicates 'grammatically similar to (parallel with)', while ≠ indicates 'grammatically dissimilar to'.

YZ 30/1 Las misteriosas actividades del invisible "Socio," a quien nadie más que Hugo conoce (*nadie*, substantive, parallels *Hugo*)

or (2) modify a substantive which bears this same parallel relationship with the element introduced by *que*:

M 248 Sin beber más líquido que aguardiente
M 165 Allí no había más pasto que el intelectual (*pasto* parallels substantivized *el intelectual*)

or (3) modify nothing, but itself be parallel with the element introduced by *que*. In (3), like English *other*, the *más* may adapt itself to paralleling (a) a substantive of any kind (including infinitives), (b) an adjective, or (c) an adverb:

(a) RA 63/1 Oh, virtud, no eres *más* que una *palabra*
M 300 No había hecho *más* que *defenderse*
(b) XY 9/1 No tienen *más* que *un* objetivo: el acrecentamiento de la fuerza militar rusa[12]
No es venerable; no es *más* que *viejo*
00 135 La culpa era suya, y nada *más* que *suya*[13]
(c) XY 41/2 No había tenido el gusto de conocer a su mamá *más* que *de vista*
RM 354 No servía *más* que *como una autorización*
Dice que no dispone *más* que *de unos pocos honderos*[14]

---

[12] Whether the parallel is with *un* 'one' or with the noun when *un* = 'a' has to be determined contextually.

[13] Construe as 'nowise other than his'; or, if preferred, take *nada* as a predicate noun paralleling the predicate adjective *suya*, and modified by *más*–in the latter case, the example belongs under (1).

[14] Marcos A. Morínigo, Sobre los Cabildos Indígenas de las Misiones, *Revista de la Academia de Entre Ríos* 1.31 (Paraná, 1946). Professor Morínigo tells me that *de más que* would be equally acceptable here; the example would then fall under (a). When, as in this amended example, a preposition is repeated on both sides of *que* (and hence 'the element introduced by *que*' contains something not paralleling the single word *más* itself), the neatest procedure is to cancel out the repeated prepositions for purposes of formulation. See below in the treatment of *otro que* a similar instance of doubling of prepositions.

Using the symbols already employed (and for the nonce taking *M* = *más* alone), and adding *B* = preferred alternative (i.e. the one NOT diminished by *NM*), *A* = unpreferred alternative, and *S* = substantive other than predicate noun,[15] we may formulate:

The entire series as *M* etc. ~ *B*, '*M* etc.' subsuming independent *M* and *M* as modifier.

The separate groupings as (1) (*N* = *A*) *MQB*, (2) *NM* (*A* = *S*)*QB*, and (3) *N*(*M* = *A*)*QB*. There is another possible order for (2), viz., *N*(*A* = *S*)*MQB*, illustrated by

No tengo dinero más que este

but this inversion does not occur in the compilation.[16] In the compilation there are ten examples of (1), thirty of (2), and seventy five of (3). Thirteen of the thirty examples of (2) use the negative *sin*, e.g.

> RM 349 Sin tener más responsabilidades que el pago de impuestos.

Where the alternatives are substantives, not only the part of speech but also the case may be reproduced in the parallel:

> CM 89 Eso . . . a nadie le ha pasado más que a mí
> M 152 No se veía . . . más que a la pobre Roseta
> ZZ 7/3 No le preocupaba más que al protagonista.

As happens with English conjunctions, however, the case may be flexible, depending in part on unambiguity. Thus in the last example

It was of no concern *to* anyone other than *to* the protagonist

---

[15] This qualification is necessary in order to exclude the type *No es más animal que hombre.*

[16] Unless one count ZZ 7/3 *No le preocupaba más que al protagonista.* Since, however, in all its other functions the conjunctive pronoun is a verbal affix and takes no modifiers of its own (its parent word may have a modifier, of course, as in CM 89 *Eso que me pasó con una víbora a nadie le ha pasado más que a mí*–here we construe *más* as qualifying *nadie* and get type [1]), it would seem better to regard *más* here as adverbial, paralleling the phrase *al protagonista*, with *le* actually repeating *B* rather than standing for *A*.

the second *to* may be omitted without confusion, whereas omitting it in Spanish would change the meaning entirely. A similar flexibility in Spanish is evident in the following invented examples, both members of each pair having been judged as correct:

> No tienen más guía que yo—No tienen más guía que a mí
> No necesitan más guía que yo—No necesitan más guía que a mí

As under rare circumstances the first member of each pair might be ambiguous, the second is available to substitute for it.

Haber, however, governs only the nominative case in disjunctive pronouns, despite its government of the objective case with conjunctive pronouns (e.g. '¿Hay suficientes? '—'Sí, *los* hay'), as witness

> JA 129 Para mí no hay más mujer que *tú* en el mundo.

No hay más guía que yo is judged as correct, *No hay más guía que a mí* as incorrect.[17]

The steps by which the normally degree-expressing *más* became exclusion-expressing are perhaps the following: From *Nadie trabaja más que yo* one infers 'Others work less than I do'. Since this does not conflict with the narrower implication 'Others do not work at all', the latter can readily come about through a shift of attachment on the part of *más*, which passes from being a modifier strictly of the verb (referring to degrees of work) to becoming a modifier rather of the subject *nadie*. This shift can be shown by intonation: *Nadie trabaja, más que yo*, equivalent to *Nadie más que yo trabaja*. Unlike the English *other*, however, which is practically unambiguous, a locution such as *Nadie trabaja más que yo* may still be given the double interpretation. The form *N*...*M*...*Q* must therefore on occasion depend upon a contextual clue.

Euphony apparently is not a factor opposing the use of correlative *que* when combined with *el* (*la*, etc.) *que* in the

---

[17] The rule in Academy §429 *b*, to the effect that *B* takes the object sign *a* if *A* has it, is inadequate in the light of these examples. In the sixteenth century (Keniston, Syn. Cast. Prose 6.743) the disjunctive pronoun could be accusative.

construction *N ... más ... Q*. The semantic distinction between *que* and *de* is respected regardless of euphony:

> JA 181 No posee más educación que la que ella misma se ha dado
> XY 38/1 Parecía no hacerle más impresión que las[18] que nos hace gracia.

There is one *N ... más ... de* plus *lo que:*

> GDB 139 No poseía ni más ni menos de lo que se necesitaba

but this means 'exactly' (referring to quantity), not 'only'. The one example with a question implying a negative likewise conforms:

> JM 199 ¿Qué tiene que hacer más que lo que tú le mandes? (implied, 'He has to do only what you command').

With a simple relative *que*, however, euphony seems to be a factor, as witness the one example:

> RM 353 Pensaron que la familia no necesitaba más *de que* el gobierno se ocupara en guiarla.[19]

Here the *de que* instead of *que que* seems to mean 'only'. The same is true of the example

> No exigimos más de que sean graduados de un instituto acreditado

suggested by a Guatemalan speaker.

Two idioms appear under *N ... más ... Q* in the compilation:

(1) *Más remedio que,* with four examples, three using *tener* and one *quedar,* e.g.

> B 147 No tienen más remedio que aguantarse.
> CS 173 No queda más remedio que estar viéndola caer.

(2) *No haber más que* with three examples, e.g.

> M 105 Su trigo tenía sed. No había más que verlo.

---

[18] Error for *la*.

[19] This example is not counted in the figures for *no más que*.

The latter is interesting in that the *que* serves a dual purpose, that of *haber que* and that of *más que*. No examples of *no poder más que* were turned up.

2.2 *N ... menos ... Q*

Just as *no más que* is 'no other than' in a minimizing sense, combining, in an example like *No es más que Juan*, the ideas of 'It is precisely John' and 'John is nothing much', so *no menos que* is 'no other than' in a maximizing sense, combining, in an example like

> XY 56/2 Siguiendo en orden al bat nada menos que Nernon, el debutante,

the ideas of 'It was precisely Nernon who came to bat' and 'Nernon is important'. Here again we are dealing with 'exclusion', not with 'degree', since the literal implication of the example, that someone 'more' than Nernon might be involved, is absurd. The English analog is most familiar in the form

> Who came to bat? Why, Nernon, *no less*.[20]

Aside from the emotional connotations noted, *no más que* and *no menos que* are synonyms, and may be combined, as in

> CM 35 Ni más ni menos que el cadáver, fresco aún, de una mujer.

Though theoretically identical in syntax with *N ... más ... Q*, *N ... menos ... Q* is more limited in application. No examples of preadjunct *menos*—type (2) of *N ... más ... Q*—appear in the compilation. The negative in six of the total of ten examples is *nada*, e.g.

> MA 6 abril, 8 Han disminuido nada menos que en un setenta y cinco por ciento.

[20] And in certain stereotypes: *I had no more than come when–*, *I had no sooner come than–*, *He did it no less than twenty times*, *No fewer than twenty people showed up*.

There is one *ni* (see the next-to-last example quoted), and *no* appears four times, three times in the idiom *no poder menos*. The counterbalanced (*A* and *B*) elements are adverb phrases (four examples), e.g.

R 29 Se trataba nada menos que de 232 peldaños,

adjective phrases (one example),

XY 52/1 También fué descubierto in fraganti Luis Venegas Torres, contralor nada menos que de la Secretaría de Economía,

substantives (two examples, already quoted), substantive phrases (three, in the idiom *no poder menos*), and one substantive clause:

ZZ 18/2 Para tan lucida reunión de figuras máximas, *no* era de esperarse *menos que*, en la parte del animador, del coordinador en la continuidad del programa, apareciese otro valor vertical en su género: el simpatiquísimo locutor Álvaro Gálvez y Fuentes, tan conocido, querido y admirado.

The *que* in this example does double duty: it is a correlative for the comparison, and a conjunction for the clause.[21]

No poder menos reveals a discrepancy with the Keniston Syntax List. The correlative in all three instances is *que*:

XY 6/1 Tan satisfactorio informe no ha podido menos que satisfacer a los dirigentes de la Nacional Financiera.
XY 26/1 Y al hojear esta nueva obra, . . . no puedo menos que evocar las vicisitudes del autor
MA 6 abril, 42 Uno no puede menos que admirarse.

There are no examples of *no poder menos de*, although this is the only form in which the idiom appears in the Syntax List.[22] The difference

---

[21] See Keniston Syn. Cast. Prose 26.345 for *que* in double function in the sixteenth century.

[22] The wording in Keniston, Spanish Syntax List §26.5 (New York, Holt, 1937) is 'When the main clause is negative it may deny any alternative "exclusion" beyond that indicated in the second element and the correlative for "than" will be *de*. Of this construction, common down to the Golden Age,

appears to be regional: the three Castilians whom I consulted preferred *menos de,* and all the Latin Americans preferred *menos que;* neither group discerned any difference in meaning.

Negative examples of *menos* which do not satisfy the syntactic conditions set down for *N . . . más . . . Q* in the preceding section, will not refer to 'exclusion'. Examples:

YZ 13/3 Y no es menos verdad que durante ese tiempo
JA 112 Él es el único para quien la Neal no es menos que los gatos y los perros.[23]

Quantitative expressions, using *menos de,* are also outside:

C 353 No tiene menos de 300 pies de anchura y no menos de 3.000 pies de longitud.

There is a type, however, which does belong here and which, if bona fide examples of it can be found, will require modifying the formulas somewhat. It is exemplified by the English

He undertook no less difficult a task than to capture the robber single-handed.

(i.e. 'he DID undertake that particular task' and 'the task was important on the side of difficulty'). No examples appear in the compilation, but the corresponding

Emprendió tarea no menos difícil que la de capturar al ladrón él solo

seems to be quite possible.[24]

---

only one example remains: in the idiom *no poder menos de.'* The phraseology should be amended (or a section added on *no más que, otro que,* etc.) so as to show that nowadays 'denying any alternative beyond that indicated in the second element' is a function of *que.*

[23] *Menos* subjective complement does not parallel *los gatos y los perros* subject of elliptical clause.

[24] The position of the negative is decisive in English. Note that we cannot substitute *not* for *no,* so as to get *He did not undertake less difficult a task than to capture, etc.,* and come out with the same implication at all; similarly with this particular construction in Spanish, where *no* must be applied directly to *menos,*

2.3 *N . . . otro . . . Q*

The eighteen examples of *otro . . . Q* in the compilation are all negative, which fact makes this phrase identical with *N . . . más . . . Q* in both construction and meaning. While the affirmative use appears to be possible,[25] it is distinctly unusual. One affirmative example of *otro* with *de* appears,

> H 143 Se encuentra muy distinta, muy otra de la que era unas semanas antes,

---

the type *No emprendió tarea menos difícil que la de, etc.* having a different meaning. So we modify formula *NM(A = S)QB* in two ways: first, by letting *M* stand for *menos* plus an adjective; second, by admitting the order *(A = S)NMQB*. It does not follow that elsewhere the position of *no* in Spanish is important. Thus *No lo dijo menos que* (or *de*) *30 veces* and *Lo dijo no menos que* (or *de*) *30 veces* are all acceptable and the shift of *no* is unimportant.

Probably the corresponding *He went no less rapidly than ninety miles per hour* is acceptable in direct translation. Here we can repeate the formula *N (M = A)QB*, with the proviso that *M* is *menos* plus an adverb and that nothing intervenes between *N* and *M*.

I have been unable to get positive evidence for a Spanish equivalent of the English use of *more* in this same type of construction, i.e. in which *more* is expanded to *more* plus an adjective or an adverb, as in *We received no more satisfactory a clue than the knowledge that the culprit was somewhere about*, implying that 'we DID get that particular clue or knowledge' and that 'it was unimportant on the side of satisfactoriness'. The same native speaker who accepted *Emprendió tarea no menos difícil* with the implication that I have assumed, rejected *Recibimos indicio no más satisfactorio*. The Castilian speaker, for many years resident in this country, felt that *The pilot climbed out of his cockpit with nothing worse than a black eye* (*Saturday Evening Post* 7 Sept. 1946 page 20) would be intelligible, though unusual, in direct translation. One Costa Rican speaker, newer to these shores, felt, however, that the literal phrasing would be untranslatable.

[25] It was used in the sixteenth century–see Keniston Syn. Cast. Prose 5.647. The invented examples *No me gusta vivir aquí; yo esperaba otra cosa que estar siempre dentro de casa cuidando de la familia* and *¿Es ésta? - No, es otra que ésta* were accepted by one speaker but rejected by another.

but this is an assimilation of *otro* to *distinto* exactly similar to that of English *another from (She is quite another from the one she was)*, and probably should not be counted among the comparatives.

The parallel of *N ... otro ... Q* with *N ... más ... Q* is perfect as far as it goes, but *N ... otro ... Q* appears with *otro* only as an adjective, while *N ... más ... Q*, like English *N ... other ... than*, may use *más* not only as an adjective but also as an adverb:

> We do not work other than at night
> No trabajamos más que de noche,

or as a substantive:

> I have no other than this No tengo más que esto

Again, despite the compilation, *otro* as a noun is doubtless possible, given the readiness with which indefinites shift between these two parts of speech.[26]

In one example the *otro*, though an adjective itself, occurs within an adverbial phrase:

> MA 23 marzo, 70 No se habló de otra cosa que de la magnificencia de los nuevos estudios.

But this is due to the fondness of Spanish for parallelism where prepositional phrases are concerned, and does not affect the logic of the construction, as witness the precisely similar example in which the parallelism is missing:

> CS 77 No conciben una persona con otra hambre que la que ellos tienen (not *que con la que*).[27]

In sixteen of the eighteen examples, *otro* is adjunct; e.g.

> MA 6 abril, 13 Sin otro derecho que el del más fuerte
> R 195 No había otra claridad que la de la luna.

---

[26] The invented examples *No llegaron otros que éstos, ¿Había otros que éstos?* and *No he visto a otro que a Juan* were accepted by one speaker but rejected by another.

[27] See footnote 13.

The two non-adjunct examples are:

YZ 5/1 El laudo . . . cuya finalidad no era otra que fraternizar y unir . . . ha sido violado

XY 13/1 Su papel . . . no era otro que el de conservar intacto el Imperio Británico

The number of instances of *otra cosa que* (four), 'anything but', indicates a high frequency for this expression among uses of *N . . . otro . . . Q*:

M 46 No les quedaba otra cosa que los fardos.

There is no evidence for *de* + article + *Q* (except the one instance of *de la que* above which was excluded from the comparatives), i.e. of replacement of *que* by *de* when followed by a clause. Two instances of *Q* + article + *Q* occur, one already quoted, the other

R 158 No disponían de otras informaciones que las que el enemigo les lanzaba.

Use of a simple *que* would obviously be ambiguous and hence unacceptable, as in the invented

La casa es otra que yo esperaba.

2.4 *Más bien . . . Q*

Only eight examples of this most specific equivalent of 'rather' appear in the compilation, which gives it a lower frequency than simple *más . . . Q* (to be treated in the next section) and only a slightly higher frequency than that of *antes . . . Q*.

In *más bien . . . Q* as in the negative phrases of 'exclusion' already treated, the *que* coordinates two grammatically similar elements, which we may designate *A* (preferred) and *B* (unpreferred). Since *más* combines with *bien* rather than with *A* or *B*, it is most convenient to use *A* ~ *B* as the overall formula. *A* and *B* may be nouns,

C 419 El interés más bien resulta un cargo indirecto que un cargo directo sobre la obra (the displacement of *más bien* is frequent, as in this last example where it is shifted in front of the verb); verbs,

> CS 65 Parecía que más bien veía que oía las palabras;

adverb phrases,

> R 359 Desarreglos sociales como de una crisis, más bien que como de uno de los lentos . . . ;

or adjective phrases,

> P 14 enero 4/3 Fué más bien la consecuencia de nuestra buena suerte que del cuidado que pusimos en conservarlo.

There would be other possibilities as well, e.g.

> Yo he de llamarte a ti más bien que tú a mí,

where subject and complement are both matched.

As *más bien* is in other ways equivalent to *mejor,* one might wonder whether *mejor* ever alternates with it. The following example resembles those of *más bien*:

> OO 99 ¿Quién mejor que el marido de su hija era el llamado a suceder al señor Higinio cuando éste faltase?

In this one detects, however, not the mere 'exclusion' implication of *más bien,* but a suggestion of 'degree'—i.e. not '*A* instead of *B*' but '*B* perhaps, though *A* more'.

No examples of *de* + article + *Q* or of *Q* + article + *Q* appear. But note the example already cited, *Más bien veía que oía las palabras,* for an instance of a finite verb introduced by simple *que* for 'than'.

There are no negative examples of *más bien* in the compilation.

2.5 *Más . . . Q*

Of the four exclusion-expressing uses of comparison, *más . . . Q* is most ambiguous. We have little difficulty in deciding, when we hear *I'd rather go than stay* or *I'd sooner go than stay,* that the speaker does NOT want to stay. *Más bien* and *antes,* like English *rather* and *sooner,* have virtually become synonyms of *not. Más . . . Q* is, in fact (and this was probably true also of *más bien que* and *antes que* in their beginnings), sometimes a euphemism for *not*. Instead of answering a question like *Mary is your favorite, isn't she?* by the blunt *Not Mary, Jane,* we spare another's feelings by saying *Well, Jane more than Mary.*

But one can never say that a given example MUST signify 'exclusion' (i.e. be a synonym of *not*) rather than 'degree'. One can only affirm that in certain positions *más* ... *Q* probably refers to exclusion, while in others it probably refers to degree. Fortunately these positions are fairly definite.

In the compilation, eight types of *más* ... *Q* conceivably with the syntax of *más bien* ... *Q* (which is the criterion for inclusion here[1]) appear. These may be classified by taking the example

---

[1] This means that the *más* must be (1) a sentence adverb, not an adjective nor a noun, (and hence cannot itself be one of the alternatives, so that *M* etc. ~ *B* becomes *A* ~ *B* here); and that the alternatives must be (2) explicit and (3) parallel. (1) The type P 6 enero, 4/8 *Sólo la Argentina ha suministrado* ... *más carne que la prometida* is excluded because *más* is adjective, while XY 21/2 *Confluyen dos influencias hereditaries: la de los Reyes, más artistas que hombres de acción* evidences *más* as an adverb accompanying a predicate noun (*be* understood) rather than an object or subject noun–and is accordingly included. Similarly the type XY 11/1 *Tenían más de lámparas de petróleo que de espiritual resplandor* is excluded because *más* is substantive. Of the latter type, one ambiguous example appears, GDB 183 *De eso debe de saber más que yo, usted que es abogado,* where *más* may be considered to modify *saber de eso* or to be a substantive and itself modified by *de eso*; it is not counted among the examples of *más* 'rather'. The adverb versus non-adverb status of *más* may be demonstrated by comparing *He has more money than I* with *He, more than I, has money.* And the sentence-adverb versus non-sentence-adverb is illustrated by YZ 52/1 *Hay chicas atractivas que no son hermosas, y éstas generalmente llaman más la atención de los hombres que las que son bellas y no expresivas,* where the position of *más* makes it impossible for *más* to be a sentence adverb–a condition which would be reversed if *más que las que son bellas* immediately followed *éstas.* (2) The type JM 215 *¿Me querrás más que tu hermana?* is excluded because the first alternative, *tú,* is unexpressed. (3) The type *A los Estados Unidos* ... *les corresponde avanzar en estas ideas más que las demás naciones* is excluded because the alternatives are not parallel; had the second alternative been *a las demás naciones* the example would have been included. Probably the type BRL 85 *Yo te amo más aún que tú me amas,* in which *A* and *B* are independent clauses, should also be excluded; but this will have to await evidence on whether *más bien* is possible in such a construction. English avoids a *rather* coordinating independent clauses; instead, it subordinates one of them: *Rather than* YOUR CALLING ME, *I'll call you.*

> Su extravagancia más se manifiesta en la impropiedad que en la novedad de las voces[2]

and arranging it in the following ways:

(1) Más se manifiesta en la impropiedad que en la novedad
(2) Se manifiesta más en la impropiedad que en la novedad
(3) Se manifiesta en la impropiedad más que en la novedad
(4) Más que en la novedad, se manifiesta en la impropiedad
(5) Se manifiesta, más que en la novedad, en la impropiedad
(6) En la impropiedad, más que en la novedad, se manifiesta
(7) En la impropiedad se manifiesta, más que en la novedad
(8) Más que en la novedad, en la impropiedad se manifiesta.

If we set *V* = governing verb, *A* = preferred alternative, and *B* = unpreferred alternative,[3] keeping the other symbols as they were before (*M* = *más* and *Q* = *que*), and disregarding interpolated words, the eight types may be identified as follows:

---

[2] Enciclopedia Universal Ilustrada, vol. 35, s.v. Modernismo, page 1231.

[3] In cases of apposition, such as XY 28/3 *No obstante el alarde de fuerza, más aparente que real,... su influencia... empezó... a debilitarse*, the *V* is considered to be an elliptical *ser* (supplying, in the example just quoted, the words *que era*), and is counted as an initial *V* in the table. Seven instances of apposition occur, four as *VMAQB* and three as *V AMQB*.

The verb does not have to be finite–e.g. GDB 266 *Santos se sentó* RENDIDO, *más que de cansancio, de desaliento*. In place of a verb (and counted as *V* in the formula), there may be an adjective in absolute construction, as in the sole example OO 81 *Los chicos,* ATENTOS, *más que a la procesión, a desprender de los cirios la cera chorreada*. Though no examples of the type appeared, a construction is possible in which *V* = *A*, *B*–as, adapting one *más bien* example already quoted, *Más que veía, oía las palabras*.

Since *más que* is now affirmative, *A* and *B*, as 'preferred alternative' versus 'unpreferred alternative', are reversed from what they were in *N*... *M*... *Q*. I deemed it best to preserve the syntactic values of *A* and *B* rather than their semantic values.

TYPE	TIMES OCCURRED IN COMPILATION[4]	EXAMPLES
(1) *MV AQB*	4	CM 112 Más parece un desgraciado que un hombre malo
(2) *VMAQB*	20	AME 94/1 Su humorismo es más de situación que de idea
(3) *V AMQB*	10	H 23 Pero sus amores eran de n suave platonismo imaginario, más que una iniciación de la llamada de la vida
		XY 27/1 ¿Amas a tu padre, a tu madre, a tu esposo, a tu hijo más que a mí?
(4) *MQBV A*	10	R 200 Más que castigo, aquel hombre merecía un premio
(5) *VMQBA*	6	R 195 Hablaban más que con palabras con suspiros
(6) *AMQBV*	2	OO 115 Al adivinar, más que ver,[5] al marido ignorante,... tuvo temor

[4] These figures include all the examples fitting the definition of *más que* as sentence adverb–44 which context allows to be considered as sentence adverb, and 22 which context marks as not sentence adverb and which are accordingly included in the statistics of *M* etc. ≠ *B*.

[5] This example shows faulty parallelism, the *ver* standing for *al ver*. Other instances of faulty parallelism are AME 16/1 *Más que el fin de la guerra* [instead of *Más que fin a la guerra* or just *Más que a la guerra*], *deseamos poner fin al inicio de todas las guerras,* and M 188 *Más parecía de desierto africano que lecho de un río* (predicate adjectives matched with predicate nouns are a common occurrence).

(7) *AVMQB*	13	GDB 78 Contigo contaba, más que con ningún otro
(8) *MQBAV*	1	RM 381 Más aún que la familia campesina de Alemania, la familia teuto-brasileña continúa.

Of the eight types, two, the fourth (*MQBV A*) and the fifth (*VMQBA*), lend themselves most readily to interpretation as sentence adverbs and accordingly would suggest 'más bien' more than 'degree' to the average native speaker of Spanish.[6] The eighth type (*MQBAV*) perhaps would also, if an example could be found in which the *más* is unmodified (*más aún* is forced to refer to degree, as *aún* itself refers to degree). In these three types, *M* is separated from *A* by *QB*, or, to put it verbally, the thing or quality that COULD by its proximity to some one element be a non-sentence adverb and therefore show degrees of that element is prevented from doing so by having the potentially degree-expressing *más* too far removed from it. Furthermore, the *MQ* stands intact at or near the beginning of the sentence, in emphatic position, which endows *más que* with unusual significance, giving it a force approaching that of 'not'.

Three other types, the second (*VMAQB*), the third (*V AMQB*), and the seventh (*AVMQB*), cannot as a rule be construed as synonymous with *más bien*. We note that in these, *M* is tied directly to *V* and *A*, i.e. that *más* is in a position to show the degrees of some more limited element of the sentence. So examples like

Es un problema que afecta más a China que a Japón[7]

[6] Three were consulted on this point. The first, who was asked, 'Assuming that there is a difference in meaning between *Témanle a él más que a la peste* and *Más que a la peste, témanle a él,* how would you identify the difference?' replied, 'In the second, *más* is equivalent to *más bien*'; *más bien* was not suggested to him. The two others, who did not think of *más bien* until I asked 'Which of the two inclines more to *más bien*?' did, however, identify the second example as the one.

[7] El Conflicto Chino-Japonés, Ojeada General, page 11 (Tokio, Nippon Gaiji Kyokai, 25 noviembre 1937).

CM 62 Labrado por los cascos más que por las picotadas y las palas
JM 102 Es una enfermedad que me desagrada más que otras

clearly refer to degree and not to ratherness.

The two remaining types, the first (*MV AQB*) and the sixth (*AMQBV*), are—as far as can be determined from so few examples—the most ambiguous. If the deductions that were made above from the position of the constituents are accurate, ambiguity is to be expected, since in *MV AQB* the *M* is in emphatic position, but this is vitiated by its standing next to *V A*; and in *AMQBV* the *MQ* is intact and in prominent position, but this is vitiated by *M*'s standing next to *A*. So it is difficult to judge

BRL 72 Más parece jifero de la puerta de la Carne que maestro de solfa
ZZ 13/1 Y estos empresarios nómadas... fueron los que—más que ningún agente comercial—llevaron 'las fotografías animadas' a todos los países.

Since, however, *más que* should probably not be taken as 'rather' except under the most favorable conditions, it is best to put these types down as expressing degree.

In the nature of the case, *MQ* must precede *B*. We may then summarize those types in which conditions are most favorable to ratherness as the ones in which *B* precedes *A*. This automatically implies that *MQ* will be in emphatic or at leat in prominent position, and that *MQ* will be intact, since the only type in which it could be divided, *MVQBA*, is logically impossible.

There may inure one other condition favorable to 'rather'—pause (comma) before *MQ*, which of course throws *MQ* to the beginning of a breath group (emphatic position) and also separates *M* from *A* and *V*. The best example is the one already cited,

Contigo contaba, más que con ningún otro.

Entirely aside from order, there are numerous contextual conditions that may force the interpretation of 'degree'. We have already seen one instance of *aún* modifying *más*. Since ratherness depends on contrasting *A* and *B*, an example like

B 102 La quiere más que a su vida

in which one finds an unemphatic pronoun, incapable of being contrastive, the interpretation has to be 'degree'.

A favorite stylistic device with the type *VMAQB* is that in which *A* and *B* are mutually exclusive adjectives. Three examples appear; e.g.

OO 28 Era más gordo que flaco
JA 133 Quedóse la Nela... más muerta que viva.

3. *Que* and *De* in Expressions of 'Degree'

The most convenient subdivision of expressions of 'degree' and one which in the main also squares with the most significant semantic differences, is a two-way division based upon the syntax of the word *más* itself. In Class I, *más* or a substantive (rarely an adverb) modified by *más* is grammatically similar to the element introduced by *que*. Letting *A* be the 'weighted' element of the comparison (i.e. the one associated with *M* = *más* or *menos*) and *B* the other element, the relationship may be expressed by the types (1) *(M = A)* ~ *B*, (2) *MA* ~ *B*, and (3) *AM* ~ *B*. This is, as we have seen, the situation obtaining in *N*... *M*... *Q* and *otro*... *Q*. Example:

P 14 enero, 10/2 Y entonces va a ser tarde... más que tarde

—here *más* and *tarde* are both predicate adjectives.

In Class II, *más* is not *A* itself, nor does it exclusively modify *A*, whence *M* or *M* plus whatever element it modifies is dissimilar to *B*. Most typical are examples on the order of

JM 185 Sois más ciego que yo,

where *más ciego* ≠ *yo*. Sometimes the clues for determining 'similarity' are tenuous, e.g. in

JA 32 Somos menos que las mulas,

where the presence of *las* tells us that *mulas* is a subject and not a predicate noun, and therefore not similar to *menos; Somos menos que mulas* would be the opposite case.

3.1 Class I, *M* etc. ~ *B*

Type (1), (*M* = *A*) ~ *B*.

Here the frontier between *que* and *de* is longest. Since the native speaker of Spanish will often hesitate, if questioned, between using *Tengo más de esa cantidad de dinero* and *Tengo más que esa cantidad de dinero,* it is best to consider *que* and *de* together. The confusion does not come, however, except when *más* stands, or appears to stand, for an adjective or a noun. Let us consider the other cases first.

Knowing that *N*...*más*...*Q* signifies 'sólo', one naturally wonders whether *más que* may be used in the sense of 'no sólo', 'not just'. The ten instances of (*M* = *A*) ~ *B* employing *que* in the compilation all show *más* used with just such force. Its special significance may be appreciated by comparing Class II *He does it more than before* (may be any degree—a tenth more or a hundred times more) with Class I *He does it more than well* ('not just well'—perhaps perfectly). There is one example each in which *más* so used parallels an adverb and a verb:

> H 158 Ya conocía más que medianamente el español
> MA 6 abril, 15 Esto, más que compensa la moderada tarifa.

Comparing now the instances of *que* and *de* where *más* parallels adjectives and nouns, we examine first the instances of adjectives, of which there are five with *que,* e.g.:

> RA 37/4 Hacían *más* que *imposible* el paso
> YZ 15/1 Comprende para ella *más* que *suficientes* problemas
> H 172 La casa era pequeña, de un solo piso. Para ellas—pensaba Isabel—*más* que *de sobra.*

In these, we observe the same 'not just' implication already pointed out. Contrast it with that of the examples with *de* (three), e.g.:

> YZ 7/1 Siendo *más* de *cien* los concursantes
> CM 18 Contó los niños, que resultaron *más* de *cien.*

With nouns, the situation is more difficult. The three examples with *que* in the compilation are all predicate nouns, e.g.:

> MA 6 abril, 17 Raleigh es más que un cigarro

M 79 Los vecinos devoraban su rabia en silencio. ¡Ladrón, más que ladrón!

Add the example of one Castilian speaker, this one with object noun; the informant avers that *de* is impossible:

Da a entender que los demás sufrieron más que rasguños.

The implication of 'not just' is plain, as it is also in the invented example

Perdió más que su territorio,

which matches

XY 38/2 Hicieron... que México perdiera más de la mitad de su territorio.

There is, necessarily, a quantitative expression somewhere about when *de* is admitted in the type ($M = A$) ~ B. But would it not also be possible to say

que México perdiera más *que* la mitad de su territorio?

Que IS possible, with the same meaning as that of *perdió más que su territorio,* i.e. we refer to a loss of prestige, warships, petroleum rights, or what-not, rather than to more territory versus less territory. Where we find *que,* then, *más* is a noun in its own right, naming something new to the context;[8] with *de, más* is more conveniently regarded as an adjective (or a cognate object, as in

CM 15 Se acostumbró a *beber más* [bebida] de lo debido)

---

[8] In *Necesito más que sólo a ese hombre* we mean 'más cosas'–*things* is new to *man.* In *Necesito a más que sólo a ese hombre* we mean 'más hombres'–men 'other than', or new to, this one. But in P 12 enero, 4/7 *Operaron a más de 500 prisioneros, más* INCLUDES the 500 and is accordingly not new to it. In *Haciendo esto, recibiremos más de la debida atención de los demás,* the meaning is 'más atención de la debida', whence *más* is not new to *debida atención,* but includes it; if *que* were employed, the implication would be something like 'más que la debida atención, protestas'.

combining with some noun (or verb) in the immediate context and matching a quantitative word, usually a numerical adjective.[9] We are obliged to say 'usually numerical' because of contrary examples like

H 69 Andrés Bustamente era de más de *mediana* estatura,[10]

and we are obliged to say 'usually an adjective' because of the frequency with which quantitative substantives, with or without *de* following, may substitute for numerical adjectives: e.g.

Tengo más de *esa cifra*

matches

Tengo más de *diez,*

and

Tengo más de *esa cantidad de* dinero

matches

---

[9] *Más* is considered an adjective when it qualifies a noun used adverbially, as in H 28 *Duró más [años] de quince años* or AME 11/1 *No varió más [libras] de cinco libras.*

[10] *Que,* referring to something 'other than' as well as 'more than', is the stronger connective, and lends itself to hyperbole. This appears to be the explanation of *Tenemos más que suficientes razones para rechazarlo* and *Las tenemos más que suficientes,* a type (not found in the compilation) where *de* is unacceptable, despite the close similarity to *más de mediana estatura.* I assume that *más que suficientes* is a stereotyped exaggeration: 'We have more (quantity) reasons AND THEN SOME(thing else)'. The same would be true of *Tengo más que poco.*

An alternative analysis of *más que suficientes* would be 'reasons that are, in addition to being sufficient, also cogent and persuasive'–alluding to the descriptive rather than to the quantitative aspect of *suficiente,* i.e. saying that the reasons are something other than sufficient as well as sufficient. Probably *que* suggests both *más que razones* and *más que suficientes,* thereby gaining in force.

De is, of course, normal in the less ambiguous *Tengo más de las razones suficientes para rechazarlo.*

Tengo más de *diez* dólares.

We now see that if in the example *Tengo más de esa cantidad de dinero* we were to substitute *que* for the first *de*, the meaning would become 'I have jewels, lands, slaves', or what-not, in addition to that amount of money.

The conclusion is thus reached that *más de*, in the type ($M = A$) ~ B, shows *más* as a quantitative adjective. In *Perdió más de diez dólares* we are saying *más de diez;* in *Perdió más que diez dólares* we are saying *más que dólares.*[11]

The substitution of quantitative nouns for adjectives of quantity produces another collision between *que* and *de*, by reason of the fact that the types discussed in this section, in which M alone or plus its modified words parallels B, overlap those in which the parallel is missing: M etc. ~ B is confused with M etc. ≁ B. This may be seen in the example

XY 25/4 Pesa... 20 gramos menos que el peso oficial.[12]

Now obviously *peso* is a quantitative noun, and would admit of *de*, just as we might say *Pesa 20 gramos menos de 30 kilos*. Why, then, the *que*? It is because we can interpret the example with *que* to mean 'It weighs 20 grams less than the official weight WEIGHS'—*peso* is a

---

[11] Fortunately the teacher does not have to depend on this necessarily roundabout description in order to explain *más de* versus *más que* in the type ($M = A$) ~ B with B other than article plus *que* (the great majority, since with article plus *que* comprises only ten per cent of the instances of *de* used in comparison), since the English prepositions *over* and *under* are practically foolproof for *más de* and *menos de*: 'He lost over ten dollars, under half that amount, etc.'. It will not, however, work for time, e.g. B 86 *Deben de ser más de las seis.*

[12] In order to get this example into the M etc. ~ B mold we may interpret in either of two ways: (1) as ($M = A$) ~ B by construing *20 gramos* as adverbial–'It weighs less BY 20 GRAMS'; or (2) as AM ~ B by taking *menos* to be an adjective modifying *gramos*. The *que-de* question remains the same in either case. Some examples will not admit of construing the specifying expression that precedes as anything but adverbial. All three examples of such expressions given by Ramsey (§546) are of this nature, e.g. *Él es tres años mayor que yo.*

subject noun, and so is dissimilar to *M*; all such constructions demand *que*. Unlike the frontier already discussed, where *que* and *de* are used in comparable constructions but with a difference in meaning, here *que* and *de* may be used with no significant difference in meaning. The difference is grammatical, not semantic.

The substantive that replaces the adjective of quantity may be a pronoun, as in

> JM 31 Gastan... más de lo que tienen
> M 6 abril, 46 65 millones más de los que ahora pueblan sus estepas y ciudades[13]
> CM 15 Se acostumbró a beber más de lo debido.

Here, instead of a noun of pure quantity (*cantidad, cifra,* etc.), a substantive referring to a thing is used as an indicator of the thing's quantity—*los* is not important to the comparison as 'people', but as 'number of people'; *lo* is not important as the nature of the thing possessed or drunk, but as the amount of it.[14] This extension is also met with in Type 2, e.g.

> RA 25/1 De allí la necesidad de atribuir a un magistrado más *autoridad* de *la* que posee un príncipe constitucional.

Deserving of attention both for the translation problem that it poses and, within Spanish, for its frequency (15), is the use of *más de un, una* where English would have 'more than ONE', as opposed to *más que un, una* for 'more than A'. *Más de una* appears seven times with *vez,* e.g.

---

[13] Type *AM* ~ *B*, but included here because the situation is the same.

[14] The substantive *lo* here is not to be confused with the adverbial *lo* to be treated later.

Lo que is frequent as a pronoun signifying 'the amount that' or 'the number that'. One occasionally has the choice of using either this general quantitative pronoun or a more specific pronoun referring to a definite antecedent and taken in the sense of the quantity-of-that-thing, e.g. *Hay más alumnos en el curso de los que* [or *de lo que*] *habíamos previsto*. The meaning of the context limits this choice; thus in *Compra más libros de los que puede leer, lo que* would probably not do, since *leer* demands a reference to something readable, not just to some quantity.

M 244 Todo esto sin contar que Teresa, más de una vez, se encerraba en su estudio,

and twice with its synonym *ocasión*. Other examples:

CM 110 La vida vale más de una carta en la baraja
XY 36/2 Kane enderezó a más de un borracho.

Had the first of these two examples signified 'more than A card', we should have found *que*. This stylistic use of *more than one, one* being emphatic and contrastive, would be encountered practically always when the word following *un, una* is not itself quantitative. When that word is itself quantitative, then the *un, una* is usually equivalent to *a* or to an unemphatic *one*, as in

M 51 El viejo estuvo más de una hora en la taberna.

This would not, of course, rule out an emphatic *one* under whatever circumstances, when the speaker reveals it through intonation.

Type (2), *MA ~ B*.

Here again we find both *de* and *que*, with the distinction of meaning already noted:

C 359 Tenemos muchos más automóviles de los que existen en Europa
JA 37 Son heroísmos de más precio que el bodrio sobrante de una mala comida.

In the latter example, we assume that the meaning is 'of another, more exalted price', the *más* analogizing here with 'other' just as it did in *N... más... Q*, e.g.

M 248 Sin beber más líquido que aguardiente.

At this point, however, two threads of the *que*-versus-*de* controversy converge in such a way as to make the choice doubtful.

First, the presence of a noun BEFORE the equivalent for 'than' may make *de* ambiguous, since the *de* phrase might appear to modify the noun; this encourages (but does not force, as witness the second-to-last example quoted) the choice of *que*. So we get

P 6 enero, 4/8 Sólo la Argentina ha suministrado a Gran Bretaña más carne que la prometida por los dos dominios juntos,

where the meaning can hardly be other than purely quantitative.[15] Even worse would be the potential confusion if *de* were substituted in

AME 61/2 Más maestros que soldados—y Costa Rica se ufana de ello,

where *que* introduces a NEW noun.[16]

Second, there is again a confusion of the types *M* etc. ~ *B* and *M* etc. ≠ *B*, coming by way of an assimilation of *más* to *mayor* and of *menos* to *menor*. *Less* is so close semantically to *smaller*, and *more* so close to *larger*, that the confusion is understandable—the more so as Spanish adds a morphological similarity in *menos* and *menor*. So in the same work we have the following examples:

C 351 La pista en la "faja de vuelo" ... no debiera de ser *menor de* 150 pies de ancho

---

[15] The one Mexican speaker to whom this was referred said that *de* would be preferable if *carne* were omitted.

A similar problem is posed by the invented example *This week we've bought more sugar than the 10,000 tons that were delivered last week.* One Costa Rican objected to the position of *sugar* in the word-for-word translation, saying that it should be phrased *más de las 10,000 toneladas de azúcar*. The Spaniard accepted both positions as correct. Both informants demanded *de*.

[16] It is difficult to find examples other than numerical in which both *A* and *B* are pictured as quantifiable and measurable on the same scale, such as would be, e.g. *red* and *pink* considered as two degrees of the same color. Thus *It is redder than merely pink* seems to be impossible in Spanish (*It is redder than pink* is not a test of this type, since it expands as 'It is redder than pink is red', giving *M* etc. ≠ *B*). With some adverbs, however, though none appear in the compilation, the conditions are satisfied: *Viaja más rápidamente que a dos millas por hora*. Here we find *que*, perhaps because of the ambiguity of the double preposition *de a*, or perhaps because the analogy is with 'Viaja más rápidamente que a dos millas por hora [es rápidamente]'.

C 351 La pista de una "faja de vuelo" no debe de ser *menor de* 150 pies de ancho
C 408 Para el sistema en conjunto, Qs debe de ser igual o *mayor que* uno
C 408 No es absolutamente necesario que Qs sea igual o *mayor que* uno.

From other sources:

AME 51/2 Lo dicho plantea el problema de lpostguerra por un término no menor de tres años
El número es mayor de treinta.[17]

No instance appears in the compilation in which *menor* or *mayor* is employed with *de* followed by anything other than a numeral. Elsewhere it is always *que*, e.g.:

MA 6 abril, 7 La guerra se inició para impedir una mutilación territorial, y terminó con otra diez veces mayor que la que había proyectado Hitler
C 368 Permitirá velocidades mayores que las que ahora se obtienen
C 403 Estas distancias son mayores que las distancias de visibilidad.

Given the frequency with which *más* and *menos* admit of words like *distancias* and *las* = 'velocidades' in a purely quantitative sense combined with *de*, there would be nothing inconsistent in using *de* in the three last examples quoted; it is not so used simply because the assimilation of *mayor* to *más* and *menor* to *menos* has got little farther than the most obvious conditions of quantity. Normally *mayor* and *menor* are used in a *M* etc. ≠ *B* construction, e.g. *The garage is smaller than the house (is small)*, where *more small* is grammatically dissimilar to *house*; whence *The number is smaller than one (is small)* is acceptable alongside of *The number is less than* (i.e. 'under') *one*. Now assimilations can work both ways. If *mayor* can take *de* under conditions most favorable to the interpretation of quantity, *más* can

[17] Example suggested by Castilian speaker, who rejected *que* here.

take *que* under conditions most favorable to the interpretation of size or greatness. Hence

> BRL 94 Un rayo cayendo de improviso a sus pies, no le hubiera causado más asombro que el que le causaron estas palabras,

where *más* = 'mayor'.

Given these conditions, it is not surprising that the native hesitates and is sometimes inconsistent in his choice of *de* and *que* in the class *M* etc. ~ *B*. *Que* is the more general connective, and tends to increase its territory; hence purely quantitative examples like

> AME 96/2 Según dice don Artemio de Valle-Arispe, sus "Andanzas de Hernán Cortés y otros excesos" han tardado *más* en llegar editadas a América, *que* lo que el personaje tardó en llegar y apoderarse de México
>
> El colombiano... aprende *más* en los periódicos sobre las otras repúblicas americanas y las naciones de otros continentes, *que* lo que aprendiera en sus días de colegial.[18]

In

> XY 25/1 Realmente no hay derecho a atacar a un pobre trabajador porque expende... el producto de su propio esfuerzo, que no tiene más pecado que ser de *mejor* calidad y de *más* peso *que* el de el de[19] los poderosos del pan,

the combination of *M* etc. ≠ *B* and *M* etc. ~ *B* is probably what accounts for the use of *que*, in addition to which *de* might be ambiguous.

---

[18] Rodolfo N. Luque, quoted in Revista de América, page 5 (Boston, Ginn, 1943). Can the separation of *más* from *lo* be an influence here? Certainly the argument that *de... que* is preferred to *que... que* for the sake of euphony is disproved, since in these two examples euphony AND logic call for *de*, but are not sufficient to compel it.

[19] Misprint–delete second *el de*.

Types (1) and (2) with adverbial *lo*

These employ *de* with the adverb *lo,* which modifies a verb in the type (*M* = *A*) ~ *B*:

> Se ha quejado usted más de lo debido
> JM 341 Has estudiado más de lo que creí [que hubiera estudiado]
> JM 277 Quizás te conviene más de lo que tú crees;[1]

or an adjective or adverb in the type *MA* ~ *B*:

> XY 36/3 Podría ser más útil a la Compañia, de lo [útil] que le soy ahora
> La leyenda ha ido más lejos de lo [lejos] que debiera haberse aventurado;[2]

or a combination of verb and adjective (through a shift of the point of view of the verb from finite or verbal to participle) in the type (*M* = *A*) ~ *B*:

> JM 222 La gruta me confunde más de lo [confuso] que estoy

---

[1] For convenience of analysis (i.e. in order to regard the *lo* as independent and so set up a pattern of regularity among all uses of adverbial *lo*) I consider *lo* to be the verb modifier here, and the accompanying clause (or adjective of the type *necesario, debido, indicado,* etc.) to be a modifier of *lo.* It would, of course, be equally valid to regard *lo* plus its adjective or clause as a unit adverbial modifier, or to regard the *lo* as an adverbial article modifying the adjective or clause which is then itself the modifier of the verb.

Examples of the *más de lo necesario* type show the error of limiting *lo* in this adverbial use to the combination *de lo que.*

In examples like *Has estudiado más de lo que creí* the decision whether to regard *lo* as adverbial or as substantive depends on whether the verb is regarded as transitive or intransitive. It is the same problem that we face in classifying *a lot* in *He eats a lot*–adverbial if we mean 'He does a lot of eating', substantive if we mean 'He eats a lot of stuff'. There is, of course, no problem in *Quizás te conviene más de lo que tú crees,* since the *más* and its co-word *lo* cannot be direct objects and so must be adverbs. The difference is semantically unimportant.

[2] R. Blanco Fombona, El Modernismo y los Poetas Modernistas, page 119 (Madrid, Mundo Latino, 1929).

GDB 216 Echarla a perder más de lo [perdida] que ya estaba.

That the *lo* is adverbial in these combinations is well illustrated by the example

> Los latinoamericanos estamos mejor [= más bien] informados respecto de los Estados Unidos, por medio de la escuela y los periódicos, de lo [bien] que el norteamericano lo [= informado] está con respecto a nosotros,[3]

where two *lo*'s are required, one adverbial and the other pro-adjective.

The adverbial *lo* furnishes two more motives for confusion between *de* and *que*. First, there is no formal difference between a substantive *lo que* and an adverbial *lo que*. In

> *Esta piedra está más dura que el acero* equivale a: *esta piedra está más dura que lo que esperaba*[4]

the parallel of the two sentences suggests that the author intends *lo* as a substantive matching *acero*, and hence to be interpreted as *M* etc. ≠ *B*, i.e. as 'Está más dura que *lo* que esperaba [*es duro*]'; but the *lo* might as readily be adverbial in the combination 'lo [dura] que esperaba [que sería]'; in the latter case, *de* would normally be used. The example

> P 10 enero, 7/4 Si la empresa aceptara un menor margen de seguridad que lo que aconseja ... la pasada experiencia

may be taken in three ways: two as *M* etc. ~ *B*, (1) as *lo* adverbial, referring to *lo pequeño* to match *menor* ('más pequeño'), (2) as *lo que*

---

[3] Rodolfo N. Luque, quoted in Revista de América, page 5 (Boston, Ginn, 1943). This example was submitted to the criticism of one Castilian speaker, who agreed that both *lo*'s were necessary, but added that it would be equally correct to say *Estamos mejor informados ... que* LO [= *bien informado*] *está el norteamericano*. The latter is analogous to the full form of *María es más bonita que Juanita* expanded to *María es más bonita que lo es Juanita*, using *que* when independent clauses are counterbalanced. See §4 for further analysis of this point.

[4] Luis Crespo in *Hispania* 29.55 footnote (1946)

for a substantive of quantity, *menor* being assimilated to *menos;* and one as *M* etc. $\neq$ *B,* (3), giving 'menor margen... que lo que aconseja... [es pequeño]'. The assimilation of *más-mayor* and *menos-menor* is thus fortified. In the example

> RM 231 Esas diferencias son mayores de lo que fueron

it makes little difference whether we analyze as 'mayores de lo [grandes] que fueron' or as 'mayores de lo [substantive of quantity] que fueron'.

Second, for a large proportion of the Spanish-speaking world there is no formal difference, or only the slightest of formal difference, between *lo* and *los.* An example like

> Encontraron peores inconvenientes que los que habían previsto

would be heard by many as *que lo que habían previsto;* and since, in the latter case, with normal *lo, de* would be called for, and there is no significant difference in meaning, *que* and *de* will be used indifferently.

In order to test this indifference, I offered, to five native speakers (one Castilian, one Catalan of long residence in Costa Rica, one Guatemalan, one Chilean, and one Mexican) a set of comparative sentences with the translation of *than* to be written in. While such a procedure is not scientific, in that after being faced with several queries of a fairly subtle turn a speaker tends to become confused, the results are consistent enough to be worth while within the limits intended. The sentences, with the number of responses of 'que', 'de', or 'either', follow (a few show only four votes, as the fifth speaker was not reached):

1. Encontraron mayores inconvenientes	D4 E1 los que habían previsto
2. Encontraron más grandes inconvenientes	Q2 D1 E2 " " " "
3. " inconvenientes mayores	Q2 D2 E1 " " " "
4. " " más grandes	Q3 E2 " " " "
5. " peores inconvenientes	D2 Q1 E2 " " " "
6. " inconvenientes peores	Q3 E2 " " " "
7. " menores inconvenientes	D3 Q1 E1 " " " "
8. " inconvenientes menores	Q2 D2 E1 " " " "
9. " " más graves	Q2 D1 E2 " " " "
10. " más y mayores inconvenientes	D2 Q2 E1 " " " "
11. " menos "	D4 E1 " " " "
12. " menos y menores "	D3 Q1 E1 " " " "

13. " inconvenientes más molestos	Q2 E2 " " " "
14. " mejores facilidades	Q2 D2 E1 las " " "
15. " facilidades mejores	Q2 D1 E2 " " " "
16. Este inconveniente es menor	Q4 los que D1 tuvimos que sufrir antes
17. " " es más pequeño	Q4 E1 " " " " " "
18. " " " mayor	Q4 E1 " " " " " "
19. " " " más grande	Q4 D1 " " " " " "
20. " " " peor	Q4 " " " " " "
21. " " " más grande	Q4 D1 " " " " " "
22. Cabe más gente	Q3 la que había D2 en el otro camión
23. Esta cifra es mayor	Q5 la que me citó usted ayer.
24. Su miedo en esta ocasión es mayor	Q3 D2 el que tenía ayer
25. Estudia más	D4 lo necesario
26. Aquí vive gente más alegre	Q3 la que se halla E1 en las ciudades

27. Esta casa es mejor	Q4 la en que usted vive
28. Asciende a más	D4 esa cifra
	Q3
29. Las maestras son mejores	E1 las que merecemos
	D3 lo que
30. Las maestras son mejores	Q1 merecemos (que sean)

We may make the following observations on the results of the test:

1. *De* is admitted by at least three of the five in all cases when *los* is used in a construction where *lo* would be equally correct. Thus we get the double interpretation of the first example, 'They encountered greater difficulties than what they had foreseen (that they would be)' and 'They encountered greater difficulties than the ones that they had foreseen'. The example

> Este inconveniente es mayor que los que tuvimos que sufrir antes

also admits of two interpretations, depending on whether *los* or *lo* is heard, but in both *que* is demanded because in neither would *lo* be adverbial: 'This difficulty is greater than those that we had to endure before' or 'greater than what (= anything) we had to endure before'.

2. When the irregular comparative stands in the normal position for a quantitative modifier (before its noun), there is a greater preference for *de* than when it stands in the normal position for a descriptive adjective (after its noun). Thus not only *mayor* and *menor*, but also to some extent *peor* and *mejor*, have assimilated to *más* and *menos*.

3. Plurality, probably by reason of its suggestion of quantity, seems to make conditions more favorable for *de*. In order to test this further, I reworded examples 16 to 21 for the Chilean, making them plural. His preference, which had previously been for *que*, then shifted to *de*.

We may conclude, from the points of interference between *que* and *de* in the written examples (the questionnaire would need many more answers in order to be probative), that while there is a rather broad no-man's land between them, especially in the *lo que, el que* sector, the choice of one or the other still obeys a grammatical distinction when adverbial *lo* is concerned, and a semantic distinction, that of 'quantity' versus 'degree', in other circumstances; in the latter, the syntactic framework seems to be breached only when test samples are chosen so as to make the situation as ambiguous as possible.

Type (3), *AM* ~ *B*.

Examples of this type are of two kinds; the first is

> XY 25/4 Pesa... 20 gramos menos que el peso oficial,

where the precise degree or absence of difference is specified by a modifying word or words preceding *M*. As the situation here is in no way different from the *M* etc. ~ *B* types already discussed, no further comment is necessary. The compilation has three examples (see above for one with *que*), two of which use *de*, e.g.

> AME 51/2 Un término no menor [assimilated to *menos*] de tres años.

In the other kind (eleven examples), *A* always appears as the word *algo*. The types *Nos ofrece más que su amor* and *Nos ofrece algo más que su amor* pair with the negatives *No nos ofrece más que su amor* and *No nos ofrece nada más que su amor*. In other words, *más* suggests 'otherness' as well as (in the affirmative, at least) degree.

Although in the type *Vivió allí algo más de tres años* the *algo* would be adverbial and would fall among the specifying expressions (*dos veces más, un año más*, etc.) discussed two paragraphs above, in the type

> R 176 El éxito significaba algo más que llegar a tener víveres,

which is the only one in which *algo M* appears in the compilation, *M* is probably best construed as the predicate of *algo*, giving 'signified something [that was] more than getting, etc.'. This being the case, *algo M* offers us nothing that has not already been considered under Type 1 with *MQ*. The addition of *algo* in some cases is necessary for clarity; in

XY 39/1 La joven no hizo intento de besar al ex-Comandante, ni éste pareció darse cuenta de la indiferencia pasajera de su novia. Aparentemente, lo preocupaba algo más que el amor

without *algo* the *más* would seem more likely to be an adverb qualifying *preocupaba*. Other examples:

RA 26/4 En esta contienda hubo algo más que el choque de ejércitos gigantescos
R 231 Es para mí algo más que un héroe
R 297 Y aunque estén hechos de algo más que de carne,[5] no son de acero.

One example testifies to a small degree of overlapping of *que* and *de* even here:

H 108 ¿Cuándo sintieron Javier y Teresa que los unía algo más de un cariño de hermanos?

3.2 Class II, *M* etc. $\neq$ *B*

Comparisons of this type comprise the majority of all comparisons not having to do with quantity, with almost half (259 examples)[6] of the total entries of the compilation. They do not fall into any clearly marked semantic-syntactic sub-types, such as were found elsewhere. There is a wealth of structural variety, however. These comparisons are of an elliptical type in which the *que* introduces a minimal syntactic element such as a noun, adjective, or adverb (unmodifying, but sometimes themselves modified), and the *M* itself functions as noun, adjective or adverb (rarely itself modified).

It should be remembered that *M* etc. $\neq$ *B* implies that *M* itself is not *A*.

[5] Note redundant *de* for parallelism.

[6] Not counted here are examples of *mayor* or *menor* with *de*, assimilated to *más* and *menos*.

In order to give some idea of the frequencies of the structural varieties, I append a table, on which the horizontal axis shows the grammatical function of *M* and the vertical axis shows the grammatical function of the element introduced by *que*. Prepositional phrases are included as 'adjectives' and 'adverbs' according to their function, and irregular comparatives are classed according to the model *mayor* = *más grande*.

(*M* sentence adverb is not counted here, inasmuch as it falls under *A* ~ *B*. In column 3 of the table, predicate noun is equated to predicate adjective, since when *M* follows a verb of being, it makes no difference which way we regard it.)

	***Más* or *menos* is**					
Element introduced by *que* is	1 Subject noun	2 Object noun	3 Adjective (or predicate noun)	4 Adverb modifying verb	5 Adverb modifying adjective	6 Adverb modifying adverb
I Subject noun or pronoun		12	*M* a pred. adj. (or pred. n.) 4; *M* other adj. 16 Total 20	19	Pred. adj. 121; non-pred. adj. 10. Total 131	9
II Predicate noun or pronoun						
III Object noun or pronoun				5	1	
IV Adjective		2 (The adj. is a phrase modifying *M*.)	1			
V Adverb modifying verb			6	8	33	7
VI Adverb modifying adjective					5	
VII Adverb modifying adverb						

I, 5. The table shows that the great majority of elliptical comparisons—191 examples—have *B* in the form of a subject noun or pronoun. Of these, the largest representation (and the largest representation of any single syntactic type in the whole of unequal comparison—121 examples) goes to *M* as an adverb modifying a predicate adjective, with the verb of being expressed or unexpressed, e.g.

B 25 Para eso es más hombre[7] que cualquiera
C 400 Factores que son un poco más críticos que los usados al estudiar el radio
CM 101 Fueron pastores de una hacienda más grande que Umay[8]
R 76 Una batalla secreta más importante que las que los generales a sus órdenes reñían en Luzón.

Where the verb of being is expressed, it occurs thirty-nine times as *ser* and eleven times as other verbs (*estar*, factitives, etc.); of the latter:

GDB 161 Estás más linda que la flor de la maravilla
JA 145 Pues aquí me tienes más contento que unas Pascuas

---

[7] Here *hombre* is an adjective; cp. *muy hombre.*

[8] The verb of being is assumed as 'unexpressed' when *B* demands it; so this example is 'Una hacienda [que era] más grande que Umay [era]'. But in MA 23 marzo, 7 *Stalin tiene mejores amigos en América que en la misma Rusia, B* demands *tiene,* whence 'amigos QUE SON mejores' is an unnecessary assumption.

On this score there is an error of analysis in Academy §428 *d.* In discussing 'el verbo que se omite en la subordinada', the example *Dionisófanes hizo . . . mayores exclamaciones aún que las que Megacles había hecho* is given as an instance of completion, i.e. of the second clause's having its verb. Actually, however, there is a missing verb *ser*: 'Dionisófanes hizo . . . mayores exclamaciones aún que las que Megacles había hecho [eran grandes]'. Only by so construing it can one make the analysis of this example square with the Academicians' own analysis of their example in the preceding paragraph: 'En *aunque él era andaluz . . . , no menos ladrón que Caco . . . ,* se comparan *él* y *Caco* con respecto al predicado *era ladrón*.' It is furthermore untrue that the *las* of the example is an object, as the Academicians call it; the *que* is objective, but the *las* (or, if you prefer, the *las* plus the whole *que* clause) is subject.

ZZ 44/1 El inglés... se hace más femenino que Marlene Dietrich.

It is in this category that set expressions, hyperboles, and other figures of speech are most frequent; for example,

RA 38/1 De él se dice que si llegara a desarrugarse, sería más grande que toda la república
JA 105 Eres más pelada que un huevo
JM 101 Mire usted a José María más colorado que un payo.

The most frequent single device is that in which *A* is denied; it is used as a substitute for the superlative:

BRL 72 No hay nada más atrevido que la ignorancia
JA 44 Jamás se vió incorrección más lastimosa... que la que el tal representaba
GDB 216 ¿Qué te parece, chica? ¿Has visto mujer más lista que yo?

The same superlative effect is achieved less frequently by making *A* or *B* all-inclusive:

JA 114 Tu cara, más linda que todas las cosas guapas y hermosas que hay en el mundo
R 27 Cualquier cosa es mejor para nosotros que esto.

One curious deviation is that in which the modifier is an adverb to one clause and an adjective to the other, as in

It goes *faster* than the speed of an airplane [is *fast*].

(This analysis is probably nearer to the truth than to assume something like *It goes faster than at the speed of an airplane.*) The compilation had no examples, but a Nicaraguan speaker volunteered

El señor corre más aprisa que el vuelo de los pájaros,

where we can only assume *es aprisa* to complete the second clause.

Following are instances in which *M* modifies an adjective other than predicative (10 examples):

R 297 Es una fuerza de más alto linaje que la meramente física: la fuerza de la fe

H 46 Daba muestras de un carácter más cerrado, de una inteligencia más nebulosa y de una voluntad menos firme que Isabel

C 394 Los caminos muy concurridos justifican mayores gastos y en consecuencia mayores velocidades de proyecto que los caminos con poco tránsito.

I, 3. Syntactically akin to the foregoing are the instances (four) in which *M* itself is the predicate adjective,

CM 120 A los hombres les disgusta que alguien que ha caído, se rehabilite, triunfe y llegue a ser más que ellos

XY 41/2 La señora de Pérez se murió, por no ser menos que su marido,

and those in which *M* itself is an adjective other than predicative (sixteen examples):

GDB 146 Este coronel tiene más vueltas que un cacho

M 36 Sus hortalizas crecían con menos rapidez que las de los vecinos.

I, 2; **I, 4**; and **I, 6** are illustrated by the following:

MA 6 abril, 46 Producimos más que España

YZ 52/1 hay chicas atractivas que no son hermosas, y éstas generalmente llaman más la atención de los hombres que las que son bellas y no expresivas

JA 83 Había aprendido mejor quizás que la mayoría de los chicos

YZ 56/3 Ese "Patio" hoy más en comadreo y chisme que cualquier quinto patio de vecindad.

Next in frequency to the instances of *B* as subject, are those in which *B* is an adverb modifying a verb (44 examples).

V, 5. As with *B* = subject, the greatest concentration of *B* = adverb modifying verb occurs when *M* is an adverb modifying an adjective, e.g.

XY 38/4 Le pareció que Violeta lucía más bella que de costumbre

C 401 Que desarrollen mayor fricción que en camino abierto.

Often a verb of being is understood:

XY 27/1 Mas vive hoy más grande y sagrado... que [fué] cuando vivió sobre la Tierra

This is due to the frequency with which adjectives are used in Spanish as predicates of other verbs than verbs of being.

Here (and in all instances of *B* = adverb modifying verb) there is approximately an even chance that *A* will be unexpressed, or only implied in a verbal inflection:

XY 35/2 Los saludos que le dirigían sus operarios eran [A = *entonces*] más respetuosas, aunque menos cordiales que antes
MA 23 marzo, 14 Comenzaron a ser [*A* = *entonces*] más irregulares que de costumbre.

The most common stereotype (eighteen examples in all of V) is that in which *B* is the word *nunca*:

CS 37 Tá más güena que nunca la fiesta
MA 23 marzo, 73 Era prodigiosa y mayor que nunca en aquellos momentos.

One example shows a confusion between *B* = subject noun and *B* = adverb:

XY 36/4 Había salido con anterioridad de situaciones más peligrosas que ahora.

V, 3; **V, 4**; and **V, 6** are illustrated by the following:

CM 108 Más moscas se cazan con miel que a palos
ZZ 34/2 Se observan más que en ninguna otra parte rostros sonrientes[9]
H 19 Vivía más en paz que nunca con sus enemigos.

III, 4 and **5**. Instances of *B* = object noun or pronoun are few, e.g.

---

[9] Here *A* = *aquí* or *allí*.

XY 7/1 Favorecieron más a los hambreadores que a los hambreados

JA 110 La persona de Dios representábasele terrible y ceñuda, más propia para infundir respeto que cariño.

The last example reveals one reason for the fewness of this type: that Spanish does not often clip a prepositional phrase. Ordinarily we should find *Más propia para infundir respeto que para infundir cariño.*

IV, 2 shows *M* not the modifier, but itself modified by *A*:

MA 23 marzo, 7 Tiene mucho más de gavilán y de buitre, que de gorrión.

The one example of **IV, 3** is

MA 6 abril, 63 Hay menos servidores del Bien que del Mal.

VI, 5. All instances of *B* = adverb modifying an adjective have the adjective in the form of a prepositional phrase, e.g.

C 403 Son más grandes para camiones que para automóviles

JA 118 ¿No te he dicho que eso es más propio de los chicuelos holgazanes del campo que de una señorita criada en la buena sociedad?

The blanks. These can all theoretically be filled, e.g.

V, 1: Más se consigue con amor que con dinero

V, 2: Aquí los exploradores han descubierto más que en otro sitio alguno

VII, 1: Más se hace parcialmente bien que completamente

There are no examples of a redundant *no* in *B* such as are described in the Academy grammar,[10] e.g.

Más vale ayunar que no enfermar.

Redundantly negatived *B* appears only in the form of the all-denying *nunca, nadie,* and *ninguno.*

[10] §428 *g, h.*

4. Complete Comparisons

So usual is ellipsis in the comparison of inequality that there are not enough examples (six) of two full clauses counterbalanced against each other to enable us to form a pattern of usage. The customary thing, of course, is to subordinate the *B* clause by using *lo* adverbial or substantive in comparisons of both degree and quantity (*Se divierte más de lo que estudia, Tiene más ahora de lo que tenía*). The compilation contains three examples where one would expect an added *de lo*:

BRL 85 Yo te amo más aún que tú me amas
JM 73 Tenemos un párroco que vale más que pesa
JM 181 Esta Gregoria vale más que pesa.

The second and third of these examples clearly use a popular saying.[11]

In two situations the *lo* is not called for:

---

[11] Their unusualness is attested by the fact that one Mexican speaker judged all three as incorrect, insisting on *de lo que*. The Castilian speaker, on the other hand, proposed *Habla más que estudia* as equally correct alongside of *Habla más de lo que estudia*, and accepted *Yo te amo más que tú me amas* as correct. It may be significant that the three examples are from Spaniards, who comprise only a third of the authors read; it may also be significant that the Castilian speaker is a specialist in Golden Age literature, with the result that colloquial norms are not so vigorously insisted on. My Latin American informants for the most part demanded the adverbial *lo*.

Though theoretically there can be no absolute semantic identity where differences of form exist, I have been unable to pin down whatever difference in meaning there may be between *Juan duerme más que trabaja* and *Juan duerme más de lo que trabaja* (I suspect, however, that *lo* quantifies it, suggesting more strongly an AMOUNT of time).

But there does seem to be a basis of distinction between *Ese señor corre más rápido que vuelan los pájaros* (acceptable–along with the same sentence with *de lo*–to one speaker who normally rejected such comparisons without *de lo*) and *Cae más de repente de lo que se desploma un árbol carcomido*. In the first, both *corre* and *vuelan* imply 'rápido'; in the second, neither *cae* nor *se desploma* necessarily implies 'de repente'. It thus is somewhat redundant, in the first example, to say *más rápido de lo [rápido] que*, etc. The same would be true of *Huyó más veloz que dispara un cañón*.

(1) In comparisons of degree, adverbial *lo* is unnecessary when *M* modifies an adjective or adverb that is matched with an explicit adjective or adverb in the *B* clause. The compilation has one example:

GDB 203 Mi soga está más tiesa que pelo es negro.

The absence of *lo* may be reasoned as follows:

(a) Ordinarily a *lo* so used modifies an understood repetition of the original adjective or adverb. Thus *Juan es más joven de lo que parece* = *Juan es más joven de lo joven que parece ser*. Since, when there is an explicit matching adjective or adverb in the *B* clause, there is nothing for *lo* to modify, *lo* is omitted.[12]

(b) Alternately, *lo* MAY be construed as a verb modifier even when *M* is combined with an adjective or adverb in the *A* clause. Thus we may construe *Juan es más joven de lo que parece* as *Juan es-joven más de lo que parece ser-joven*. The analysis is possible, since my Castilian informant accepted *Juan es más joven de lo que lo es María*, where we must analyze as *Juan es-joven más de lo que lo-(= joven)-es María*—in other words, we cannot here fall back upon considering the first *lo* as a modifier of understood *joven*, as we did in (a), but must regard it as a verb modifier. I do not recommend this analysis, however, because several speakers rejected the parallel *Juan es más joven de lo que Mara es vieja* (in favor of *Juan es más joven que María es vieja*), where theoretically we could analyze as *Juan es-joven más de lo que María es-vieja*.[13]

---

[12] The same is true of *Ud. vive más indiferentemente que Juan vive enérgicamente*, contrasted with *Ud. vive más indiferentemente de lo [indiferentemente] que vive Juan*.

[13] As with adjectives, so with adverbs. The example in footnote 57 could be given a *lo que* and analyzed as *Ud. vive-indiferentemente más de lo que Juan vive-enérgicamente*.

Instead of a specific new adjective, we may find the pro-adjective *lo*. This we have encountered in examples of the type *Juan es más joven que lo es María.*[14]

(2) In comparisons of quantity, substantive *lo* is superfluous when two explicit nouns are compared in the aspect of their quantity, since the quantitative *lo que* is displaced in *B* by the specific noun. Likewise, a *de* would be just as ambiguous as in the quantitative comparisons where *B* is a simple noun. So the connective is just *que*, and we get the one example

> OO 52 ¡Si creerá semejante barbilampiño que sabe más que yo, yo que he tratao más de estas garroteras que dolores padeció María Santísima!

The example

> CS 76 Ud. pide aclaraciones más que oraciones las ánimas benditas

is ambiguous.[15]

The last example quoted is the only one in the compilation showing a complex *B* without a verb. Theoretically, all combinations of I to VII in the table would be possible.[16]

---

[14] See footnote 48. A pro-adverb *lo* is unlikely because of ambiguity: thus, in order to paraphrase the example in footnotes 57 and 58 as *Ud. vive más indiferentemente que lo vive Juan* we should have to run the risk of having our second verb considered transitive and the *lo* regarded as a pronoun.

[15] Taking *más* as a quantitative modifier of *aclaraciones*, we should expect no *de lo que*; but taking it as an adverb, *de lo que* would be admis-sible, even with the verb missing from the *B* clause, as witness RM 371 *La familia urbana está, entre nosotros, más próxima a la familia rural de lo que en Alemania y en Europa en general.* So *Ud. pide aclaraciones más de lo que las ánimas benditas piden oraciones* is possible. But in the original, the position of *oraciones* probably influences the quantitative interpretation. Note the Academy example with a similar inversion: *Se ofrecen a mi remedio más inconvenientes que estrellas tiene el cielo.*

[16] Similar examples of complex *B* without the verb are in Keniston Syn. Cast. Prose 6.744 and 37.46.

5. Conclusions and Summary

The extreme intricacy and subtlety of unequal comparison is due mainly to the fact that it is highly elliptical, compelling us to expand sentences constantly in order to find their immediate constituents, and to the fact that the three words most used, *de, que,* and *lo,* have more than one function; these omissions and ambiguities interlace in a way that taxes the analyst's powers in unraveling them. The worst complicating factor is the triple function of *lo,* which may be an adverb, a substantive, or a pro-adjective.

The compilation proves that two generalizations often made about the comparison of inequality are false: (1) That *que* and *de* are frequently used indifferently. Since the total frequency of all exceptions to the analysis here made is only five, we see that indifference to the distinction is highly infrequent. (2) That *del que* etc. replaces *que el que* etc. The compilation furnishes no evidence to support this view, but firmly establishes the semantic differentiation where clauses are concerned as well as elsewhere.

We may outline the analysis as follows, with numbers in parentheses referring to frequencies in a total frequency of 623:

I. Complete Comparison (6 *que*)
- 1. Where adverbial *lo* would be more normal
  - *Yo te amo más aún que tú me amas*
- 2. Where *lo* is unlikely
  - A. With explicit adjectives or adverbs in contrast of degree
    - *Mi soga está más tiesa que pelo es negro*
  - B. With explicit nouns in quantitative contrast
    - *Yo he tratao más de estas garroteras que dolores padeció María Santísima*

II. Elliptical Comparison (617)
- 1. Type *M* etc. ~ *B* (306). (*Que* conflicts with *de* here only)
  - A. Normally with *que* (165 *que,* 3 *de*), referring to 'exclusion' and 'otherness'
    - (1) *NM...Q* (125 *que,* 1 *de*)
      - a. *M* = *más,* 'only', 'just' (115 *que,* 1 *de*)
        - *No hago más que cumplir*

No necesitaba más de que el gobierno se ocupara en guiarla (*de* to avoid *que que*)

b. *M* = *menos*, 'none other than'—enhancement (10 *que*)

Nada menos que Nernon, el debutante

(2) Affirmative *M* . . . *Q* (22 *que*, 1 *de*)

Hacían más que imposible el paso

Significa algo más que llegar

Los unía algo más de un cariño (see under exceptions)

(3) *Otro que* (18 *que*, 1 *de*)

No había otra claridad que la luna

Se encuentra muy otra de la que era (*otra* assimilated to *distinta*)

B. Normally with *de* (131 *de*, 7 *que*), referring to 'measurable' quantity or degree

(1) *B* = substantive of quantity (116 *de*, 6 *que*)

a. *B* not new-to-context noun (116 *de*, 4 *que*—see under exceptions for *que*)

Era de más de mediana estatura

Se gasta más de lo que se gana

b. *B a new-to-context noun* (2 *que*)

Más maestros que soldados—y se ufana de ello

(2) *B* = adverbial *lo* + relative *que* (15 *de*, 1 *que*—see exceptions for *que*)

Has estudiado más de lo que creí

2. Type *A* ~ *B*, meaning 'rather'—a nuance of 'exclusion' (52 *que*)

A. *Más* a sentence adverb (44 *que*)

(1) Inversions favoring 'rather than' interpretation, with *B* before *A* (16 *que*)

Más que castigo, aquel hombre merecía un premio

(2) Inversions (and other syntactic conditions) requiring 'degree' interpretation (counted under *M* etc. ≠ *B* and included here only for contrast)

El caballo sabe más que el hombre

(3) Ambiguous (28 *que*)

Insinuando más que diciendo

B. Explicit *más bien* (8 *que*)

Más bien veía que oía

3. Type *M* etc. ≠ *B* (259 *que*)

Eres más pelada que un huevo

III. Rationale of Exceptions

1. Confusion of *M* etc. ~ *B* with *M* etc. ≠ *B*, with negligible semantic difference

Pesa 20 gramos menos que el peso oficial

2. Assimilation of *menor* to *menos* and *mayor* to *más*, plus confusion of *M* etc. ~ *B* with *M* etc. ≠ *B*, with negligible semantic difference

No debiera de ser menor de 150 pies de ancho (Cp. *Qs debe de ser mayor que uno)*

No le hubiera causado más asombro que el que le causaron estas palabras

3. Confusion of *lo* substantive with *lo* adverb

Tardó más ... que lo que tardó el personaje

4. Confusion of *un* article with *un* numeral (?)

Los unía algo más de un cariño de hermanos

It is best to define the uses of *que* negatively, stating the description as '*que* is used for *than* except under such-and-such conditions'. A positive synthesis would either be too complicated for practical use, or too general for specific application.[17] I therefore offer the

[17] The latter is illustrated by the rule of Hilario Sáenz (*Hispania* 23.327, 1940), stating: "¿'Than" is translated by *que* when both members of the comparison are of the same nature' (illustrated by examples from Bello in which parallel elements, e.g. two nouns or two verbs or two adverbs, stand on either side of *que*), which, without extensive rationalization, does not help us with examples like *Habla más que nunca* (where the parallel *ahora* is not expressed) or *No habla más que a Juan* (where *más* itself is the parallel of *a Juan*). Probably the best working rule for *de* so far proposed is that of Sáenz (page 330), that *de* is employed when the compared elements stand in a part-whole relationship, e.g. *Tengo más de veinte años*, where *más* includes *veinte*, or *Trabajo más de lo que deseo [trabajar]*, where the amount that I do work includes, and surpasses, the amount that I want to work. Still, there are considerations which make even this definition faulty at times, e.g. the type *Raleigh es más que un cigarro*, where what Raleigh is includes its cigaret-ness and surpasses it. We use *que* here despite the part-whole relationship, probably because there is no

following brief statement as a 'rule' that covers the norms for *que* and *de*:

Use *que* to correlate all comparisons

EXCEPT that *de* is used in the elliptical type *M* etc. ~ *B* (i.e. where *más* or *menos* or its phrase is grammatically similar to the element introduced by the correlative), where *B* is a literally or figuratively 'measurable' (a) quantity (e.g. *Tiene más de esa cifra, Tiene más maestros de los* [*maestros*] que *tenía antes)* or (b) degree (with adverbial *lo*, e.g. *Es menos bonita de lo [bonita] que parece*)

EXCEPT that *que* is used when *B* is a literally non-quantitative and new-to-context noun used quantitatively (*Tiene más maestros que soldados*)

As a textbook rule we may say that *de* is used if three conditions are satisfied: (1) EXPLICIT (2) AMOUNTS of the (3) SAME THING are compared. 'Explicit' defines the type *M* etc. ~ *B* (i.e. both amounts must be named). 'Same thing' eliminates the new-to-context noun, and includes qualities (measured by degrees) as well as substances (measured by quantities).

---

hint of QUANTITY. QUANTITATIVENESS seems to be the criterion for *de*, whether quantity as applied to countable or weighable or otherwise measurable things (*más de veinte, más de esa altura*), or as applied to the imagined quantification of actions and qualities (*Habla más de lo que debe, Es más bonita de lo que parece*). In the latter case, since quantification is imagined and figurative, we should not be surprised to find *de* alternating with *que*, the *que* revealing (when it is not used simply to avoid some ambiguity) that the speaker is not picturing the relationship as quantitative.

Addenda to the Comparison Of Inequality in Spanish

THIS EXTENSION OF remarks on the subject of my article, "The comparison of inequality in Spanish" (*Language* 26.28-62 [1950]), has two chief motives. First is my inexcusable oversight in failing to collate Hayward Keniston's article, "Expressions for *than* after a comparative in sixteenth century Spanish prose,"[1] with my own data. While Keniston treats another epoch, it is important to note that the two descriptions are nearly identical, save for two sharp deviations noted below. Second is the discovery of an apparent contradiction which turns out to be predictable on the basis of the theory and hence confirms it.

1. The first of the two respects in which contemporary Spanish differs radically from 16th-century Spanish was noted in the original study (31 and note 21). It is the reversal of *no más de*, the earlier stereotype for 'not other than' = 'only', reserved now for the true quantitative 'not more than' and replaced in the sense of 'only' with *no más que*. Keniston's article (148), however, gives the impression of a sharper cleavage than was noted there on the basis of his *Syntax of Castilian prose* (§26.345 and §26/541 (Chicago, 1937), leading one to posit a reorientation of *que* and *de*: the *que* of 'otherness' has been generalized, and the *de* of 'fromness', which Keniston regarded as the natural method of indicating 'no different from', hence 'only', has shrunk to the orbit of straight quantification, analogous to English

[1] This article was first published in *Language* 29 (1953): 62-66, reprinted with permission. Keniston's article was published in *Revue de linguistique romane* 6.129-51 (1930).

upwards of. The two are exemplified in the following citation from Palacio Valdés:[2]

> Hace media hora que ustedes están juntos, y las reglas de la casa no permiten más que quince minutos... Ninguno puede estar junto a una niña más de ese tiempo.

The second is that contemporary Spanish with very few exceptions avoids the type *Habla más que sabe* 'He does more talking than knowing', frequent in 16th-century Spanish,[3] in favor of the type *Habla más de lo que sabe* 'He talks more than what he knows' (cf. my article, note 56).

2. The apparent contradiction is evidenced in the following (Grismer-Arjona 29):

> Yo os perdono, y más aún, hija mía, te felicito por haber escogido un marido mucho mejor del que yo hubiera podido darte.

According to the formula, this should have *que el que*, but my two Spanish colleagues prefer *de*. There is clearly no question of confusing *mayor* with *más*, as I noted (my article 48) with previous instances of interchanged *que* and *de*.[4] The native speaker's first guess is euphony, but this is obviously the usual failure to see 'sounding good' as an effect rather than a cause. The test for the example cited lies in making the second term refer to a definite individual: when I changed the subordinate clause to *el que yo le había escogido*, both speakers shifted their preference to *que*. In the following they reacted according to the standard pattern, demanding *que* in all:

---

[2] Raymond L. Grismer and Doris King Arjona, *The pageant of Spain* 122 (New york, 1938).

[3] Keniston, Expressions for *than* 138.

[4] Cf. this additional example of *mayor* for *más: mayor mal del que me ha sucedido no puede sucederme* (G. A. Becquer, *Legends, tales, and poems* 40 [ed. Olmstead; New York, 1907]); and the invented example *La parte es menos que el todo*, judged possible by a Castilian speaker alongside of *menos de* (but *menos de*, not *que, mi porción, parte, cuota*, etc.).

> Este aparato es más complicado que el que tengo en mi laboratorio—Estas señoras son mayores que las que viven en el otro piso—Estas reliquias son más antiguas que las que nos mostraron en Roma

But in the last example, when the second term was changed to *las que hubiéramos podido hallar en Roma,* they accepted *de.* In the following, where the second term is vague, *de* was acceptable; but as soon as a definite, concrete individual or thing replaced the hypothetical one, they again demanded *que*:

> Este reducto es más fuerte del que habría sido posible construir en la colina [*but* que el que se construyó, etc.]—Sus inventos son más ingeniosos de los que otro hubiera podido idear—La vida del reconcentrado ha sido más terrible de la que cualquiera haya soñado en las pesadillas del delirio—Una fortuna más grata de la que nunca nos imagináramos

Thus when the second member is vague, the speaker ceases to think of counterbalancing two different things, and reverts to the more powerful suggestion of a different degree of the same thing. If it is true that *que* yields to *de* under the impulse of indefiniteness, then *de* should yield to *que* under the impulse of excessive definiteness. One condition of definiteness is singularity. In *Tiene más autoridad de/que la que tiene un príncipe,* if *autoridad* is construed as a mass noun the choice is *de*; if as a countable, *que*: four native speakers—a Spaniard, a Costa Rican, an Argentinian, and a Peruvian—preferred *que* here but accepted *de.* The extreme case is where we have a purely quantitative comparison, with the second term a countable in the singular naming a precise object. The utter quantitativeness demands *de,* the utter definiteness demands *que,* and apparently no regular construction with an explicit second member is possible. For example, if only one man attended a dance on a previous occasion, we cannot use the Spanish equivalent for *There are more men at the dance than* (supply *he who*) *attended last time.* With the slightly less precise but still quantitative 'one vote', *que* would be used:

> Hubo más votos por el candidato republicano que el solo voto [*but* de los 1.347 votos] que recibió en las elecciones anteriores.

A reexamination of the examples shows that the polarity definite-indefinite also helps the confusion in the formal likeness of *menor-menos, mayor-más*: note the use of *que* with the singular 'one' in *mayor que uno,* against *mayor de treinta* (48).[5]

Another condition of definite and precise 'otherness' in which the pattern is overbalanced is found in the speaker's intent to exaggerate. In *Las manos eran, en efecto, tan bellas, más bellas que lo que D. Luis había dicho en sus cartas,*[6] Valera enhances the contrast more than with the lukewarm *de lo que.* In *Este* [sic—miners' usage] *agua sube más que lo que me dijo* (invented by L. Moreno), the speaker might be expressing angry surprise, or calling the other person a liar. In *El matrimonio pesa más que lo que yo creía* (similarly), the speaker implies that marriage is something quite different from what he had expected. The effect achieved is predictable from the regular pattern. *Que* normally substantivizes a following *lo que,* thus contrasting two names of separate things rather than two aspects of the same thing.

In the following example,[7] a singular is used in the same vague, undifferentiated way as the plurals above:

> Me parece que no se me puede tener en peor opinión de la que ya he logrado

The 'otherness' of two distinct opinions is submerged in the gradation of a single opinion; the expression is equivalent to *no puede ser peor de lo que es.*

3. 'As has happened with English *different,* certain other expressions have by their close similarity in meaning been made similar to comparisons in form as well' (29).[8] The Academy (§428 j) notes this for

---

[5] Bello (§1021) implies that *mayor (menor) de veinticinco años* is elliptical for *que de.* The contamination described here is probably a factor.

[6] Pepita Jiménez 124 (Clásicos castellanos).

[7] J. Figueroa Campos, *El misterio de los guantes negros* 30 (Buenos Aires, 1947). This reference, and others marked GPS, were supplied by G. P. Sullivan.

[8] Subsequent references are to pages of my earlier study.

diferente, distinto, diverso, and *primero.* It extends, however, all the way to the comparison of identity, as might be expected, since *mismo* likewise takes the same correlative *que.* Here it is with the antonym of *mismo, contrario:*[9]

> Con las mujeres ocurre lo contrario que con las lanchas de salvamento: nos gustan más las de los otros que las que consideramos como nuestras

From there it passes to fractional and multiple comparisons, e.g. *Tiene doble (triple, la tercera parte,* etc.) *que antes,* or with *mitad:*[10]

> El tipo de cambio actualmente es muy ventajoso y los libros les resultan a mitad de precio que antes

The multiples analogize even farther: *Tiene doble de lo que debe tener Tiene más de lo que debe tener.* But with *veces* the comparison is expressed as an outright multiplication: *Tiene dos veces lo que debe tener.*

The Academy's argument from ellipsis (§428 j), that *acaban de comer con costumbres diferentes que* equals *diferentes de las costumbres con que,* is weakened by the type *El suyo es muy diferente que el mío,* accepted by my Castilian colleagues, where no ellipsis is possible. There is likewise no relevant ellipsis in *amar a una persona de distinta patria que la nuestra.*[11] As it is more usual in English to employ *than* where *from* would be wordy (e.g. *It caused quite different reactions in a man than [from those which it caused] in a woman*[12]), so Pereda writes:[13]

> La madre iba por caminos diferentes [de los caminos por los] que su marido.

---

[9] Enrique Jardiel Poncela, *Amor se escribe sin hache* (Buenos Aires, 1945). GPS.

[10] Letter from León Sánchez Cuesta, 7 July 1949.

[11] Antonio Azorín, *Old Spain* 82 (New York, 1928). GPS.

[12] Advertisement in Collier's for 12 August 1939, p. 48.

[13] J. M. Pereda, *Peñas arriba* 1.82 (Buenos Aires, 1942). GPS.

The vacillation between *que* and the prepositions *de* and *a* is seen in this instance of *a* with a true comparative and in the following *otro de*:[14]

> Las palabras españolas terminadas en consonante representan un promedio de un 38%, en tanto que en inglés ese mismo tipo de vocablos suele aparecer... en proporción no menor al 67%—Es, evidentemente, la vida más otra de la nuestra que cabe imaginar

4. 'As with English *prefer, preferir* may govern *que*' (29). Numerous written examples now confirm the oral one cited, for instance these:[15]

> Prefiero aburrirme con la cartera llena que con la carta vacía—Góngora prefiere ser condenado por ignorante que por hereje

So for *ser preferible*:[16]

> Es preferible gustar las cosas hora por hora...que pasar vertiginosamente por la vida

5. The assimilation of *antes* and *después* to the comparatives in *antes que* and *después que* (rather than *antes de que* and *después de que*) was noted in my earlier paper (30). This is corroborated by the use with them of the quantifier *mucho*, which, like English *much*,[17] is employed with regular comparatives (*mucho mayor, much older*). An example:[18]

> comienzan a evolucionar las formas compuestas mucho antes que en castellano

---

[14] Tomás Navarro, *Fonología española* 49 (Syracuse, 1946); and J. Ortega y Gasset, Revista de occidente 5.30 (1927). The latter reference supplied by Joseph Silverman.

[15] Azorín 32; and Agapito Rey, Hispania 32.403 (1949).

[16] Azorín 56.

[17] *Much* is also a test for the assimilation of *prefer* to the comparative: *I much prefer it*, but not *I much like it*.

[18] Samuel Gili Gaya, Revista de filología española 30.116 (1946).

6. Besides the type *La gruta me confunde más de lo [confuso] que estoy* (49), where *más* modifies a combination of verb and adjective instead of the more customary single element, one may get other overlappings like *Lo hace con más frecuencia de lo que creo conveniente*, where if the single element were modified one would expect *de la que*. Obviously *con frecuencia* functions as a unit equivalent to *frecuentemente*, and the sentence is construed *más con frecuencia de lo que*, etc.[19] But in *Hay más distancia de lo que yo creo conveniente*[20] the noun is apparently lost sight of.[21]

7. *Suficiente* occurs in a transposed order, *Tenemos más que suficientes razones para rechazarlo*, which seems to parallel *perdió más de diez dólares* (45) and hence to call for *de*. Native speakers prefer *que*, however, and the following examples[22] show that the phrase was inverted, and equivalent to *Tenemos razones más que suficientes*, not to *Tenemos más razones que suficientes*:

> un torrente circulatorio imperfecto, un hígado tórpido . . . son motivos más que suficientes para que el cerebro de un anciano no trabaje con la regularidad debida—¿Fué este un motivo más que suficiente para que incurriera en el odio profundo de los abolicionistas

For *de* to be acceptable, *suficiente* has to be made quantitative rather than descriptive by adding the article: *Tenemos más de las suficientes razones*.

[19] The parallel example from Keniston, *Syntax of Castilian prose* §26.441, is *lo tal creo con más veras de lo que se me puede decir*, where *más* 'logically modifies the adverbial phrase *con veras*'.

[20] Pío Baroja, Paradox, *Rey* 51 (New York, 1937).

[21] Keniston, *Syntax of Castilian prose* §26.441, cites *porque no uuiesse dentro del Alhambra más mal de lo que podía aver con la gente que avía dentro*.

[22] Revista de los archivos nacionales de Costa Rica 12:1/2.52; ibid. 48.

The Infinitive as Complement Of Nouns in Spanish

[*Author's Note*: This final piece of governance is the most recently published, though not the most recently written. It claims a place here both because of the neglect of the infinitive in most textbooks and as an illustration of how transformational grammar (in its classical form) can be exploited to show a relationship between two languages, of which one represents a "deeper" phase than the other. In effect we derive the English construction from the Spanish one by a deletion rule.]

* * *

THE INFINITIVE IS the no-man's land of contrast grammars of English and Spanish.[1] No other part of the verb system is so carefully avoided in textbooks, and a look at the situation in English supplies a ready explanation: ambiguity is rampant. Robert Lees (1960) once referred to the infinitive after the adjective in English as a "multiply ambiguous construction," and to back him up I offered (Bolinger 1961: 381) the first example in the list below (Appendix), where, by indulging in a little profanity, I was able to extract six interpretations of one sentence.

The situation in Spanish is not so bad. A good deal of the ambiguity on the English side is cleared up by adding a relator word. But the semantic distinctions are often so slight that one can sympa-

[1] From Josef Klegraf and Dietrich Nehls (eds.), Essays on the English language and applied linguistics on the occasion of Gerhard Nickel's 60th birthday, 219-226. Heidelberg: Julius Groos Verlag, 1988.

thize with our English forbears for dumping them all together, and even more with the English-speaking student who has to decide when he wants to give a Spanish equivalent for the phrase *the best road to follow* whether to say *el mejor camino para seguir, el mejor camino que seguir, el mejor camino a seguir*, or *el mejor camino de seguir*.

The remarks to follow are based on my own casual collecting, some 150 examples from the infinitive file of W. E. Bull, and some rather concentrated questioning of eleven native speakers of Spanish from various areas of Spanish America by students of mine (a large number of original examples were contributed by Ida Catalina Salazar). I shall attempt no more than to touch on the main points of comparison between English and Spanish, but I also offer as an illustration of a more exact treatment something that I call a transformulation (see Bolinger 1966), by which I mean a transformation put to the service of translation. This is appropriate in a tribute to Gerhard Nickel who in his seminal works on contrastive grammar has more than once resorted to the graphic displays of generative grammar. The area is one in which a view of old-style deep structure helps one to understand the relationship between the two languages, because in the process of making the ambiguous English sentence unambiguous one passes through stages in which some of them resemble the Spanish constructions rather closely.

To limit the discussion I omit the consideration of adjectives. I also leave out deverbal nouns, which are less troublesome since they call for the same connectives as their parent verbs. The examples numbered (3) illustrate this.

In effect, the field is thus reduced to nouns followed by the prepositions *a, de, para,* and *por,* and the relative *que*. I shall try to give semantic interpretations as well as to peel off some of the layers of structural ambiguity.

First the preposition *a*. This represents an innovating usage. See examples (4)-(13). Alfaro (1964, s.v. *a*) condemns it as a Gallicism or an Anglicism, but as can be seen by the sources of the quotations it seems to be pretty firmly settled on both sides of the Atlantic. It competes chiefly with *por*, but there is an intimacy between the thing and the action, and also a kind of immediacy, that is absent with *por*. Careful speakers preserve the intimacy—note example (7)—but for others this goes by the board and only the notion of 'immediate future' remains.

Example (13), a more conventional one with the noun as the implied subject rather than the object of the infinitive, suggests one entering wedge for the construction and also shows—by its ellipsis of the word *próximo*—a possible basis for the notion of 'immediacy'.

Second is *por*, the classical preposition of futurity in infinitive phrases modifying nouns. This future is indefinite, whereas that of *a* was definite. *Trabajos por hacer* are labors yet to be done. It differs from the same construction with *sin* in that there is an expectation: *trabajos sin hacer* may imply simply neglect.

Third are *de* and *para*. I take them together because they have the largest area in common. *Para* is the loosest-fitting of all the connectives under discussion. In an example like (16), *Se han dado los pasos iniciales para erigir una . . . fábrica*, it is impossible to tell whether the immediate constituent of the *para* phrase is the noun *pasos* or the entire preceding clause. In fact, the majority of the instances of *para* admit of transposing its phrase to the beginning of the sentence. For instance, (17) can be changed from *Es una magnífica mañana para salir* to *Para salir es una magnífica mañana*. *De*, on the other hand, cannot be separated from the noun without doing violence to the sentence: whereas *Tenemos los medios para hacerlo* (19) can be changed to *Para hacerlo tenemos los medios*, no such transposition can be made using (21), with its *de*. The indivisibility of the *de* phrase is obvious in the unacceptability of (23) as against (22). This comparison suggests that phrases with *para* are hybrids, functioning adjectivally or adverbially or somewhere between. *De* phrases are purely adjectival. The contrast in meaning follows suit. *Para* covers anything that leads to the action of the infinitive: (24), *libro para leer*, a book that leads to or opens the way to reading; (25), *un hueso para roer*, a bone that opens the way to gnawing. By contrast to this, *de* characterizes the noun, like any adjective. A couple of minimal pairs will illustrate: (26), *lugar de comer*, is an eating place, a restaurant, while (27) *lugar para comer*, could be a shady spot at the side of the road; (28), *traje de lucir (de dominguear, de presumir)* is Sunday-go-to-meetin' garb, whereas (29), *traje para lucir*, could be anything that makes *lucir* possible—it may get the results but lacks the design.

The last and most interesting connective is *que*, which textbooks generally tag with the semantic label of 'obligation', limiting it to examples like (30) and (31), or, with more daring, going as far as (32) with a verb other than *tener* or *haber*. Obligation is a limiting case, and of course with *tener que* and *haber que* it has become quite definitely stereotyped. But elsewhere *que* is freely used in a more inclusive sense, as can be seen in the clearly non-obligatory examples from Galdós and Sender, (33) and (34). Compare Spaulding (1931: §126) and Keniston (1937*b*: §§37.483-37.485). The trick is to find an English analogy. We obviously do not say things like (35), but we do have a literary paraphrase for combinations of verb plus preposition, as in (36), (37), and (38): *He brought me a chair on which to sit* and the like. The difference between the two languages is that Spanish uses the relative consistently whereas English leaves it out most of the time. The semantic area in the two langauges is the same. It refers to an action that is given, with a noun that names something on which the action can be carried out. Typically the noun is a means to the action. Of my eleven informants, eight accepted (40), where filling bottles in that kind of job is an action that is given, but only two accepted (39), in which *para meterlas* would be the normal thing. The primacy of the action is most evident in the freedom with which Spanish omits the antecedent noun—in Keniston's example (41) the desire to speak is there and is seeking unsuccessfully to find something to operate on.

As a relative, of course, *que* is not unique. In examples (42)-(44) we find the same construction with *como, donde,* and *quien.*

To sum up: *A* and *por* are temporal, immediate and indefinite respectively. *De* represents the infinitive as an attribute of the noun, while *que* practically reverses this. *Para* establishes the loosest kind of relationship between infinitive and noun, suggesting scarcely more than that the noun is compatible with the action—it leads to it, opens the way for it.

I turn now to the question of syntax and the underlying kinship between the languages. We find that Spanish exhibits at the surface what English reveals only with a bit of probing. (By the surface I mean the way the sentence is finally coded as it comes out.) This can best be appreciated with a set of mixed examples in which infinitives form only a part, (45)-(51) in the list. It is obvious from these examples that English uses its prepositions in much the same way as Spanish where ordinary nouns are concerned—*to a dinner, to the train, on the truth, of his arrival,* and so on, the first sentence in each of the sets. And with the *-ing* nominal, (51), the parallel with Spanish is especially close: *a rag for cleaning shoes, un trapo para limpiar zapatos*. It seems clear that in

English there is a deletion rule applying before infinitives and before clauses with *that;* in transformational syntax, *a rag to clean shoes* is the end result of a series of steps in which *a rag for to clean shoes,* (52), appears earlier. I have shown under the examples the rewrite steps for prepositional phrases. Example (53) is the rewrite that shows a prepositional phrase to contain a preposition plus a noun phrase. Example (54) is the rewrite of the noun phrase into two types, a choice between what I have labeled VNP to stand for verbal noun phrase, and NP_1 for all other noun phrases; the VNP is by definition an infinitive or a *that* clause. Example (55) inserts VNP as the alternative that is selected; an example would be *a rag for to clean shoes* or *the news of that he had arrived.* Example (56) is the deletion rule: *a rag for to clean shoes* becomes *a rag to clean shoes* and *the news of that he had arrived* becomes *the news that he had arrived.* Example (57) is the step that I have called a transformulation. English is on the left-hand side and Spanish is on the right. It is intended to say that where English has deleted a preposition, Spanish will restore it. Example (58) is a diagram showing the same thing. The left-hand side shows the need in English to distinguish two kinds of noun phrase; the right-hand side shows that Spanish makes no such distinction.

If this seems like laboring the obvious, I can only point to the importance of the deletion rule in comparative syntax. It brings together a number of things that are generally treated as unrelated phenomena. Not only is the English infinitive in types like (52) affected, but the separate rule on verbs of motion, in (46), and on noun clauses in apposition to nouns, (48) and (49), are seen as special cases of the same phenomenon, which is that Spanish is generally opposed to deleting prepositions before noun phrases.

In the next group of examples we see the extent to which transformulation can be applied in cases where Spanish would use the preposition *de.* I have simply translated to English fourteen examples from Bull's material. In (59) and (60) English uses only an *-ing* nominal and nothing needs to be done. In (61)-(66), transformulation applies directly—English is normal either way. In (67) and (68) transformulation applies, but there are idiomatic restrictions on the English that force a slight change—for instance, the word *care* has to be replaced by its synonym *precaution,* very likely because of a conflict of homonyms—*taking care of* would suggest an unintended meaning. In the next three, (69)-(71), transformulation with *of* does not work. *For* does, but fails to parallel the Spanish. I do not know what the conditions are, but no doubt they could be defined. The last example of this set, (72), can be squeezed into the mold of *máquina de coser, sewing machine,* and we can say *stamp-issuing decision,* which is a type of transformulation needed for other purposes anyway, or we can regard this one example as intractable. All in all, instances of *de* do yield to transformulation, and most of them relate to the parallel English preposition *of.*

A similar transformulation can be set up for infinitive phrases with *que* in Spanish, but part of the time these involve tracing the English back more than just the one step that was necessary with the preposition. In *a tool to work with,* (73), from *a tool with which to work,* we have a rule for end-shifting the preposition and then a rule for deleting the relative. In a transformulation both of these rules must be reversed, but the main thing is simply the English rule for deleting the word *which,* a step that is already clear enough in familiar examples like (74), *the house which I bought* reduced to *the house I bought.*

The preposition *por* is harder to deal with because there has been a deletion in Spanish, and English has no deeper-lying parallel as far as I can see. The deletion appears to be the verb *quedar,* as in (75): *cartas por echar al correo* is *cartas que quedan por echar al correo.* There is nothing here of much help toward matching structures in the two languages. One has to be satisfied with the semantic label of indefinite futurity.

As for the preposition *a,* it behaves like the loan translation from French that many consider it to be, and this may explain why so many native speakers of Spanish reject it. It has come in at the top layer and has no firm ties in the structure of the language. Once again there is nothing on which to base a transformulation from English.

Like transformations, transformulations are really nothing new. We have made them all along, for example in dealing with possessives, where we trace *John's house* back to *house of John* as a bridge to *casa de Juan.* But the procedure can be exploited more systematically, to learn facts about the structure of both languages that may have been missed before. Consider (77), where we find that the English sentence *I keep tools to work with* is ambiguous and needs to be transformulated in two different ways. In the first it answers the question *What kind of tools do* *you keep?*, and is transformulated *I keep tools with which to work, Tengo herramientas con que trabajar*. In the second it answers the question *Why do you keep tools?*, which calls for *I keep tools to work with them* and in turn *I keep tools for working with them, Tengo herramientas para trabajar con ellas*. And this, finally, offers the bonus of clues that might otherwise be overlooked, for example the parallel in (78). There is no essential difference between *things to talk about, things about which to talk, cosas de que hablar*, and *things to discuss, *things which to discuss, cosas que discutir*. The same relative is "underlyingly" ¿ present in both.

Appendix

(53) Phr_{prep} → Prep + NP

(54) NP → $\left\{ \begin{matrix} \text{NP}_1 \\ \text{VNP} \end{matrix} \right\}$ (VNP = infinitive or noun clause with *that*)

(55) Prep + NP → Prep + VNP (*a rag for to clean shoes; the news of that he had arrived)*

(56) Prep + VNP → VNP (the deletion rule: *a rag to clean shoes, the news that he had arrived)*

(57) $\overline{\underline{\text{Prep}}}$ + VNP → Prep + VNP (the transformulation rule: 'the preposition that was deleted in English is restored in Spanish')

(58) English: 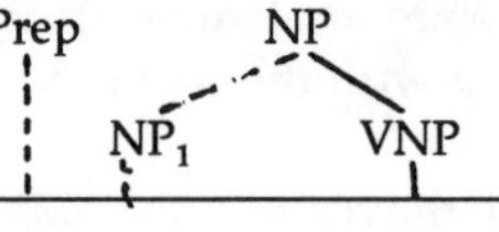

Spanish: Prep NP

NP_1 VNP

Infinitive	*-ing* Nominal
(59) (no equivalent)	*a question of performing this operation*
(60) (no equivalent)	*on the pretext of being oppressive*
(61) *the way to carry out the calculations*	*the way of carrying out . . .*
(62) *the duty to serve*	*the duty of serving*
(63) *the intention to solve the problem*	*the intention of solving. . . .*
(64) *the obligation to correct it*	*the obligation of correcting it*
(65) *the need to create*	*the need of creating*

(66) *the hope to win a wife*	*the hope of winning a wife*
(67) *without taking the trouble to inform himself*	?*without going to the trouble of informing himself*
(68) *without taking care to investigate seriously*	?*without taking the precaution of investigating seriously*
(69) *This is no time to get sad.*	??*This is no time for getting sad.*
(70) *that passion to humble himself*	??*that passion for humbling himself*
(71) *He was not a man to lose heart.*	??*He was not a man for losing heart*
(72) *the decision to issue a stamp*	(no equivalent; or, *stamp-issuing decision*?)

(73) *a tool to work with*
a tool with which to work
(74) *the house which I bought*
the house I bought
(75) *cartas por echar al correo* = *cartas que quedan por echar . . . .*

(76) *house* | *of* | *John* → *John's house*
casa | *de* | *Juan*

(77) *What kind of tools do you keep? I keep tools to work with* = *I keep tools with which to work* = *herramientas con que trabajar*
Why do you keep tools? I keep tools to work with = *I keep tools to work with them* = *para trabajar con ellas*

(78) **a book which to read, un libro que leer*

(1) *But it's so damned glorious to yield!* 'It's too glorious a day for us to admit defeat'; 'Yielding is glorious'; 'The thing is too glorious for us to give it up'; 'The thing is too glorious for it to stoop to admitting defeat'; 'It lends itself so gloriously to our yielding it'; 'It [the enemy nation] is so glorious in yielding (to our demands) [It is glorious of it to etc.].'
(2) *The best road to follow: el mejor camino para seguir, el mejor camino que seguir, el mejor camino a seguir, el mejor camino de seguir.*
(3) *Nos invitaron A comer: la invitación A comer. Se empeñaron EN discutir: su empeño EN discutir.*
(4) *el procedimiento a seguir para la preparación de un Atlas . . . .* Mosén Antoni Griera, *Curso de lingüística*, p. 84. San Sebastián: 1921.
(5) *si en esta Unversidad la plaza a cubrir estuviera provista.* Letter from Angel Benito Durán (Spaniard), 21 Aug. 1949.
(6) *el camino a seguir, el asunto a tratar, letras a cobrar.* Cited from Cuban popular speech in Padrón (1949: 172).
(7) *ruta a seguir.* Accepted by Antonio Heras (Spaniard), who rejected *medicina a tomar.*
(8) *criterio a seguir, trabajos a realizar.* Cited by Flórez (1963: 284) as something avoided by ¿"los colombianos cultos"¿.

(9) *Problemas a Discutir.* Title of student paper, corrected from *Problemas de Discutir*, by instructor, Oswaldo Arana (Peruvian), 1959.
(10) *Ex texto a estudiar debe tener una unidad de interés.* Memo from Marcos Morínigo, 1 Mar, 1948, who explained that even *las cortinas a comprar* and *El hombre a ver es su dentista* can be heard in the Plata region.
(11) *Lo primero a tener presente* .... Arturo Posnansky (Bolivian), in *La Revista Belga*, febrero 1945 p. 64.
(12) *Hay, sin duda, más dificultades a vencer* .... Emilio Carilla, *Pedro Henríquez Ureña y otros estudios*, p. 98. Buenos Aires: 1949.
(13) [*el XI Congreso Panamericano del Niño, a realizarse en Bogotá* = próximo a realizarse] .... *Boletín Indigenista* (México), marzo 1959, p. 8.

(14) *trabajos por hacer*
(15) *trabajos sin hacer*

(16) *Se han dado los pasos iniciales para erigir una . . . fábrica.*
(17) *Es una magnífica mañana para salir.*
(18) *Para salir es una magnífica mañana.*
(19) *Tenemos los medios para hacerlo.*
(20) *Para hacerlo tenemos los medios.*
(21) *No hay medios de conseguirlo.*

(22) *Necesarias son algunas líneas para esclarecer determinados puntos.*
(23) **Necesarias son algunas líneas de esclarecer determinados puntos.*
(24) *libro para leer*
(25) *un hueso para roer*

(26) *lugar de comer* 'eating place, restaurant'
(27) *lugar para comer*
(28) *traje de lucir* 'best clothes'
(29) *traje para lucir*

(30) *Tengo varias cartas que contestar.*
(31) *Hay mucho que leer.*
(32) *Me dieron mucho trabajo que hacer.*

(33) *Dejo mi mujer y tres hijos, únicos bienes que poseo. Nada más tengo* QUE PODER DEJAR. Galdós, *Zumalacárregui*, p. 307.

(34) *Las ratas siguen su loca carrera por todo el parapeto. Por eso el soldado que tiene algo* QUE COMER *no lo deja nunca en el suelo.* Grismer and Arjona, *The pageant of Spain*, p. 130. New York: 1938. From story by Ramón Sender.

(35) **He gave me a book which to read.*

(36) *He brought me a chair to sit on = on which to sit.*

(37) *They gave me money to buy it with = with which to buy it.*
(38) *There was no target to shoot at = at which to shoot.*
(39) **Me entregó un par de botellas que meter en la nevera.*
(40) *Me entregó un par de botellas que llenar* (dairy employee speaking).
(41) *No halló que decirle.* Keniston (1937a: §37.485).

(42) *Me explicó la manera como hacerlo.*
(43) *Nos prestaron un lugar donde vivir.*
(44) *tener un marido a quien pedírselo.* Keniston 1937*b*: §37.484).

(45) *He invited me TO a dinner at his house.*
He invited me (to) to dine at his house.
(46) *They ran TO the train*
They ran (to) to catch the train.
(47) *I insist ON the truth.*
I insist (on) that you tell me the truth.
(48) *The news OF his arrival.*
The news (of) that he had arrived.
(49) *His promise OF help.*
His promise (of) to help.
(50) *This is good FOR cleaning shoes.*
This is good (for) to clean shoes.

(51) *A rag for cleaning shoes.*
A rag to clean shoes.
(52) **A rag for to clean shoes.*

References

Alfaro, Ricardo. (1964): *Diccionario de anglicismos,* segunda edicion. Madrid: Gredos.

Bolinger, Dwight. (1961): "Syntactic blends and other matters," *Language* 37, 366-81.

Bolinger, Dwight. (1966). "Transformulation: structural translation," *Acta Linguistica Hafniensia* 9, 130-44.

Flórez, Luis. (1963): "El español hablado en Colombia y su Atlas Linguístico," *Thesaurus (Boletín del Instituto Caro y Cuervo)* 18, 268-356.

Keniston, Hayward. (1937*a*): *Spanish Syntax List.* New York: Holt.

Keniston, Hayward. (1937*b*): *The Syntax of Castilian Prose: The Sixteenth Century.* Chicago: University of Chicago Press.

Lees, R. B. (1960): "A multiply ambiguous adjectival construction in English," *Language* 36, 207-21.

Padrón, Alfredo F. (1949): "Giros sintácticos usados en Cuba," *Boletín del Instituto Caro y Cuervo* 5, 163-75.

Spaulding, Robert K. (1931): *Syntax of the Spanish Verb.* New York: Holt.

Part III

Word Classes

Articles in Old Familiar Places

[*Author's Note*: For the non-journalist sensitive to such matters, it comes as something of a surprise to read the following sentence from I. F. Stone's *Weekly* (June 14, 1954, p.1): *This may explain the attitude of Secretary Dulles at press conference last week.* Why not *his* or *the* press conference? The answer seems to be, as P. A. Erades quotes one of his correspondents as saying, that omission of the article "expresses the insider's point of view" (*English Studies* 39 [1958] 2.2). When the noun refers to some routine, it no longer requires a *the*: we treat it in just as familiar a way as something for which there is a proper name. This comes clearest in referring to places associated with some kind of familiar *activity*. A plumber on his way to take communion is headed *for church*; on his way to repair a leak, he is headed for *the church.*

"Familiarity" is so personal that it is no wonder usage varies from group to group, region to region, and (since Spanish and English are the same in this respect) from language to language. The Britisher goes *to hospital*, the American *to the hospital*; Mrs. Mary Foster, according to the *Congressional Record* (Feb. 9, 1965, 2382-85), *stood in courthouse trying to register*, in Selma, Alabama; Mark Twain writes, *After lesson, Catasauqua gave Catiline some rushes (Letters from the earth*, 1962, p. 131). The closer we are to something the less definite its outlines appear, and the less need there is for a definitizing definite article.]

* * *

ONE OF THE coincidences between English and Spanish is the dropping of the definite article before certain place names.[1] The two languages agree (as against French, with which in most other respects each has more in common) in the over-all semantics of the loss, in the identities of certain of the places, in the apparent inconsistency between one name that loses the article and a synonym that does not, and in a certain discrepancy between dialects.

Most textbook grammars of medium to ample coverage mention *casa* at least, and sometimes *clase,* as two nouns that resemble English *home, camp, school, class,* etc. in dropping, permissibly, the definite article in prepositional phrases. Even reference grammars, however, give little more information than this.[2] Bello makes a casual reference to *casa* and *palacio* (§877), Ramsey (§1345) adds *misa* and *caza* (the latter certainly no place name and the former doubtful), Fernández[3] and Alonso-Henríquez[4] and also Alfredo F. Padrón[5] mention names of theaters.

The works that go into more detail all have something to offer. I shall quote, with comment, and then try to draw the threads together.

---

[1] Originally published in *Hispania* 37 (1954): 79-82). I wish to acknowledge the benefit of discussion by my students, especially Father Robert G. Dodson and Patrick R. Stingley. As usual, I am indebted to my colleague Dr. Laudelino Moreno.

[2] I find nothing in Lenz, *La oración y sus partes;* Keniston, *Spanish Syntax List;* Gili Gaya, *Curso superior de sintaxis española;* Spanish Academy, *Gramática de la lengua española;* and Alonso, "Estilística y gramática del artículo en español," in *Estudios lingüísticos,* Madrid, ed. Gredos, 1951. The source that should offer most, Cuervo's *Diccionario de construcción y régimen,* "el, la, los, las," Bogotá, 1946, has little more than the others except for two citations from Martínez de la Rosa with *casa* in adverbial use without preposition, possibly a Gallicism.

[3] Salvador Fernández, *Gramática española; los sonidos, el nombre y el pronombre,* Madrid: Revista de Occidente, 1951, p. 153 fn.

[4] Amado Alonso and Pedro Henríquez Ureña, *Gramática castellana, segundo curso,* Buenos Aires: Losada, 1949, p. 51.

[5] Alfredo F. Padrón, "Giros sintácticos en las hablas popular y semiculta cubanas," mimeographed pamphlet, Havana, 1949, p. 4.

Kany[6] says: "With a few nouns, like *casa, palacio,* etc., standard Spanish has from early times omitted the definite article, possibly because the 'noun was originally felt as unique and in effect a proper noun' (Keniston, p. 237). The usage has in a few cases been extended in American Spanish but, more generally, has fallen into disuse. Thus in Mexico, *catedral* and *Cámara de Diputados* are often used without *la*: 'Las campanas de Catedral . . . '; ' . . . *frente a Catedral*' . . . . In Spanish America the article is general with *casa* while standard peninsular Spanish omits it: *voy a la casa* for standard *voy a casa* . . . ." There is a question whether the matter of *casa* is linguistic or more broadly cultural. One of my students points out that if a man is working in his garage, he does not then go *home,* but *to the house;* he already is home. On a farm the same is potentially true; from the farthest corner of it one might still go *to the house,* but go *home* from some outside point. It is easy to imagine the effect that this broadening of the horizon would have in predominantly rural Spanish America. The terms retain their meaning (*a casa* 'home,' *a la casa* 'to the house'), but the frequencies are drastically changed. Three Argentine speakers confirm the nuances that I have mentioned for Spanish.[7] Padrón adds for Cuba, "Decimos siempre *Voy a casa* y no *Voy a la casa,*"[8] commenting on Kany's observations. One dialectal difference, however, does affect the meaning of the phrases: a number of Spanish American speakers (several Mexican, one Costa Rican) assure me that they do not omit the article unless the subject's own home is referred to; others use it either way (cp. "No era raro ver discurrir . . . tal o cual linterna . . . con que respetuoso servidor alumbraba a sus magníficos amos, quienes se

[6] *American-Spanish Syntax,* University of Chicago Press, 1945, pp. 19-20.

[7] The cultural facts are not uniform. Two Castilians tell me that they would say *Voy a la casa,* not *Voy a casa,* speaking to a total stranger, regardless of distance or of location on or off one's own property, and that *Voy a casa* would be normal even for just garage-to-house if speaking to a friend. The conclusion is the same as far as frequencies in Spanish America are concerned: that in a sparsely settled comunity with few intimacies, *a la casa* would be used more.

[8] "Apuntaciones sobre el libro *Spanish-American Syntax,* de . . . Kany," mimeographed pamphlet, Havana, 1949, p. 1.

dirigían a la habitual tertulia o de visita *a casa de sus parientes*."[9] The English analog is *I'm going home with my friends*.)

H. L. Mencken traces the omission of the article before nouns that become proper nouns because of a new official status. His remarks are pertinent to the Mexican *Cámara de Diputados*: "In many American cities ... the newspapers now omit [the article] even before *City Hall* and similar terms. The custom of omitting it before *Congress* arose during the days of the Continental Congress.... John Pickering, in his pioneer *Vocabulary* of 1816, said: 'This word, originally a common noun, and still so used in England, has with us become a proper noun. We, of course, use it without the article, but English writers, in speaking of American affairs, generally use it with the article.' The NED shows that in England it began to be customary to omit *the* before *Parliament* so long ago as the Fourteenth Century.... In New Zealand it seems to be the custom to omit it even before *Cabinet*...."[10]

Keniston[11] has already been quoted by Kany. He includes *concejo* (compare English *in council*) with *casa* and *palacio*, and concedes that *sierra* and *tierra* in similar phrases are "in reality compound prepositions," e.g. *paso entre tierra de Guadix i la mar*.

Benot and Curme make similar statements, for Spanish and English respectively. Benot says, "La falta de artículo es ... signo de individualidad: *Voy a palacio* (el del rey, el del obispo); *Voy a Apolo* (el

[9] Alarcón, *El sombrero de tres picos*, New York: Holt, 1907, p. 45. Cuervo, op. cit., p. 33, describes what is probably the true state of affairs for the standard language: "*Casa* no lleva artículo cuando en absoluto denota la de la persona que habla ni cuando se trata de la de la persona denotada en el complemento siguiente."

[10] "American street names," *American Speech*, 23.86 (1948).

[11] *The Syntax of Castilian Prose, The Sixteenth Century*, University of Chicago Press, 1937, §18.72. Cuervo, op. cit. pp. 32-33, mentions *palacio* and explains as possibly analogical to *palacio* the two examples of *en corte* and *a tesorería general* that he quotes. From the pre-Classical period he quotes, p. 72, *fuese luego para Corte* and *los sacramentos de Santa Iglesia*.

café de Apolo)."[12] Curme says, "All things living and lifeless were conceived as individuals, and were used without the article, just as names of persons had no article [this, which describes early vs. modern English, also describes Latin vs. Spanish]. In set expressions there are many survivals of this old usage: 'He is going to bed, to school, to ruin, on foot, by water,' etc."[13] This is much the same as Keniston's remark about proper names, but with a different perspective: instead of "acquiring the loss," so to speak, by reason of being felt as proper nouns, the examples given always "had the loss." The wording is not a quibble, for in the present state of both languages dropping the article has taken on a positive value, with the result that not all instances of absence of the article are traditional ones: English *I'm going to lab* and Spanish *Fuimos a Telégrafos* are new.

Kruisinga improves the statement for this new positive value: "Many class-nouns denoting PLACES are used without an article when the USE of the place is referred to, e.g., *school* when meaning 'a session of school', or 'the set time of attendance at school'. The construction is especially common in prepositional adjuncts."[14] He gives examples of *before school, school begins, before bed, after church, in court, bed felt comfortable, from table, to camp, into hospital, in hall, prison... should be the last... resort,* etc.

"Use" suggests adverbial modification. The new positive value implies a manner of acting or behaving that is normal to the subject in connection with the place referred to. 'Going' and 'home,' 'school,' 'church,' etc. imply, together, certain conventional modes of behavior. What strikes our attention in these phrases is not that the kind of adverbial modification in question is unusual (*in session, at sea, from abroad, by air, on horseback, a caballo, en avión,* etc. are common enough), but that the places named are definite: in the commoner phrases the relationship is either to no particular place or thing (*a caballo*) or to something too broad or inclusive to pinpoint (*por tierra, de oro*). For

---

[12] Eduardo Benot, *Arquitectura de las lenguas,* Buenos Aires: Glem, n.d., II, 80, fn.

[13] George O. Curme, *Syntax,* New York: Heath, 1931, p. 511.

[14] E. Kruisinga, *A Handbook of Present-Day English,* Part II, Groningen: Noordhoff, 1932, §1376.

names of definite places to enter the pattern, the places must be rather special: something lying near the home base of the subject. *Home,* of course, is the ideal example. How intimate the connection has to be is shown in the impossibility, to most speakers, of saying *The sheriff is in jail,* unless he has been arrested, or, to a truck-driver about to deliver a load of books, *Let's go to college.* The phrases have all to some extent been fossilized.

But since genuine proper nouns, which do not necessarily refer to something as intimately connected with the subject as home, school, class (if one is a student), camp (if one is a soldier), etc., also drop the article, it is impossible at times to tell whether a given noun should be considered one way or the other. Spanish, but not English, can apply the test of using the noun as a grammatical subject. Of the following, 1. Casa es el lugar más querido, 2. Misa tendrá lugar a las seis, 3. Palacio es el lugar más anhelado, 4. Clase de español sigue a clase de historia, 5. Presidio es el lugar menos anhelado, 6. Correos queda en la próxima esquina, 7. Coro sigue a confesión, 8. Catedral queda en la próxima esquina, and 9. Química es la próxima clase, all the relevant nouns were judged acceptable in other contexts without the article, but here only those in 3, 6, 8, and 9 (and as for 4, the modification is not a factor since *Voy a clase de español* was accepted). Of the nouns most frequently mentioned by the grammars (*casa, misa, clase, palacio*), *palacio* would seem therefore to stand a little to one side, and to resemble *Correos, Cámara de Diputados,* and English *Parliament* and *Congress* as a more nearly exclusive example of a proper name.

Química is significant. In departmentalized institutions it is the practise in both languages to label departments by the name of their function in the whole; in the Spanish bank there are *Valores, Caja, Créditos, Depósitos, Préstamos, Hipotecas* (but *el archivo,* a service to, not of); in the American hospital there are *Surgery, Maternity* (but *the pharmacy,* similarly); in the university there are the names of classes (*I'm on my way to chemistry; Voy a química*). These are proper names as used, but also designate functions, and are close to the "home base" of the speaker. The name of a place that is in but not of the institution (cp. *He is in *washroom*) is not likely to be turned into a proper noun. The three threads, properness, function, and familiarity, are intertwined even here.

As properness is usually primary with the nouns just mentioned, function may be with others. Function implies process, and process takes time: we can therefore test with prepositions of time. *Durante* was accepted with *clase, misa, presidio, confesión, coro,* and *corte,* but rejected with *casa, palacio, correos, catedral,* and others. *A través de,* which is purely spatial, was accepted with *palacio, presidio,* and *correos.* To the extent that the artificial conditions of questioning an informant are reliable, it would follow that function is primary with *clase, misa, confesión, coro,* and *corte,* and that *presidio* shares function and properness in about equal proportions. Results in English are similar (*during school* but not *during campus; across campus* but less likely *across school*). With nouns of pure function, omission of the article is of course common: *I'm on my way to rehearsal, practise, work; a ejercicios, prácticas, servicio, trabajo, paseo,* etc. The adverbialness of certain phrases of location in English is shown in their conversion to straight adverbs: *abed, ashore, afield,* and *home* itself.

Spanish reference grammars overlook the possibilities with different prepositions; mostly they consider only *a, de,* and *en.* Yet, within the limits of sense, practically any preposition can be used. My Castilian informant accepts *clase* after *a, de, en, desde, hacia, para, por, durante, cerca de,* and *antes de* (rejecting *sobre, entre, hasta,* and *a través de*). That *sobre clase* should be rejected and *sobre Correos* accepted follows from the meaning of the words—*Correos* was accepted with all but the purely functional prepositions *durante* and *antes de* (and even with *antes de* in the spatial sense 'antes de llegar a'). But use with prepositions is limited not only by sense but also by the tendency of prepositional phrases to fossilize, with the result that in both English and Spanish there are arbitrary inconsistencies. In my speech *in* is acceptable with *gym, jail, camp, school, church,* etc., but not with *market* without the article. In Spanish my informant accepts *por* with *casa, clase, misa,* and *palacio,* but not with *presidio.* Differences from speaker to speaker are to be expected whenever the rather personal sense of "home base" counts.

Fossilization makes for inconsistencies between synonyms. I can say *They sent him to jail* (or *prison*) but not *They sent him to penitentiary;* my Castilian informant accepts *Fué a presidio* but not *Fué a cárcel.*

Fernández notes[15] that in Madrid "se dice vamos *al María Guerrero, al Infanta Isabel, al Beatriz,* pero *a Eslava, a Lara."*

Similarly, there are differences among dialects in both languages. Carter Dickson's "the plain Briton would arise in all his majesty, saying: 'To hell with common sense; stick him *in clink*"'[16] sounds strange to us, and the Britisher's *in hall* and *in hospital* are also unfamiliar to most Americans. British proper noun *the High Street* contrasts with American *High Street.*[17] Kany records *colegio* as typical of Bolivia in the type *Un libro de los que traje de colegio,*[18] rejected by my Castilian informant, as he also rejected the Mexican *a Catedral* and *a Cámara de Diputados.*[19] The "home base" feeling writ somewhat smaller is seen in the outburst of the profane Quaker: "Well, they may turn me *out of meeting,* but I'll be damned if they can stop me from using the plain language."[20]

To summarize: names of places that (1) suggest functions occurring within the place, or that (2) are quasi-proper nouns, and that (3) at the same time are more or less on the "home base" of the speaker, are likely to drop the definite article; but it is hard to predict what ones will actually do so.

---

[15] Ibid.

[16] *The Reader Is Warned,* New York: Pocket Books, 1945, p. 210.

[17] American usage originally accorded with British. See Mencken, op. cit.

[18] "Bolivian popular speech," *Hispanic Review,* Jan. 1947.

[19] Cf. J. González Moreno, *Etimologías del español,* México: Patria, 1942, p. 134.

[20] *Word Study,* Feb. 1949, p. 1, col. 2.

Prepositions in English and Spanish

[*Author's Note*: Not much has changed, in the uncertainty over what makes a preposition, since this little survey made its appearance. Following is a list of the candidates for prepositionhood mentioned in the article (plus one more, *inclusive*), along with the classification found in three more recent dictionaries, Moliner (1966), Collins (1971), and American Heritage (1986):

	Moliner	Collins	AmH
DURANTE	prep	prep	prep
INCLUSO	adv	adv	adv
EXCEPTO	adv	prep	prep
MÁS	adv (= *y*)	conj	prep
MENOS	adv	prep	prep
CUANDO	"can be replaced by prep"	prep	prep
SALVO	adv	prep	adv
MEDIANTE	prep	prep	adv
NO OBSTANTE	(unclassified)	prep	(unclassified)
NO EMBARGANTE	(unclassified)	(absent)	(unclassified)
ALLENDE	(unclassified)	adv (but + de =prep)	prep
PREVIO	"adj used as abl. abs."	"as prep"	adj
CONSIDERANDO	gerundio (but defined by preps)	(verb)	(verb)
DADO	(no sep. sense)	p.p.	adj
INCLUYENDO	(no sep. sense)	(no. sep.)	(no. sep.)
INCLUSIVE	(unclassified)	prep	adv

Collins is obviously the most progressive, but the confusion is apparent even there in the treatment of the mathematical senses of *más* and *menos*, the one a conjunction and the other a preposition.

One often hears prepositions and other clusters of function words referred to as "closed classes," since they seem not to take on new members. The psychologist Murray Glanzer was of the opinion that "while new nouns, adjectives, and verbs are being introduced each year ..., no new pronoun, preposition, or conjunction has come into the language in the last hundred years" (*Journal of Verbal Learning and Verbal Behavior*, 1 [1962] 31). It is probably true that nobody reaches out to the raw syllables of English or Spanish to patch together a new preposition, but that does not mean that an occasional existing word will not make its way across the line by stealth. *See if... lemons are grown adjacent your property* advises the *Los Angeles Times Home Magazine* (Feb. 4, 1951, p. 32). *Flowers courtesy the Rose Shop* is a natural abbreviation of *by courtesy of*. The Webster Ninth Collegiate gives 1945 as the earliest date for the prepositional use of *absent*, as in *Absent* (in the absence of) *more favorable conditions, we shall have to wait.*

It is fun to read signs and portents into one's own piercing insights. The way the category of prepositions is pictured here can be hailed as a precursor of Prototype Theory.]

* * *

THE TEACHER WHO looks at the diminutive list of prepositions in Spanish as the Academy and its followers set them out, says to himself, "No wonder my students have trouble distinguishing *para* and *por*."[1] The list contains nineteen items: *a, ante, bajo, cabe, con, contra, de, desde, en, entre, hacia, hasta, para, por, según, sin, so, sobre,* and *tras*. This apparently is expected to match the list given by Curme[2] for English, in which there are 286 entries.

---

[1]A paper read at the 38th Annual Meeting of the AATSP, Washington, December 29-30, 1956 and originally published in *Hispania* 40 (1957): 212-14.

[2] George O. Curme, *A grammar of the English language: syntax*, New York: Heath, 1931, pp. 562-566.

Part of the disproportion vanishes when we realize that Curme includes everything, from unit morphemes to phrases like *to the south of,* while the Academy, with accustomed conservatism, disregards things as familiar as *dentro de* and *frente a*. But there still remains a striking difference, and one wonders whether Spanish is really so lacking in resources of this kind as the numbers imply. We have been hearing for a long time that English is more hospitable to innovations than Spanish. Is this another instance of the same thing?

One way to find out is to look up equivalents of some of the English prepositions which appear to lack counterparts in Spanish. When we do so, Spanish comes out with distinction. *During* has its *durante, including* its *incluso, except* its *excepto, plus* and *minus* their *más* and *menos,* and so on. But the monolingual Spanish dictionaries put them down as adverbs, while the bilingual dictionaries develop a kind of split personality: in Cuyás, *except* is a preposition on the English side, but its opposite number *excepto* is an adverb, and both Cuyás and Williams call *incluso* an adverb, but bravely put *durante* down as a preposition.

This begins to look like a mere question of terminology. If it were only that, it would deserve two lines. But when we try to explain why different labels are applied in the two languages, we uncover some interesting facts about the way their forms are clustered.

Evidently there must be a hard core of prepositions, with an outer envelope that grows more and more diffuse, like the atmosphere of the earth, the farther out you go. We can imagine that if the earth were a double planet, with its twin not too far away, it might be hard to decide, sometimes, which twin the atmosphere belonged to. Are prepositions in Spanish subject to some such double pull, which does not exist to confuse the classes in English?

Since Spanish grammarians and lexicographers are so determined to call the outer layer of forms adverbs, we should expect that the extraneous pull, if there is one, comes from the class of adverbs. So we ask ourselves, in what sense can a word like *excepto* be considered an adverb? Does it modify a verb? *Él come excepto.* Nonsense. Does it modify an adjective or another adverb? *Esa mujer es excepto hermosa, Esa mujer es excepto excepcionalmente hermosa.* More nonsense. Obviously adverbs as a class cannot constitute the outside pull, for we should have to revise the definition of the adverb in order to include these forms under it. When the *Vox* dictionary records *excepto*, adv., A excepción de, fuera de, using prepositions to define a supposed adverb, it obviously does not believe in its own classification. I suspect that there are three reasons for it: the debatable forms are uninflected, like adverbs; the part is confused with the whole (*Trabajaban más durante la guerra* includes an element, *durante la guerra*, which is adverbial); and "adverb" has long been a convenient name for assorted leftovers.

We shall have to look in another direction for our competing center of attraction. We find it pointed by Andrés Bello, who adds to his list of central prepositions a list of near-prepositions in which he includes *cuando* (as in *cuando la guerra*), *excepto, salvo, durante, mediante, obstante*, and *embargante*.[3] For some reason he excludes *allende*, continuing to regard it as an adverb despite its construction with nouns, as in *allende los mares*. But his comment, and those appended by Cuervo, concerning the origin of forms like *durante* and *excepto*, locate the outside pull. *Durante* and *excepto* are, of course, fossilized participles, which continued to be used up to the seventeenth century in agreement with the noun to which they were joined: *durante la guerra*, but *durantes las guerras*.

Our near-prepositions have not come to be felt fully as prepositions because they still reflect the absolute construction from which they were derived. There is still occasional wavering, as in this from an Argentine novel: "¡Cuántos lograrán, *mediantes mis palabras*, llegar hasta la voz secreta que me anima..."[4] The absolute construction, *hecho el trabajo, aprobadas las leyes, hallado el tesoro*, is still so much alive that the native speaker of Spanish cannot shake the near-preposition free even though it no longer agrees in number and gender. Furthermore, there is a link between the fossils and the still active construction, in the shape of forms that are still inflected but are stereotyped in meaning, for example *previo* as a synonym of *después de*:

---

[3] Andrés Bello and Rufino J. Cuervo, *Gramática de la lengua castellana*, Buenos Aires: Sopena, 1949, §§1183-1190.

[4] Julio Ardiles Gray, *La grieta*, Tucumán, 1952, p. 98.

"Previa una laboriosa preparación ... el 21 de septiembre... quedó inaugurada formalmente la sociedad."[5]

Granted that the link between the absolute construction and near-prepositions explains the reluctance to call them prepositions in Spanish, why the willingness in English, which also has an absolute construction? Partly, it is the comparative infrequency of absolutes in English. In greater measure, however, it is due to word order in the two languages. Except for a fossil or two like *Dios mediante,* the Spanish absolute puts the modifier before the head: *hecho el trabajo,* not *el trabajo hecho;* in fact, *el trabajo hecho* has been usurped by another construction, so that word order is virtually the contrastive marker of the absolute construction in Spanish. The result is that *mediante un gran esfuerzo* is still normal word order for the absolute construction. In English the opposite is true. The few literary absolutes that are left, like *The house clean, she was able to sit down and read awhile,* put the modifier after the head, and do not point the slightest resemblance to a prepositional phrase. Only a few remnants keep the opposite order, like *pending an investigation, notwithstanding their objections,* and they, isolated from other absolutes, are pulled into the orbit of the prepositions. Or it might be more accurate to say that their resemblance to prepositions in meaning enabled them to retain a preposition-like word order.[6] And in English, just as in Spanish, the vacated premises have been occupied by another construction. *The work done* means, to your freshmen, only 'the work that has been done.'

If near-prepositions hover about the hard core of inherited prepositions, do they all hover at the same distance? No, not if the process is a living one. We have already located *previo* on the outer fringe. Moving from the periphery toward the center, we can divide the process into a series of arbitrary steps.

At the farthest extreme are those forms which still maintain obvious contact with some other construction. In Spanish, one contact is with the absolute construction. But in both languages there is

---

[5] *La casa del estudiante indígena,* Publicaciones de la Secretaría de Educación Pública, México, 1927, p. 139.

[6] See Curme, p. 156.

another external contact that we have not considered yet, and that nowadays is a more active emitter of prepositional electrons than the absolute construction. I refer to the *-ing* form in English and the *-ndo* in Spanish. Their activeness is evidenced in the impossibility of drawing any line between verb and near-preposition. I doubt that any Spanish dictionary would even list a word like *considerando* or a phrase like *dejando a un lado* in the near-prepositional sense, let alone recognize it as a preposition. Practice varies in English. My *Oxford Universal* omits *considering,* but others list it as a preposition. None list *including* as a preposition. Yet Spanish is, if anything freer than English to use the *-ndo* without a subject to attach it to. Perhaps here, again, is the reason we are more generous with the preposition label in English: we react against dangling participles, so when one begins to dangle beyond repair we prefer to call it a preposition. In Spanish the contact with the verb is still solid.

A step farther in are forms that have become detached from their source but not yet drawn far in the direction of anything else. In English we have *failing,* commonest in the fossilized absolute phrase *failing that.* Jespersen quotes an example of *failing him* from Shaw.[7] Perhaps English *given* and Spanish *dado* are in this preliminary stage, which is one of frequency and meaning rather than of formal marking.

Next we find clear formal indications of detachment from the source but incomplete indications of attachment to the prepositions. In Spanish it may be the loss of an inflection: *mediantes* becomes *mediante; inclusa* becomes *incluso.* In English it may be detachment from a subject: *Counting all of them we have six* becomes *Counting all of them there are six.* Some of the freedom of non-prepositions may still be retained, as with English *except,* which readily combines with *that* to give *except that,* a rarity among prepositions in English.[8] Evolution in the direction of prepositions may be evidenced in the exclusion of some constructions that would be possible if the forms were still attached to their origins. For example, *mediante* excludes the explicitly nominative pronoun in Spanish, but has not gone so far as to accept

---

[7] Otto Jespersen, *A modern English grammar,* Copenhagen, 1940, Vol. 5 §6.3_3

[8] Jesperson, op. cit., London, 1928, Vol. 3 §2.2_2

the objective: *mediante yo* is as bad as *mediante mí.*[9] In English I might say *They'll have to go minus their friends* or *minus you* but I don't think I'd say *minus me* or *minus him,* and I'm sure I'd not say *minus I.* English *than* and *but* waver.

The inner circle is composed of forms that take the objective case of the pronoun. In English, newly arrived prepositions can still make the grade. In Spanish I believe that this is impossible. Even as firmly entrenched a form as *según,* which every Spanish grammar and dictionary recognizes as a preposition, cannot take it. The pronouns *mí, ti,* and *sí* have come to be felt as terminals of the inherited prepositions, and can no more be detached from them than a suffix like *-able* can be detached from its stem. It is as impossible to say *Lo hizo para él y mí* as to say *Es conta y conmensurable.*

On this account I feel that if prepositions in Spanish are not to become a dead class, Spanish grammarians and lexicographers had better abandon the objective case of the pronoun as their criterion. If *según* cannot take the objective case, it should not be necessary for other forms to pass an impossible test in order to get themselves included. In its place I suggest the more realistic criterion of nexus with the noun. The first benefit that this will bring will be the elimination of foolishness about forms like *excepto* being adverbs. Adverbs don't construe with nouns. As a secondary criterion we need some formal sign of detachment from other constructions. With former participles this is obviously the loss of inflection. With some possible future addition from the *-ndo* forms it might be loss of personal *a,* for example *incluyendo a Juan* becoming *incluyendo Juan.* This still leaves a few words to be decided arbitrarily or by feel. In *Tengo todos menos ése* the native speaker may be able to decide whether this belongs among absolute constructions in the sense 'that one not being counted,' or among conjunctions in the sense 'pero no tengo ése,' or among prepositions, as it would be classed in English.

In short, it is time to take up where Bello left off, and not try to turn back the clock as his commentator Alcalá-Zamora does when he

[9] Bello-Cuervo, §1189.

says of *durante, mediante, obstante, excepto,* and *salvo,* that "resulta indudable que les faltan los caracteres de preposición."[10]

[10] Bello-Cuervo, p. 367.

Verbs of Being

[*Author's Note*: The student who has assiduously learned what a transitive verb is and what a personal noun is, and diligently puts an "object-sign *a*" between them, feels cheated when a sentence like *Perdió un hijo* comes along. Of course there was always *Tiene un hijo*, but *tener* with a direct personal object was excused as a "special case."

We have a better idea now of existentials as a class with peculiarities of its own. This brief article was an early treatment of such verbs showing how Spanish uses the preposition *a* to distinguish ordinary operated-on objects from objects that are "brought on the scene" or "removed from the scene."

Had I thought of it at the time, I might have used presentative *there* as an illustration from English—it works with existentials but not with other verbs:

> There were created several useless products.
> *There were sold several useless products.]

* * *

THE TRANSLATED TITLE of Dale Carnegie's book begins *Cómo ganar amigos*.[1] The absence of the object-sign *a* might seem to follow just from the fact that *amigos* is indefinite, since indefinite-noun personal direct objects often omit *a* (Keniston, *Spanish Syntax List* §2.18). This is probably true, but at the same time *ganar* belongs to a semantic class

[1] I am indebted to my colleague Dr. Laudelino Moreno for supplying several of the quoted examples, inventing others, and patiently answering the test questions that I put to him. This article was originally published in *Hispania* 36 (1953): 343-45

of verbs whose performance is pretty regular in this regard, and which constitute accordingly a special case. It is more than a coincidence that all three of Ramsey's examples of the "impersonal" and "indeterminate" (§1322) are with verbs of the type that I shall discuss here: *nombrar, formar*, and *elegir*.

Afredo F. Padrón (*Cuestiones lingüísticas y gramaticales*, Habana, 1947, p. 147) notes for *perder*: "Sería muy distinto el sentido en *José perdió su hijo* and *José perdió a su hijo*. En el primer caso significamos que perdió su hijo porque dejó de tenerlo, bien por muerte o desafecto de éste, al paso que con el segundo indicamos que perdió a su hijo por haber sido demasiado indulgente o por haberlo corrompido con malos ejemplos." (Ramsey, §1320, and Bello, §899, note the same.) Here the contrast is clearly shown in English by using different verbs: *to lose* and *to ruin*. What one loses, in a sense passes out of existence. Similarly *ganar* as cited would be 'to win,' while if *a* had been added, English might prefer 'to win over.'

The classical examples of the type are *haber* and *tener*. *Haber*, though it governs the accusative pronoun (*Los hay*), does not call for *a* with nouns, and the same is true of *tener*, regardless of the definiteness of the object (*Tengo un amigo; se llama Juan*), when used in its commonest sense. That sense is what characterizes the type: *Tengo un amigo* is really an expression of existence—the only purpose in such an utterance is to create the individual for the benefit of the person spoken to. That sense is exclusive for *haber*, and only in the comparatively infrequent *Tengo a mi amigo en casa* do we find a conceptually pre-existing individual serving as object of *tener*, and so introduced by *a*.

With *ganar*, though the individuals pre-existed as people, only in winning them do they come to exist as friends; it is a creative verb. The synonymous *adquirir* behaves identically: *Adquirió un nuevo amigo llamado Juan*.

Compare *dejar*: "Con la apagada voz que le quedaba, respondió el General: '*Dejo mi mujer y tres hijos*, únicos bienes que poseo"' (Galdós, *Zumalacárregui*, p. 307). Here *dejar* is 'to leave' in the sense 'to have as survivors,' 'to have continuing to exist'; one going away on a trip, on the other hand, and "leaving" (i.e. *putting*) one's wife and children in the hands of a relative, would add *a*. The Galdós item suggests *poseer*, which behaves like *tener*: *poseer el diablo una persona* would (if context clears up the ambiguity) refer to ownership, while *poseer el diablo a una persona* would refer to one possessed (seized, frenzied).

In *El ataque fracasó dejando algunas víctimas (Revista de los Archivos de Costa Rica,* enero-febrero 1948, p. 36) *dejar* implies 'to have as a result.'

In "Los Pah-ah-tun antes de la conquista *representaban los dioses de la lluvia*" (L. Moreno, *Tradiciones mayas,* Universidad de Yucatán, Mérida de Yucatán, 1943) *representar* is a synonym of *ser.* In its more usual sense of serving someone, an employer for example, as agent, *a* would be used.

With *señalar* we might say *Señaló un hombre* in the sense 'Señaló que era un hombre,' and *Señaló a un hombre* in the sense 'apuntó'.

With *anunciar, Anunciaron los campeones* might mean 'announced who they were,' i.e. brought them into existence as champions, while *Anunciaron a los campeones* would be suitable at a post-game banquet, to introduce them to the audience.

With *conocer,* one for whom the Blanco family looms for the first time over the mental horizon in the act of getting acquainted with it might say *Conocí la familia Blanco* (cp. Keniston *Sp. Syn. List* §2.296, *Amigo mío, se hacen viajes para conocer mujeres*), but *Espero que conozcas a la familia Blanco cuando vayas a Madrid* is the view of a third party to whom the family is already an entity-in-being on which the act of acquaintance is to be performed.

The de-personalized *Dios creó la primera mujer de una costilla de Adán* contrasts with *Dios castigó a la primera mujer;* in the first, *a* would be possible, of course, but in the second its omission would be unlikely. Like *crear* is Bello's *formar,* §899: *La escuela de guerra es la que forma los grandes capitanes.* But Bello puts *formar* in the class of verbs that omit *a* because they so often have nonpersons as their objects. Semantically such a class of verbs is doubtful; it is not the frequency with which *dejar* is used with nonpersons that makes for *Dejo mi mujer,* but the particular meaning under the circumstances.

With verbs of selection, where the object becomes what it is called in the very act of making the choice, *a* may be omitted: *Ella escogió un marido, Voy a elegir un compañero.* In a political election one might find either *¿Cuándo elegimos el nuevo gobernador?* or *¿Cuándo elegimos al nuevo gobernador?,* but the latter is probably an after-the-fact contamination.

Nombrar likewise has 'choice' as one of its meanings: *El presidente nombró dos embajadores*. But if the ambassadors were implicated in some scandal and the finger of suspicion were pointed at them, the phrase would be *Nombró a dos embajadores*. The number of verbs of selection among the examples cited by Keniston (*Sp. Syn. List* §§2.282-2.294) is significantly high: *elegir, escoger, diputar*. Bello (§895) attributes the effect to the nature of the noun object; his examples: *El presidente eligió los intendentes y gobernadores; El papa ha creado cuatro cardinales*.

Verbs of identification are like those of selection—until the act of identifying is carried out, the individuals named are not known to be what the name calls them. Thus Keniston's example (*Sp. Syn. List* §2.281) *El mérito del gallo consiste en descubrir a los embusteros* means to expose pre-existing (though unknown) cheats, but without the *a* would signify to find out whether there are any such. Similarly *En la picota veremos a los ladrones* and *En la picota veremos los ladrones* are both indefinite, but in the first the speaker refers to seeing the thieves, whoever they are, exposed there, and in the second he refers to finding out, by the exposure, who the thieves are. In the second the pillory is used as a test, and innocent persons may be subjected to it. Similarly contrasting uses of *buscar* are common.

What one finds after *como* leads to the same inferences, for *como* has two functions, one of which is to make a comparison and the other of which is similar to the verb *ser* (the analogy of *como* and *ser* extends to the use of the indefinite article: *como abogado, es abogado*). Keniston cites as examples of the use and omission of *a* after *como* the following (*Sp. Syn. List* §§2.421, 2.422): *El Conde quiere a su hija como a un dolor de muelas* and *Maquiavelo le hubiera saludado como aventajadísimo precursor de sus máximas*. In the first of these the writer does not imply that the daughter *is* a toothache, but that she is like one, metaphorically; in the second example, the writer does imply that the person in question is regarded as a precursor, and is not merely like a precursor—with the omission of *a*, the expression becomes one of being. Making the contrast a minimal one, we might have *Yo siempre he considerado a Juan como mi mejor amigo* (he has actually been considered to be that person) versus *Yo siempre he considerado a Juan como a mi mejor amigo* (I have shown him the same consideration that I might show my best friend, though he is not necessarily that friend). Bello (§1235) chooses, unfortunately, a situation which leads him to a false conclusion: "¿Es indiferente poner o no la preposición en 'Le miran como padre;' 'Los trata como a hijos'? Me parece que *le miran como padre* se dice de los que miran como un padre al que no lo es; y que, por el contrario, 'los trata como a hijos' sugeriría la idea de verdadera paternidad." This is quite true, but for a reason only incidental to the use and omission of *a*. In both examples we are speaking of a peculiar relationship, that of parenthood, which ordinarily, unlike friendship (which is often a matter of viewpoint), either exists or does not exist—the fact that *como* is used at all indicates that true parenthood is not the question here. *Le miran como padre* is 'They regard him as their father, even though he may not be': *mirar* has the special sense of 'choose-to-consider-to-be'—a verb of being. Similarly with *tratar*: in *Los trata como hijos, tratar* is another such verb of being; but in *Los trata como a hijos* ('he treats them the way he would treat his children'), *tratar* takes on the active sense of the love, discipline, condescension, etc. of his treatment of them. In neither case is he necessarily the actual father, but in the latter the more colorful meaning of *tratar* suggess true parenthood more strongly.

Similar examples from the sixteenth century are Keniston's *Pero dadme un príncipe que haga eso.—Doos el Emperador* ('Hay el Emperador') (*Syntax of Castilian Prose* §2.242) and all "exclamatory expressions used in the sense of 'here is,"' *ves aquí, he aquí*, etc., except when followed by proper names: *Ves aquí mi señora (Syn. Cast. Pr.* §2.253). The latter might still be used without *a* nowadays, and it is worth noting that the omission, unusual by textbook standards, is in the area of verbs of being. Other modern analogs: *¿Ha visto usted nunca tal majadero?* would probably be more likely without than with *a*; "—¡Chicas, es don Luis!—se gritaban unas a otras—. Señor doctor, ¡aquí! *¡Míreme usted este chico!...* ¡Entre a ver a mi madre!" (V. Blasco Ibánez, *El intruso*, Valencia: Editorial Prometeo, 1916, p. 25). Keniston (*Sp. Syn. List* §2.264) gives *¿Ves este joven?* as the only example quoted, but the significance of *ver*, if any, is unexplained.

For the *leísta* who uses both *les* and *los* accusative (the singular is less reliable as a test), there is a loose correlation between *los* and the omission of *a* on the one hand, and *les* and the use of *a* on the other hand. I have the following preferences from my *leísta* colleague:

1. ¿Ha nombrado el presidente los dos embajadores?—No, no los ha nombrado todavía. 2. ¿Cuándo anunciaron los campeones?—Creo que los anunciaron anoche. 3. ¿Tiene usted amigos en Chicago?—No, no los tengo. 4. ¿Dónde tiene usted a sus padres?—Les tengo en el hospital. 5. Ha ganado dos amigos, pero no sé como los ha ganado. 6. Escogió dos ayudantes, pero debe ser que no los sabía escoger bien. 7. Voy a elegir dos compañeros, pues los necesito para que me acompañen. 8. Los Pah-ah-tun etc. (see above). Los habían representado desde siglos atrás (but if *representar* meant 'serve as vicegerent,' then *les*). 9. Tenemos que designar dos representantes, y los tenemos que designar antes de vencer el plazo. 10. Ahí están los niños, jugando. ¿Les ve? 11. Pero ¿dónde están mis compañeros? No les veo.

The meaning of the verbs is, however, only incidental here to the over-all personalizing effect of *les*. Thus for the verb-of-being *perder* the same speaker gives *Murieron en la guerra. Así perdí mis hijos. Así les perdí.* And, as a teacher, he would personalize more in *Reunimos tres alumnos—les hallamos cerca,* and less in *Reunimos tres carpinteros—los hallamos cerca.*

Part IV

Word Order

The Position of the Adverb in English—A Convenient Analogy to the Position of the Adjective in Spanish

[*Author's Note*: As with most of the themes in this book, that of the next piece and the one following was inspired by the wish to find some hook in the memory store of English-speaking students that might snare a difficult point that they were trying to learn. Adjective position, with the freedom in Spanish to place most attributive adjectives either before or after the noun, has always been exasperatingly hard to understand, even though it obviously responds to some distinction in the minds of native speakers. How get a handle on it?

There was obviously little help on the English side—in fact, the English side is the main cause of the problem, if one looks just at the position of adjectives. The key must be somewhere else. It occurred to me that modifiers are modifiers, and maybe adverbs-modifying-verbs in English might illuminate adjectives-modifying-nouns in Spanish. And so it turned out. The similarities are remarkable, and have a bearing on much broader concepts of word order in both languages, and in general.

(The farthest ripple—touching Spanish as well as English—is a later piece, "Adjectives in English: Attribution and predication," *Lingua* 18 [1967] 1-34.)]

* * *

ENGLISH GRAMMAR offers no foothold, as far as its adjectives are concerned, to the teaching of adjective position in Spanish.[1] Though its adjectives are variously placed—"money enough" and "enough money," "knight errant" and "arrant rogue," "eternal life" and "life eternal"—their position in no way resembles the working of logic, and is of practically no help to the Spanish teacher.

The English adverb, on the other hand, shows virtually the same peculiarities of position, with reference to its verb, as does the Spanish adjective with reference to its noun.

(1) English adverbs which determine but do not describe precede their verbs:

	Compare:
He *just* had to come	La *única* razón
They *even* hated me	Una *verdadera* ganga

(2) Determinative adverbs become descriptive when placed after their verbs:

	Compare:
We often eat	Cierta cosa
We eat often	Una cosa cierta
He once hit me	Varios libros
He hit me once	Libros varios
She simply told me	La pura verdad
She told me simply	La verdad pura

(3) Qualitative-descriptive adverbs tend to precede when the action modified is regarded as "to be expected" or "taken for granted," but follow when the intention is more that of giving information:

	Compare:
He angrily refused (the situation is such that anger is to be expected)	El furioso león se abalanzó sobre su víctima

[1] Originally published in *Hispania* 26 (1943): 191-92

He refused angrily (no expectation)	De repente apareció un león furioso
They rudely interrupted me (interruptions are naturally rude)	Vive en una ruda cabaña
They interrupted me rudely (this came as a surprise)	No me gusta una cabaña ruda
They joyously sang the Christmas carols	Veo su alegre cara
They sang the Christmas carols joyously	Tiene la cara alegre
She lightly brushed it aside	Se lo quitó con un ligero movimiento
She brushed it aside lightly	Se lo quitó con un movimiento ligero
He carefully looked through the paper	Lo miró con cuidadosa atención
He looked through the paper carefully	Lo miró con atención cuidadosa
She majestically strode from the room	Me repugnan sus majestuosos ademanes
She strode from the room majestically	Me repugnan sus ademanes majestuosos

(4) As a first corollary to (3), differentiating adverbs, which are the most strongly informative, tend to follow:

	Compare:
He did this carefully and that indifferently	Llevaba un sombrero viejo y zapatos nuevos
It is essential to think quickly and act promptly	Quédese con este libro cansado y déme uno interesante

(5) As a second corollary to (3), eulogistic and dyslogistic adverbs tend to precede:

	Compare:
They magnanimously remitted our debts	Le agradezco su generosa acción
He considerately opened the door for us	Soy su atento servidor
He viciously spat at us	¡Malo, falso, ruin traidor!

The motive here is, of course, the idea of "just what would be expected of that sort of person."

The shade of meaning which attaches to adverb-position in English is so firmly rooted that here and there an adverb has become stereotyped in meaning because of the position that it most frequently occupies: *scarcely* and *hardly* are examples; they are now exclusively prepositive. *Fast* is almost restricted to post-position, which gives it a distinctive shade when it occasionally goes before: "He fast walked out" is inadmissible, but "These customs are fast disappearing" is correct.

The exceptions to the analogy which I have attempted to trace are mainly due to the greater flexibility of adverb-position. Thus in the last example under (3), actually three shades are possible: "She majestically strode from the room," "She strode majestically from the room," and "She strode from the room majestically"—gaining in informativeness from first to third. Also, especially with temporal and locative adverbs (this problem naturally does not arise with adjectives), almost any position may be possible, with or without a change in meaning: "Sometimes I think there's no use," "I think sometimes there's no use," and "I think there's no use, sometimes"; "Now it's too late" and "It's too late now"; "There he goes" and "He goes there." But where the adverb and adjective functions parallel each other, the resemblance in position is remarkable.

Adjective Position Again

PEDAGOGICALLY THE ARTICLE by Raymond Moody is a fine position paper.[1] His advice to deal with semantic problems on their own terms in the native language of the learner, freeing them from the limitations imposed by insufficient vocabulary at the early stages, is something we all need to heed. The criticisms he makes of the transformational approach are probably valid. As applied to adjective position it is too indirect, and does not really tap the students' awareness of restrictivity, assuming that such an awareness does lurk somewhere in the unconscious. My own preference for demonstrating that it does exist, and for enticing the student to utilize his own feel for word order when there actually are options, has been to compare Spanish adjective position with English adverb position. I tell them, "You already know how to put adverbs before or after their verbs, and what you mean when you do one or the other. Spanish does the same in its noun phrases as English does in its verb phrases." It is not too difficult to find parallel examples:

Tenía ricos ornamentos.	It was richly ornamented.
Tenía ornamentos ricos.	It was ornamented richly.
Sufrió terribles daños.	It was terribly damaged.
Sufrió daños terribles.	It was damaged terribly.
Le dio un dulce beso.	He sweetly kissed her.
Le dio un beso dulce.	He kissed her sweetly.
Noté un barato perfume.	I noticed it was cheaply perfumed.
Noté un perfume barato.	I noticed it was perfumed cheaply.

[1] "More on Teaching Adjective Position: Some Theoretical and Practical Considerations," *Hispania* 54 (May 1971), 315-21. This article was originally published in *Hispania* 55 (1972): 91-94

The effect of postposition is the same in both cases: it gives the most contrastive information, which in many cases, perhaps the majority, means that it is differentiating. *Un perfume barato* discriminates a type of perfume; *perfumed cheaply* discriminates a type of perfuming. (Spanish adverb position makes the same distinctions [see "The Position of Adverbs in English," above].)

But Moody's discussion of adjective position is proof of how much must still be done before we can be confident that we are giving our students the best statement of the facts. Inductive grammar at least had the merit of not misleading anyone, provided the examples were varied; if we are again to take the responsibility of feeding the rules along with the examples, we have to make them accurate.

The discussion presents adjective position as based fundamentally on the mathematical organization of reality: "In talking about parts (differentiating some or one of many) the adjective follows; in talking about totals (all or one unique, where no differentiation is concerned), the adjective precedes" (p. 318). What this amounts to is labeling a principle by one of its applications. It is true that differentiating part from whole is one of the uses to which adjective position is put. But the principle itself is broader and not only embraces a wider range of applications in the position of adjectives but also covers the relative position of verb and subject, of adverb and verb, and of main and subordinate clauses. It has been for many years one of the main concerns of the Prague school of linguists, who call it Functional Sentence Perspective. Their starting point was the contrast between the relatively grammaticized word order of English and the "free" order of Czech. Most of what they say about English versus Czech[2] is true

[2]For example, the series of studies by Jan Firbas in *Brno Studies in English* starting with "Thoughts on the Communicative Function of the Verb in English, German and Czech" in Vol. 1 (Prague, 1959). The work goes back to that of Vilém Mathesius in the 30's and 40's. My own "Linear Modification" (*PMLA* 67 [1952], 1117-44), written before I was aware of the Czechs' work, has essentially the same point of view. Anna Hatcher's articles are in similar vein; see especially her monograph *Theme and Underlying Question*, supplement to *Word* vol. 12 (1956).

of English versus Spanish. The controlling principle is the "communicative dynamism" of the elements that are balanced against one another. Recent work in generative grammar on presuppositions and topic-comment is finally attempting to grapple with the same problems.

A word about the mathematical organization of reality. Most linguists prefer to think that reality is organized linguistically, not mathematically. Mathematics is a special code, secondary to natural language and excerpting very special parts of it. William Bull has brilliantly demonstrated what some of those parts are. But mathematics cannot be promoted above language. If there are mathematical aspects to adjective position, they are secondary and derivative.

The principle of differentiation is a useful entry device for adjective position in Spanish because it is easy to state and easy to grasp. But counterexamples are not hard to find. In the following I give each a paragraph, to provide for comments. The first four are contained in a personal note from Gordon T. Fish; they are cited here along with his annotations. The same examples are also given in his 1961 *Hispania* article ("Adjectives Fore and Aft: Position and Function in Spanish," 44, 700-08). One remark of his is worth quoting. "I have found ... in the literature ... a persistent effort to cram all embarrassing cases into the Procrustean bed of the restrictive."

Volvió a su Mallorca natal. "There is no question of distinguishing one city from another; *natal* tells why he returned."

No perder el tiempo en calaveradas estúpidas. "There is no implication that some escapades are not stupid; the adjective tells why they are a waste of time."

Furioso porque le arrancamos de su casona triste. "Which was so wretched."

Dios misericordioso me ha dejado el consuelo de poder evocar aquel mundo mágico. Fish underlined *consuelo* to show why *misericordioso* is postposed: it explains the consolatory act.

La actividad desplegada y la experiencia acumulada [por el ASTP] *en los años densos de la guerra planteó ... el problema de la enseñanza de una segunda lengua*[3]. This does not distinguish dense war years from thin war years; they were all dense by reason of being war years. The purpose of postponing the adjective is to point out that they were dense; preposing it would have taken that fact for granted.

Examples of the opposite, the preposing of differentiating adjectives, are not so common, but are still abundant:

¿Y se dedica una porporcional suma a las atenciones benéficas?
This example, from Laudelino Moreno, is, according to him, something that might easily be heard in ordinary conversation.

La entonación emocional... es seguida constantemente con especial atención, como signo demostrativo de las interiores reacciones del interlocutor. In the context of this passage from Navarro's textbook[5] the concept of 'reaction' is newly introduced and carries more semantic weight than its modifier *interiores*.

Actualmente trabajo en... la Universidad de Tulane con un contrato que expirará en mayo del corriente año. Letter from a Colombian.

El accidente fue causado por un falso movimiento. Falso is essential to discriminate the kind of movement referred to; but if it were postponed it would make the irrelevant suggestion that there actually were other movements under consideration.

Es un estupendo estudiante. In the context of this remark, made by a Spaniard in relaxed conversation, the person's studiousness was the center of interest.

The relative weight of the noun can be assessed also by native speakers' reactions to phrases in which a descriptive adjective precedes a semantically empty noun, constrasted with phrases containing semantically heavier nouns. Thus *el irresoluto óptico* is more likely than *el irresoluto hombre*. This is analogous to what happens with accent in phrases containing empty nouns in English: *He acted like a crázy màn* contrasts with *He acted like a crázy fóol. He acted like a crázy mán* and *el irresoluto hombre* are about equally hard to contextualize.

Especially interesting are the corrections that a native speaker makes on manuscripts submitted by non-natives. The following was made by Moreno on a thesis he was directing:

---

[3] *Revista de la Universidad de Buenos Aires*, 3 (1958), 7.

[5] *Manual de entonación española*, New York: Hispanic Institute, 1944, p. 214.

Siempre los montones de trapos y de paja en el suelo, donde duerme la numerosa familia. Corrected to *familia numerosa*. Moreno explained that as he corrected it, the sentence suggested that even the animals might be counted as part of the family. Putting *familia* at the end—this is my interpretation—gave too much emphasis to its literal value; the thing primarily signaled is the numerousness, counting the animals.

The examples cited up to this point have all had their main accent in the normal position, on the last element of the phrase, adjective or noun. What of the additional possibility, so common in English, that of a differentiating adjective not only preceding the noun but accented to boot? (Sentences like

It was an ea
sy job.

are typical.) Though this resource is not often called on in Spanish, it is nevertheless there to be used when needed. Examples:

Y esto se hace, según insiste Spitzer, a pesar de que el más concreto aspecto de una palabra es su significado.[6] *Concreto* was italicized in the original.

[Los españoles], que vinieron en opuesta dirección. Introduction to a speech by Juan Rodríguez Castellano, who accented *opuesta* when he said it, and de-accented *dirección*. He was referring humorously to himself as crossing the continent in the opposite direction to that taken by the explorers.

Yo hablo de las hermósas casas, no de las féas. In repeated trials with examples like this, I have never found a native speaker who boggled at them.

So what is it that leads to the misconceptions? One factor is surely frequency. English is forced to use constructions like these; Spanish is not. Contexts in which the broad semantic value of the device of position is narrowed to the specific meaning of differentiation are probably most numerous of all and create an overriding impression about Spanish word order. But there are other contexts. Here is one suggested by a Venezuelan colleague, whom I tried in vain to persuade to accept *Quiero que conozcas a mi mujer adorable.* He proposed

[6]*Boletín del Instituto Caro y Cuervo*, 4 (1948), 127.

Quiero que conozcas a mi sobrinita adorable as natural for him, regardless of whether there were one niece or many. A little reflection locates the reason in the social situation. There are strong reasons for referring to one's wife as adorable in a self-evident sense, and for not putting her adorableness explicitly on display as if she were up for admiration; the opposite may readily be true in the case of one's niece. (A test of the same pair on a native speaker of French revealed the same preferences. A second native speaker of Spanish offered the four sentences *Le presento a mi mujer adorable, Le presento a mi adorable mujer, Le presento a mi sobrinita adorable, Le presento a mi adorable sobrinita,* unhesitatingly picked the first example as least acceptable and gave essentially the same explanation as mine. It had nothing to do with how many nieces there might be.) Postposing the adjective makes it explicit, exactly as with *su único hijo* and *su hijo único,* both meaning 'only' and neither differentiating.

I return to my analogy of adverb position in English. There is one place where the match with adjectives in Spanish is almost perfect. This is with *-ing* nominals; the verb has become a noun and the adverb in the verb phrase parallels an adjective: *Comfortably sitting back is no way to face an issue; Sitting back comfortably is no way to face an issue.* The first of these examples refers to sitting back; no point is made of its being the comfortable thing to do—that is pictured as self-evident. The second is not differentiating; it does not imply that sitting back uncomfortably is a way to face an issue; it only makes the comfortableness explicit. On the other hand, if it is wished to postpone in order to point out a contrast, that can be done: *Wrongly deciding would be fatal; Deciding wrongly would be fatal*[7]. The second clearly suggests that there are right decisions as well as wrong ones. But this is only a way of USING a semantic device that can be used in other ways as well.

Another distractor, I suspect, is the reliance on noun phrases containing definite articles and premodifying possessives, which introduces the extraneous factor of anaphoric and cataphoric determiners. When we say *La mujer me habló,* the article implies that

[7] The accents are assumed to be in their normal position on the second of the two elements.

mujer is already known from the context; it is anaphoric. Adding a premodifying descriptive adjective does not usually alter this: *La linda mujer me habló* still means the *mujer* is known from the context, and *linda* is therefore as a rule (but not necessarily) known, too. But when we say *La mujer linda me habló,* the article is cataphoric: *linda* is needed to specify it. (If a speaker misuses an article anaphorically he is immediately brought to book. *La mujer me habló.—¿Qué mujer?—La mujer linda.*) There is thus an intersection of two grammatical facts: a cataphoric article in need of specification, and an adjective placed in the accent position of information focus which is therefore best able to satisfy the need. Adjective position has broader implications than merely that of differentiating one nominal concept from another.

Natural language is like that. It cannot afford to limit its semantic resources to mathematically precise formulas, but must define them broadly and leave the rest to situations of use.

Meaningful Word Order in Spanish

[*Author's Note*: In this longer piece I tried to carry the notions originally confined to adverb and adjective position into the larger realm of sentence constituents in general—to show, for example, that the same principle accounts for the position of a subject in relation to its verb as for the adjective in relation to its noun. Along the way I had to make the best use I could of vocabulary then available. The kind of prosodic highlighting described in this article I later renamed *accent* (or *pitch accent*). (The overwrought *passionate stress* I now term *accent of power*.) The concepts of theme and rheme (or topic and comment), presupposition, and focus have since become familiar, but at the time were novel, at least in American linguistics.]

* * *

IN THIS ARTICLE[1] I shall tentatively outline a theory of Spanish word order in accordance with the general principles of Linear Modification set forth in the article of the same name.[2]

Explanations of why speakers prefer one sequence over another are many and varied. Gili Gaya speaks of a "synthetic" versus an "analytical" style in reference to adjectives and nouns, and is alone in recognizing a similar tendency in phrases with the gerundio.[3] Numerous grammars offer a principle of "longest element last" in reference to subject and verb. Others call attention to the "poetic" effect of putting adjectives before their nouns. Supposing that such

---

[1] Published originally in *Boletín de Filología* (Universidad de Chile) 8 (1954-55): 45-56.

[2] *PMLA*, LXVII: 7, Dec. 1952, 1117-44.

[3] *Curso superior de sintaxis española*, México, 1943, 171.

principles are true as far as they apply, it is still the linguist's job to suspect the presence of some underlying force that ties them together. Symptoms are comparatively easy to discern, in semantics as in medicine; what is not so easy is to coordinate the symptoms into a pattern.

We must begin by distinguishing between two manifestations of sentence order, "free" and "petrified." The latter comprise those combinations where the speaker has little or no choice: *Lo hago* can hardly become *Hago lo* in modern Spanish; *entre los dos* cannot become *los dos entre*. In them there is no question of what a different combination would "mean," since only one combination exists. The main instances of free order are the following:

1. Subject-verb: *Juan trabaja, Trabaja Juan.*
2. Verb-object: *Vi a Juan, A Juan lo vi.*
3. Adjective-noun: *Roja alba, Alba roja.*
4. Adverb-verb: *Bien lo sabe, Lo sabe bien.*
5. Coordinate-coordinate: *Juan y Maria, Maria y Juan.*
6. Superordinate-subordinate: *Lo mato si lo veo, Si lo veo lo mato.*

Actually the first four classes, or at least the third and fourth, could be made subsidiary to the sixth; but it is so customary to treat subject-verb and adjective-noun as classes to themselves that it is more convenient to treat all six as equals, and limit the sixth to phrases and clauses.

The second step is to distinguish three manifestations of stress, which we may call alliteratively "petrified," "prosodic," and "passionate." Petrified stress is the phonemic stress by which *habló* is differentiated from *hablo*; we shall not be concerned with it. Prosodic stress is that which occurs normally in the second element of the phrases *roja álba* and *alba rója, Bien lo sábe* and *Lo sabe bién*, etc. It is often referred to as "sentence stress," and has been thought by some to be an automatic component of the sentence just as the stress in *habló* is an automatic component of the word, and hence to be essentially different from the contrastive stress on *Juan* in *Juán lo dice, no Eduardo*. Prosodic stress is the one we shall be concerned with here, in its interrelationships with free position, and I hope to show that it is not altogether automatic, but akin to the stress on *Juan* in the last example.

The third stress, which I have labeled *passionate,* is evidenced in *esa maldíta casa;* our emotions about a particular thing at times cause us to distort the "logical" stress that it normally carries. We shall not be concerned with passionate stress. It must be admitted, however, that there is no sharp dividing line between prosodic and passionate—where prosodic stress highlights something considered "important," it is to that extent passionate. But the two can be separated clearly enough to make discussing one without the other significant.

Two cautions before continuing. First, "free" is not to be taken in an absolute sense. Just as a rigid convention determines the order of *entre los dos,* so the intent of the speaker determines the order of *alba roja.* The difference between the two is not that one is determined and the other not, but that one is determined wholly by convention while the other is determined, within certain limits, by a meaning which the speaker wishes to convey. It is precisely this determining intent or meaning that we are called upon to track down. Second, rigid convention and speaker's forethought are only two of the several ingredients of sentence order, which is probably the chief reason why the forethought has escaped detection. In any long sentence a good deal has to be crowded in, and there are only two directions in which it can be done, fore and aft; when a long modifier of incidental importance is inserted, or when a speaker bethinks himself of something to add in the course of saying what he had intended to say, the more systematic ordering of elements will be disrupted. On this account what I hope to demonstrate here will not explain everything; where it can be seen best will be in relatively short groups, in which the ordering of the elements visibly proceeds along the lines of the preexisting linguistic pattern which the speaker carries in his head.

1. Subject-verb. Imagine a store with merchandise for sale. One clerk notices that a certain article is gone, and asks a second about it. The second replies *Lo compró algún señor viejo.* In a store-situation, buying and selling is the regular thing, and consequently *Lo compró* offers nothing unexpected or especially informative; the identity of the buyer, however, was not predictable, and *algún señor viejo* is accordingly a new and unexpected datum.

Imagine, in contrast, a private home in which things are not normally offered for sale. A visitor calls, and notes the absence of a piece of furniture that had been there before. He asks what became of it, and receives the reply *Algún señor viejo lo compró*. The fact of the article's having been sold is now the most unexpected datum, and the sentence reverts to the more usual subject-verb order—probably reflecting the fact that if an action is performed, someone has to perform it, whence subjects (particularly indefinite ones) are presupposed.

Imagine someone asking *¿Por qué no se puede usar papel para taparlo?* Of the two answers *Porque el papel se rasga* and *Porque se rasga el papel* the former is more likely—'paper' has been mentioned and is accordingly presupposed, but what happens to the paper is a new, unpredicted, and contrastive datum (what happens when in the second example *rasga* is loud-stressed and *papel* is de-stressed we shall examine later). But if the question had been *¿Cómo no terminaste la carta?* the answer *Es que se rasgó el papel* would be if anything more likely than *Es que el papel se rasgó*, since the reference to the paper as a cause is unexpected.

In answer to the question *¿Por qué se ven tantos paquetes por aquí?* the form *Los dejó olvidados el cartero* would be more likely than *El cartero los dejó olvidados*. Since the packages are in a place where they should not be, it is to be supposed that someone left them there, and consequently *Los dejó olvidados* is less new and informative than the identity of the person responsible.

I have chosen examples in which the situation could be carefully defined in order to illustrate something that might have been more easily illustrated with a simpler set of examples. It is easy to see the operation of the principle in the pairs "*¿Quién trabaja?*"—"*Trabaja Juan*" and "*¿Qué hace Juan?*"—"*Juan trabaja,*" because the element presupposed has already appeared verbatim in the preceding question and the new or contrasting element has not. It is more difficult to trace a "presupposition" that is present by implication but not explicitly; yet we see the same principle at work: that which is presupposed, but needs to be stated in order to clarify or remind, precedes; that which is new, unexpected, informative, and contrastive follows. The "point" of the utterance is toward the end.

I used the qualification "needs to be stated" because a good part of the time the element that is presupposed is not uttered at all. Thus it is superfluous to answer *¿Quién trabaja?* with *Trabaja Juan*—normally it is sufficient to say merely *Juan*. And here is another reason why the underlying principle has gone unnoticed—it is most obvious in the kind of sentence that is least frequent. Most of the time a presupposed element will not be expressed unless it has to be captured from an environment that implies but does not explicate it, or from an environment that only vaguely implies something of the general class of which the actual element is a specific.

To repeat: the normal thing is that a presupposed element that is clearly understood will not be uttered, while one that is not clearly understood will be uttered and will precede; the non-presupposed element, or "point," will always be uttered, and when it combines with the presupposed one it normally follows.

But sometimes, for special effects, a presupposed element, even a lengthy one, is repeated though specifically known from the immediate context. Thus in answer to *¿Quién lo dice?* one may find simply *Yo*, or, *Quien lo dice soy yo* alternating with *Yo soy quien lo dice* (*digo*). We may call such a verbatim or near-verbatim presupposed element a "resumptive," and we find that resumptives offer a free choice between the two orders of words, with the principal difference between them being what is conveyed by the difference in intonation. *Quien lo dice soy yo* has loud rising-falling stress at the end, and partakes of the firmness of that characteristic intonation contour: it would be suitable, e.g., in a sharp rebuke, and could hardly be used if the intent were kindly or humorous. *Yo soy quien lo dice* (*digo*) has its loud stress at the beginning followed by a fall that is first fairly abrupt and then gradual. Its mood is one of tension-relaxation, and is suitable for (though does not necessarily imply) a humorous or kindly intent. Inasmuch as most resumptives do not need to be uttered at all, it is not surprising that one purpose of their utterance is to create an intonation contour that otherwise could not be managed for lack of a sufficient number of syllables.

To clarify the difference between resumptives and other prosodically unstressed elements, let us look again at one of the preceding examples. In answer to *¿Por qué se ven tantos paquetes por aquí?* it would be unusual if not impossible to say *El cartero los dejó olvidados* with loud stress on *cartero* and the remainder de-stressed. But if the question were *¿Quien dejó olvidados todos estos paquetes?* the answer might readily be the one, intonation and all, that could not be used before. We conclude that a prosodic stress followed by non-stress implies that the non-stressed element is a resumptive, while the more normal arrangement, where prosodic stress is *preceded* by non-stress, implies that the non-stressed element inheres in the total situation and is presupposed or at any rate non-contrastive, and may or may not be resumptive. In other words, an element which is explicitly resumptive comes after prosodic stress.

A resumptive need not be verbatim. Sometimes it is paraphrased. In answer to *¿Cómo sabías que se entregaría la mercancía a tiempo?* one might have *Mis amigos me dieron la noticia,* with prosodic stress on *amigos.* What follows is resumptive: *noticia* = *que se entregaría la mercancía a tiempo;* in place of the repeated clause there is a surrogate noun. Observe now the incongruousness of putting. in the position of *noticia,* some noun which cannot serve as a surrogate: *Mis amigos me dieron su palabra*—here, if we attempt to de-stress *palabra* as we de-stresed *noticia,* the effect is jarring. On the other hand, if *palabra* is given prosodic stress, the utterance is normal. Since 'promise' is new to the context, and is the "point" of the utterance, it must have prosodic stress.

This gives us a clue to the function of normal prosodic stress in the Spanish sentence: this stress, as is well known, comes toward the end of the breath group. The stress marks the point of the utterance, that portion of it which answers the question (asked or implicit) uppermost in the minds of the interlocutors. The contrastive, new, informative element tends to follow, and with it goes the prosodic stress. This norm enables the speaker to choose between which grammatical segment he chooses to highlight, subject or verb, by putting now one, now the other, in the position of stress.[4]

---

[4] It can be argued that many sentences in Spanish do not reveal any necessary emphasis of one part over the other, that in answer to *¿Cómo perdiste el anillo?,* for example, one might as readily find *Lo hurtó algún pillo* as *Algún pillo lo hurtó.* In the first, according to the principle, the concept of 'perdiste' is taken to suggest a theft, with the result that 'hurtó' is presupposed; in the second, 'hurtó' is not taken as implied by 'perdiste' but as a new datum. But as far as a speaker is concerned there might be occasions when either element is equally contrastive. The answer to the argument is that this is only one of

One matter remains to be disposed of in connection with subject/verb order: the notion of longest-element-last. Measuring sentences by the yard we should probably find that in the main the longest element does come last. But if my argument is right, it does not come last because it is long, but it tends to be long for the same reason that it comes last, viz., because it is a new datum. One of our elementary grammars gives *¿Tiene una mesa el alumno?* as an example of a relatively long subject following the verb and its object. Now if *el alumno* had been known between both speakers to be the subject, it would probably not have been mentioned; the sentence would have been simply *¿Tiene una mesa?* The fact that it is there at all suggests that it is a new datum, and it follows because it is new, not because it is long. Obviously in answer to *¿Qué hace en la tienda a estas horas aquel señor de la barba larga, los zapatos negros y el traje gris?* the interlocutor is not going to repeat the whole description; it is now a resumptive, and will be abbreviated, replaced by a pronoun, or omitted altogether.

---

many instances where the language forces its speakers into an either-or choice. Another such instance is the contrast between perfective *Lo vi salir* and imperfective *Lo vi saliendo*. The speaker may be indifferent to the distinction, but he nevertheless has to choose one or the other. In all probability he is never totally indifferent to the distinction, and picks the one toward which he leans however slightly. The fact that this leaning may be almost infinitely slight is another explanation of why the real semantic contrast has escaped detection. It also explains why the catchall explanation of "euphony" is so often invoked. It is worth repeating, for the benefit of those who call upon euphony to explain phenomena like the one under consideration here, that we do not say things because they are euphonious, but they are euphonious because we say them. What a writer does may to a fair extent be conditioned by euphony because he is able to go back over his text and cull out unwanted repetitions and other cacophonies; but the speaker is guided by more vigorously functioning linguistic and semantic frames. Part of the over-stress on euphony is conceivably due to the literary orientation of much linguistic research.

To repeat: long elements usually come last because they are usually contrastive, not because they are long.[5]

The order subject-verb predominates over the order verb-subject in Spanish, but this statistical fact is not to be interpreted mechanically. In a given discourse one actor is more likely to carry through a series of different and hence contrastive actions. In any given setting the actors are more stable, relatively speaking, than their actions; the actors are therefore more readily presupposed, while their actions are more unpredictable and hence more contrastive.

2. Verb-object. The same principle operates here, but is partly obscured by another powerful tendency in word order, that of arranging elements according to time. When we say *Entró y se sentó* we do not put *se sentó* last because it is necessarily more contrastive but because it occurs AFTER *entró*. Similarly the preponderance of the order action-goal is probably due in part at least to our viewing the action as terminating in the object, and hence as preceding it in time. But instances like *Cada centavo que ganó lo jugó* in answer to *¿Cómo llegó a su actual estado?* are common enough and prove that here, too, the point of the utterance (in this example 'gambling') comes last. Furthermore, the passive voice enables the speaker to invert at will in order to get the action at the end: *Los enemigos fueron derrotados* makes

---

[5] It is possible, of course, that Spanish is witnessing one of those linguistic petrifications that occur periodically along the course of every language. We find, to start with, an order determined by the contrast presupposed-contrastive. Purely by accident this order coincides most of the time with the contrast short-long. In the course of time speakers reinterpret a semantic principle into a mechanical one, and the determinant actually turns out to be the contrast short-long. Exactly this has happened with the conjunctive pronouns: *Lo tengo* is mechanically determined, whereas formerly speakers were free to say *Tengo lo* and their choice was undoubtedly then determined by meaning. English has already experienced a shift from semantic to mechanical determinants in the order subject-verb (in its remaining zones of freedom the same general principles of presupposition and contrast apply as in Spanish), and Spanish may yet undergo it, but the petrification has not proceeded far enough to outweigh at this date the factor of meaning.

'derrota' the point; *Derrotaron a sus enemigos* makes 'enemigos' the point.

3. Adjective-noun. This is the phenomenon of word order that has been commented on most in Spanish, probably because the units, unlike those of subject-plus-modifiers and verb-plus-modifiers, are short and the contrasts achieved by altering the sequence are striking.

Yet adjective-noun order has evolved farther toward being mechanically determined than has subject-verb order. Only descriptive adjectives, in the main, are free to roam, and even they stand far more often in one position than in the other. In part, the mechanization of adjective order is due to the relative superfluousness of descriptive adjectives in any but a defining or contrastive sense. Most of the time when we use the word *rojo* it is not to paint a picture but to discriminate one object that is red from others that are not. And if this is true of single descriptive adjectives, it is cumulatively true of grouped descriptive adjectives; only the story-teller has much use for two or three descriptive adjectives all modifying one noun at the same time. One result of this is that afterthoughtive parentheses make up a high percentage of all grouped adjectives; the type *El tibio, suave y soñoliento atardecer nos adormecía* is outnumbered by *El atardecer, tibio, suave y soñoliento* (or, with the parenthesis in better balance, *El tibio atardecer, suave y soñoliento*).

But in combinations of noun plus single descriptive adjective the principle of presupposed-first and contrastive-last still operates. In *casa blanca* the adjective narrows the reference of the noun; in *blanca casa* the noun narrows the reference of the adjective (as Gili Gaya points out, the same applies to appositives: *madre viuda* vs. *viuda madre*). Further, when there are no parentheses a series will give step-by-step narrowings: *vino blanco italiano* is primarily about 'vino blanco' narrowed, for this particular occasion, to 'vino blanco' which happens to be 'italiano'; while *vino italiano blanco* is primarily about 'vino italiano' narrowed, for this particular occasion, to 'blanco'. The more adventitious and contrastive the adjective, the more it moves toward the end.

Prosodic stress functions as with subject-verb. In *casa blanca* the normal loud stress is on *blanca;* in *blanca casa* it is on *casa.* If in *casa blanca* the stress falls on *casa,* we know again, exactly as with subject-verb, that *blanca* is a resumptive *(No he dicho "casi blanca" sino cása blanca)*. What we are most unlikely to find, unless with passionate stress, is *blanca casa* with stress on *blanca* and *casa* de-stressed.[6]

What gives the obvious poetic flavor to a pre-posed descriptive adjective? The answer to this is the same as to why descriptive adjectives are not often pre-posed: the poet sees things in qualitative terms—a color 'white' is likely to be, for him, predominant, while the particular objects which are white may in his poetic mood be secondary. So for the poet the color is sometimes presupposed and the things which carry the color are then adventitious, unpredictable, and contrastive. In the practical world the reverse is true. We can set up the same opposition of stability-instability for noun-adjective as for subject-verb: the noun, or thing, is more likely to be durable, and to take on in the course of its existence the accidents of poses (verbs) and qualities (adjectives). This does not mean that all pre-posed adjectives are poetic. The speaker is free to put an adjective first whenever it pleases him to imply that the meaning of that adjective is presupposed: *deliciosas comidas, hermosa hija, malos consejos, infernal ruido,* etc., illustrate the circumstance of being complimentary or uncomplimentary in Spanish, where presupposition is the rule.

4. Adverb-verb. The contrast between *Furiosamente atacaron* and *Atacaron furiosamente* is the same as that between *furioso ataque* and *ataque furioso.* When the modifier follows, it is the new, unpredicted, or adventitious datum; when it precedes, it is presupposed and overspreading, and the modified verb or noun is then the narrowing and contrasting element. The same occurs with non-descriptive adverbs: *Ayer llegó* tells what happened yesterday; *Llegó ayer* tells when the arrival took place.

In the type *Felizmente lo comprendieron todo* (which transposed with parenthesis, gives *Lo comprendieron todo, felizmente*) we have the

---

[6] What follows a passionate stress is not so completely de-stressed as is an ordinary resumptive. Another example is *Pero sí hay perfecto acuerdo entre la gente aquí,* with passionate stress on *acuerdo,* spoken as a lively protest against someone who has maintained a view that the existence of an 'acuerdo' refutes. Instead of an abrupt drop in pitch on the last syllable of *acuerdo,* such as one would have with a resumptive, the tonal curve descends more gradually.

equivalent of "Es cosa feliz que..." The broad, all-enveloping judgment precedes, and the event is narrowing and definitive.

5. Coordinate-coordinate. Where two elements are of equal status and joined by *y*, it should make no difference which comes first. And it is here, as one might expect, that factors other than the ones under consideration are most likely to sway the choice. There is, first, temporal sequence: *ayer y hoy, leer y escribir, llegué y me senté, primero y segundo, etc.*, are not ordinarily reversed. Second, stereotyped sequences which may have, partially, phonetic causes (more sonorous word gravitating into position of stress): English *pick and shovel*, Spanish *picos y vagonetas*[7] (in these the order of use may influence). Third, social dictates: *señoras y señores* (as against *hombres y mujeres*). Probably the order tends to be fossilized whenever two things are frequently juxtaposed.

It becomes accordingly harder to find examples of the sort of thing we want. Certain combinations, nevertheless, seem to exhibit it, with a tendency toward the general principle of more probable or more inclusive (broader) first vs. less probable or less inclusive (narrower) last. The order *sortijas y pendientes* is more usual than *pendientes y sortijas; soldados y marinos, ración de pan y agua* ('bread' is to be expected in practially any ration, but 'water' stands in contrast with all the other things that might combine with bread), *por tierra y por mar* from the standpoint of the landsman, *mesas y sillas, café y crema* (the explicit subordination in *café con crema*, as against *crema con café*, comes to mind), *crema y azúcar, pan y mantequilla*, are more likely than the inverse order. Frequently the second element is what typifies the combination. In *el acero es una mezcla de hierro y carbono* we refer to iron as the main ingredient but carbon as what differentiates ordinary iron or other alloys from steel; carbon is contrastive. Of course, there is a possibility of temporal sequence here, too: "*First* you take your iron, *and then* you add some carbon." But we can imagine a case where the temporal sequence is reversed: suppose that in making a certain kind of leaded glass the lead is first fused and then the sand is added; despite the change in the order of operations, *arena y plomo* would be

[7] I am indebted for this example, and for numerous others, besides criticism of my own inventions, to my colleague, Dr. Laudelino Moreno.

the more likely arrangement; sand is presupposed for glass, and lead is the contrastive marker of a particular variety.[8]

6. Superordinate-subordinate. In *Cuando murió su esposa, él murió* the situational 'when his wife died' covers not only time, but also suggests cause. In *El murió cuando murió su esposa* the temporal clause is now only temporal. In both cases the first element is broad and situational, the second is narrow and specific. In *leyendo aprendemos* one infers learning as an incidental benefit, among other conceivable benefits (such as entertainment) to be had by reading; in *aprendemos leyendo* one infers reading as one of the possible ways of learning, among other possible ways such as writing and listening. In the first, reading is broader, learning narrower; in the second, learning is broader, reading narrower. In the first, one describes *what* (the "point") can be accomplished by *reading* (the "situation"); in the second, one describes *what way* (the point) one can go about the general problem of *learning* (the situation). Note the association of the question-asking *qué* with the point of the utterance. We can frame it in so many words: "*¿Qué se puede hacer leyendo?*" "*Leyendo aprendemos.*" "*De qué manera se aprende?*"—"*Aprendemos leyendo.*"

7. Conclusions. It seems clear that the possibilities of free arrangement outlined here follow essentially the same pattern, which can be diagrammed as follows:

Sentence or phrase
Situation/Point/Resumptive

The situation sums up what is presupposed, overshadowing, non-contrastive, known from or attributed to the context. This potentially includes resumptives, but resumptives are only one of many situational possibilities. The point is the new, contrastive, narrow,

---

[8] This raises the question of "importance." It is often maintained that the important member of a sequence tends to precede, and in a sense this is true; but one also hears that the important member is stressed, and here we see that the stress comes on the second member, not the first. So "importance" in the abstract seems to carry little meaning. One member may be important in that it comes first to mind, while the other is important in that it sets the combinations apart from other combinations.

typifying, unpredicted element, the 'what' of the utterance that focuses it, and is marked by prosodic stress. The resumptive is a verbatim or near-verbatim repetition of something from a preceding utterance, and is de-stressed.

No utterance is complete without a point. Possible complete utterances are then point alone, situation-point, point-resumptive, and situation-point-resumptive. Examples:

1. Point: "*¿Quién vino?*"—"*Juan.*"
2. Situation-point: "*¿Quién vino?*"—"*Si no me equivoco fué Juan*" (or, *Vino Juan*, with the situation a resumptive).
3. Point-resumptive: "*¿Quién vino?*"—"*Juan vino.*"
4. Situation-point-resumptive: "*¿Quién vino*"—"*Si no me equivoco fué Juan quien vino.*"

In more complex sentences, we may find these three divisions of the sentence built up hierarchically. In the example *Cuando murió su esposa él murió* we can analyze the first clause separately and then the sentence as a whole:

First clause:	*Cuando murió*	/ *su esposa*	/ ...
	Situation	/ Point	/ Resumptive

Sentence:	*Cuando murió su esposa*	/ *él*	/ *murió*
	Situation	/ Point	/ Resumptive

Such a hierarchy implies a parallel build-up of stresses, which is exactly what we find: the point of the sentence as a whole has a heavier prosodic stress than the point of the subordinated part.[9]

[9] In order not to complicate matters I have left intonation largely out of account. This much needs to be said, however: that what is usually referred to as "contrastive stress" is rather contrastive intonation. For example, in the following exchange, "*Me pregunto qué habría pasado si mi hermano hubiera heredado esa fortuna*"—"*Su hermano la habría desperdiciado,*" *hermano* will get the usual stress that it gets in the situation but in addition (without necessarily increasing the stress) it may receive a higher pitch, with the implication 'your brother by contrast with the person who actually did inherit'. The loudest stress is still on the point *desperdiciado*, but the pitch of the point may be lower

Discontinuity of the Spanish Conjunctive Pronoun

[*Author's Note*: Three things are perhaps striking about this piece on the "clitic" pronouns. One was the need that I felt to justify the use of "negative evidence," that is, of expressions that native speakers reject when experimentally confronted with them. All such judgments, in the view of the structuralism of the day, were subjective, and hence unreliable. (The same taboo did not permit classroom teachers to dwell on "mistakes.") It took the advent of transformational-generative grammar a decade later to open the floodgates to such "starred forms"—and to create new problems of excessive use.[1]

The second is the foretaste here of something that has recently occupied the attention of investigators such as John Haiman and Talmy Givón: the universal likelihood that, other things being equal, connectedness will signify connectedness and separation, separation. Thus *John came and Mary came,* with a verb separating *John* and *Mary,* is apt to suggest that they came separately, but *John and Mary came* that they came together. *Lo estoy haciendo* "suggests something that might be interrupted and then resumed, while *Estoy haciéndolo* suggests something done in a single session."

The third is the possibility of having a constituent that functions in more than one way at a time—a syntactic blend. *Lo quiero ver* can be 'lo quiero' without ceasing to be 'verlo'.]

---

than the highest pitch of the situation. Investigators have sometimes confused high pitch with loud stress. The two are more often than not combined in the same syllable, but need not be.

[1] See my "Judgments of grammaticality," *Lingua* 21 (1968) 34-40.

1. It is a commonplace that the Spanish conjunctive pronoun has more than one possible position with respect to a series of interdependent verbs.[2] Constructions of the type *Lo quiero ver* ~ *Quiero verlo, Lo estoy viendo* ~ *Estoy viéndolo, Lo vamos a tratar de hacer* ~ *Vamos a tratarlo de hacer* ~ *Vamos a tratar de hacerlo* are of everyday occurrence; they have been counted and to some extent classified by Keniston.[3] Detailed as Keniston's list is, however, it leaves some important questions unanswered:

(1) Discontinuous constituents of the type *Lo (quiero) ver*, which we shall designate as D, are far less common than continuous constituents of the type *(Quiero) verlo*, which we shall designate as C. Shall we infer that D is used in the same situations as C but less frequently, or that D is used in fewer situations than C, or both?

(2) If D is used in fewer situations than C, what are those situations?

(3) Keniston supplies[4] a partial answer to (2) in the statement 'with verbs other than auxiliary verbs followed by a complementary infinitive... the pronoun regularly follows the infinitive' (no exceptions are listed). But what is an auxiliary verb in Spanish? If it develops that the very flexibility of the pronoun is the only test, or the chief test, of the classification 'auxiliary', then a statement of this sort is circular. Spanish has no such neat formal test of auxiliaries as the use of an infinitive without *to* in English *(He made me come* vs. *He forced me to come, Come see us* vs. *Come to see us*, and the like); all complementary infinitives are the same.

(4) All examples of D in modern Spanish offered by the grammars show the pronoun before the verb (that is, in graphic terms, to the left of the verb—here called DL). Is a position after the verb (to the right of it—here called DR) also possible? And if so, when?

[2] This article was originally published in *Language* 25 (1949) 253-60, reprinted with permission.

[3] Hayward Keniston, Spanish syntax list; New York, 1937.

[4] Spanish Syntax List §10.73 and §10.75.

(5) Can there be discontinuity between two pronouns that are objects of the same verb? For example, can *Quiero dárselo* become *Le quiero darlo*?

(6) Keniston mentions 'the degree to which the combination of verb and dependent infinitive is felt to be a unit'[5] as determining D and C. Are there other differences in meaning?

2. Slightly over a thousand examples were studied, gathered[6] from fifteen Spanish and Spanish American sources dated between 1867 and 1946. The types of writing examined include novel, essay, history, short story, and magazine articles.

The citations of this compilation comprise a body of affirmative data, useful in applying J. S. Mill's 'method of agreement'. To answer some of the questions set forth above, however, the 'method of difference' is required. In order to test (2), for example, we require not only examples which the Spaniard uses, but examples which he rejects. To this end, a number of doubtful constructions were invented and submitted to several native speakers of Spanish. A similar procedure was used to ascertain meanings: minimally different constructions (differing only by C and D) were submitted for comment.

A few casual sources reinforced the data, especially in the matter of DR.

3. Since the study was not aimed at discovering frequencies, what it contributes to Keniston's findings is only incidental. In general, Keniston's figures are confirmed. The following observations may be more or less significant:

(1) DR appeared, with a frequency of only 1. This may have been eliminated from the Keniston list as insignificant, or it may not have appeared. As a structural phenomenon, however, it is important.

---

[5] Spanish Syntax List §10.61 and §10.72

[6] Thanks are due to Professor R. M. Duncan and to his class in Spanish syntax at the University of Southern California in the summer of 1946, for collecting the material; to my Spanish-speaking colleagues for patiently answering many questions; and especially to Mrs. Betty Haeber Maynor for collating the material.

(2) Keniston's observation[7] about the progressive tenses, namely, that two pronouns show DL more readily than one, is confirmed for infinitives. Two pronouns show DL three times as often as one pronoun alone. This suggests in some cases a prosodic reason for DL.

(3) A third of the examples (23) of *haber de* show DL.

(4) There are wide divergences in individual preference for C or D. In Baroja's Zalacaín el Aventurero, a third of the examples have D (37 out of 110; 16 of the 37 show *ir a*). In Benito Lynch's Los Caranchos de la Florida, C and D are almost evenly divided (and four-fifths of the examples with D show *ir a*). Many other sources yield almost no examples of D.

4. Since the great majority of immediate constituents are continuous, it requires a special justification to class two discontinuous elements as a constituent. The type *Lo quiero* is exceedingly common, and suggests the division *Lo quiero/ver* rather than *Lo . . . ver/quiero*. In addition, as we shall see, native speakers report a hint of the meaning of *Lo quiero* in *Lo quiero ver*. The existence of an extensive series of transitive verbs without objects, however, would not be congruent with the fact that elsewhere *ver* and its related verbs regularly take objects. More cogently, the common-sense report of all speakers of Spanish, that *Lo quiero ver* and *Quiero verlo* are substantially equivalent, is evidence that in *Lo quiero ver* we are really dealing with a discontinuous constituent.

5. Since D occurs with the infinitive and the present participle when combined with other verbs, each species of such combination must be examined separately. The potential constructions with the infinitive are: the infinitive with its object pronoun(s) as the object of a verb §5.1; the infinitive with its object pronoun(s) as the complement of a verb but separated from it by a preposition or by *que* or *no* or by the definite article §5.2; the infinitive with its object pronoun(s) as the subject of a verb §5.3; split objects, i.e. one going with one verb and the other with another—this being possible in any of the three preceding environments (§5.4). As there is no such flexibility with the

---

[7] Spanish Syntax List §10.65.

present participle, we need only consider the types of verb with which the participle is combined (§7).

5.1 As the pronoun shows DL with apparently unlimited freedom when it is the object of an infinitive that is itself the object of another verb, the question arises whether there are, in fact, any such 'non-auxiliary' verbs as Keniston assumes with which DL does not occur. Our compilation confirms the fact that the verbs which Keniston lists as auxiliaries are the ones where DL most commonly occurs. But as his list of non-auxiliaries is short, none of the verbs included in it happens to occur among our examples with DL. It would be a pretty safe guess, however, that *creer* would fall among his non-auxiliaries, and we have: *En ocasiones la creía ver al borde de la locura*[8] and *En las palabras de su madre creyó ver—y lo creyó ver por primera vez en su vida—un odio.*[9] But as this is conjectural, we took the list of non-auxiliaries, invented the following examples, and submitted them to several native speakers: *Lo decidió abandonar, Lo deseo explicar, Lo intentó conseguir, Lo logró comprar, Lo necesito explicar, Lo parece creer, Lo pienso pedir, Lo pretendo ofrecer, Lo procuraré hacer, Lo temo saber*. All were accepted by at least one speaker, and most by more than one.

Six speakers of diverse origins rejected *Lo dijo saber*, and only one of six accepted *Lo celebro hallar*. The criterion seems to be not auxiliariness but meaning, with two factors making the DL acceptable: (1) the governing verb does not regularly, or does not in the given sense or given context, take an object of its own in such a way that the hearer might be confused (thus *decidir* probably takes an infinitive as its object much more often than a noun or pronoun, so that the speaker's intention in *Lo decidió abandonar* would manifestly be *abandonar*, not *lo*, as object of *decidió*); (2) it makes little difference to the general sense whether the infinitive or the pronoun be taken as the object of the governing verb (thus the general meaning of the accepted *Lo siento decir* is not in the least interfered with by the suggestion of *Lo siento*). On the other hand *Lo dijo saber* is too suggestive of *Lo dijo*, since *decir* takes pronouns as its complements far oftener than infinitives,

[8] Antonio Heras, Vorágine sin fondo 103 (Madrid, 1936).
[9] Ibid. 26.

and the meaning of *Lo dijo* interferes with that of *Dijo saberlo*. Similarly with the rejected *Las determiné ver* as opposed to the accepted *Determiné verlas*.

We may conclude that per se the CONSTRUCTION with infinitive object admits of DL, whether or not the governing verb is an auxiliary. As this removes one of the props from under the whole auxiliary class, it raises a serious doubt whether there is such a thing as an auxiliary class where infinitives are concerned. (Individual verbs might be established as auxiliary to infinitives in certain dialects where they entirely supplant non-auxiliary forms; this would be true of *ir a* where it replaces the future tense.)

Our data offer no evidence that when both of two pronouns are objects of the infinitive, one may precede while the other follows. The sentence *No le puedo prestarlo ahora*, reported to us as used by a Panamanian speaker, was condemned by other native speakers.

Our data were also not sufficient to enable us to draw any conclusions about DL with more than one verb. Structurally there is no antipathy to attaching the pronoun to any preceding infinitive or present participle: *Tenía hecha intención de irla a oír a la parroquia,*[10] *Está tratándolo de hacer*, and the like are acceptable though infrequent. Meaning again, however, sets up a barrier. Thus the same speaker who accepted *Lo puede ir a hacer, Lo debe ir a ver, Lo solía ir a ver, Lo espero seguir haciendo*, and *Espero seguirlo haciendo*, rejected *Lo quiero comenzar a hacer*. We note again the relatively greater frequency of *querer* with pronoun objects, with the result that *Lo quiero* suggests an extraneous meaning.

5.2 Besides other verbs, elements standing before infinitives include prepositions, *que, el*, and *no*.

DL with the prepositions *a* and *de* is practically as free as when there is no intervening element. The compilation shows examples of DL with *ir a, volver a, acertar a, llegar a, tornar a, venir a, haber de*, and *acabar de*. In addition, the following have been judged as correct by native speakers: *Lo viene a ver, Lo entraron a comprar, Lo llegaron a*

---

[10] Gustavo Adolfo Bécquer, Legends, tales, and poems 107 (New York, 1907).

pensar, Lo trato de explicar, Trátelo usted de hacer, Lo debe tratar de hacer, Debe tratarlo de hacer, Lo acerté a ver, and *Lo cesó de creer.* Two pronouns appear to admit DL more readily than one: *Nadie se lo acertaba a explicar.*[11]

DL is blocked, however, when the governing verb and its preposition do not form part of a stereotype. Thus *Lo habla de hacer* is rejected. (Again we note an incongruous meaning in *Lo habla.*)

We have no written evidence of DL with prepositions other than *a* and *de.* The native speakers whom we have consulted judge as incorrect the following: *Lo acabó por hacer, Lo entraron para comprar,* and *Lo insiste en hacer. Acabar por* is certainly a stereotype, but DL results in extraneous meanings for both *acabó* and *por hacer.* We have found ready oral acceptance, however, for *Lo piensa en hacer,* in which *Lo piensa* is congruent, and somewhat grudging acceptance for *Lo tardaron en hacer.*

Two stereotypes are involved in *que* plus infinitive: *tener que* and *haber que.* There is abundant evidence for DL with *tener que* but none for DL with *haber que.* Our informants rejected *Lo hay que hacer* unconditionally. But while *Lo siento tener que decir* is judged as correct, and testifies to the readiness of DL with *tener que,* it is probably wrong to regard *Tengo que hacerlo* and *Lo tengo que hacer* as alternating constructions, in view of the semantic difference between *Tengo que escribir muchas cartas* and *Tengo muchas cartas que escribir* (exactly parallel to the difference between *I have to write many letters* and *I have many letters to write*).

We have no indication, oral or written, that DL may occur with *el* or *no.* While sentences of the type *Prefiero no hacerlo ahora* are common, *Lo prefiero no hacer ahora* is rejected.

Other conceivable intervening elements, as in *Me es capaz de matar,* also have proved to be impossible so far as tested.

5.3. DL seems to be impossible, or nearly so, when the infinitive is the grammatical subject of the preceding verb. There is no written evidence for it, and speakers reject *No lo cabe hacer, Lo urge decir, Se lo quiere saber* (for *Se quiere saberlo*) and *Se lo debe creer* (for *Se debe creerlo*),

---

[11] Ibid. 131.

along with analogous constructions involving neutral impersonal verbs such as *Se lo trato de hacer* (for *Se trata de hacerlo*) and *Se lo llegó a creer* (for *Se llegó a creerlo*). DR is also found repugnant: *Debe creérselo* (for *Se debe creerlo*) and *Puede creérselo* (for *Se puede creerlo*). Three speakers, however, two Mexicans and one Spaniard, accepted as possible the combination *Lo precisa decir*, and two others, Argentinians, would not entirely reject *Lo conviene explicar* (for *Conviene explicarlo*). Lacking spontaneous inventions by native speakers, however, we must class such forms as doubtful.

5.4. When one pronoun is the object of the infinitive and the other is the object of the governing verb, each pronoun normally goes with its own verb: *Tomó el papel y se puso a leerlo;*[12] *¿Cómo se puede verla?*.[13] DL of the pronoun belonging to the infinitive readily occurs under certain conditions, however: *¿Cuándo se la quiere suponer existente?;*[14] *Se le podía oír aun estando muy lejos de la iglesia;*[15] *Ya ves que me la has hecho olvidar.*[16]

With the more common verbs of suasion and perception the language has retained a large part of its former fluidity. *Me los hizo llamar* was accepted as equivalent to both the split objects (with DL of the second) *Me hizo llamarlos* and the coupled objects *Hizo llamármelos* (~ *Hizo que me los llamasen*). *Me los mandó comprar* alternates with *Me mandó comprarlo* and *Mandó comprármelo. Se los oí cantar* alternates with *Le oí cantarlos* and *Oí cantárselos* (~ *Oí que se los cantaron a él*). The greater ambiguity of *Se lo mandó dar* for *Le mandó darlo* seems to be what caused two speakers to reject it, though a third admitted it as a bare possibility.

In constructions of the type *Se le podía oír*, however, where *poder* (and possibly some other verbs such as *deber* and *necesitar*, admitting of a grammatical subject, whether infinitive or ordinary noun) combines with an infinitive which may take either the accusative or

[12] Pío Baroja, Zalacaín el aventurero 169 (Madrid, 1920).
[13] Ibid. 155.
[14] Alfonso Toro, Compendio de historia de México 185 (México, D.F., 1933).
[15] Jorge Isaacs, María 154 (Buenos Aires, 1943).
[16] Ciro Alegría, La serpiente de oro 122 (Santiago de Chile, 1936).

the dative of the person (*oír, ver, enseñar*, and the like), it is impossible to tell whether we are dealing with split or with coupled objects, for two constructions have converged. These are (1) *Se podía oírlo* 'hearing him possibilized itself' = 'hearing him was possible' = 'it was possible for me to hear him', where the accusative is the person, and (2) *Podía oírsele (cantar)* '(singing) could hear itself with-respect-to-him' = '(singing) could be heard with-respect-to-him' = 'he could be heard (singing)'. Now since any finite verb in Spanish is complete without an expressed subject, the parenthesized *cantar* can be omitted, giving 'he could be heard (doing whatever he was doing)', with an implied subject. The two are virtually identical in meaning, for it makes no difference whether we think of hearing the person or hearing the noise that he is making. (There probobly is not a third construction involved, *Se podía oírle cantar*, since *cantar* here would be the OBJECT of *oír*, and while as subject it could be omitted and still be implied, as object it probably could not). It might seem that the two constructions would not necessarily merge owing to the fact that one uses *le* and the other *lo*, and a *Se lo podía oír* would be unambiguous. But here a peculiar thing occurs: even for the loísta, a *lo* in the continuous construction may become *le* in DL position next to *se*. One cultured loísta rejected *¿Se lo puede tratar como a un cualquiera?* in favor of *se le*, despite the fact that the sentence is equivalent to *¿Se puede tratarlo como a un cualquiera?*—and *tratar*, unlike *oír* and its related verbs, does not offer the dative-accusative complication.

Split objects with verbs other than those of suasion and perception appear to admit of DL if the meaning is clear. Thus in *Me lo propuse comprar* the idea of 'propose it (the plan) to myself' is not inimical to the full meaning 'buy it', and is accordingly acceptable. Keniston'a example *Déxamelo abrazar*[17] would be considered correct in contemporary Spanish because the idea of 'leave him to me (since I want him)' is not inimical to the idea of 'to embrace him.' This sort of compatibility leads to blends, such as *Déjamela ponerla aquí*, reported to us as used by an undertaker in reference to the body of a woman, combining *Déjame ponerla* and *Déjamela para ponerla*.

[17] Syntax of Castilian Prose: The Sixteenth Century §10.761 (Chicago, 1937).

DL with a preposition seems to be uniformly avoided with split objects because of resulting ambiguity. Thus *Me lo voy a comprar* is accepted as equivalent to *Voy a comprármelo* but not as equivalent to *Me voy a comprarlo*. Likewise rejected were the split-object equivalents of *Me lo persuadieron a comprar, Me lo obligaron a creer, Me lo niego a comprar, Me lo decidí a comprar,* and *Me los obligó a llamar*. *Me* and *a* were chosen because under other conditions they lend themselves more readily to DL than *se* and other prepositions.

We have already seen in §5.3 that DL does not occur with split objects when the infinitive is a subject.

6. The example of DR that occurred in our compilation is *Empezó a encontrársele algunas veces en compañía de Manolo Peñalosa,*[18] which is unanalyzable except as an alternant of *Se empezó a encontrarle*. From other sources we have *Dijérase que sólo la corteza de aquel hombre era tosca y fea; que tan pronto como empezaba a penetrarse dentro de él aparecían sus perfecciones*[19] (~ *Se empezaba a penetrar*); *Verdad es que por terreno tan resbaladizo puede caerse con facilidad en el desvarío de la lingüística funambulesca*[20] (~ *Se puede caer*); *Si usted cree que hay facilidades para que la Universidad me proporcione estudios y una beca con la cual pueda vivirse honestamente, le suplico no deje de contestarme*[21] (~ *Se pueda vivir*); *Cuando surja otro muchacho como él . . . , debe salvársele antes de que sea demasiado tarde*[22] (~ *Se debe salvarle*); *César . . . abandonó . . . las grandes tragedias del teatro romántico, por las frivolidades del circo. Y solía vérsele, los días festivos por la tarde, ocupar una silla de pista*[23] (~ *Se solía verle*); *También conocí sus penas, aunque a simple vista pudiera creérseles felices*[24] (~ *Se pudiera creerles felices*).

---

[18] Antonio Heras, op.cit. 166.

[19] Pedro A. de Alarcón, El sombrero de tres picos 18 (New York, 1907).

[20] T.Navarro Tomás, Fonología española 113 (Syracuse, 1946).

[21] Personal letter from a Mexican, 1947.

[22] Hoy, 25 Oct. 1947, p. 6 (México, D.F.).

[23] Antonio Heras, El laberinto de los espejos 121 (Madrid, 1928).

[24] Augusto D'Halmar, in Algunos cuentos chilenos 48 (ed. Armando Donoso; Buenos Aires, 1943).

For as much as these examples can determine, we note (1) that only the pronoun *se* is involved, and (2) that DR occurs when the construction is strongly reminiscent of some other construction, i.e. there is a kind of contamination. *Vivirse* is so frequent that *pueda vivirse* has its way made smooth; the same is true with *caerse* and *puede caerse. Se le encuentra* is so frequent that *encontrársele* does not sound strange even when the *se* pertains to another verb. Observe also the similarity of some of the examples quoted with the following one in which there is continuity, not DR, since the main verb has a grammatical subject other than the infinitive: *Tal vez por esto ha podido reprochársele a Latorre que en su cualidad objetiva esencial reside el defecto de sus mejores cuentos.*[25]

7. Our compilation did not include the progressive tenses, but we offer the following on the basis of tests with native speakers.

In general the verbs that admit of DL with the progressive tenses are those nonce auxiliaries which have indesinent (durative) meanings that may be interpreted as continuous motion in one direction, in addition to continuing state such as *estar* and *quedar*. *Seguir, continuar, andar, venir, ir, pasar,* and *quedarse* were approved in the following phrases: *Lo sigue (viene, continúa, anda) diciendo; Se me quedó mirando* and *Se qiuedó mirándome; Lo anduvo (pasó, vino, fué) llamando.* The potentially desinent (point-action) and potentially transitive verbs were rejected, however: *Lo entró (salió, apareció) llamando, Se lo fué llamando, Lo prosiguió estudiando, Lo bajó (subió) llamando.*

More than with the infinitive, however, there is a question with many of these whether the DL form really is a more-or-less mechanical alternant of the continuous form; for the divergences of meaning are wider. Native speakers report the following. *Lo fué llamando* suggests repeated action, while *Fué llamándolo* suggests a single act; the same is true of *vino* in place of *fué. Lo pasó mirando* suggests concentrated effort, while *Pasó mirándolo* refers to a casual momentary act. *Lo estoy haciendo* suggests something that might be interrupted and then resumed, while *Estoy haciéndolo* suggests something done in a single session. While these reports differ somewhat, they have in common the fact that

[25] Armando Donoso, op. cit. 13.

discontinuity in syntax implies potential discontinuity in action as well.

8. Statements in handbooks and grammars give us to understand that pronouns admit of discontinuous constructions with dependent infinitives and present participles, but do not clearly recognize the limits of this discontinuity. We find the following.

(1) Pronouns belonging to infinitives that are themselves the direct objects of other verbs may show DL if no ambiguity is created; but if there are two pronouns belonging with the same infinitive, either both show DL or neither does.

(2) DL occurs under the same conditions as (1) if there is an intervening *a* or *de* (or possibly *en* in a few limited combinations), but not when there are other prepositions intervening, or any other elements than another dependent verb.

(3) DL occurs with *tener que*, but with a difference in meaning.

(4) No clear evidence favors DL with a subject infinitive.

(5) DL occurs with split object involving the common verbs of suasion and perception even when some ambiguity may result, and with other verbs when no ambiguity results, but does not occur with a preposition.

(6) DR is possible with *se* when there are split objects in a context that suggests some other common construction, i.e. in the presence of contamination.

(7) DL may occur in progressive tenses when the auxiliary is one of continuing state or uniform motion.

(8) Slight differences in meaning are found between DL and a continuous construction (*Lo quiero hacer* suggests *lo quiero* along with *hacerlo*), and these differences become more marked in the progressive tenses. Occasional marked differences occur with the infinitive, as in *Lo vamos a hacer* and the potentially hortatory *Vamos a hacerlo.*

Part V

Modality

Indicative and Subjunctive—

One Subjunctive or Two?

[*Author's Note*: Modality is grammatically encoded in Spanish in the contrast between indicative and subjunctive, which gives pride of place to the first article in this section.

Each of the two modes comprises a set of systematically distinct verb forms. Accordingly it makes sense to look for separate meanings to match the separate forms. But should we expect all subjunctives to mean one thing and all indicatives another, or does each mode subsume a collection of meanings? The most casual look confirms that if the subjunctive has various meanings, they must at least be related—as common sense suggests they should be, else why express them with the same form? The challenge—if you believe that the most economical semantic description is the one with the fewest entities—is to find a single underlying meaning.

That is the burden of the first article in this section.[1] It responds to a contrary argument by Anthony Lozano (1972) that the meaning of the subjunctive has to be subdivided in order to be properly analyzed.

The position I take is summarized in Bolinger (1968, 28-29): "both the Romance languages and English make a distinction on the one hand between presentments, representations to the mind, mental pictures—however one wants to characterize them, whether intense or dim, dreamlike or real—and, on the other hand, the volitional involvement of the participant, which in turn can have to do with a willingness or unwillingness to accept, or with a desire to influence." Without realizing it I had tapped a stream that was about to become

[1] Lightly edited for this edition, chiefly to eliminate an erroneous use of the term *performative*.

a flood when linguists discovered the philosopher J. L. Austin's *How to do things with words* (Oxford, 1962) and began talking about performatives and illocutionary forces, the stuff that is about the message rather than in it (in *He's a liar I tell you!* the *I tell you* has both an assertive and an iterative force applied to the message *He's a liar*). What I hit upon was the fact that English relies on the same principle that determines the choice of mode in Spanish, but does so in the context of syntactically "exposing" the message. We can say any of the following:

> I was in Madrid and all the bells were ringing. (fact? dream?)
> I dreamed (knew, felt, saw, could tell, sensed, it was clear that) I was in Madrid . . .
> I was in Madrid, I dreamed (knew, felt, etc.), and . . .

The message *I was in Madrid* is fronted—or, to put it the other way around, the main verb *I dreamed* is postposed, adverbialized—and the possibility of doing this practically guarantees that the verb in the exposed message will be indicative in Spanish, no matter what the order of the words: *Soñé que estaba en Madrid.* I pick the verb *to dream* because it shows that "fact," however tempting, is irrelevant; what counts is the transmission of a message about the world, either "out there" or in imagination. The opposite case is the impossible **I was in Madrid, I regretted (doubted, denied, saw to it that)* (OK *I regretted to say,* but that is another story), and its impossibility—in spite of the perfectly normal *I regretted that I was in Madrid*—is the clue to the fact that *regret* does not have as its main function that of presenting a picture to the mind, but of conveying involvement. *Regret,* as our piecemeal grammar rules tell us, "takes the subjunctive." The beauty of the illocutionary test is that it corrals just about all the verbs that take noun-clause *that* complements. And this consistency is the strongest indication that indicative and subjunctive do have each its proper coherent and cohesive meaning.

Readers who wish to follow this debate to its conclusion may consult Lozano (1975) and Bolinger (1976). I have not included the latter here because of the large number of cross references and because the first article is a clear enough statement of the principle that there is only one subjunctive.

The second piece in this section antedates the first one (I was still talking about "fact"), but also anticipates it: I was aware of *temer* as a special case involving a 'suponer' alongside an adverbial 'con temor'. Both this piece and the third one (*CLM* is *College Language Manual,* the working title of what became the MLA's textbook *Modern Spanish*) give an idea of the encroachment of the indicative on what is supposed to be subjunctive territory. The last piece on the subjunctive again sustains the thesis that if there is a difference in form there must be a difference in function. Prof. Emilio Lorenzo (p.c. May 1972) independently came to the same conclusion: the past subjunctives *-ra* and *-se* do not mean the same.

References

Bolinger, Dwight. 1968. Postposed main phrases: An English rule for the Romance subjunctive. *Canadian Journal of Linguistics* 14.3-30.
———. 1976. Again—One or two subjunctives? *Hispania* 59.41-49.
Lozano, Anthony. 1972. Subjunctives, transformations and features in Spanish. *Hispania* 55.76-90.
———. 1975. In defense of two subjunctives. *Hispania* 58.277-83.]

* * *

IN COMMON WITH other Romance tongues, Spanish has a formal contrast in its verb system between two modes, indicative and subjunctive.[2] Though the forms vary, they are in such a tight paradigmatic relationship to each other that there can be no question of the internal unity of either mode: *tenga* is the same, in this respect, as *alce,* and *salí* the same as *tuve.* Given a clear-cut formal opposition, one expects to find—and traditional grammar thought it had found—a clear-cut semantic opposition as well. The indicative was the mode of reality, of reporting; the subjunctive was the mode of the inner light, of such things as desiring and approving or rejecting.

[2] Originally published in *Hispania* 57 (1974), 462-471.

Against the traditional view of one subjunctive, Anthony Lozano[3] has advanced the theory that there are two, distinguished by the features [+optative] and [±dubitative]. Traditional grammar was guilty of "overemphasis on surface structures" and "little regard to deep structures" in its failure to perceive the essential difference between them.

In what follows I shall try to show that splitting the subjunctive is not only unnecessary but harmful in that it destroys intuitive insights that were obvious to native speakers and teachers alike, however badly they may have stated them. I hold that there are neither syntactic nor semantic justifications for a separation and that the supposed reasons for it are an artifact of the style of analysis.

A number of ways can be found to put the notion of two subjunctives to an empirical test. One is with zeugma, the figure of speech that results when two things each connected to a third, but in different senses, are conjoined. We may say *Before breakfast I wash my face and hands* because washing the face and washing the hands are essentially the same kind of operation. We do not normally say **After breakfast I brush my teeth and hair* because brushing teeth and brushing hair are fundamentally different. (The *Heritage* example of zeugma is *She left in high spirits and a Cadillac.*) If there are two features as distinct as Lozano would have them appear, then conjoining them with a single subjunctive should produce a zeugma. As the following examples show, nothing of the sort happens:

> Es posible, tal vez necesario, pero sin embargo deplorable, que él sea nuestro representante.[4]
>
> Es curioso pero innecesario que él piense así.

(Compare the zeugma on the English side when two verbs are conjoined, one of which would take indicative and the other subjunctive, and the lack of zeugma when both would take indicative:

---

[3] "Subjunctives, transformations and features in Spanish," *Hispania* 55 (1972), 76-90.

[4] For judging the examples, thanks go herewith to David Nasjleti, Alberto and Guadalupe Castilla, Ninfa Flores, and Herlinda Cancino. They are not responsible for any possible misinterpretation on my part.

It is evident that they have his permission + It is not desirable that
they have his permission ≠ *It is evident but not desirable that they have his permission.
It is evident that they have his permission + It is not generally understood that they have his permission = It is evident but not generally understood that they have his permission.)[5]

In the first of the Spanish examples above I have given a [+dubitative] *es posible,* a [+ optative] *es necesario,* and for good measure the emotional *es deplorable* (just in case anyone might care to claim that there is a [+emotive] separate from [+optative]). It makes no difference; a single subjunctive handles all three. By Lozano's analysis the *sea* would have to be marked BOTH [+optative] and [±dubitative].

Traditional grammar would not deny that there are features of willing and doubting in these sentences; but it would attach them to the governing expressions. There is nothing odd about saying that *es posible* is [+dubitative] and *es necesario* is [+optative]. But Lozano goes a step further and lodges these features in the subjunctive itself. This has the effect, in a sentence like *Es posible que lo sea,* of giving the feature [+dubitative] twice, once for *es posible* and again for *sea. Es posible* does not of itself bring the dubitative meaning to the sentence; instead, or in addition, it selects that meaning from one of the two general meanings of the subjunctive. For traditional grammar, the meaning of the subjunctive is not ambiguous in this way as regards the two features, but vague; it is more abstract and embraces both of them.

It also, I would claim, embraces more. One can find instances of governing expressions that are not characterized semantically as either [+optative] or [±dubitative] and yet require the subjunctive:

Es interesante que usted haya dicho eso.

---

[5] On the Spanish side the zeugma would be even more obvious because two different forms of the subordinate verb would be required: **Es evidente pero no es de desear que tienen/tengan su permiso.*

Es típicamente profesorial que D. Andrés se haya olvidado de sus gafas.
Es inútil que ellos hayan ensayado tal cosa.
No tiene ninguna importancia que ellos hayan hablado mal de mí.
Es desdeñable que hayan hablado mal de mí.

To judge something to be interesting, contemptible, useless, or typically professorial is not to doubt it or to will it. But it IS to take an attitudinal stance toward it.

The concept of abstractness for the subjunctive, with resulting vagueness, also implies that there will be instances where we cannot (except arbitrarily) decide between [+optative] and [±dubitative]. A good many governing expressions can be taken either way:

Ni pensar que él lo haga.
Es inconcebible que él lo haga.
No admito que ésa sea su opinión.

There is the same vagueness as in English sentences like *It's out of the question that he should have it*: they may refer to disbelief or to negative willing. The adjective *inconcebible* literally refers to doubt, but by stretching doubt to incredulity that such an idea could even be suggested, one can express will. In the first of the above sentences we can extend contextually the notion of willing or of doubting:

Ni pensar que él lo haga; no lo vamos a permitir.
Ni pensar que él lo haga; las condiciones no lo permiten.

Or, contextually, one of the possibilities may be canceled. Since willing looks to the future, a past reference may eliminate it.[6] *No acepto que usted lo haga* is optative; *No acepto que usted lo haya hecho* is dubitative, at least in the sense that the speaker is rejecting the idea. Of course, it is also optative, and here we can see the difficulty of trying to separate the two domains. The speaker not only does not affirm the idea intellectually; he is UNWILLING to affirm it. To say that something is

[6] It does not eliminate optativeness in general, only that part of it that inclines to the imperative. *I approve his having been arrested* refers to the past and is still optative.

incredible is to say that you regard it as false but also to say that you are DISPOSED to regard it that way. *Creer* is (normally) the intellectual [±dubitative], *aceptar* is the attitudinal [±dubitative]. This will be important in the discussion of negation.

Such a broad area of overlap can hardly signify anything but that the distinction between the two features within the subjunctive is an artificial one, with performance variables intervening to pinpoint this or that meaning in a particular context.

This covers, in part, the semantic arguments. But Lozano relies more heavily on syntactic ones. "The crucial contrast between [+optative] and [±dubitative] involves negation" (p. 77). When a *no* precedes a governing expression of the [+optative] class, the requirement of subjunctive is not affected: *Me mandó que viniera* and *No me mandó que viniera* must both have subjunctive. But when it precedes [±dubitative] there is a choice: *No dudo que lo hagas (haces); No creo que lo hagas (haces).*

It is at this point that the style of analysis creates the problem which in turn imposes the solution that Lozano adopts. In a classical transformational-generative framework the trigger- ing effect of a morpheme such as *no* is seen as a power in its own right. In reality, no such importance attaches to it. Everything depends on how *no* affects the meaning.

At this point we must appeal to a type of analysis that is essential to understanding the modes in Romance: the theory of illocutionary forces which holds that underlying every utterance there is a declaration that indicates the type to which the utterance belongs: *John ate the beans* is equivalent to *I declare John ate the beans; Did John eat the beans?* is equivalent to *I ask did John eat the beans?; Eat the beans* is equivalent to *I order you to eat the beans.* Sometimes the illocutionary verb is explicitly given: we may actually say *I declare, I ask,* or *I order.* More often it is not verbally explicit, though there is always an intonation: the terminal fall in a declarative sentence is illocutionary in the broad sense.

From illocutionary theory comes strong support for the traditional notion of the indicative as the "mode of reporting." It explains what otherwise would appear as an odd coincidence: that sentences beginning with expressions such as *I report, I declare, I say, I affirm,* etc.

have the same mode as sentences with no subordinating expression at all:

Juan *está* enfermo.
Declaro que Juan *está* enfermo.

If adding an explicit illocutionary verb makes no real difference (since there is always one anyway in deep structure[7]), then it is to be expected that the same mode will be used in both. Where traditional grammar failed was in taking the indicative for granted and in neglecting to wonder why it is that virtually all subjunctives but only some indicatives occur in subordinate clauses. What is needed is to recognize that Spanish has formalized these illocutions: the indicative mode makes it explicit whether an utterance is intended to convey "intelligence." Grammatically superordinate verbs such as *digo, declaro, pienso, creo, sé, veo,* etc. add information on how we acquired the intelligence (*esta mañana yo leí que*...), what vehicle we are using for its expression (*le escribí que*...), what universe of reality it exists in (*anoche yo soñé que*...), what part of our own storage it comes from (*me imagino que*..., *predigo que*...), and other similar ideas; but the underlying meaning of "intelligence" remains the same, embodied in the indicative mode.

With illocutions in our arsenal we can now take on the problem of negation, and the first question is whether the facts are correct. Are dubitative expressions AS A CLASS free to take either indicative or subjunctive when negated? This appears to be Lozano's claim,[8] but it

---

[7] Or remote structure or whatever is the term quoted on today's market.

[8] But whether it actually is I cannot say for certain. At one point (p. 77) he states that "the feature [±dubitative] may or may not obligate subjunctives if the matrix verb in the main clause is preceded by the preverb *no*." This can be taken to mean that ANY expression containing the feature has a free choice, or that SOME expressions always have it and others do not, or that some REQUIRE subjunctive while others have a choice or REQUIRE indicative. Later, in setting out the transformations (p. 85), he says that in the formulas "*creer* represents *parecer*; *dudar* represents *negar*." This sounds as if only four verbs were being covered by what we have been led to expect would be a transformation affecting the dubitative feature as a whole. I assume that these are instances

cannot be substantiated. If "dubitative" means anything it must apply to the following, where there is no choice; only the subjunctive is normal:[9]

No es inconcebible que él lo haya (*ha) hecho.
No desconfío de que llegue (*llega) a tiempo.[10]
No es imposible que sea (*es) así.

Negating *dudar* and *negar* makes the indicative acceptable; negating at least some other verbs of the dubitative class has no such effect. It is simply a fact of the idiom structure of Spanish (one which a complete dictionary would have to record) that *no dudar* may be given the meaning 'afirmar.' There is no universal effect of negation, only a local one. Anticipating a point that will be made later concerning word order in English, we can see that *doubt* and *deny* occupy a special place among dubitative expressions in English, too, where negating them is concerned:

They are well known to you, I don't doubt.
The church has been a factor, it is not to be denied (I don't deny).
*The church has been a factor, I don't question.
*The church has been a factor, it is not inconceivable (unimaginable).
*The church has been a factor, I don't dispute.

If there is no automatic triggering effect of negation, what effect does it have? The answer lies in the semantic spectrum of particular words, and in the intent of the speaker. The sentence *Sabía que él era mi amigo* conveys an intelligence: the fact is part of a stock of information. The negative *No sabía (ignoraba) que era mi amigo* does the same except to say that information is not part of the stock. In neither case is it colored with an attitude. *Saber* is difficult to construe in any

---

of careless wording. Since he has elected to give us an entire class of dubitative expressions, he must intend his treatment to cover the class.

[9] Except for people for whom the subjunctive is recessive anyway.

[10] The affirmative example, *Desconfío de que llegue a tiempo,* is from the Moliner dictionary.

other way.[11] *Creer* is less restricted. It has the two possibilities, affirmative and negative, with the indicative, to convey an intelligence. In addition, especially when negated, it may express the RECEPTIVITY of the subject toward the intelligence. This is merely to say that it is within the competence of the speaker to use *creer* as a partial synonym of *ser posible* and *no creer* as a partial synonym of *no aceptar*. The intention of the speaker is paramount, though given the commonest meanings of words we can usually predict which way he will turn. Our prediction here is that affirmative *creer* will govern indicative; but that is by no means certain:

> Creo, señor Gordon, que la prensa de su país no esté informada correctamente respecto al Dr. Fidel Castro.
>
> ¡Qué padres! Le digo a usted, señor, que porque no he conocido otros creo que sean mis padres.[12]

As for *no creer,* we predict that it is more apt than *creer* to govern subjunctive. Our prediction here is based on what we know about negation. Whether for courtesy, hesitation, or what-not, it is more apt to be tinged with an attitude.[13]

---

[11] But not impossible: "No tengo más que una pequeña cantidad de dinero en soles.... Esto no lo sabe don Julio y tendrá que recibir dólares en pago, cosa que *no sé* que aceptación *tenga.*" José Miguel Quintana, Jr., in *América Indigena* 21 (1961) 204. If the accentuation is to be trusted, this is *no saber* with the meaning of doubt. Compare English *Oh, I don't know that it's so good.*

[12] I have these two examples from Col. Gordon T. Fish. The first is a remark by a Cuban, age 31. The second is from a Quintero play. Even such a verb as *explicar* may take subjunctive if it is attitudinal: *La selva es baja; el P. Avencio en su libro ... explica que ésta no tenga árboles descomunales ... debido al suelo gredoso....* (Quintana, op. cit. p. 206.) *Explicar* carries the connotation 'hacer comprensible': it breaks down our resistance, makes us receptive to the information.

[13] There is a way to formalize the effect of negation by using the "negative hopping" transformation. I relegate it to this footnote because I do not believe it gives a true answer; it will not work for *no dudar,* for example. But it is worth a paragraph because it does shed some light n the complexity of negation. As is well known, certain "higher" elements, including interrogation

---

as well as negation, have a hovering effect on a sentence; it is not always clear where they are intended as a constituent. The sentences

He saw no one.
He didn't see anyone.
It's not true that he saw anyone.

show what is apparently the same denial attaching at three different points. Certain illocutionary verbs are particularly susceptible to this:

It seems that he didn't do it.
It doesn't seem that he did it.
I think it's no good.
I don't think it's any good.

"Negative hopping" says that the negative element in the subordinate clause is lifted into the main clause by a movement transformation. It might be possible then to order the transformations so as to account for the indicative after *no creer*. Suppose that in deep structure *no creer* always governs subjunctive and *creer* always governs indicative. The deep structure representation of *Creo que esto no sirve* would thus have indicative by rule, with the movement transformation then yielding *No creo que esto sirve.* The sentence *No creo que esto sirva* would have *no creer* in its deep structure. The main difficulty with this is that it assumes a paraphrase relationship between *Creo que no sirve* and *No creo que sirve,* a question that not all native speakers are agreed upon. One has the same misgivings about the English equivalents. Sometimes the meanings are obviously not the same. *I am not prepared to say that* tells us that the speaker will not say it, but *I am prepared not to say that* means something different. Even when there is no practical difference the two constructions are still not quite identical. This can be sensed by comparing cases where the illocutionary verb is postposed.

I think he isn't ready = He isn't ready, I think.
I don't think he's ready = He isn't ready, I don't think.

So it appears that negation is only a clue that forces one to look deeper. The indicative-subjunctive contrast is a phenomenon in its own right. It does not depend on other structures except in a loose statistical way. The speaker chooses the subjunctive morpheme as a direct reflection of his meaning, precisely as he chooses the word *gato* when he intends to speak of cats.[14] And if he wishes, he may turn an expression that normally governs indicative into one that governs subjunctive—which is to say that in the light of intentions we may not be dealing with grammatical government but with a set of more or less powerful tendencies. "The glue that holds the elements together into a speech act is the semantic intentions of the speaker."[15]

I have tried to show that Spanish has no RULES whereby the modes can be determined through features of dubitativeness, optativeness, negation, or the like. It is a mistake, says William Haas, "to present as rules what are in fact concurrent semantic tendencies," adding that "however strong a semantic tendency may be, what happens 'as a rule' is not to be stated by a rule."[16] Affirmative *creer* can be used with the subjunctive, *ser posible* can be used with the indicative;[17] all depends on the intent of the speaker, and our best generalizations are only statistical. The traditional rules of

—in the latter example the range of the negation is seen in our freedom to repeat it: it belongs BOTH with the performative and with the subordinate verb. *I don't think he's ready* is simply more inclusive. It embraces everything from mild lack of conviction to firm contrary conviction. *I don't think he meant it* is more diffuse, and hence potentially milder, than *I think he didn't mean it. I don't suppose you'd like a cup of tea* could even be used as an invitation, where *I suppose you wouldn't like a cup of tea* could not.

[14] For a good statement of the dependence on attitudes, see Vicente Pérez Soler, "Construcciones con verbos de duda en español," *Hispania* 49 (1966) 287-9.

[15] John Searle, "Chomsky's revolution in linguistics," *The New York Times Review of Books*, 29 June 1972, p. 23. Searle regards the failure to take account of intentions as the major weakness in Chomsky's edifice.

[16] "Rivalry among the deep structures," preprint, 1972.

[17] *¿Es posible que está vuesa merced en esta tierra?* Cervantes, *Novelas ejemplares* (Bib. Emecé), p. 545. The speakers are face-to-face.

thumb—willing, emotion, indefinite antecedents, unreality, unrealized future, etc.—are hints at the underlying semantic tendencies, and are pedagogically useful; but neither they nor any refinement of them will serve as rules in the formal sense.

What, then, is the recourse of the teacher? He is left with a field of meaning, to describe as best he can, using his rules of thumb and any parallels that come to hand in the students' native language. It is at this point that illocutionary theory comes home, for it can be used to show the student that he is already making in his own language the same distinction that Spanish makes in its modal system. In English our freedom to move the illocutionary verb—structurally the "main" verb—away from the beginning of the sentence, and to place it in the middle or at the end, mirrors exactly the choice of mode in Spanish. The parallel is found in Figure 1.

FIGURE 1

English		Spanish
The "main" verb is postposable	=	The "subordinate" verb is indicative
The "main" verb is not postposable	=	The "subordinate" verb is subjunctive
Examples:		
I think he's coming. He's coming, I think.		Creo que viene.
I'm sorry you broke it. *You broke it, I'm sorry.[18]		Siento que lo hayas roto.
I see you know each other. You know each other, I see.		Veo que se conocen.

[18] With a comma split this is of course acceptable; but that is not the intent here.

I insist that it stop. *It stop, I insist.	Insisto en que pare.
It seems they're ready. They're ready, it seems.	Parece que están listos.
It's good that they're ready. *They're ready, it's good.	Es bueno que estén listos.
It's probable that they know. *They know, it's probable.	Es probable que sepan.

The fact that the illocutionary verb is postposable in English and that it does not alter the mode in Spanish, which retains the indicative that it has when there is no subordinating verb present, shows the essential adverbiality of these expressions. In fact, their insertion, after commas or between commas, exactly parallels the insertion of sentence adverbs:

I suppose he's coming.
He's coming, I suppose.
He's coming, supposedly.

I don't doubt he will do it as soon as he can.
He will do it, I don't doubt, as soon as he can.
He will do it, undoubtedly, as soon as he can.

Such expressions therefore do not alter the intelligence-conveying function of the "subordinate" clause. They only take the declarative black and dilute it to some shade of gray. By fronting the "subordinate" clause the speaker actually makes it independent. The same phenomenon can be observed in Spanish[19] but it is less common. The reason is obvious. The indicative mode alone does for Spanish what clause-fronting does for English. The illocutionary verb is moved only to play down its importance or because it is an afterthought.

---

[19] *Sin perder ... de vista el primero de los factores ..., debemos, creo considerar el segundo.* Germán de Granda in *Thesaurus, Boletín del Instituto Caro y Cuervo* 25 (1970), 450.

In my earlier formulation of the English parallel[20] I was unable to carry it to adjective and adverb clauses. With noun clauses plus indicative, an illocutionary-type expression is present by definition, and can be tested by postposing it. With adjective and adverb clauses explicit illocutionary verbs are infrequent, and the test lies in whether one can be inserted. The fact that they do occur occasionally gives some assurance that the test is valid. In the pair

He was looking for a house that I think had ten rooms.
He was looking for a house that had ten rooms.

the illocutionary *I think* in the first sentence makes it clear that the adjective clause is asserting something about a particular house. Lacking it, the second sentence is ambiguous; it might refer to a particular house or to any one of a number of houses that could fill the bill. What is interesting about these examples is that they show how adjective clauses may converge with noun clauses. In the first sentence the *that* clause both modifies *house* and serves as object of *think*. The speaker both describes and conveys the intelligence that there WAS such a house and that it HAD ten rooms.[21]

In Figure 2, the illocutionary *I assure you* is used as a test in adjective clauses:

FIGURE 2

I bought a house which, I assure you, has ten rooms.	Compré una casa que tiene diez cuartos.
*I need a house which, I assure you, has ten rooms.	Necesito una casa que tenga diez cuartos.

[20] "Postposed main phrases: an English rule for the Romance subjunctive ," *Canadian Journal of Linguistics*, 14 (1968) 3-30.

[21] The notion of "definite antecedent" is a semantic clue to the same phenomenon. We ask the student to imagine whether the reference is to some particular thing that exists already in the speaker's mind. If what we describe is real, we describe it in real, intelligence-conveying terms. The advantage of illocutionary verb insertion is that it gives the same insight concretely.

There was someone who would, I assure you, help us.	Había alguien que nos ayudaría.
*There was no one who would, I assure you, help us.	No había nadie que nos ayudara.[22]

With adverb clauses, explicit illocutionary verbs are quite rare. Following are a few that strike me as normal, paired with others which are not and in Spanish would require subjunctive:

It happened when I gather you were unable to cope with it.
*I'll let you know when I gather you'll call me.

He escaped after it seems he was able to bribe a guard.
*He promised to help me after it seems I paid up the debt.

The two were caught after they had traveled—we understand—more than two miles.
*The two were caught before they had traveled—we understand—more than two miles.

I wasn't there when you say he turned up.
*I won't be there when you say he turns up.

The sentence *I wasn't there when you say he turned up* does not state that I was absent at the time of your saying, but at the time of his turning up; *you say* is an inserted illocutionary verb, and presents *he turned up* as an assertion. (*You said* in this same context would be ambiguous.)

The comparative unusualness of illocutionary verbs with adverb clauses makes the insertion test less useful to apply in individual cases, but examples of it are still helpful in developing a sense of the distinctions. The student is expected to conceive that in a sentence like *I was there when he came, he came* says exactly what it would say as an independent sentence, whereas in one like *I promised I would be there when he came,* the same two words bear no such relationship to the fact of his coming. Our ability to say *I was there when we know he came,* but

[22] If the illocutionary verb precedes or follows the subordinate clause it is construed with the sentence as a whole. Thus *There was no one who would help us, I assure you* is acceptable but irrelevant to this discussion.

not to say **I promised I would be there when we know he came,* helps to see this difference.

One type of sentence remains to be looked at both for how it relates to illocutionary-type subordination and for what might be termed a purely attitudinal context without any particular coloration of doubt, will, or whatever. It can be illustrated by a sentence like *Que venga ahora—Dios mío, no sé qué decirle; puede ser necesario, además de ser cosa cierta, pero me cuesta pensarlo.* The speaker starts out unsure of what attitude he is to adopt, and proceeds to weigh the considerations—one of which, *ser cosa cierta,* would not, in normal order, govern the subjunctive. Preposing a subjunctive clause appears to mean 'this is something to adopt an attitude toward.' In English such clauses tend to be of questionable acceptability except in those cases where Spanish would require subjunctive in normal order:

> *That he was there I heard.
> That he was there I doubt.
>
> ?That he was sincere I know.
> That he was sincere I accept.
>
> ?That you felt insulted I can understand.

(In the last pair, the first would tend to be interpreted as calling for the intellectual *entender,* the second for the attitudinal *comprender.*) This suggests that in English too the purpose of preposing the clause is to weigh it for attitude. What Spanish can do more freely than English, since it can count on the subjunctive to show the meaning, is to prepose attitudinal clauses even when there is a single main verb which in normal order would govern indicative: *Que Juan sea el mejor alumno no cabe la menor duda (lo creemos absolutamente; lo tenemos por una verdad innegable).* Since movement transformations are normally among the last to apply, this cannot be handled within Lozano's framework. But semantically there is no problem. The speaker offers the idea as something toward which it may be necessary to adopt an attitude, before he shows his hand and, instead of attitudinizing, affirms it.

Such preposings differ from the illocutionary-type preposings in that they are explicitly subordinated. In English the relative *that* must be retained. Compare the following, where the lexical illocutionary status of *guess* is apparent in the fact that using a relative with it is actually a bit unusual:

?I guess that he just wants to.
I guess he just wants to.
*That he just wants to I guess.
He just wants to, I guess.

I can't conceive that you did it.
*I can't conceive you did it.[23]
That you did it I can't conceive.
*You did it, I can't conceive.

The directions of acceptability and of use and omission of *that* in these two sets are exactly reversed. It is no coincidence that the Spanish parallel using the subjunctive shows subordination *par excellence*—subordination to an attitude. The indicative shows independence, with only a casual, adverb-like "main" verb if there is any subordination at all, which there usually is not; the speaker is making a pronouncement about something which he regards as out there, in the world, with no glandular attachment to him.

The value of parallels such as the one I have drawn is perhaps more in what they show of the nature of language than in their usefulness as classroom guides. But if one of the advantages of learning a foreign language is that it provides such insight, as we are fond of claiming, then we cannot afford to dismiss them. All the better if some practical dividend accrues as well. I offer two instances where the illocutionary tests I have suggested do a better job than verbal generalizations.

The first is with noun clauses and has to do with the interpretation of *es probable*. If we think of the indicative as the "mode

[23] The starring of this example does not imply that others using verbs that would govern subjunctive in Spanish might not omit *that*. *I'm sorry you said that*, *I insist he do it*, *It's nice you could come*, etc., are all normal. But in the main *that* is used more, and in some cases must be used, with meanings that in Spanish would call for subjunctive; whereas with illocutionary verb meanings it is usually omitted. See my *That's that*. (The Hague: Mouton, 1972).

of fact," it is hard to discuss this phrase in the context of impersonal expressions, for it seems to lean substantially more toward factuality than *es posible*, and hence at least potentially to call for indicative. Yet even in the form *es muy probable* or *es del todo probable* it requires subjunctive. Whatever the psychological reason may be, the English parallel holds; *it is probable* cannot be postposed, as can be seen by comparing it with *it is evident*:

It is evident that they have accepted —>
They have accepted, it is evident.

It is probable that they have accepted -/->
*They have accepted, it is probable.

The second example is that of adverb clauses after *mientras*. This conjunction (as well as *en tanto que*) is puzzling in that it seems to violate the traditional rule for using the subjunctive in a clause that refers to unrealized future. The indicative is normal, as the following by Simón Bolívar shows: *Para efectuar este viaje necesito de los auxilios más indispensable* [sic] *para permanecer en Londres, mientras obtengo algún resultado favorable.* (The example is from Col. Gordon T. Fish.) The clue to futurity in this case seems to be the same as with noun clauses: in the sentence *El meteorólogo pronostica que va a llover* the *va a llover* is unrealized, hence "unreal"; but it is PREDICTED. Similarly *mientras*, and English *while* also, can view the future as predicted rather than contingent. And *while* stands the illocutionary test, whereas other temporal conjunctions do not:

While the two kids *I suppose* are there taking it all in, you and your wife are going to stage a free-for-all.
*As soon as the two kids *I suppose* are there taking it all in, you and your wife are going to stage a free-for-all.

Both sentences are normal without the illocutionary verb.

I hope to have done more in this rejoinder than clarify some points about the indicative and subjunctive modes. I would like to have succeeded in showing the wisdom of building on our intuitions rather than disowning them; the traditional view of the Spanish modes was correct: their significance is semantic; they represent two ways of looking at reality, one intellectual, the other attitudinal. At the same time, linguistic theory, if it is the right kind, puts a foundation under what we know intuitively. Such is the case with illocutions. Theory in turn must be distinguished from formalization, which in spite of its impressively scientific appearance is never better than what it formalizes. Even in these latter days it makes for communication to use ordinary language in talking about language.[24]

---

[24] Because it has only minor interest pedagogically, I place here an extension of remarks on an earlier point of considerable theoretical importance: how much of the explanatory apparatus is needed only because the style of analysis creates artificial problems? The earlier example was the effect of negation. I give one more here.

Instead of recognizing the presence or absence of a dative of interest and an impersonal reflexive as phenomena that are free to intersect with the subjunctive, Lozano takes them to require a further chopping of the subjunctive into optative-impersonal, dubitative-impersonal, and their opposites. The over-structuring that results is much the same as if one were to sub-classify on the basis of number and tense, creating a dubitative-plural (*Dudo que vayan* contrasting with *Dudo que vaya*), a dubitative-past, etc. The evidence cited for the subclasses is of the following sort (p. 80):

Será preciso que intentes la fuga.
Te será preciso intentar la fuga.
Será preciso que se intente la fuga.
Será preciso intentar la fuga.

The two pairs are supposed to have within them a paraphrase relationship: the first has the same deep structure as the second, and the third the same as the fourth. And since the first two contain a reference to person and the last two do not, with quite different transformations in the infinitives, it is necessary to recognize a separate optative-impersonal. The subset containing sentences like *Ella deja que Rufo me acompañe* and *Será preciso que intentes la fuga* must be distinguished from the one containing *Será preciso que se intente la fuga* etc. (One wonders about *Mandan hablar* and *Mandan que se hable* as against *Te mandan hablar* and *Mandan que hables—mandar* is not listed among the impersonals.)

The difficulty lies with the notion of paraphrase, which one soon discovers cannot be extended beyond a narrow range of sentences. In the following set,

> Sería agradable que habláramos de nuestros amigos.
> Nos sería agradable hablar de nuestros amigos.
> Sería agradable que se hablara de nuestros amigos.
> Sería agradable hablar de nuestros amigos.

the fourth sentence agrees semantically not with the third but with the first and second. The simple fact of the matter is that the infinitive is noncommittal as to its underlying subject, picking it up from whatever contextual clue is most obvious, whereas the *se* construction is explicitly impersonal. What creates the difference between Lozano's set and mine is the semantic properties of the adjectives: *preciso* is normally said of everyone and requires a dative or a verb with a personal subject to confine it to a single person, whereas *agradable* more often applies to present company, and lets us infer a personal reference, specifically *Nos sería agradable,* when we say *Sería agradable que se hablara.* If in addition there is a contextual clue such as the *nuestros* in the last example, the infinitive immediately picks it up and the personal reference is obvious. If I look you in the eye and say *Conviene llegar a tiempo, ¿entiendes?* you will understand that *llegar* means *llegues,* something which is not so easily inferred from *Conviene que se llegue a tiempo, ¿entiendes?* The whole problem of the infinitive and its subjects needs to be explored before a generalization such as Lozano's can be made safely.

From the standpoint of transformational theory the importance of these facts is that they undermine the cornerstone of paraphrase. Why should a language be cluttered with two or more constructions that mean the same? Words, perhaps yes, because there are thousands of them and one can afford to be extravagant. But constructions? Of course sameness may result when performance variables happen to converge, as they do in the case of *Será preciso que intentes* and *Te será preciso intentar.* Here transformational grammarians have simply turned things upside down: they have looked to competence for samenesses and to performance for differences. The opposite is just as apt to be true.

Verbs of Emotion

THE CONTRAST OF factuality and non-factuality determines pretty well most uses of the indicative and subjunctive in noun clauses except after verbs of emotion.[1] With the latter Spanish is supposed to demand the subjunctive automatically, regardless of the reality of what the subordinate verb reports: *Lamento que estén enfermos* has to do with an event that the speaker knows to be true and which he affirms as true,[2] but the subjunctive is "required" exactly as in *Ojalá que se*

[1] J. Francis Lemon, "A Psychological Study on the Subjunctive in Spanish," *MLJ*, XI (1926-27), 195-99 says that the "subjunctive after verbs of emotion could not be explained under this rule," i.e. the rule that it is used when the speaker does not present something as an actual fact. This article was originally published in *Hispania* 36 (1953): 459-61

[2] Lemon's example *Es la costumbre ... que demos los recados,* even when spoken on an occasion when the messages were actually being given, is not parallel in factuality. Whereas *estén enfermos* is affirmed as true now, *demos* is timeless—it may be used appropriately of an actual situation, but is no more intrinsically assertive of that situation than *When it rains we get wet* uttered during a rainstorm is intrinsically assertive of the rain. What assertion there may be is derived from the occasion of its use. Compare the obvious contradiction in the factual *Me alegro que estés bien, pero veo que no lo estás* with the lack of contradiction in *Es la costumbre que demos los recados, pero no los damos ahora.* G. P. Sullivan calls my attention to a similar distinction between *propositions* and *assertions* made by Clarence Irving Lewis *(An Analysis of Knowledge and Valuation,* La Salle, Ill., 1946, p. 49).

mejore, where the event is hypothetical. Even in the type *Que lo haya dicho no lo niego* there is an explicit tentativeness that is lacking in the example with *lamento.*

With the normal tendency to make the form of a given meaning agree with the form which that meaning usually takes, it would be surprising if the indicative were never to be found after verbs of emotion. Whether through analogy or otherwise, conversational Spanish does not exclude the indicative here, as the following spontaneous examples show:

Lemon and others have striven to find a frame of reference that would accommodate both the ordinary non-factual subjunctive and the factual ones like those treated here. Mostly this has meant devising a kind of fictitious nonfactuality, so as to make it cover all cases. Gili Gaya (*Curso Superior de Sintaxis Española*. Mexico, 1943, §110, 2^0) refers to 'una apariencia de irrealidad objetiva." While this may work in theory, and perhaps correctly sums up the origin of the subjunctive after expressions of emotion (*estés enfermo* held conceptually and not denotatively), I believe that it misses the point as a description of the linguistic mechanism, partly through failure to define what is meant by emotion. If we try to fabricate expressions with neutral, physiological words having to do with emotions, we get forms that would hardly ever be uttered: *The dog is stimulated that he is touched by an electric wire, My endocrine functions are stirred that it turned out all right.* Broadly speaking, noun clauses are governed by expressions that fall into two classes: those which treat the proposition in the clause as an item of information (getting it, having it, giving it, regardless of whether the information is true or false, real or imagined), and those which treat it with some personal or social bias. The latter fall into categories which are all alike, but for which we have no adequate name, each with polar extremes: acceptance-rejection, goodness-badness, like-dislike, and—here emotion enters—pleasure-pain. *I understand that he refused* is a (true or false) item of information; *I understand his refusing* shows me receptive to an idea, which is probably straight fact, but which will be expressed with subjunctive in Spanish. The poles of "inclination" and "disinclination" are probably as close as we can come to naming the attitudinal function of the subjunctive. (I exclude the suasive or "willing" type, as one much easier to define.)

1. . . . lástima que no tengo (Prof. H. Corbató, 14 May 1950; later in the same talk he used the identical phrase bu with *tenga*).
2. Me alegro mucho de que así es (Prof. L. Moreno, in conversation, 5 May 1953).
3. Lástima que yo no tengo el informe (Moreno, 13 Dec. 1951).
4. ¡Lástima que se acaba ya! (A. Casona, *Nuestra Natacha*, ed. Shoemaker, New York 1947, p. 69).[3]

All the Spanish American students—a dozen or so, of diverse origins—that I have queried on this point declare that the indicative is perfectly normal to them. A Mexican, a New Mexican, a Nicaraguan, and a Puerto Rican all judged as correct the sentences *Aplaudo que él está de acuerdo, Lamento que no ha podido asistir, Me alegro de que tiene el dinero, Aplaudo que decides quedarte.* Two Mexican students reported the type *Siento que está enfermo* to be current in Mexico.

Persons with a literary background are more reluctant to accept the indicative, but despite this, a Guatemalan colleague reported the type *Me alegro de que usted está aquí* as in use, a Spanish colleague (Ciudarealeño) regarded it as possible, and, going farthest of all, another Spanish colleague[4] (Burgalés) not only accepted *Me alegro que estás contento* as common in Spain but averred that it represented a more outspoken concern than the formal and relatively perfunctory *estés contento;* likewise more outspoken—and here, in view of the context, blunt—is, he feels, *Siento que estás enfermo* (as if to say 'That's the way things are,' or 'You brought it on yourself'—what has to be accepted, opposed to the subjunctive, which pictures a world that the speaker creates and in which he might, by wishing, make the sick well again).

With *temer: Temo que no lo puedo hacer,* accepted by a Spanish colleague. *Si llegamos a tener guerra con la Nigricia Oriental, me temo que este hombre no nos va a llevar a la victoria* (Pío Baroja, *Paradox, Rey,* New York, Macmillan, 1937, p. 30)—but this latter example is with an auxiliary of certainty. *Temer* seems to be a special case, to judge by the space (§§392-5) devoted to "Oraciones de temor" in the Academy

[3] Item from Joseph Silverman.

[4] Dr. Laudelino Moreno, whose fertile help as informant was invaluable.

grammar—which, for reasons hard to understand, does not treat verbs of emotion as a separate class in the chapter (XXIV) on noun clauses. *Temer* comes close, at times, to what F. C. Tarr[5] refers to as "asseverative verbs." The example given by Keniston (*Spanish Syntax List*, New York 1937, §28.261) illustrates the point: *El conde tendió la mano a Julia, temiendo que se la rechazaría*, i.e. 'suponiendo con temor.' English makes the contrast by *I am afraid that it will happen* versus *I am afraid of its happening*—the first is a prediction, the second is a state of mind (it is a slovenly contrast, for both expressions cover the entire range, but the tendency is as indicated). The Keniston example employs *rechazaría* exactly in the sense 'había de rechazar,' a parallel which is not only etymologically valid but attested in other examples of current usage. The Academy grammar (§393*d*) also admits the indicative of *haber de* after *temer*.

Grammars of contemporary Spanish reject the indicative after expressions of emotion. Bello (*Gramática*..., Paris, 1936, §462) states: "no tiene cabida el indicativo...porque en estos casos...prevalece sobre la regla que asigna el indicativo a los juicios, la que pide el subjuntivo para las emociones del ánimo." Keniston gives one other example besides the *temer* one quoted, and states that the only common verb is *esperar*. Since *esperar* covers the range of 'hope' and 'expect,' it is not probative, and there may be valid—and similarly extraneous—reasons for the indicative in the one remaining example counted but not quoted by Keniston, as in the one with *temer*.

As to the source of the indicative after expressions of emotion, one may look in two directions: analogy and oral tradition. Most likely conversational Spanish has kept alive what Tarr notes (160 fn) as prevalent in Old Spanish, the indicative after verbs of emotion owing to the fact that the clause was not fully subordinate to the governing verb, i.e., *He was glad that it happened* = 'He was glad because it happened.' Tarr adds (259): "These *de que, de lo que*, etc. clauses with the indicative after expressions of emotion disappear in Spanish in the

---

[5]"Prepositional Complementary Clauses in Spanish, with Special Reference to the Works of Pérez Galdós," *RH* No. 129 (Oct. 1922), pp. 1-264.

fourteenth century, while their French counterpart (*de ce que* with the indicative after *être content, blâmer, remercier,* etc.) is alive today."[6] Keniston's later work (*The Syntax of Castilian Prose: the Sixteenth Century,* Chicago, 1937, §28.265), however, gives examples from the sixteenth century, after *pesar, placer, recelarse, regocijarse,* and *espantarse,* to quote only those verbs which are most emotional and least asseverative (he recognizes the causal origin of the indicative after *pesar* and *placer,* which Tarr attributes to all such indicatives). A still later example from Lope de Vega (*Las Batuecas del Duque de Alba,* Obras, Ac. XII, 534*a*)[7]: *Por Dios, mucho siento / Que no son monstruos*—the context forces this to be 'regret' and not an asseverative 'feel.'

So the indicative probably went underground, but never disappeared in familiar speech. Given other archaisms in Spanish America, it is not surprising that this one should appear there. It is not noted by Kany, *Spanish American Syntax,* Chicago 1945, so far as I have found.

---

[6] The Academy grammar makes the same statement (§395*b*), giving evidence later than the fifteenth century, but the examples quoted are with pause before *que,* making it clearly equivalent to 'porque.' The one exception is from Tirso, *Hombre os llamé, y temo y dudo que no lo fuiste jamás,* where there is no question about complete subordination; but this is *temer* again, and the equally assertive *dudar*—for a similar assertive *doubt* in English, see the *Century Dictionary* definition II 2.

[7]Another item from Joseph Silverman.

Gleanings from CLM: Indicative vs. Subjunctive In Exclamations

THE WORKING COMMITTEE OF the MLA Spanish college textbook discovered early in its efforts to order thoughts into chapters that not all questions of Spanish grammar had been settled beyond a doubt.[1] Not that it had begun with the comfortable assumption that only pedagogical problems lay in its path, but it did seem that for a beginning text there ought to be pretty plain sailing. Instead, it turned out that several things that had been closed to inquiry for a long time had to be dusted off and given a fresh look. Of these, a few that may be of more general interest will be given from time to time in "Notes on Usage."

Besides the two authors (one a Costa Rican, the other a Chilean) and the six members of the Working Committee, some thirty people—the Advisory Committee, critics, and others—examined the twenty-four dialogs that form the basis of the text. The one thing that arrested more eyes than any other was a sentence that appears in the second dialog: *Lástima que yo no hablo inglés*. It was taken to be a mistake by so many that we felt we had to learn more about the circumstances that might have elicited the indicative from writers who were, after all, native speakers of Spanish. They might have been guilty of a lapse, or they might have had good reason.

The subjunctive is not always used after expressions of emotion, as I have shown here, and *lástima* seems to be rather frequent in selecting the indicative. But are these instances only rare exceptions,

[1] Originally published in *Hispania* 42 (1959): 372-73.

or is there some set of circumstances in which the indicative is regular with expressions of emotion? Besides the earlier examples I have the following: *Milagro que no le ha cogido* (José Robles, *Cartilla Española,* New York, 1935, p. 32); *Estoy tan triste que renunció el Sr. Roberts* (translation offered by a Chilean informant for the English *I'm so sorry that Mr. Roberts resigned the job*); *¡Cuánto me alegro de que estás ya bien!* (volunteered by Castilian informant); and—ironically these examples from the dialogs themselves passed unnoticed by all those who read them— *Qué bueno que llamaste* and *Qué suerte que no fui.*

What these examples have in common, of course, is that all are to some extent exclamatory. Could it be that exclamations are one place where the speaker is more likely to mean that he has the feeling as a result of the circumstance, rather than that he projects his feeling on the circumstance, as Tarr explained the medieval examples of indicative after expressions of emotion? We decided to find out whether the indicative correlates with exclamations.

We used a Mexican informant who was given the non-exclamatory sentence *Me preocupa que no están aquí* and rejected it (she accepted the sentence with *estén*); she also rejected the indicative in the merely declarative *Es una fortuna que estés aquí* but rejected the subjunctive in the exclamatory *Por fortuna que estás aquí.* In the following she accepted either indicative or subjunctive:

¡Qué desgracia que has perdido!
¡Magnífico que le tocó el premio!
¡Qué lástima que se ha portado así!
¡Cuánto me alegro de que todo ha salido bien!
Gracias a Dios que nada te ha pasado.

In all but the last, her preference was about equal. In the last, she preferred the indicative. On another occasion we tried her with the sentence *Qué suerte que no nos fuéramos* (or *hayamos ido*—offering both alternatives); she corrected it to *nos fuimos,* and we had to use the less exclamatory *me alegro* in order to elicit a subjunctive.

The indicative with *lástima* turns up too often, in the speech if not in the writings of cultivated persons all over the Hispanic world, not to be regarded as perfectly normal—and of a piece with the indicative accompanying expressions like *qué bueno,* which no one appears to question. In a classroom lecture my Castilian colleague used the sentence *¡Lástima que no me acuerde!*, and was questioned about it by his students; he replied that *acuerdo* would be MORE usual here, and justified the subjunctive on the grounds of showing more sentiment on his part.

Why is it then that the indicative with *lástima* flags down the attention of so many people? I can only explain it as one of those scapegoats, like *his'n* and *he don't* (or perhaps more appropriately like *I want in*, shunned by speakers who in their next breath will say *He let me in*), that are the stock in trade of a purism that deals in items rather than patterns. We are conditioned to react to them like a bull sensitized to red flannel but indifferent to red silk.

I am not sure that the category of "exclamations" is fundamental here. It does seem that in exclamations the leading expression might well become more detached from the clause (*Too bad I don't speak English* = *Too bad. I don't speak English*), but it is hard in language to be sure that one has cut beneath the symptoms into the cause itself. At least it seems to be true that exclamations are an easily identified set of utterances where the subjunctive after expressioons of emotion regularly gives way to the indicative.

The Subjunctive *-ra* and *-se*: "Free Variation"?

MOST AUTHORITIES have held that there is no difference in meaning between the *-ra* and *-se* forms of the imperfect subjunctive. Gili y Gaya says "los significados de ambas formas han quedado identificados."[1] According to Ramsey-Spaulding, "the imperfect tense forms are interchangeable."[2] Lenz is most emphatic: "si *cantara* se usa como subjuntivo, es absoluto sinónimo de *cantase,* una mera variante formal."[3]

But in which of its two senses is one to take "interchangeable?" One sense is interlinguistic: Dialect *A* uses *-ra* and Dialect *B* under identical conditions uses *-se*. The other sense is intralinguistic: a single dialect uses either form without contrast in meaning. Critics have left the senses undistinguished, for coupled with the remarks on interchangeability one usually finds observations about the frequency of *-se* in Spain and of *-ra* in Spanish America. In the search for a possible semantic contrast the interlinguistic sense is of no concern to us except as a warning: a speaker in whose dialect the assumed difference has been leveled is not in a good position to judge it. And if the difference, assuming it exists, is a ticklish one, even the speaker who uses both forms may be fooled into identifying them. So in order to make any sort of test we must look to a dialect where both forms

---

[1] This article was originally published in *Hispania* 39 (1956): 345-49. The Samuel Gili y Gaya reference is to his *Curso superior de sintaxis española,* Barcelona, 1954, §135.

[2] M. M. Ramsey, *A textbook of modern Spanish,* revised by Robert K. Spaulding, New York, 1956, §23, 36.

[3] Rodolfo Lenz, *La oración y sus partes,* Santiago de Chile, 1944, §306.

are in vigorous colloquial use, and stimulate an informant to look for differences, varying the examples so that if the differences are imaginary the results will be random.

Two linguistic theories are in conflict here. One, old and well established, is that there is no such thing as an exact synonym. The endings *-ra* and *-se* are not words in the ordinary sense and accordingly might not be thought of in connection with synonyms, but since they communicate meaning the theory is the same. The second is a recent borrowing from phonology: that it is possible to have two or more forms in "free variation"—for example, a given speaker uses either a plosive or a continuant [b] in a given position with no resulting contrast of any kind. Free variation has proved itself in phonology. It has not proved itself at higher levels, and if it is not true of *-ra* and *-se,* where it has been affirmed for so long, one may well question it wherever it has been applied in syntax.

I have found only two written intimations that *-ra* and *-se* differ in meaning. The first is by Aristóbulo Pardo V.: "Para mí personalmente, y tal vez por la modalidad idiomática en que me he criado, si alguien me dijese 'Me gustaría que escribiese usted un comentario,' y otro 'Me gustaría que no lo escribiera,' el uso de la segunda me daría mejor la impresión del deseo del interlocutor; la primera no me dejaría completamente convencido del 'gusto' que el solicitante decía tener."[4] The second is by M. Criado de Val: "En cambio, es plenamente actual el significado *desiderativo* [de *-ra*], que suele ir unido a verbos como *querer, pedir, desear,* etc.": QUISIERA *que se* HICIERA *algo semejante.* La forma en *-se*... tiene un significado más general y menos preciso que *amara,* aunque su tendencia actual es asimiladora. Puede usarse como *hipotético: No faltaría excusa que darle, si allí las* HALLASE, y *comparativo: Jugaremos como si* FUESE *de veras.*"[5] The latter came to my attention after all the conclusions of this article had been drawn, and confirms them substantially, though Criado de Val limits his comparisons to a few contexts.

[4] *Boletín del Instituto Caro y Cuervo,* IX (1953), 315.

[5] *Fisonomía del idioma español,* Madrid, 1954, pp. 118-119.

The dialect that I have examined is that of my Castilian colleague,[6] who freely uses both forms and consciously distinguishes between them. In the following examples the model interpretations were supplied by him:

In conditional sentences, *if*-clause: "Si yo (1) *fuera* (2) *fuese* usted [en este momento], no lo haría." No. 2 suggests less authority than No. 1; 2 is advice, 1 is recommendation. "Lástima que esté lloviendo; si (3) *hubiera* (4) *hubiese* sol, podríamos salir." No. 4 is spoken by someone who doesn't care to go out even if the sun were shining—he is glad of an excuse to stay in. "Si me (5) *sintiera* (6) *sintiese* mejor, me levantaría." The speaker in No. 6 does not feel like getting up at all. In 5 he has a real desire to get up and thinks he may well get up later. "El médico me dijo que si me (7) *sintiera* (8) *sintiese* mejor podría levantarme." Either the doctor in 8 has used poor psychology or the patient is looking for an excuse not to get up. "Si [yo] (9) *pudiera* (10) *pudiese* hacerle ese favor, lo haría." No. 9 might be said the first time by someone who has been asked a favor, in order to show a real desire to help; but if the petitioner keeps insisting, he might in annoyance use 10 to push the idea farther away. "Si (11) *estuviera* (23) *estuviese* aquí mañana, ¿qué haríamos?" Here the reference is future, but there is the same contrast of more likely versus less likely.

In other subordinate clauses: "Siento que no (13) *hayas estado* (14) *estuvieras* (15) *estuvieses* aquí anoche." These represent a gradient of 'nearness to the speaker.' In 13 the issue is still pending—the speaker perhaps is wondering why the other was not there. In 14 the issue is settled, e.g. the speaker may have known beforehand that the other would be absent, and why. In 15 the issue is no longer of much interest; it is vague and detached from the speaker. "En caso de que lo (16) *hiciera* (17) *hiciese,* ¿qué diría usted?" Again the reference is to future time, and 17 envisages a more remote possibility; objective time is evidently not a determinant in the *-ra, -se* contrast. "Prepáreles la comida en caso de que (18) *vengan* (19) *vinieran* (20) *viniesen.*" Once more the real time is future, and the three subjunctives represent

[6] Dr. Laudelino Moreno, whose help I gratefully acknowledge, and whose linguistic sensitivity and imagination have avoided those stubborn and unconscious mental sets that have invalidated more than one study in syntax.

diminishing degrees of likelihood. (21) 'Bien, vamos a suponer que Vd. se *llamara* Gretchen Schrafft,"[7] vs. (22) *llamase*. The reference is to present time; same contrast of more or less plausible supposition vs. mere hypothesis. "Vamos a suponer que usted (23) *fuera* (24) *fuese* ese criminal." My informant volunteers 23 as a potential insult and 24 as an inoffensive hypothesis. "No creo que lo (25) *sea* (26) *fuera* (27) *fuese*." These were explicitly set up to refer to present time. In 25 the speaker implies that he has evidence, in 26 that he is expressing an opinion, and in 27 that the opinion is uncertain. "Ojalá que (28) *pudiera* (29) *pudiese*—casi creo que pueda." The context in 29 is contradictory, which makes the utterance itself unlikely to occur. "En tal caso, ¿qué harías con los recursos que (30) *tengas* (31) *tuvieras* (32) *tuvieses?*" The three-step contrast remains the same in these adjective clauses. "¡Quien lo (33) *supiera* (34) *supiese* hacer!" If in reference to a third person, 34 suggests less likelihood of finding him; if to the speaker, remoter possibility of realization.

The inference is that *-se* implies 'remoteness, detachment, hypothesis, lack of interest, vagueness, greater unlikelihood,' while *-ra* brings everything into relatively sharper focus. If this is true, it is confirmed by the tendency of the *-se* form to grow less frequent and in some dialects to disappear. In the 20th-century Peninsular dramatic works studied by Francis B. Lemon,[8] *-ra* forms outnumbered *-se* forms by 172 to 26, indicating a preference for *-ra* in everyday speech which is just what one would expect if *-ra* signals meanings that are warmer and more immediate. This of course assumes that the *-ra, -se* contrast here outlined extends back in time; evidence favors the assumption.[9]

The examples cited thus far test the contrast in a variety of grammatical environments (noun, adjective, and adverb clauses) and in a variety of objective environments (past, present, and future time, plus other circumstantial differences). It overrides these mutations. All

---

[7] Pedro Villa Fernández, *Por esas Españas*, New York, 1945, p. 126.

[8] *Hispania*, VIII (1925), 300-302.

[9] Criado de Val, op. cit. p. 119, says "Es arcaico el uso con valor *ponderativo: No lo dejaría de hacer, si* NEVASE *y* VENTISCASE"—'even under such impossible circumstances as these.' But would this be archaic after *aunque* ("No lo hago aunque *caigan, cayeran, cayesen* los cielos")?

instances, however, are where subjunctive would normally be found—subordinate clauses or clauses on the borderline. It remains to be asked whether the uneven grammatical distribution of the two forms has any bearing. The *-se* form is virtually excluded from independent clauses, but has maintained itself in some. What ones are they?

Of the 1657 *-se* forms collected by Leavitt O. Wright[10] from 38 texts published since 1800, 27 occurred in independent clauses. Of these, 25 were examples of *hubiese* plus past participle, in the result clause of conditional sentences. That seems to be the answer.

Now the simple tenses of the subjunctive in conditional sentences are mixed in function. *Si tuviera el dinero, lo compraría* may mean either 'If I had the money tomorrow, I'd buy it,' a future-less-vivid condition that may still be realized, or 'If I had the money now, I'd buy it,' a contrary-to-fact condition that cannot be realized. The pluperfect subjunctive, however, is almost uniformly contrary-to-fact. Circumstances are more propitious here than anywhere else for a verb form meaning 'unlikelihood' to elbow its way. Though widely condemned,[11] *hubiese* is pretty freely used in the result clause of conditional sentences, especially when the *if*-clause precedes it. A second Castilian, a Guatemalan, and a Nicaraguan assented to a number of test sentences, including the following: "Si lo hubiera sabido, no se los *hubiese* dado." "De haber admitido tal razonamiento, no se *hubiese* salido con la suya." "Si les hubiera revelado el documento, ¿me *hubiesen* aceptado?"

Whether the *-ra, -se* contrast is maintained here may be judged from context. Following are two of the examples cited by Spaulding:[12] "Si existiese en la mirada el poder que algunos autores le atribuyeron, yo me *hubiese* caído allí mismo redondo" (Pardo Bazán). "Silvestre,

---

[10] *HR*, I (1933), 335-336.

[11] For example by Eduardo Benot, *Arquitectura de las lenguas*, Buenos Aires, III, 304 footnote; by Academia Española, *Gramática* . . . , Madrid, 1931, §300; by Rufino J. Cuervo, *Apuntaciones* . . . Bogotá, 1939, §320; by Félix Fano, *Indice gramatical*, Mexico, 1947, pp. 133-134. but see Gili y Gaya, op. cit., §131.

[12] Robert K. Spaulding, "An Inexact Analogy, the *-ra* Form as a Substitute for the *-ría*," *Hispania*, XII (1929), 374.

cuando trabajaba en su mesa, lo hacía sobre un mar. Victor Hugo le *hubiese* admirado" (Baroja). Others, from independent sources, and with the *if*-clause suppressed: "Era un hijo de usted y había de ser generoso. ¡*Hubiese* tenido que nacer de otra madre, para pensar de otro modo!"[13] "Si esto es cierto, una conjetura se impone: sin la invasión musulmana, los hispano-visigodos *hubiesen* creado una nacionalidad 'moderna' mucho más parecida a Francia."[14] "Un extraño nos *hubiese* creído apesadumbrados por una desgracia."[15] The situations are fanciful: being slain by a look, matched by a figure now dead, born of another mother, observed by a nonexistent stranger; and in one, the explicit term *conjetura*.

Wright's remaining two examples, both from the Duque de Rivas, are worth quoting: "Cualquiera juzgara que tornar nunca pudiese." "Si aquí estuviera mi cuerpo . . . hiciese honor a la cena." By contemporary standards the simple tense here is practically impossible; but the situations again are remote and hypothetical. I have two additional instances of simple-tense -*se*: "*Pudiese* que los reinos hubieran unido a la península," from a composition by a Spaniard, dealing with an imaginary recasting of history, and "Eso *pudiese* suceder," accepted by a Panamanian who judges it more vague than the same utterance with *pudiera*.

But to determine whether "vagueness" etc. is decisive in the distribution of forms in conditions and near-conditions, we need to extend the contrast to include the indicative endings -*ría* and -*aba* (-*aba* covers -*ía* as well). They compete with -*ra* and -*se* in result clauses, and their frequency may have something to tell us.

First, the contrast between -*ra* and -*ría*. Says Alfredo F. Padrón, "En el habla popular [de Cuba] hay preferencia por las formas en -*ara*, -*era* en la expresión de deseo, conveniencia o posibilidad: 'No quisiera (querría) morir sin haberlo visto'; 'Bueno fuera (sería) no olvidar esta experiencia.'"[16] This is the well-known diffident use of -*ra* rather than -*ría* so frequent in the auxiliaries *quisiera, debiera,* and *pudiera,* to avoid

[13] Sánchez Galarraga, *El héroe,* New York, 1941, p. 6.
[14] Pedro Laín Entralgo in *Cuadernos Hispanoamericanos,* XV (1950), 475.
[15] Ricardo Güiraldes, *Don Segundo Sombra,* Buenos Aires, 1928, p. 74.
[16] *BICC,* V (1949), 167.

excessive positiveness. But more positiveness (*-ría*) versus less positiveness (*-ra*) is not limited to situations of courtesy. An Ecuadoran speaker finds "Si tuviera tiempo lo *hiciera*" more unreal than the same with *haría*. My Castilian informant finds "¿Qué *hiciera* usted en ese caso?" more provisional or dubitative than the same with *haría,* and in "Si hubiera tenido el dinero, lo *habría* comprado" considers the conditional to signal a natural consequence of having had the money, but *hubiera comprado* a possible consequence of having had it. The roughly corresponding forms in English are *I'd have bought it* and *I might have bought it.*

If the *-ra* is more unreal than the *-ría,* we should expect it to be more frequent in contrary-to-fact conditions than in future-less-vivid conditions. This argues relatively more examples of *hubiera* but relatively fewer examples of other verbs in *-ra* as against *-ría.* Spaulding's statistics, gathered from ten authors active in the fifty years prior to the date of his article (1929),[17] confirm this: In simple tenses, with both clauses of the condition expressed, 257 *-ría* in the result clause as against 8 *-ra.* In the perfect tenses, with both clauses expressed, 14 *-ría* in the result clause as against 70 *-ra,* and with only the result clause expressed, 13 *-ría* as againt 185 *-ra,* making a total of 27 *-ría* and 255 *-ra.* The *-ra* predominates in situations of greater unreality, just as the *-se* became possible in situations of greatest unreality.

The second contrast is between *-ría* and *-aba.* This may be found as a past-future as well as in the result clause of conditions: "Dijeron que *llovía*" 'The weather man said it would rain' was interpreted by the speaker (who had said it spontaneously) to mean 'there is now no possibility of rain' as against *llovería* where the possibility remains undecided. The imperfect is a step farther toward positiveness. In the following, the subject exudes self-confidence: "Si caía en alguna república americana . . . , con dedicar unos versitos al cacique de tanda, en caso de necesidad, se *había* salvado."[18] This enables us to line up four primary tenses along an axis of likelihood or positiveness vs. unlikelihood or uncertainty: "Si hubiera aceptado la proposición, es

[17] Op. cit., pp. 371-376.

[18] Antonio Heras, *El laberinto de los espejos,* Madrid, 1928, p. 192.

seguro que *estaba (estaría, estuviera, estuviese)* en el puesto ahora." The noun clause opens the door to all four; without *es seguro, estuviese* drops out, but *hubiese estado* is still possible.

In result clauses the scale is still more extensive when the condition is contrary-to-fact because the *if*-clause with its *hubiera* or *hubiese* renders the utterance practically unambiguous as far as real time is concerned and the tenses in the result clause may then be used figuratively. (This same redundancy of "tense" has resulted in the type "If I *knew* you was coming I'd have baked a cake" in English, where the result clause fixes the time and the contrast between *knew* and *had known* becomes redundant). Taking Padrón's example[19] "Si yo fuera el Papa, *negaba* la licencia," my informant accepts the following, arranged on the same positiveness-uncertainty axis as before: "Si yo fuera el Papa, *negaba (negaría, habría negado, hubiera negado, hubiese negado, negara)* la licencia." It is even possible to have *niego* at the left-hand extreme, but this I exclude because positiveness is absolute and there is no longer any degree of that unreality which we have been measuring.

CONCLUSION

Disregarding the perfect tenses used for real anteriority,[20] we may set up the following scales:

A. Non-conditional utterances:

Present and future
- ame
- amara
- amase

Past
- haya amado
- amara
- amase

[19] *BICC*, V (1949), 167.

[20] The pluperfect in past contrary-to-fact conditions does not signal 'anteriority' but 'past': "If I *hadn't been* there" analogizes with "But you *were* there." Anteriority requires periphrasis: "If I *had already* arrived."

B. Conditional utterances:

Present and future

past future	amaba amaría	result clause
if-clause	amara amase	result clause
Past	amaba amaría habría amado	result clause
if-clause	hubiera amado hubiese amado amara	result clause

The purpose is to show the approximate position of *-ra* and *-se* in the over-all scheme. I do not guarantee that more information might not alter or add to some of the other items, particularly in the second set under *B*.

One school of linguists maintains that all contrasts are two-way. We need not accept this in order to agree that a multi-point scale is a luxury that is bound to prove unstable. It is no wonder that in some dialects of Spanish the *-se* form has all but disappeared, or the imperfect is crowding out the conditional; or that the *-se* form in its feeble estate has assumed new contrastive functions, such as that of "greater elegance" noted by Kany.[21] But in dialects like the one described, where both *-ra* and *-se* have remained vigorous, they are not in free variation, and if they are in complementary distribution it is a distribution that accords with the difference in meaning.

---

[21] *American Spanish Syntax*, Chicago, 1951, pp. 182-183.

Ser bien

[*Author's Note*: A language presumably starts with meanings that are concrete and directly related to the external world—or, if to the inner world of our feelings, to their gut level. But eventually they etherealize, and one way in which we can be pretty confident that all do is in setting up some kind of transcendent world, representing a range of hovering meanings all the way from social duty to fate. Certain verbs characteristically undergo this sort of refinement, and the clearest examples in English and Spanish are the modal verbs. Take the two common senses of *could*:

> He tried to lift the weights but couldn't.
> It's risky business—you could lose your shirt.

In the first the subject lacks the physical power; in the second there is a force beyond his control: 'the possibility exists that you will lose'. We call the first the "root" meaning, the second the "epistemic."

I start my three samples of epistemicity with a brief piece on a formulaic expression in Spanish, interesting both because of its apparent illogicality and because English has the same illogicality. If *well* and *bien* are adverbs, what business do they have passing themselves off as predicate adjectives following noun phrase subjects? As will be seen, the speaker is pretending to speak for some higher intelligence.

The second piece looks at epistemic meanings wedging themselves into the system of verb inflections. The future and conditional tenses appear with the epistemic sense of *must*, a little more freely in Spanish than in English (except perhaps Hibernian English):

> Where's John? — He must be working (it must be that he is working).

¿Dónde está Juan? — Estará trabajando.

The speaker pretends to clairvoyance: John *will turn out* to have been working. An example of the same from an English novel:

> Southward above spiky pines you could see . . . the great castle of Argyll. . . . Beyond *would be* the estate office. (J.D. Carr, *The case of the constant suicides.*)

The final piece looks at an atempt to apply classical transformational grammar to an explanation of Spanish modal verbs. My critique takes a position similar to that of generative semantics, which was being promoted at the time by a number of MIT scholars who had become disenchanted with Chomsky's relegation of *meaning* to a last-stage operation instead of placing it at the center of things. I argued that underlying meaning determined the use of modals, that they lie along a gradient of meaning, and that there is no need, at bottom, to split them into root and epistemic. (The story of this rift among generative grammarians is entertainingly—and somewhat wistfully—told by Robin Lakoff in "The way we were"[1])]

* * *

THERE IS MORE to the difference between *bien* and *bueno* as modifiers than the formal difference of parts of speech, though the two kinds of differences are closely intertwined.[2] The same is true of English, where the competition between the personal-satisfaction "He fights *good*" and the social-satisfaction "He fights *well*" goes beyond the issue of grammatical correctness.

The same social implication is present in *ser bien* as opposed to *ser bueno* and *estar bien*. The construction merits attention because of its peculiarity of syntax (*ser* + adverb) and because some native speakers tend to reject the following type: "Muy cierto es todo lo que dice usted . . . , pero *es bien que diga* algo relativo al uso actual." The citation is

---

[1] "The way we were; or, The real actual truth about generative semantics: A memoir." To appear (1990) in *Journal of Semantics*.

[2] This article was first published in *Hispania* 35 (1952): 474-75.

from Alfredo F. Padrón, Comentarios a *Arcaísmos Españoles Usados en América* de Carlos Martínez Vigil (pamphlet, Havana 1941, p. 30), who comes vigorously to his own defense with a quote from Cejador (*Fraseología o Estilística Castellana,* I, 159), and the following from Keniston (*Syntax of Catilian Prose, the Sixteenth Century,* §29.314): *bien será que entremos.* In another recent example (Wilhelm Giese, *Boletín del Instituto Caro y Cuervo,* VI, 1, p. 119: "Al enumerar las diferentes lenguas románicas se debe mencionar el dalmata . . . , y *sería bien llamar* la atención hacia los elementos latinos en albanés") foreign influence seems ruled out, in that German does not admit *wohl* here.

English and French share this use of *well* for 'advisability,' an approval with overtones of duty. Compare "*It is well to realize* ['you had better realize'] that you are in the presence of a judge" (*good* in the same context is more inclusive), or "We waited, and *it was well that* we did, because they turned up after all" ['anything else would have been unwise'].

Only Cuervo (*Diccionario de Construcción y Régimen,* s.v. *bien*) seems to have properly heeded *ser bien* in this sense. He implies, by the location (*8b*) of his definition, a belief that *bien* here represents a transition toward the noun, and the definition, with its noun equivalents, implies the same: "Con el verbo *ser* se allega al valor que tendrían como predicados las expresiones *cosa oportuna, cosa conveniente.*"

The *Oxford Dictionary* of English, however, puts the equivalent *well* flatly among the adjectives (Definition 6). This seems more practical, in view of the Academia's 196*d* (from which, however, *bien* is missing). That we are here in a kind of limbo between adverb and adjective is borne out, on the adverb side, by the need of *ser bien* to qualify an action. Cuervo's eleven examples (two under período anteclásico) are all either with infinitives (three) or clauses (eight), and the English *it is well* can not, with its vicarious *it,* take any other kind of subject (I have elicited "*Sería bien* un castigo ejemplar," "*Sería bien* el empleo de un mayor esfuerzo," but even here the nouns denote actions). And it is borne out on the adjective side by the resemblance to sentence adverbs such as *seguramente, afortunadamente,* which necessarily convert to adjectives when they become predicative like *bien*: "*Seguramente* lo dirá" becomes "*Es seguro que* lo dirá." Like the sentence adverbs *bien* does not describe the action of the verb, but judges the action in relation to something else: compare "He died happily" (manner of dying) and "Happily he died" ('it was a good thing that . . .').

The Future and Conditional of Probability

THIS STUDY WAS undertaken to discover three things: (1) whether the future (F) and conditional (C) of probability (P) can be taught chiefly as a mode of certain verbs, especially the "have" and "be" verbs (*tener—haber* and *ser—estar*); (2) whether there is any correlation between particular FCP tenses and particular normal tenses, such as CP with imperfect rather than with preterit; (3) whether the dividing line between normal FC and FCP can be fixed with accuracy. More or less satisfactory answers to these, and incidentally to other, questions came to light.[1]

The examples were culled from twelve Spanish and Spanish American authors and one magazine. The *genres* include verse, prose poem, drama, formal and informal essay, short story, and novel,[2] and

[1] This article ws originally publlished in *Hispania* 29 (1946) 363-76.

[2] The works studied, and the initials used to refer to them in this article, are as follows: A = P. A. de Alarcón, *Novelas cortas*, 3ª serie, Madrid, Sucesores de Rivadeneyra, 1920; Am = *América*, Havana, 24: 1, 2, 3, 1945; B = V. Blasco Ibáñez, *Los cuatro jinetes del apocalipsis*, Valencia, Prometeo, 1919; CAM = Ciro Alegría, *El mundo es ancho y ajeno*, Santiago de Chile, Ercilla, 1941; CAS = Ciro Alegría, *La serpiente de oro*, Santiago de Chile, Nacimiento, 1936; FR = Fernando Robles, *La virgen de los cristeros*, Buenos Aires, Claridad; G = Rómulo Gallegos, *Doña Bárbara*, 5ª ed., Barcelona, 1929; JD = J. R. Jiménez, *Diario de un poeta recién casado*, Madrid, Calleja, 1917; JE = J. R. Jiménez, *Estío*, Madrid, Calleja, 1916; L = M. J. de Larra, *El pobrecito hablador* (in *Obras completas*, vol. I), Barcelona, Sopena; M = A. Machado, *Poesías completas*, Madrid, Residencia de Estudiantes, 1917; P = A. Palacio Valdés, *La hermana San Sulpicio*, Heath, 1925;

cover slightly more than three thousand pages of text.

1. FCP versus normal FC.

"Reliable" and "unreliable" FCP cases are carefully distinguished from each other and from positive normal FC. Any case which can be interpreted in two ways, as normal FC or as FCP, is classed as unreliable. There are almost a third as many unreliable examples as reliable ones (sixty-three against 209). This line is sharply drawn in order to make the study as objective as possible. Instances of unreliable examples are:

> "¡Señor, / cuánto te bendecirán (will bless, future; probably are blessing, present) los sembradores del pan!" (M, 200).
>
> "¡Y además, te repito que he de darte la felicidad de este mundo y la del otro! Para ello bastará (it will suffice; it probably does suffice) con lo siguiente: Yo, amigo mío, no soy la Omnipotencia." (A, 24).
>
> "A pesar de nuestros amores, Concha no se condenaría (would not condemn; probably did not condemn—English 'would not be condemning')." (V, 57).

The best index of reliability is the presence of some temporal expression which fixes the time of the verb in question. Among the 209 reliable examples there were thirty-four such expressions in the immediate environment of the verb, as follows:

ya	15
a estas horas	3
ahora	3
(References to a specific event: "el día de la	

Q = S. and J. Alvarez Quintero, *Los galeotes*, Madrid, Calleja, 1917; R = J. E. Rodó, *El que vendrá*, Montevideo, García, 1941; V = R. del Valle-Inclán, *Sonata de otoño*, Buenos Aires, Losada, 1940. Grateful acknowledgement goes to the readers, Miss Anna Berg, Mr. Lawrence Chávez, Mrs. R. B. Duncan, Miss D. M. Hawley, Miss Celestine Labat, Miss Patricia Luby, Mrs. Emma B. Meier, Mrs. E. J. Mohr, Miss Ulla Person, Mr. Gerald P. Sullivan, Miss Teresa Vietti, Miss Dorothy M. Wilson, and Miss Mae E. Wilson.

creación," "durante su vida," "en tu gloriosa carrera") 3
en este momento 2
a la sazón 2
todavía 2
hoy 1
esta vez 1
hacer (time idiom) 1
un día 1

Besides these, there were seven instances of modification of the verb in question by an adverbial clause containing a verb in normal tense which determined the time, and eight instances of coordination with an adjoining verb in normal tense having this same determining effect. Elsewhere, less specific elements in the context fixed the time. *Ya*, though the most frequently-used adverb, is the least dependable, for it is used with both FP and normal F: "Ya vendrán" can signify 'They are probably on their way already' or 'They will come in due time'; in M, 184 we see this: 'Ya verdearán de chopos las márgenes del río . . . /Ya los rebaños blancos . . . hacia los altos prados conducirá el pastor." We cannot tell for certain whether this is something imagined to be probably happening now, or expected to happen soon in the future.

Correlation of reliability and tense. Of the sixty-three unreliable examples, sixty-one are simple FC (fifty-four simple F and seven simple C), only two are in the corresponding perfect tenses (two F perfect and no C perfect), and none are progressive.[3] Of the 209 reliable examples, 150 are simple FC (113 simple F and thirty-seven simple C), fifty-four, or more than a fourth, are in the perfect tenses (forty-five F perfect and nine C perfect), and five are progressive (three F progressive and two C progressive). It follows that the compound tenses—or, if the examples of progressive are deemed insufficient, at least the perfect tenses—are more unambiguous than other P forms.

Correlation of reliability and particular verbs. Certain verbs turned

[3] "Progressive" here means *estar* plus the gerundio. Only one example with another auxiliary turned up: "habrán ido llegando," (M, 194).

out to have a much higher percentage of unreliable examples than others. In order to attempt an explanation of this fact, we may tabulate the ten verbs occurring five or more times:

		Occurrences		Percentages	
Verb	Total	Reliable	Unreliable	Reliable	Unreliable
ser[4]	64	53	11	83	17
tener	22	20	2	91	9
haber[5]	17	11	6	65	35
saber	12	10	2	83	17
hacer	9	9	0	100	0
estar[6]	8	7	1	87.5	12.5
querer	7	3	4	43	57
ir	6	2	4	33	67
poder	6	2	4	33	67
decir	5	5	0	100	0

The high percentages of unreliable cases unfortunately occur in the lowest frequencies, which makes it difficult to speak with assurance; but nevertheless some explanation can be offered where the discrepancies are widest. Since unreliable examples represent only twenty-three per cent of the total, the figures fifty-seven, sixty-seven, and sixty-seven, for *querer, ir,* and *poder* respectively, are suggestive.

Querer and *poder* are distinguished by the fact (which they share with *haber,* also having a large number of unreliable cases) of not relating, as a rule, to overt action, which blurs their reference to time. So when Larra writes (L, 169), "No habiendo usted de reunir, pues, honra y provecho, querrá una u otra," he may be taken to mean 'you will want' when the time comes or when you face the problem, or 'you perhaps do want' now, whether for present or future use. And when he writes (L, 31), "De que podrás inferir, Andrés, cuán dañoso

[4] None in passive voice, of which no examples were found.
[5] Uses as auxiliary of perfect tenses not counted here.
[6] Uses as auxiliary of progressive tenses not counted here.

es el saber," he may mean a future inference or a possible present one.

Ir and its companion *venir* (all three of whose examples are unreliable) are distinguished by the fact that they may stress either movement ("Venían, iban a pie") or arrival and departure ("Vino, vamos, se fué a las dos"). It is this double meaning of the words, not any peculiarity of their reference to time, which causes them to be unreliable. Thus when Alegría writes (CAM, 108), "Me voy. Vendrán muchos a querer pegarme," he may mean 'Many are probably on their way' or 'Many will presently be here.' Similarly Machado's (M, 225) "Cantad conmigo en coro: Saber, nada sabemos, / de arcano mar vinimos, a ignota mar iremos" may signify 'we shall some day depart for or reach' or 'We are probably on our way.'

Other examples result from the ambiguity of the tenses. Since the simple present often substitutes for the future, as in "Van mañana" ('They are going tomorrow'), the superimposition of a future form ("Irán mañana"—'They are probably going tomorrow') could be for probability, not necessarily for futurity.

Still others result from the circumstances which—along with the fact that all future involves prediction and hence probability—doubtless gave rise to FCP in the first place. When, in English, we say, "I can't tell you, but my mother will know," we mean "will turn out to know when we ask her,' though of course it is understood that she has the information now. Or, when a current magazine writes of a military column approaching a desert oasis, "Nowadays you can't tell whether it will be a water-hole or an artillery battery," the meaning is 'will turn out to be,' though whatever it is, it is now. Rodó's (R, 172) "Una justificación que ninguna estética... será osada a negarle" signifies 'will turn out to be,' hence either 'will be in the future' or 'probably is now.'

Some derive from the kind of imagery in which the distinction does not matter, or in which indistinctness is perhaps deliberately sought. We should expect this to be true occasionally of verse; and, in fact, Machado offers us (M, 184 and 256-257) two extended passages in which repeated examples of F might be considered either way.

Finally, some result from the similarity, in metaphorical use, between a C which implies a suppressed *if* and a C which is merely past future. In Am, 28, "No pude menos que preguntarme si las muchachas americanas serían capaces de trabajar bajo semejantes condiciones," the writer may imply 'if put to the test,' whence the C is normal; or the statement may be indirect discourse for "Me pregunté: '¿Serán capaces, etc.?"' In this dual possibility we see that a normal C when it correlates with *if* does not depend any more upon real time than does CP: the same C tenses would be used for the past-oriented "I wondered then whether they *would be* capable if they had to" as for the present-oriented "I wonder now whether they *would be* capable if they had to"—and both are the same as that of 'I wondered whether *they were possibly* capable," *were* by nature, hence timeless. Another way of matching normal C and CP is that "Lo haría Juan" can mean, normally, 'John is the sort of person who would do it' (ultimately derived from some elliptical condition such as 'John would do it if it were put to him'), which is close akin to the CP meaning, 'John probably did it.'

2. *Direct combination with other speculative devices.*

In order to find soemthing about the immediate context that involves FCP, we may tabulate the other devices that are used with it and that contribute to the general notion of P. I do not count general context (such as presence of other FCP nearby, a *tal vez* or other expression in an adjoining clause, etc.) but only a device within the clause whose verb is the FCP in question.

In the following table, questions are counted as a speculative device. Exclamations are not counted *per se*, but are counted as questions when they really ask. If a speculative expression occurs with the FCP in a question, it is counted under that expression, not as a question:

Combined with questions (57 direct, 3 indirect)	60
si (mostly questions and exclamations)	12
phrases denoting uncertain identity (*algún* and *algo*, 4; *qué*, exclamation, 1; *en el mundo*, 1; *sabe Dios lo que*, 1; *Dios sabe dónde*, 1)	8
phrases denoting uncertain quantity (*unos*—all in the phrase "tendría unos... años," 3; *como* 'approximately,' 2; *las veces que*, 1; *cuántos*, exclamation, 1; *cuatro o cinco*, 1)	8

phrases denoting uncertain likelihood (*tal vez,* 2; *acaso,* 2; *quizás,* 1; *probablemente,* 1; *¿no es verdad?* following the statement, 1) 7

phrases with half-positive literal meaning (*por supuesto,* 1; *presumiendo que,* 1; *indudablemente,* 1) 3

It is apparent from the last item in the table that, like the English *I'm sure,* some Spanish expressions of certainty are used to suggest uncertainty.

3. Type of discourse.

With the current emphasis on the spoken language, it is interesting to know what proportion of reliable FCP are in quotations. The examples are counted in two ways:

I. There are 122 statements, fifty-four questions, and nineteen exclamations, punctuation being used as a basis for this classification.

II. There are 118 examples in *direct discourse,* ten in *quotative indirect discourse* (e.g., "El instinto le hizo ir ... hasta la 'rue de la Pompe' ... ¿Qué haría su hijo? ... De seguro que continuaba su vida alegre . . . ," B, 205), and sixty-seven in *non-quotative indirect discourse* (e.g., "No era, como muchos habrían quizás imaginado, una mujer vieja," A, 56, the author recording his own opinion). The editorial *I* is not counted as direct, nor are the fanciful conversations in Machado so counted; this weights the scales in favor of non-quotative discourse, since only those utterances supposed to have been made outside the covers of the book and repeated in the book, are counted as direct.

4. Correlation of verbs and tenses.

The seven verbs occurring five or more times in reliable examples divide among the tenses as follows:

	Simple F	F progressive	Simple C	C progressive	F perfect	C perfect	Total
ser	39	0	11	0	4	0	54
tener	11	0	9	0	1	0	21
haber[7]	11	0	0	0	0	0	11
saber	10	0	0	0	0	0	10
hacer	5	0	3	0	1	1	10
estar[6]	7	0	1	0	0	0	8
decir	1	0	0	0	4	0	5
all others	29	3	13	2	35	8	90

The fact that stands out most boldly here is the heavy representation of "all others" in the perfect tenses, and the relatively light representation of the most frequent verbs in the perfect tenses. The correlation is obviously one of meaning. "All others" includes virtually all the verbs of action. And if we look at the meanings of the most frequent verbs, we find that *hacer* and *decir*, both verbs of action, are the only ones a large proportion of whose examples are in the perfect tenses. Seeking further, we find that two of the three simple C examples of *hacer* are in the time idiom (e.g., P, 84, "Haría ya una hora"), which is non-action, raising still higher the proportion of properly ACTION meanings of *hacer* that are encountered only in the perfect tenses; we also find that two of the four examples of *ser* in the perfect tenses are in the action idiom *ser de*, 'to become of' (Q, 40, "¿ Qué habría sido de Fulano, aquel que se fué a América?"). From the "all others" list we pick the verbs *acordar, consistir, creer, dudar, importar*, and *mediar* as those least likely to suggest action in any context; on investigation we find them all, with the exception of *mediar*, occurring in simple FC (and *mediar* has fooled us by being used in an action sense: A, 264, "Marzo habrá mediado ya"—'to intervene'). We infer that if the non-action verbs, and the non-action uses of potentially action verbs, were eliminated from the "all others" list, the proportion of perfect tenses would be higher still.

---

[7] Perfect and auxiliary uses are not counted.

The evident conclusion is that action in past time, as opposed to duration in past time, has most of its P representation in the future perfect tense. And since Spanish in its normal tenses splits the past into imperfect and preterit, the question immediately arises whether all or some of the F perfect of P may not correspond to one rather than the other of these two normal tenses. We naturally infer a correspondence of the F perfect with the preterit rather than with the imperfect, knowing the kinship, both historical and in current usage, between the present perfect and the preterit. This relationship, with what it implies for meaning, will be developed in the next section.

5. *Correlation of FCP and time-reference.*

English distinguishes with a high degree of consistency between the progressive tenses emphasizing "nowness" and "thenness" ("John is eating," "John was eating") and other tenses lacking this emphasis ("John eats, ate, used to eat," etc.). Spanish in turn distinguishes with a like degree of consistency between an indefinite (i.e., uncircumscribed) past and a definite (i.e., circumscribed) past ("Juan comía" *vs.* "Juan comió"). Does FCP carry out these distinctions?

Before making the comparison we should be cautioned that neither language is absolutely consistent in its specialty. "Here comes John" emphasizes nowness, but is not progressive; with certain verbs the distinction is made only in special senses: "John is having (undergoing) an attack"; "John is being (acting) very foolish." In "Fué Juan quien lo dijo," *fué* assumes the tense of *dijo,* and might as well be *era.* These exceptions are not frequent enough, however, to vitiate the comparison.

Since we are concerned with two sets of tenses, normal and P, it will be convenient to give labels to those features of time-reference which are common to both sets, rather than to attempt to handle the features by means of the names of the tenses. Let us therefore use the term *going-on* for the reference to time that is normally represented by the English and Spanish progressive tenses, the term *extended* for the reference to time that is normally represented by the English simple present and the non-progressive uses of the Spanish imperfect, and the term *narrative* for the reference to time that is normally represented by the Spanish preterit. Features other than time (the customary "used to," the interrogative "did you?," the persistence-of-effects "ha dicho," etc.), are disregarded. As with all questions of semantics, the distinctions are subtle, and we shall simply have to do the best we can.

I. The present.

1. *The extended present* overspreads both past and future. It is the normal use of the English simple present tense: "John eats"—yesterday and tomorrow as well as now. In Spanish it is also the simple present tense, though this tense has in Spanish a going-on reference as well. Of the 113 reliable instances of simple FP, ninety-seven unquestionably belong here. This includes, in the nature of their meaning, all examples of *ser* and *haber*.[8] Example: (FR, 174) "¿Conque tan amigo del Gobierno y no tiene armas? ¡Las tendrá muy escondidas!"

2. *The going-on present*. This is the Spanish present progressive and the English present progressive when present in time-reference (the future "He is coming tomorrow" is excluded). It may also be the Spanish (and rarely the English) simple present. In the P usage we have the corresponding simple F and the F progressive.

The important question here is to determine whether the proportion of simple, used as going-on present, versus progressive, remains the same in FCP as in the normal tenses. Since the simple present is one of the eliminated constructions in the Keniston list, no statistics are available on the relative frequency of simple present versus present progressive in NORMAL going-on use. The very fact that it is eliminated, however, and that the frequency of the progressive IN ALL TENSES (including FCP) is not unusually high (304—almost exactly the same as for FP), argues a much smaller figure for present progressive and hence a disproportionately small number of present progressives as compared with simple presents in going-on use.

The comparison between simple FP and F progressive of P therefore becomes significant, for of the reliable cases there belong here definitely only seven examples of simple FP as compared with four of F progressive of P in going-on use. In addition, there are nine simple FP that might be considered as either extended or going-on—giving a

[8] Perfect and progressive auxiliary uses are not counted.

maximum of sixteen versus four and a minimum of seven versus four. Either figure seems weighted more heavily in favor of the progressive tense as a sign of going-on time-reference than one would find in the normal tenses. Whether this is because where going-on present is concerned we tend in Spanish FP to do what we would do in English normal present, i.e., favor the progressive, or whether the apparent disproportion is rather due to the fact that in conversation—FCP being primarily a quotative device, as we have seen—the speaker of Spanish would always favor the progressive more than the literature-based Keniston figures would lead us to believe, in both normal and FCP tenses, I cannot say.

Examples: (1) definitely going-on simple FP: (A, 262) "¡Cuántos brillantes salones se abrirán en este momento . . . !"; (2) possibly going-on or possibly extended: (L, 140) "¿Si aludirá ('is his reference to' or 'is he alluding to') a que se casó en agosto?"; (3) progressive: (CAS, 38) "Array, questarán pensando los cristianos."

3. *The narrative present* or historical present is exemplified by "He takes the medicine, drops into a chair, and falls into a dead faint." No examples of a corresponding FP were turned up.[9]

II. The past.

1. *The extended past* is the simple past in English (along with the habitual and other non-time variants) and the simple imperfect in Spanish. Its P analog is the simple C: (G, 49) "La mayor, Genoveva, no pasaría de diecisiete años."

2. *The going-on past*, as with the present, is shared in Spanish by simple imperfect and imperfect progressive, with corresponding simple CP and C progressive of P. Examples: (B, 41) "De seguro que había salido, adivinando una visita próxima. . . . Andaría por las calles en busca de noticias"; (P, 31) "¡Oh diablo! ¿Estaría galanteando a la hermana San Sulpicio?"

A comparison of the relative frequency of simple and progressive

[9] Kany (*American Spanish Syntax*, 1945, 15) points out the narrative future, "Voy a echar una mirada." English similarly makes use of the auxiliary *take*: "I'm going to take a look, a swim, a turn around the block," etc.

tenses in going-on past use is impossible because only one C progressive turned up (the last example quoted). Even with abundant examples the comparison would be difficult, since CP blankets the whole past—there are, as we shall see, instances of CP for normal preterit—and even intrudes upon the present.

3. *The narrative past* comprises the normal Spanish preterit and present perfect. The manner of its transposition into P tenses affords the most interesting comparison between those tenses and normal tenses.

Of the thirty-seven reliable CP, only five appear at all likely as standing for preterit. Three occur in one passage (A, 271):

> "¡Salve, cabello luminoso, desprendido de la dorada frente del sol!
> "¡Ya es de día!
> "Así despertaría el mundo el día de la creación.
> "Así saldría la creación de las tinieblas del caos.
> "Así renacería la especie humana cuando volvió la paloma al arca de Noé."

The fourth and fifth are (A, 294, A, 242):

> "¿Qué habrá sido de Alonso? ¿Se suicidaría?"
> "—Ese abogado debió de enviar el manuscrito a un español de Ceuta....
> "—¡Toma! ¡Ya caigo! Se lo enviaría a un sobrino que tiene de músico en aquella catedral."

It was suggested in section 4 that the large number of F perfect indicates that this tense is the P analogue of the preterit. The fact that there are only five instances of CP standing for preterit confirms this view. We must therefore try to determine (1) whether there is something about the relationship between the preterit and the present perfect which would tend to make a speaker prefer the latter as the point from which to jump into a P tense (hence into F perfect); and (2) under what conditions the CP is preferred to the F perfect of P as a narrative past.

(1) The present perfect has two main uses. The first is as a substitute for the F perfect: "Luego que lo haya leído, llámeme." Since this type of construction would have to be subjunctive, with no possibility of FP, we may put it aside.

The second is to show persistence of effects. In "They've caught him" we imply that he is still in their hands. In "They caught him" we imply nothing more than the action. In "Have they caught him?" we imply a continued search or a continued interest in the search. The action *per se* is the same in preterit and present perfect,[10] and Spanish, as we know, makes heavier use of the "persistence of effects" implication than English does, i.e., uses the perfect where English would not; in the following example we see a F perfect of P correlated with a normal present perfect, for neither of which would English use a perfect tense:

"Llegué a casa, después de caminar entre calles algún tiempo, a la hora precisa de comer. Mi diminuta huéspeda me salió al encuentro y me abocó con familiaridad . . . .
—Se *habrá* usted *perdido,* por supuesto.
—Alguna vez; pero *he preguntado* y fuí saliendo adelante." (P. 65).

Now since the central idea of P is that of something "unsettled," and since so long as it is unsettled its effects persist vividly in the mind of the speaker, the tense of persistent effects, the perfect, is well suited to express a process that is presumably finished but cannot be completely dismissed; other things being equal, "I suppose he's found them" implies more doubt, more of the kind of dwelling upon the idea that is characteristic of P, than does "I suppose he found them."
So we are not surprised that while thirty-one of the forty-five reliable examples of F perfect of P CAN be translated by the preterit, most of them seem more natural as present perfect:

"Sí; pero un sabio de la reputación de don Timoteo habrá publicado ('probably published'; more likely as 'has probably published') además obras de fondo." (L, 187.)
"Las casitas del poblacho le hacen señas con sus fogones trémulos.

[10]Where the verb itself is one of a continuing state, e.g., "¿Cuánto tiempo ha esperado usted?," where the waiting may continue, the process itself may go on into the present; but that is a function of the meaning of the particular verb, not specifically a function of the perfect tense.

También de la capilla sale un tenue resplandor. Algún devoto habrá prendido (more likely as 'has probably') ceras en el ara." (CA, 33).

"—Vino a... pedirme permiso para buscar sus mulas en las ranchería ....'

"Y se lo habrás dado, ¿verdad? ('have given' or 'gave')

"—Claro que sí...." (FR, 115-116).

Context forces the remaining fourteen to be perfect:

"Es decir, que marzo habrá mediado ya y que el sol lucirá en el horizonte." (A, 264).

"¡Jesús, qué chica! Parecía hecho de rabos de lagartijas. Aun hoy habrá usted advertido que su carácter es bastante distinto del de su prima." (P, 33).

It is obvious that while preterits come over to P as F perfects, it is impossible to disentangle them from verbs which may have been present perfects to begin with.

(2) The C seems to be preferred to F perfect of P in narrative use when there is a greater suggestion of vagueness. Thus while for "Where can the book be?"—"You probably left it at home" we should most likely say "¿Dónde estará el libro?"—"Lo habrá dejado en su casa," if the second part is made into a question, e.g., "Where can the book be? Did you perhaps leave it at home?" we might readily use "¿Dónde estará el libro? ¿Lo dejaría en su casa?"[11] That is, for the question, where the speaker is even more hesitant than for the statement, the C fits.

The ordinary, fairly positive interpretation of narrative past, then, calls for the F perfect; the more hesitant, or imaginary, interpretation calls for C. The example (A, 294) "¿Qué habrá sido de Alonso? ¿Se suicidaría?" shows the two in contrast. *Habrá sido* involves little guesswork, for something had to become of him; *se suicidaría*, however, is only one of many calamities that might have befallen him, and is therefore more imaginary. In the example (A, 242) where *debió de enviar* contrasts with *enviaría*, the second speaker is hazarding a guess which

---

[11] Example suggested by Srta. Carmen Roldán.

receives only the answer "Puede ser." This hesitant or imaginary use of CP may even invade the territory of FP, as in "¿Dónde está mi libro? ¿Estaría en el otro cuarto?"[12] Note that English has an identical construction. "¿Estará en el otro cuarto?" would be less hesitant.

4. No comment on the C perfect of P is necessary, as it corresponds to the normal past perfect. Example: (B, 82) "Pensando con delectación en que las dos chinas habrían atropellado la dignidad de la cocinera francesa."

6. *FCP a "sentence adverb."*

Though in form, only the VERB undergoes a change for FCP, actually FCP may modify smaller or larger units in the utterance. In (B, 137) "A estas horas gritarán de entusiasmo," the implication is 'probably-shouting,' But in (Q, 95) "¿Qué hará que no viene?" the implication is not *probably-doing,* since we are always doing something, but *probably-what*—the identity of the *qué* is in doubt, and the sentence means "¿Qué será lo que hace?"

7. *Idiosyncrasies.*

FCP is a construction that can be eschewed, since there are a number of substitutes for it. This fact leaves it free to appear or not appear according to the taste of the writer or speaker, and consequently makes it something of a stylistic device. It is therefore bound to vary widely from one author to another, both in its total frequency and in its frequency as applied to particular verbs or situations. Rodó is fond of *será,* and of the FP in general in the sense of 'must'—almost as a synonym of *haber de.* Larra likes *sabrá.* Machado uses no CP. The total frequencies, expressed in percentages of the number of pages on which FCP occurs, are as follows:

[12] Example suggested by Sr. Rómulo Herrera.

Author and Book	Total pages	Cases[13]	Percent
A	322	47	14.6
Am	26	2	7.7
B	250	16	6.4
CAM and CAS	433	21	4.85
FR	300	5	1.67
G	225	22	9.78
JD and JE	200	2	1
L	200	38	19
M	268	14	5.22
P	150	7	4.67
Q	260	17	6.54
R	201	12	5.97
V	189	6	3.17

8. Summary and conclusions.

1. The FCP, especially in the simple tenses, is often ambiguous. Since it is also a construction that can be avoided for all practical purposes, it is probably wrong to present it to students as something to be used at will.

2. If auxiliary and non-auxiliary uses are counted together, the four verbs showing the highest frequency are the *be* and *have* verbs *ser, estar, haber,* and *tener,* with over twice as many examples as all others combined. One possible method, then, would be to teach FCP as a mode of these verbs.

3. The FCP occurs almost twice as often in quotative as in non-quotative discourse. It is therefore primarily a device of the spoken language, and should be given due emphasis by those who place the spoken language first.

---

[13] Since each author was studied by a different reader, individual differences, shift of criteria in judging material to be discarded, etc., among the readers would make this table unsafe to use as a precise indication of the frequency of a given author. I vouch for the accuracy of M, however, and since five figures are substantially higher than that of M, the general conclusion, that of wide individual variation, is not affected.

4. With certain exceptions that need not be stressed for purposes of teaching, the correspondence of FCP with normal tenses may be tabulated as follows:

Normal	*P*
Simple present extended	Simple future
Simple present going-on	Simple future or future progressive
Present progressive	Future progressive
Imperfect (extended and going-on)	Simple conditional
Imperfect progressive	Conditional progressive
Preterit	Future perfect
Present perfect	Future perfect
Past perfect	Conditional perfect

Modes of Modality in Spanish and English

DOES SPANISH HAVE modal auxiliary verbs? Traditional grammars have always recognized a class of modals, the two most typical being *poder* and *deber*, but have lacked explicit ways to demonstrate its existence.[1] Stockwell, Bowen, and Martin, in their *Grammatical Structures of English and Spanish*,[2] questioned whether modals were needed, given the resemblance between modals and main verbs: Spanish modals are fully inflected and take infinitive objects like many main verbs (*Puedo salir, Quiero salir*).

But a doubt had already been raised about this solution by E. L. Blansitt (*The Verb Phrase in Spanish: Classes and Relations*, Univ. of Texas diss., 1963), who claimed that *querer*, but not *poder* nor *deber*, could enter into constructions like *Lo que quiero es trabajar*. *?Lo que puedo (debo) es trabajar*.—this is to say, that the object of *querer* can be "theme-predicated" or produce a "pseudo-cleft" sentence while that of *poder* and *deber* cannot.

The most obvious candidate now for explicating the structure of the supposed auxiliaries is transformational-generative grammar. Philip W. Klein has undertaken the job, and despite the apparent modesty of the auspices (a master's thesis at the Univ. of Washington), he has acquitted himself handsomely. His *Modal Auxiliaries in Spanish*[3]

---

[1] This article was first published in *Romance Philology* 23 (1970): 572-80.

[2] Robert P. Stockwell, J. Donald Bowen, and John W. Martin, *The Grammatical Structures of English and Spanish* (Chicago, 1965), p. 165.

[3] Studies in Linguistics and Language Learning, IV. Seattle: University of Washington, 1968.

is an up-to-date transformational treatment which benefits from recent research by Rosenbaum, McCawley, Lakoff, and Ross, and shows better than any previous study the underlying structure of *poder* and *deber*.

The work has two failings, which I will get around to analyzing after I have sketched his treatment. The first is not K.'s fault. It is the failure of transformational grammar in its current form to capture a relatedness in syntax that cannot be quantified, i.e., cannot be expressed in terms of precise items and precise processes. I intend to propose a partial solution to this. The other is the inference that K. apparently intends to be drawn, namely that Stockwell et al. were right in their decision to merge the modals with "verbs": "They are simply verbs which happen to carry lexical meanings that overlap with the meanings of English modals." This invites our considering what "being a modal" signifies. In the first place, traditional grammar did not deny the modals the status of verbs—they were referred to as *modal verbs*, which can only mean verbs sharing some peculiarity not shared by other verbs. It is only with recent formal grammars that we find the practice of classing elements of the predicate phrase into "verbs" and "modals," among other things—it is not something that should be read back into the traditional terminology. In the second place, K., by showing exactly how modals differ from other verbs in their underlying grammar, has simply defined the class of modal verbs, in the same way that the class of transitive verbs is defined in terms of how they fit into the underlying structure in relation to complement noun phrases. What K. has shown is that it is unnecessary to assume a syntactic FEATURE + M—that *poder* and *deber* can be handled as ordinary verbs, restricted by rules already needed in other parts of the grammar. By eliminating the feature, he may give the impression that he has eliminated the need to recognize the class. But again, the feature from the standpoint of traditional grammar is a straw man:[4] Classes depend on criteria, not features. There is a close analogy in the transformational treatment of English questions. It has long assumed

---

[4] K.'s assertion (28) that I had the "idea of a grammar that postulates a category [+ M]" attributes the straw man to me. It is true that I postulated a class, but the feature concept is his.

a constituent Q, responsible for triggering the transformations that turn an underlying structure into a surface question. Recently A. Koutsoudas has claimed that wh- questions can be merged with commands, thus eliminating, at least from that kind of question, the need for the Q constituent.[5] But this does not abolish the class of wh-questions, which is now simply defined in a different way. We shall also need to continue to talk about modals in Spanish. I hope to show later that unless this is true, we cannot talk about modals in English either. For the moment, it is enough to repeat that the Stockwell team was wrong in denying the modals any special status.

But these considerations are not the meat of K.'s study. Its merit is in clarifying what a modal is. The treatment is roughly as follows:

1. *Poder* (to simplify, this verb will stand for its class) has an underlying structure similar to that of *querer* except that in place of a noun-phrase complement it takes a verb-phrase complement directly. This can be shown by looking at the phrase marker for *Yo quiero invitar a Juan:*

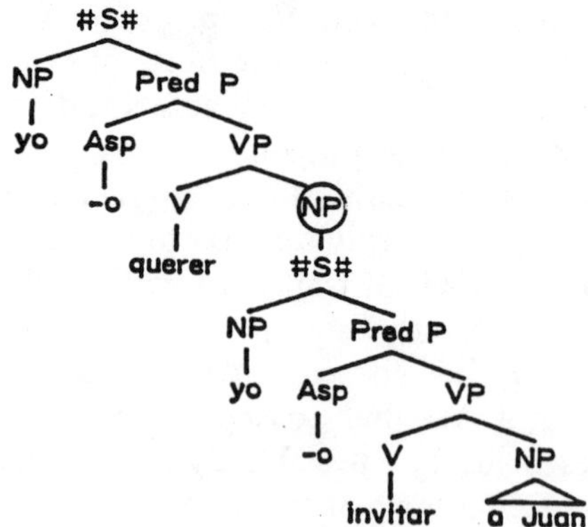

The marker for *poder* would differ in that the circled NP would be eliminated. This expresses the assumption that while *Lo que yo quiero es invitar a Juan* is grammatical, ?*Lo que yo puedo es invitar a Juan* is not—the object of *poder* is not a noun phrase and cannot be fronted like a noun phrase.

[5] "On wh- words in English," *J L*, IV (1968), 271-273.

My comment on this point only strengthens K.'s argument, for it develops that his restriction is not necessary and the underlying structure for *poder* and *deber* can be written exactly as for *querer*. It embarrasses me to be the one to call attention to this, since I appear to have been the conduit through which Blansitt's supposed restriction found its way into K.'s grammar. The fact is that sentences with *poder* and *deber* can be pseudo-cleft, not, apparently, with complete freedom nor to the satisfaction of every native speaker of Spanish, but readily enough. I heard the following in a spontaneous conversation: *Lo que debemos es continuar*,[6] and these have been accepted (in fact, insisted upon) as normal by Colombian and Castilian speakers: *Lo que podemos es esperar hasta mañana, Lo que tengo es que trabajar*. Though at least some Spanish American speakers reject it (because *haber de* in any position is not colloquial for them?), the example *De lo que hemos es de continuar* was accepted as normal by my *madrileño* informant.

2. *Poder* will be marked in the lexicon with the same feature that distinguishes *tender a* from *insistir. Tender a* occurs only in constructions that have the same subject for the main sentence and for the embedded sentence: *Él tendió a criticar a Juan*, not **Él tendió a que yo criticara a Juan. Insistir en* allows either possibility: *Él insistió en criticar a Juan, Él insistió en que yo criticara a Juan*. Since the feature is already required for these cases, nothing further needs to be assumed to account for *Yo puedo trabajar, *Yo puedo que usted trabaje; Yo quiero trabajar, Yo quiero que usted trabaje.*

3. There are actually two verbs *poder*: *poder*$_1$ 'possibility' and *poder*$_2$ 'ability'. The argument up to this point has concerned *poder*$_2$. *Poder*$_1$ is found in sentences like *Puede llover, Juan puede invitar a Pedro* in the sense 'John may (it may be that John will) invite Peter', etc. The underlying phrase marker for *poder*$_1$ is

[6] Prof. Juan Marichal, 30 Nov. 1964.

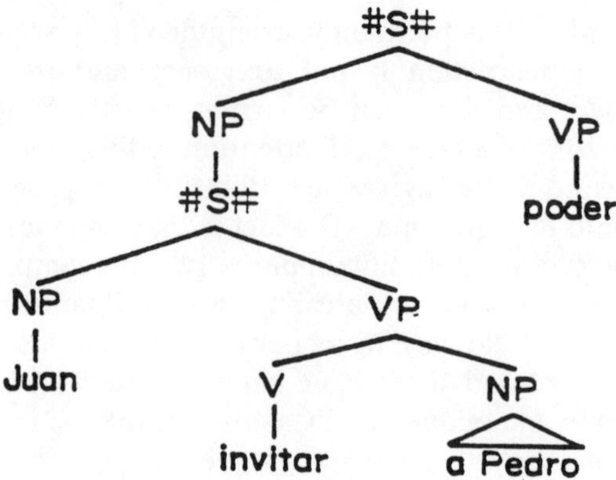

—'John's inviting Peter is-possible'. This is no fanciful construct, for it has to be assumed for a number of other verbs, e.g. *parecer*. It is unnecessary to go into the transformations which produce the surface structure *Juan puede invitar a Pedro.*

At this point K. weakens his argument somewhat by introducing a *poder*$_3$, as in *Puedo invitar a Juan* not in the sense of *poder*$_1$, 'It is possible that I may invite Juan', nor that of *poder*$_2$, 'I am capable of inviting Juan', but in that of 'Someone permits me to invite Juan'. Since *deber* divides only into a *deber*$_1$ and *deber*$_2$, it would improve matters if the parallel could be maintained. I believe that his mistake was to analyze the paraphrases or translations rather than the meaning of the Spanish sentence. The distinction is that between *Mama, can I go out and play?*, where Mama, if she is on her toes, will correct the *can* to *may*, and *I can lift the weight*, where my inner capacity is referred to. But if we are to have a poder$_3$ on the strength of the 'permission' meaning, we shall need a *poder*$_4$ on the strength of examples like *No puedo levantar el peso.—¿Por qué?—Porque no lo puedo alcanzar.*, in which it is not one's ability to lift the weight that is referred to but the interference with applying the ability. At bottom besides *poder*$_1$ there is only *poder*$_2$ meaning 'nihil obstat'—it makes no difference whether the absent obstruction be one's inner weaknesses, some intervening obstacle, or the moral or physical opposition of another human being. These differences are supplied by the context. (I shall try to show later that even the *poder*$_1$—*poder*$_2$ split is superfluous.) Transformational grammar is sometimes guilty of over-structuring on the basis of unnecessary semantic splits.[7]

K.'s treatment makes it possible to handle a number of characteristics of *poder, deber*, etc. that apparently would be difficult to rationalize if they were regarded as modals. First, negation. Both *No puedo hablar* and *Puedo no hablar* are possible, and they differ in meaning. If *poder* is a modal, there is no embedded sentence, and without an embedded sentence the negation should affect both examples in the same way. Yet clearly in *Puedo no hablar* something negative is judged to be affirmatively possible. If *poder* is not a modal, there are two sentences, and the negation can be arranged accordingly, including *No puedo no hablar*. Second, multiple occurrence. If a modal is allowed in the Aux (the constituent of the predicate phrase which also contains tense and aspect), it presumably can be taken only once: cf. *He may do it* and *He can do it*, but not **He may can do it*. But Spanish has no problem with this multiplication: *He de haber debido poder cantar*. Viewed not as multiple modals but as multiple embeddings, the problem disappears.

Has K.'s sword two edges—has he, after cutting the jugular of Spanish modals, inadvertently severed that of English modals too? The importance of the question arises from the fact that in the context of Stockwell-Bowen-Martin the notion of "modal" derives from English in the first place: For comparative purposes, it is assumed that English has modals. Either English must escape K.'s treatment or, if we are to continue talking about modals, they must be defined for both languages in the less rigorous terms that I proposed at the outset.

Consider first negation. Both of the following are acceptable: *How can I avoid that party?—You could just stay away./ How can I avoid that party?—You could just not show up.* As the latter does not mean the same as *You couldn't show up*, the argument for *can, could* as main verbs

---

[7] If it is to be contended that paraphrases must have the same deep structure because all things meaning the same must be the same at bottom, and therefore, since there are distinct paraphrases for the three *poder*'s, the three exist, then I would again insist on a fourth *poder* on the basis of the paraphrase *No se me impide que levante el peso* for *Puedo levantar el peso* in the sense that it is within reach or that I am not otherwise being restrained by physical circumstances.

applies in English as in Spanish. If it is argued that somehow the contraction of the negative points to two verbs, *can, could*$_1$ and *can, could*$_2$, only one of which is a main verb, then we could cite emphatic forms which do not contract but which, except for emphasis, mean the same as contracted ones: *I múst nót fáil! I mustn't fail.* All we can say is that if the negation belongs to the embedded sentence, it will not contract; if it belongs to the main sentence, it may or may not.

Second, multiple occurrence. The existence of *might could* in the dialects proves that English does allow more than one so-called modal at a time. Furthermore, we need to take a wider look at what other verbs should be included along with *can, may,* etc., in the class of modals, if there is such a class. Is *have to* in the same class as Sp. *poder*? If it is not, we are in trouble trying to explain *Smith simply has to own this property! I saw the record in the Recorder's Office!/ This property simply has to be owned by Smith! I saw the record,* etc., where *have to* analogizes with *poder*$_1$ and *deber*$_1$: the underlying structure is the same for both active and passive, 'It simply has to be that Smith owns', etc., unlike what happens with *Smith desired to own the property, *The property desired to be owned by Smith.* If *have to* is admitted to the class, then there are many possibilities of multiple occurrence: *We might have to wait. Nobody need have to feel concerned. Could anybody ever have to be so careful?* The evidence for *had ought* in *He had ought to do it.* is also dialectal, but in tag questions it is closer to the standard: *He ought to do it, had he?* In short, the class of verbs represented by *can* and *ought* has essentially the same underlying syntax as *poder* and *deber*. Where the English and Spanish verbs do differ is in the impossibility of the pseudo-cleft sentence in English: **What I can (should, may, etc.) is write.*[8] But this is only one score, and did not prevent John R. Ross from sustaining what the title of his unpublished paper announced: "Auxiliaries as Main Verbs" (16 May 1967). K. of course is not to be accused of having claimed the opposite. The point is simply that Spanish is in no important way different from English—the oddities of contraction with the negative and inversion with questions are low-

[8] I disregard the type *What I can't do is compose; what I can is write,* where the ellipsis is based on a sentence that is already pseudo-cleft.

level rules.[9]

I come now to the question of how well the transformational treatment expounds the facts about verbs of the *poder, deber* class.

First, it brings out starkly, and by that fact intelligibly, the peculiar means by which impersonal verbs are personalized. This has been a historical process as well as a descriptive fact: OSp. *parecer* exhibited no such personalization as we see in *Juan parece tener el dinero* which "really means" not that John seems anything but that IT seems that John has the money.[10] By way of contrast, *constar* has not yet been personalized: *Consta que Juan tiene el dinero* is not matched by **Juan consta tener el dinero.*

But starkness makes the syntax seem clearer than it is. If there were not some deep semantic kinship between the personal and the impersonal constructions, they could not have merged in the first place. Indeed, without such kinship the fact that both English and Spanish have gone the same route would be an incredible coincidence.

---

[9] There is a further similarity—though a partial one—between the languages in the possibility of deleting the embedded sentence. Consider

¿Por qué lo haces?—Porque debo (puedo).

Why do you do it?—Because I should (I can, I must).

But more verbs permit it in Spanish than in English. Except for

¿Por qué lo haces?—*Porque he (*Porque tengo),

in which the particles *de* and *que* are required, the scope of deletion includes a sizable number of the verbs that may take infinitive complements. There are varying degrees of acceptability in the following, but the outlines are mainly correct:

¿Por qué no lo haces?—Porque no quiero (deseo, anhelo, necesito).

¿Por qué no lo haces?—*Porque odio (*Porque no acostumbro, n proyecto, no prefiero, no acepto).

The modals in Spanish seem to be included in a larger class that also embraces some quasi-modals. (English of course has a type of deletion that applies to all non-modals, including extraposed subject infinitives: *I want to, I hate to, I'd like to, I forced him to, It's easy to,* etc., but not **To is easy.* How would one class *have to,* so much like an auxiliary in its phonetic reduction?)

[10] See "The syntax of *parecer.*"

Take the verb *want*. It is used in both the sense of 'need' and the sense of 'desire', and the semantic bridge is obvious. When we say *You want to be more careful* we are imputing a need as if it were a desire: It wants for you to be more careful, hence you ought to desire to be more careful. We can draw a phrase marker for the two senses of *want* such that *you* is shown not to be the subject of the main verb in the deep structure, but it nevertheless IS the deep structure subject—it both is and is not, and the requirement that we must choose, which is forced on us by current transformational grammar, presents a false picture.

If language has more in-betweens than on-targets, then the class of modals, or whatever we want to call it, should turn out to be a gradient class, one manifested by a cline, in the neo-Firthian sense. There should be some modals that are more modals than others. Take the E. verb *need*. In negative, interrogative, and conditional sentences it may be used uninflected to refer to external obligation: *All he need do* [= he need do no more, neg.] *is wait a bit. You needn't be so sharp with me*. But the inflected form can still refer to external obligation, and can be passivized like *poder*,

We need to understand these facts. = It (to understand these facts) is necessary for us.

These facts need to be understood by us.

and it admits the pseudo-cleft construction for either the external or internal need, but gradiently:

What we need is to understand these facts.
What these facts need is to be understood by us.
What we need is to treat this water with chlorine.
What this water needs is to be treated with chlorine.
What I need is to drink some water.
*What the water needs is to be drunk by me.

This freedom of *need* would be impossible if what is imposed from outside and what wells up from within were not confused in the mind of the speaker.

So when we say *You can catch cold that way*, and aver that it means not ability but possibility, we overlook the blending that mediates between structures: This one happens also to mean 'You that way (i.e., you by behaving that way) make yourself susceptible of catching cold'. Even with weather expressions we cannot be sure that the construction is one or the other: *Puede llover* looks like a pure case of *poder*$_1$ with a sentential subject; yet we also find *Quiere llover, Está tratando de llover,* which suggest that the *poder*$_1$ may not be as pure as it seems. The outer becomes inner all along the line, metaphorically:

> He must be here, he hás to be here!
> He could be here, you know, and we just don't see him.
> He needs to be here if we are to make any use of him.
> He ought to be around here somewhere, I just know it.

Is it possible to show, in terms of structural descriptions and transformations, the kind of double vision with which a sentence like *Debo vivir aquí* 'Debe ser que vivo aquí, (said by a man groping in the dark for his apartment) presents us? It cannot be done by a transformation that maps a single underlying structure onto a surface sentence, for that explicitly denies any change in meaning. Transformations are a device for representing an output, and have nothing to do with sense. It would seem that two deep structures are actually involved, one undoubtedly more than the other in some cases but in others (such as several examples with *need*) striking a balance more nearly equal. I suggest then that *Debo vivir aquí* 'Debe ser que vivo aquí' be represented by two deep structures, one added to the other, rather than transformed into it by the subject-incorporation transformation plus the VP-promotion transformation plus assorted agreement transformations. We might adopt the convention that the phrase marker providing the simplest route to the final result should be the one given last. (This would express a kind of "grammar simplification" principle: a language probably tends to blend more roundabout structures into more direct ones.) Thus *Debo vivir aquí* 'Debe ser que vivo aquí' could be represented as follows:

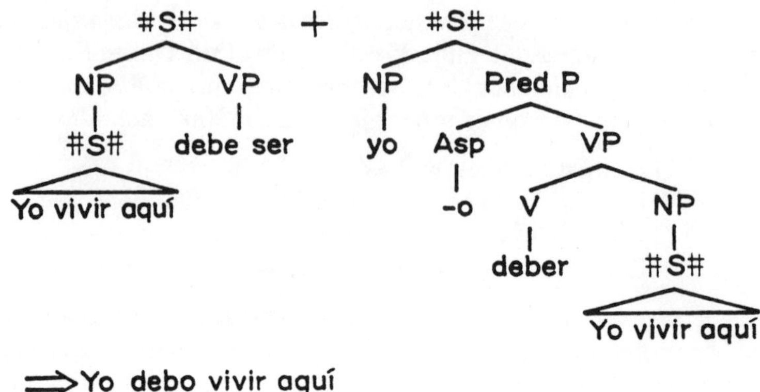

The paired phrase markers could be referred to as a blending transformation. It says something like this: "The speaker has within his competence two structures which have influenced each other as wholes"; the process by which certain surface structures carry certain meanings is not a transition through various transformational steps, but a LEAP. In other words, the phrase marker to the left is not restructured along the lines of the one to the right, but retains its identity; the surface sentence *Yo debo vivir aquí* counts both of them as its deep structure.

I must explain why I have included *ser* along with *deber*. There are three reasons:

(1) The *ser* of existence or factuality is already in the grammar. The relationship between *Es que lo ha dicho* and *Debe ser que lo haya dicho* is obvious.

(2) Including *ser* saves the day for K.'s probably correct intuition about an NP-dominated S in his interpretation (Ex. 30) of *yo-invitar-a Juan poder*. By changing it to *yo-invitar-a-Juan puede-ser* we get a sentence that can be pseudo-cleft: *Lo que puede ser es que yo invite a Juan.* Without it, the NP description fails: **Lo que puede es que*... (The fact that *puede* can occur without *ser* in *puede que* probably deserves to be marked in the lexicon as a peculiarity of *poder*; I doubt that any other verb permits this deletion and in other situations *poder* itself does

not do so: *¿Juan pasar a ser presidente de la compañía? ¡No puede ser!*, not **No puede* in the same sense.)

(3) Most importantly, including *ser* simplifies the lexicon by eliminating $deber_1$ and $poder_1$. The impersonality is already carried by the *ser* of existence. *Poder, deber,* etc. can be viewed as saying, metaphorically: 'By its nature this event has within it the capacity (obligation, etc.) to be'. This accords well with our feeling toward metaphors underlying the notion of fate: *Why did things turn out like that?—It just had to be, that's all.*

Blending is a fact of language. It has to be represented somehow. There may be a better way to do it, but the one I propose can be fitted with the least disruption into the transformational-generative framework.[11]

---

[11] Some incidental observations on K.'s thesis—p. 3.: *Saber* is alleged to behave differently from *querer*: While the latter allows both *Quiero salir* and *Quiero que tú salgas*, the former admits *Sé manejar* but not **Sé que él maneje*. In the negative we have both *No sé manejar* and *No sé que él maneje.*

P. 47: Fn. 4 appears to disagree with the passage to which it refers. The latter (36) characterizes $poder_1$ as taking "abstract, sentential subjects." The note cites the example *La campaña contra el analfabetismo puede tener mucho éxito* as a case of *campaña* being [+ Abstr]. If the note responds to the text, the subject in the deep structure is the embedded sentence *la campaña contra el analfabetismo tener mucho éxito*. It is probably true, though, that abstract subjects facilitate the blending that I have indicated: *What these facts need is to be understood by us* is a better sentence than **What this water needs is to be drunk by me.*

Part VI

Postscript

Reference and inference: Inceptiveness in the Spanish preterit

[*Author's Note*: No matter how wide the net is cast, a fish or two always escapes. The Parts into which this book is divided were designed to stretch around almost anything, but I come at the end to two leftovers that ought to go in somewhere but don't fit the rest. The first is on a question of verbal aspect (akin to modality, but not quite the same), which I felt should be included because of its approach to meaning and its early use of the opposing concepts of *reference* and *inference*.

A key question now for the burgeoning school of linguistic pragmatics—the study of language not as pure system but as instrument—is to distinguish between what is lodged IN the code and what is grafted from outside. If a married couple says *We're going to build a new house,* no one is apt to assume that the husband is a plumber and the wife a carpenter, or that they are planning to build something for sale. The verb *build* (unlike *construct*) stretches enough to include the planners and payers. As for who the owners will be, the word *new* (seemingly redundant—how could one build an *old* house?) clinches that: it is the *new* of *Our new house is the old Danforth mansion.* The meanings of *build* and *new* have a relatively constant inner part, or reference, and an outer part, the inference or inferences to be drawn when the abstract meaning encounters a concrete situation.

It was my belief that the Spanish preterit had a referential meaning that covered its uses for starting as well as for stopping an action, and that these latter two aspects were inferred from that more inclusive meaning. Later I learned indirectly that the same claim had been made for the Greek aorist by M. S. Ruipérez in his *Estructura del sistema de tiempos y aspectos del verbo griego antiguo,* Salamanca 1954.]

* * *

THE NOTION THAT the Spanish preterit may refer to the inception of an action as well as to its termination is not new.[1] Bello distinguishes between two classes of verbs, *desinentes* and *permanentes,* the latter admitting a preterit which, he says, "denota la anterioridad de aquel solo instante en que el atributo ha llegado a su perfección: *Dijo Dios: Sea la luz, y la luz fue* [sic; my version has *fue la luz*]: *fue* vale lo mismo que 'principió a tener una existencia perfecta.'"[2] Keniston refers to this class of verbs as *durative,* but is more cautious. With "a number" of them, he says, "the preterit may stress the beginning of the state," as in *después que estuve sano.*[3] The most recent and clearest statement of the thesis is by W. E. Bull, who calls the class of verbs in question *noncyclic* (a cyclic verb is one that embodies a succession of different events leading to a conclusion, e.g., *to dress* involves picking up the clothes, inserting the arms or legs, buttoning, etc., and terminates when one "is dressed"—Gordon T. Fish terms such events "self-limiting"). Bull assigns a terminative meaning to the preterit with all cyclic verbs (that is, with all cyclic functions of verbs—a given verb morpheme may operate in more than one sphere) and an inceptive meaning as normal to the preterit with noncyclic verbs.[4]

Most textbook grammars ignore the inceptive side of the preterit and focus on the terminative. When they do include some inceptive meanings, as with *saber* or *conocer,* they usually treat them just as a translation problem: *Supe que había estado aquí* has the special meaning 'to find out'; *Conocí a su hermano* has the special meaning 'to get acquainted with.' This practice has all the ear-marks of the old, and bad, habit of imposing the grammar of one language on that of

[1] This article was originally published in *Hispania* 46 (1963) 128-35.

[2] *Gramática de la lengua castellana,* §626.

[3] *The syntax of Castilian prose, the sixteenth century* (Chicago, 1937), §32.47.

[4] *Time, tense, and the verb* (Berkeley and Los Angeles: University of California Press, 1960), p. 47 and passim.

another. But widespread and pernicious as the habit is in general, let us withhold judgment on whether we really have an example of it here. Possibly there is another interpretation.

For the moment I adopt Bull's terms and refer to *cyclic* and *noncyclic* as he has defined them, since what follows is mainly a discussion of that part of his *Time, Tense, and the Verb* which has to do with the functions of the preterit. This is not an attempt to reexamine the main thesis of Bull's valuable monograph, with which I agree, but only to look into one detail which happens to be an important problem for teaching and about which, consequently, practical decisions have to be made. If there is an element of inceptiveness in the Spanish verb SYSTEM, specifically in the preterit "tense" at the point where it crosses one of two main classes of events, we shall have to organize our teaching materials one way; if inceptiveness is, instead, only a trait of certain individual verbs, then we shall have to organize them differently. That is the question I want to try to answer.

The Preterit of Cyclic and Noncyclic Events

Is it true that in the preterit "a cyclic event can only be terminative"? With the majority of verbs this seems plausible. In *Murió ayer a la una* the person became moribund earlier and at one o'clock he breathed his last—this is clearly terminative. In *Llegamos a la una* we were on our way earlier and came to a stop at the time mentioned. But does the terminative implication perhaps depend on the verb? In dying and arriving we are interested in the end point. What about a verb like *almorzar?* It is cyclic—having lunch involves sitting down at the table, eating to satiety or until all the food is gone, and finally wiping the mouth or getting up or some other terminal act. But if I say *Almorzamos ayer a la una* I probably refer to the time we started eating, not the time we finished: *Tenemos cita para almorzar a la una* expects the other party to arrive at one, not leave at one. A medical examination is a cyclic event; but if I say *El médico me examinó a la una* I refer to the—probably appointed—time for the start of the examination, not its end.

Apparently, then, a cyclic event can be oriented any way it pleases to a starting point or an end point. *A la una* adjusts itself to the event in terms of the nature of the event. It has no essential relevance to the inceptive or terminative aspect of the preterit applied to a cyclic event.

The companion question is whether "noncyclic events are initiative,"[5] e.g. *Habló ayer a la una*. Without denying that many of them are, I want to cite examples of a few verbs labeling noncyclic events that seem to me not to be necessarily initiative.

1. *Costar*. This seems to label a noncyclic event. Something can cost a given amount as long as the price tag hangs on it. But in the preterit—*Costó cinco dólares*—the price has been paid, the event has come to an end, the merchandise is no longer priced for sale at anything. *Costó* does not signal the beginning of the costing period but its end.

2. *Seguir*. The spontaneous translation that I get for *I tried to interrupt him but he kept on talking* is *Traté de interrumpirlo pero siguió hablando*. If the noncyclic *siguió* were initiative, this should mean that he began to continue, perhaps 'He resumed talking' (as it appears to mean in the *Visual Grammar* example *La tormenta pasó... y la selva siguió como antes*). But it hardly seems to be initiative in the ordinary sense of the word. Certainly the act of going on does not begin at this point. Nor does it end. Here we are interested in the middle.

3. *Querer*. In what sense is *quiso* initiative in *Quiso hacerse respetar* (Bull, p. 95)? One might say that the total phrase is initiative, that there is an effort to initiate an attitude of respect. But if this is the case, then *Empezó a hacerse respetar* is also initiative, and the initiativeness of the preterit slips from our grasp, since here what is initiative is the verb *empezar*, in whatever form. Surely we have to disregard the total phrase and ask whether *quiso* per se is initiative, i.e., whether it indicates a beginning of desire. But the desire, if there was one, must have antedated the *quiso*. If the attempt was unsuccessful, then perhaps the desire continued; if it succeeded, then I should think that that particular desire must have come to an end. I return to *quiso* later.

4. *Poder*. Does *Trató varias veces y por fin pudo hacerlo* refer to a beginning of being able? If so, being able should continue, if ever so

---

[5] Bull permits context to impose a terminative aspect of noncyclic events (p. 96), but I try here to use examples that he has classed as initiative, or others like them.

little, beyond that point; but there is no guarantee that it does. *Pudo hacerlo* means, practically, no more than *Lo hizo*. A second attempt five seconds later might fail. *Pudo hacerlo* tells us 'There was an ability that lasted long enough to get the act performed.' Maybe longer, too; but that is not part of the reference of this verb.

Meaning Imposed or Meaning Selected?

So it appears that the nature of the event contributes to its inceptiveness or terminativeness, whether the event is cyclic or noncyclic. Let us see whether this may be reflected in a straddling of the cyclic and the noncyclic.

The sturdiest representatives of preterit-for-inceptiveness are verbs like *saber, conocer, entender, comprender, quedar, recordar, guardar, continuar, retener, atraer*, etc., verbs apparently involving an active or acquisitive phase (e.g. acquiring knowledge—setting in motion) and a passive or retentive phase (e.g. holding on to knowledge—continuing in motion). It is obvious that *Supe los nombres* probably implies *Sé los nombres:* my knowing the names does not end with acquiring the knowledge, but continues indefinitely (or anyway continued—I may since have forgotten them).

Now the question is, are these verbs univocal, combining in one homogenous event both the acquisitive phase and the retentive phase, or are they equivocal (like a pair of homonyms), referring to the two phases separately and distinctly? If they are univocal, then when the preterit is added and we get an inceptive result, the preterit must be responsible for it—we can say that the preterit has inceptiveness as one of its references. But if the verbs are equivocal, then the addition of the preterit may have as its result simply the selection of a meaning that is already there, the meaning most compatible with the preterit in some other of its characteristics; it will not be a case of inceptiveness "of" a total event, since there are really two events, two references of the verb. Let us say that the preterit refers to termination. Then, when we add the preterit to an equivocal verb, it will select the meaning that fits the notion of termination; if the verb labels both a cyclic event and a noncyclic one, the preterit will tend to select the former.[6] So conceived, "inception" with these verbs is a synthetic view of the two phases as if they were one, seeing the verb falsely as a unit, whereas the actual reference is to the END OF A BEGINNING. This idea carries us back to the wording in Bello's definition. "La anterioridad de aquel solo instante en que el atributo ha llegado a su perfección" suggests, with its *ha llegado*, a terminus.

If the notion of "beginning" inheres in the verb, and what the preterit does is simply to block it off, then it ought to be possible to use these same verbs inceptively in the imperfect or imperfect progressive. We can do exactly that: *Yo tenía una carta de ella casi todos los días* 'I had a letter from her almost every day'; *Nos llamaron precisamente cuando estábamos conociendo a su familia* 'They called us right when we were getting acquainted with your family.' This is hardly surprising where *conocer* is concerned, if we are willing to admit that *conocer* simply retains, as part of its semantic range, the fundamentally inceptive meaning of *cognosco*.

That *saber, conocer*, etc., form a special class of verbs shows up when we compare them with other verbs labeling noncyclic events. Here is where we take note of Keniston's caution in applying his rule only to "a number" of verbs of the durative type. The noncyclic class is really a superclass, including, besides the acquisitive-retentive events, others that involve no mere steady state after the agony of getting started is over, but a continued doing: *to dance, ride, walk, fly, soar, hover, rise, dwell, live.*

It also includes a few where the steady state is the whole show. If the preterit conferred inceptiveness on all noncyclic events AS A CLASS and as a prime characteristic of the preterit, then a sentence like *La caja contuvo el tesoro* would mean that the box acquired the treasure. So with *pertenecer*; but *El dinero le perteneció a él* I doubt would ever

[6] It is possible, of course, for the preterit to apply to the retentive phase if it is viewed as an anterior segment. An old man recalling a lost skill may say *Supe todo eso, pero ya se me olvidó.*

clearly mean that he got possession of the money.[7] Here, it seems, we cannot have an inceptive meaning because there was none there to begin with.

The special condition of the *saber-conocer* type shows up again in the restrictions on its inceptiveness. If *supe* were fully and generally inceptive, i.e., preliminary to continuation in the broadest sense, it ought to be possible to say *Supe español* with the meaning 'I learned Spanish'; similarly with *Entendí español.* Instead, the inceptiveness is limited to events whose inceptive phase can be viewed as point action, as happening-and-then-over-with: *Supe la verdad,* I caught on, it dawned on me, I grasped it.

Finally, we can test different classes of noncyclic events with formulas that are explicitly terminative. The most useful is *acabar de.* In *Acabo de conocer a su hermano* I am saying that I am making an end of the acquisitive phase. The retentive one is not affected—I still know your brother. But in *Acabo de llorar* the entire action is affected; I am not still performing that act of weeping. If this reasoning holds, the preterit has the same effect: *Conocí a su hermano* selects an acquisitive reference and marks its terminus; *Lloré* has no acquisitive reference to select, and marks the anteriority of the action as a whole.

English offers some analogies that are suggestive, though of course not probative. English *to be able* is equivocal, like Spanish *poder,* and we can say *I've just been able to do it* as we can say *Acabo de poder hacerlo,* to refer to one of the two meanings of these verbs, namely, 'success'—not a continuing ability but an ability that lasted as long as the performance of the act. But English *know* is not like Spanish *conocer*: it is univocal, and we do not say *I've just known your brother* with the meaning of 'met.' Nouns as well as verbs may be equivocal. In *At this time of year, daylight lasts eighteen hours, daylight* refers to an extent of time. In *It was windy until past daylight, daylight* refers to the beginning of the day. But *daytime* is univocal: it can go into the first

[7] The idea could be inferred in *Primero le perteneció a mi hermano y luego me perteneció a mí,* but the reference of these two instances of *perteneció* is the same—a belonging that covered a period of time. The *luego* separates them and suggests termination for the first and initiation for the second, but this is read in from the context.

sentence but not the second. The alternative to saying 'These two meanings inhere in the word" is an extreme view of meaning in relation to context which says, in effect, "The *daylight* of the phrase *past daylight* has no meaning outside the phrase itself." This logical, but know-nothing, view of meaning would make it impossible for us to say that the verb *saber* "has" two meanings,[8] but would make it equally impossible to say that the preterit "has" the meaning of inceptiveness. In other words, it creates a stalemate. I prefer to agree that there is a separable inceptiveness, but that it belongs to the verb rather than to the preterit.

The Last Event in a Series; Reference vs. Inference

In the sentence *Primero hizo sol y luego llovió* the first event is contextually limited at its end point but the second is not. We therefore have the ingredients for regarding the first as terminative and the second as inceptive. The fact that we may prefer instead to take the latter in the sense 'then there was a rainy spell' (i.e., something that came to a stop) probably reflects our experience with rainstorms—they come and they go. The reverse order, *Primero llovió y luego hizo sol,* poses a stronger temptation: the sun is always up there shining somewhere, and it seems as if *hizo sol* means not so much 'there was a sunny spell' as 'the sun shone,' something that might go on indefinitely.

I submit that position in an utterance is an unsafe hitching post for inceptiveness; it makes the reference of the preterit too precarious. Yet this lack of a contextual end point seems to me to be the most persuasive argument for inceptiveness in the following, from the *Visual Grammar* series:

La tormenta pasó, { brilló el sol,
cantaron los pájaros y
la selva siguió como
antes

[8] Or, in stricter terms, to say that we can recognize two clear distributions for the verb *saber* only one of which is shared, e.g., by the verb *ignorar.*

The last three verbs, parallel to one another but consecutive with the first, all suggest events that can continue.

Consider first *brillar*. To INFER a continuation of sunshine one does not need a noncyclic event; it would do just as well in this context to say *apareció el sol*—the cyclic expression carries just as clearly the promise of continued sunshine. We cannot then jump to the conclusion that *brilló* is either noncyclic or inceptive. The verb obviously includes cyclic meanings: *Brilló su espada; eso me dio a saber que mi enemigo estaba en acecho* refers to a single gleam of light. As far as the context tells us, *brilló* refers to a burst of light, a dazzling first impression of light after dark. Whether *brilló* refers to the start of an event that continues, or to a stopped event from which a certain kind of continuation (a more subdued glow, e.g.) can be inferred, is not demonstrable in this context.

Cantaron and *siguió*, however, obviously cover events that embrace more than a small beginning. Like the *hizo sol* in the earlier example, their position at the end of the utterance leaves them free to cover an unspecified time. I cannot prove that they are not inceptive, but I can offer an alternative explanation: that the function of the preterit is neither to start nor to stop, but to segment: 'The storm passed and there followed a time when the sun shone, the birds sang, and the forest went on as before.' We may be noncommittal as to how long the time lasted, as we were in the *Almorzamos a la una* example, but the preterit still confines it. It is confinement (plus anteriority) that seems to me to be the continuing, consistent reference of the preterit; the inception and termination are inferences, not references.

Performance vs. Ability

The last event in a series has another implication: CULMINATION.

If *Acabo de llorar* means that the weeping is past, *Acabo de volar* should mean that the flying is past. But *Acabo de volar* can suggest a continued ability to fly. In this same connection it has been claimed that a form such as *volé* can have an inceptive reference in a context like this: *Después de muchos esfuerzos y un sin fin de tentativas, por fin volé (anduve, caminé, nadé, leí, escribí,* etc.). *Volé (anduve,* etc.), one is prone to think, represents the start of an activity that lasts the rest of a lifetime.

But there is a fundamental difference between *anduve* and a verb like *supe*. When I say *Supe que era Juan* it necessarily follows (unless I forget) that *Sé que era Juan* is continuously true. If I say *Conocí a su hermano* it follows that *Conozoco a su hermano* is uninterruptedly factual. It does not mean that I CAN know him; it means that I DO know him. *Anduve* is different. It does not follow that *ando* is continuously factual unless we include the transferred meaning 'I can walk' rather than 'I do walk.' This would be mixing meanings, since *por fin anduve* refers to the act, not the ability. It proves the ability; we infer the ability; but *ando* (or *seguí andando)* is not the reference of *anduve* but an inference from it.

Again we can demonstrate by substituting a clearly cyclic event. In *Después de muchos esfuerzos y un sin fin de tentativas, por fin di un paso* we can infer *ando* or *seguí andando*. This is an inference, and not the reference of *di un paso*.

This is not to say that the inference may not be compelling. In *¡Mire, mire! ¡Acabo de andar!* the best translation is 'Look, look! I'm finally walking!' But as this can be said standing still, and as *acabo de* is explicitly terminative, the reference is to something that has occurred, not to something occurring. Or the speaker may be walking again as he says it, and the ability is continuing; but the act referred to, on which the inference is based and which is confirmed by the continuation, is itself terminated. One can as readily say *¡Mire, mire! ¡Acabo de dar un paso!* under identical circumstances and with identical inferences.

Inference depends on what we know of the structure of people and of things about us. When one learns to walk, one normally retains the skill, and from the first step we infer a continuation. But a situation like *Jugué no sé cuántas veces, y por fin gané* is different. Here we are not so prone to pass off *gané* as anything more than the first win or the first winning occasion. It is physically possible to keep on winning just as it is physically possible to keep on walking, if we view both activities as the repetition of a cycle. But we know the aleatory nature of winning and losing, and what we infer about a continued ability to walk we are less likely to infer about a continued ability to win.

Subclasses of Noncyclic Events

I have tried to show, in verbs of the *saber-conocer* type, that it is possible for such verbs to include among their meanings two that are inherently distinct, selected but not imposed by some exterior formula.[8] The question of multiple labeling needs to be extended to other classes of verbs. I single out two, quotative verbs and verbs of perception.

The quotative verbs include *decir* and its synonyms: *afirmar, declarar, alegar, aseverar,* etc. They embrace both cyclic and noncyclic events: *Dijo que era Juan, Dice que era Juan,* the one referring to what is uttered, the other to what is maintained.[9] Verbs of this class differ from the *saber-conocer* type in that the noncyclic phase cannot be inferred from the cyclic one. *Supo que era Juan* suggests *Sabe que era Juan; Dijo que era Juan* does not suggest *Dice que era Juan,* nor even that he actually maintained it when he said it; the only thing reported is

---

[8]This is not alien to Bull's views. "Many stems may label both cyclic and noncyclic events," p. 46.

[9] For Bull, pp. 84-85, this use of *decir* is "nonsystemic." *Dice* is present tense, or "present imperfect" in Bull's system, by virtue of which, if *dice* were systemic, it would have to be imperfect with respect to the point present; actually, however, according to Bull's reasoning, the saying has already been done, i.e., is perfected with respect to the point present.

This assumes a normal meaning for *decir* from which the meaning in question is a deviation. In order for *dice* NOT to be systemic, it is necessary to assume that *decir* means 'to utter' and not 'to maintain.' Aside from etymology, I see no reason for making this assumption; *decir* in the present tense is probably used more often than not to mean 'maintain,' and this surely must qualify as a regular usage. If it is claimed otherwise, then we should look at the whole set of *verba dicendi* from *pronunciar* to *sostener* to see whether there is not a gradation from verbs that appear to refer primarily to utterance to verbs that appear to refer primarily to sustained belief, with the constant possibility, at either end of the gradient, of shifting from one semantic area to the other. The English verb *claim* is defined as 'to assert or maintain as a fact'—putting it about the middle of the gradient. *He claims that it was John* seems to be noncyclic, with a reference to the belief held. *He claimed that it was John* probably means 'he said,' cyclic and with reference to utterance. I should think that one would always favor a systemic interpretation where possible, to avoid ad hoc solutions. *Dice* seems amenable.

that the words were uttered. In fact, whereas *Supo que era Juan pero ahora sabe que no era Juan* is probably a non-sequitur, *Dijo que era Juan pero ahora dice* ('sostiene') *que no era Juan* is a normal sequence. The same is true of *creer*. These verbs express a viewpoint, not a fact, and viewpoints can change. They form a class about which it is impossible to claim that noncyclicness makes for an inceptive use of the preterit. The preterit selects a point-action or terminative meaning, one of two broad meanings inherent in the verb (i.e., one of two clear-cut ways in which utterances with the verb *decir* are distributed with respect to other utterances). The *Vox* definition of *opinar* is 'formar o tener opinion.' The two meanings do not imply each other.

Verbs of perception such as *ver, observar, notar, advertir*, are akin to *saber* in that the latter is etymologically a verb of perception and in the similarity of contexts like *Supe que era Juan* and *Vi que era Juan*. They are significant in that as a class they indicate point action, and in the light that this sheds on the dual aspects of a verb like *saber*. In *Vi que era Juan* it has been argued that *ver* is noncyclic (*vio* appears twice among the examples in Bull, p. 95). The reasoning is apparently that if one sees something and that something remains visible, one continues to see it. But even in the most literal sense this depends on an act of attention. The seeing terminates when one turns the gaze elsewhere. Perception typically refers to the interception of a piece of sense data, not its retention. We have developed transferred meanings for some verbs of perception by which we apply them to the apprehension and retention of truth. *Vi que era Juan* suggests that I kept on "seeing" it in this metaphorical sense of *see*. But this does not justify viewing the primary point action as the inceptive aspect of a secondary figure of speech even if we grant that both meanings are now firmly fixed. The nature of the metaphor is perhaps clearer if we compare *ver* with another point-action verb, *aceptar*. *Acepté el regalo* and *Acepté la verdad* are alike in that when "accepting" terminates, "having" begins; but for the first example we do not employ *Acepto el regalo* for 'having,' while for the second we do employ *Acepto la verdad* for 'having.' The accident that *aceptar* has been extended in a non-literal sense to signify an attitude of acceptance (therefore noncyclic) does not then react on the primary sense of the verb to make *Acepté la verdad* the inceptive aspect of a noncyclic event. *Acepté la verdad* continues to be cyclic, to refer to the initial act of grasping, which terminates when the object is within the grasp. We can, I feel, apply the same reasoning to *Supe la verdad. Saber* comes to represent a pair of homonyms, one of which, the acquisitive one, is cyclic, the other, the retentive one, noncyclic.

Whether a verb will have this duality depends on the verb. It exists for *aceptar*—a primary point action and a secondary attitude. It does not exist in the same way for *recibir*. As for *oir*, its metaphorical extension is quite distinct from that of *ver*: *Oí que lo van a hacer* means 'Oí decir que lo van a hacer,' and does not suggest a continued hearing of the same thing; the extension of *oir* has not got itself mixed up with truth values. Similarly *leer* in *Leí que lo van a hacer. Leer* and *oir* operate in the realm of opinion, *ver, notar*, etc., in the realm of truth, but all are equally confined, not inceptive, in the preterit. The fact that truth continues to be truth whereas opinion changes has caused us to read the continuation of the truth back into a continuation of the point event labeled by the verb.

Summary

I have called into question the claim that there is an inceptive reference to the preterit because I do not believe that the preterit is either explicitly inceptive or explicitly terminative. The preterit, as I see it, refers to a SEGMENT of anteriority, which may be of any extent, from the infinitesimal (point action) to the infinite (reckoning infinity backwards, as in *Hasta la creación, hubo sólo la nada).* We may at various times be more interested in one end of the segment than in the other, but that is a preference imposed by particular verbs in particular contexts. It is more likely that we shall be interested in the end than in the beginning, because the end is what determines WHETHER there is anteriority; but WHAT is anterior is the segment. It is not necessary that the anteriority be demonstrable on external grounds: *Estuvo en Los Angeles* may represent a decision of the speaker simply to ignore possible extensions of the span—maybe the person stayed on, but the speaker uses the preterit to carve out the span that interests him. This is just to say that the preterit HAS a reference not derived circularly from a context.

The segmental vs. inceptive-terminative reference of the preterit can be illustrated by an example of Bull's, *Hace dos horas que estuvo aquí*, which, he says, "measures the time between the termination of the event... and PP [point present]" (p. 49). But if that were true, *Hace dos horas que estuvo aquí* would imply a denial of *Hace una hora que estuvo aquí* referring to a single span of 'being here.' The two are not, however, incompatible. An exchange such as the following is normal: A: "Hace dos horas que estuvo aquí" (or "Estuvo aquí hace dos horas"). B: "¿Y hace una hora?" A: "También. Estuvo aquí toda la tarde." *Estuvo aquí* refers to a segment of time and not either an inception or a termination (though of course it had both); the sequence of two "ago's" poses no contradiction. *Hace dos horas que estuvo aquí* tells us this: 'Measure two hours back and you will hit somewhere within the time span when he was here.'

I have tried to show that the claim for inceptiveness in the preterit is based on the misinterpretation of a number of sets of data:

1. The apparent correlation between inceptiveness or terminativeness and classes of events (cyclic vs. noncyclic). But this appears to depend on the nature of the event as signaled by the verb. *Murió a la una* and *Almorzamos a la una* are both cyclic, but one is terminative and the other inceptive—by inference. As labels of noncyclic events, *saber* and *ignorar* are companion verbs; yet *Supe cuántos había* seems to be inceptive whereas *Ignoré cuántos había* is not—the point-action meaning incorporated in the semantic spectrum of *saber* is lacking in that of *ignorar*.[10]

2. Information conveyed by reference and information conveyed by inference. The reference of *I want some sugar* is one thing; the inference that we base on it—'Please pass the sugar'—is something else. References are always clues to inferences, else there would be no continuity between utterances—we would have to have verbalizations of everything; but we have to distinguish them (even as we also recognize that in the course of time a repeated inference may become a reference).

---

[10] For speakers influenced by English, *ignorar* may mean 'to ignore' (see R. J. Alfaro, *Diccionario de anglicismos* [Panamá: Imprenta Nacional, 1950], s.v. *ignorar*). But this is not the inceptive phase of 'not knowing.' If *ignoré* marked the transition from *saber* to *ignorar* (as *supe* marks that between *ignorar* and *saber*), it would have to mean 'I forgot.'

3. The presence of multiple labeling within lexical units, i.e. homonymy. It was a semantic accident that *morir* classically was both transitive and intransitive, with a context such as *Han muerto al rey* selecting the transitive meaning. Other such semantic accidents occur in the coupling of cyclic and noncyclic events under a single label. The semantic kinship of the two events then leads to a confusion. The verb *querer* is an example. Originally it named events more cyclic than noncyclic ('to seek,' prolongable but normally terminated with the act of finding; 'to beg,' 'to aim,' 'to get'); but in Castilian it was extended through "innovación semántica" (Corominas) to mean 'want, desire.' The old sense is still present in the Cid, with noun objects, and with infinitive objects it apparently survives still in the type *Quiso hacerlo,* exactly paired with English *He sought (tried) to do it. Quiso hacerlo* and *Quería hacerlo* are close enough in meaning to suggest that both are phases of a single event. But in such cases I believe we have to do with two events, one of which is selected, and segmented, by the preterit. This conclusion is supported by the fact that while the two meanings of *querer* are close, they may contrast in the same context: *Quise hacerlo pero en realidad no tenía ganas* strips *quise* of its volitive ties; except that it is bad stylistically, one could even say *Quise hacerlo pero en realidad no quería.*

4. The lack of an explicit termination for acts that occur at the end of a series. When events are strung chain-wise, as happens with narration in the preterit, each succeeding event cuts off the preceding one. But in *Bailaron, luego dejaron de bailar y descansaron* the event 'descansaron' is a segment that follows segments explicitly given, and we therefore infer a beginning. The reference, however, is to 'there followed a rest period.' Our interest may be on the beginning or the middle or the end, but the preterit does not "mean" any one of the three.

5. Events that not only stand at the end of a series, but cap the series with success. The performance of the act promises further performances. The preterit, however, refers to the event, not to the ability to perform again or keep on performing.

6. Verbs whose reference is apprehension or perception, plus the nature of truth, which is timeless. When such verbs acquire a second reference, a phase of retention, the stage is set for a misinterpretation: *Supe (vi,* etc.) *que era Juan* contains the timeless truth 'que era Juan,'

and the language permits us to use the same verb stem in *Sé que era Juan;* so we conclude, "*Supe* can't be something terminated; it has to be inceptive." In *Oí que era Juan* and *Oigo que era Juan* we do not come to such a conclusion because one of the two essential ingredients is missing: we are dealing not with truth but with hearsay. In both cases, however, the reference of the preterit is the same: a point-action apprehension of a sense datum.

If my analysis is correct, the reference of the preterit is a constant. If it appears to vary, the variation is in the context. We can say that the construction *Supo la verdad* "has" the meaning of inceptiveness the way *más fuerte que nadie* "has" the meaning of superlativeness. It is something imported from outside. Fundamentally, *más* signals the comparative degree; fundamentally, the preterit signals segmentation and anteriority.

Qué tan, qué tanto

[*Author's Note*: This final piece is all I have to show for several years of poring over *papeletas* recording the wisdom of Alfonso X and his scribes. In my college days I earned my keep selling "tailoring," and many of my customers were Mexican. I was struck by the fact that when they wanted to say *how much* they split the expression exactly as in English, *qué tanto,* instead of the standard *cuánto.* Later, in graduate school, I discovered that what appeared to be a corrupting influence from English was actually a respectable bequest from the Middle Ages.

In a subsequent informal survey involving informants from various Spanish-speaking countries, Ninfa Flores found some confirmation for my impression that *qué tan(to)* may, at least for some speakers, suggest greater precision than *cuán(to).* Her results also made it clear that dialectal differences are rampant in the whole area of quantification, from the quite decided regional preference for one form over the other to the well-known fact that Modern Spanish is reluctant to use *cuán* in any interrogative sense at all, preferring, for example, *¿Qué altura tiene?* or *¿Cómo es de alto?* or *¿Es muy alto?* to *¿Cuán alto es?* Speakers who use *qué tan(to)* have no problem with *¿Qué tan alto es?*]

* * *

KANY'S *AMERICAN SPANISH SYNTAX*[1] offers the only important note, to my knowledge, on the interrogatives *qué tan* and *qué tanto,* so common in our own Southwest and in northern Mexico, the one to replace the unused *cuán* and the other alternating with *cuánto.*[2]

---

[1] Chicago, 1945, pp. 330-331.

[2] This article was originally published in *Hispanic Review* 14 (1946): 167-69.

Kany points out that the usage "is a survival from the older language," and quotes the *Celestina*, Melchor de Santa Cruz, and Quevedo. *Qué tanto* is, in fact, medieval, for it appears in two Alfonsine astronomical works, the *Cánones de Albateni* (a translation) and the *Libros de Astronomía* (original compilation). The Wisconsin files do not show that it appears elsewhere in Alfonso. It is irregular, predominating over *quanto* in some portions of the manuscripts and in other portions not appearing at all, apparently being a pet of some particular scribe or scribes. The following are among the many instances of its use in *Albateni:*

si tu quisieres saber esto por otra carrera, sabe que tantos son aquellos menudo s que tu as demas. 4Vb.

auemos començado del signo de Capricornio por que se a sabudo que tantos son los sobimientos de los signos en midiel cielo. 6Rb.

esso sera que cates a los menudos que tu as demas, e sabe que tantos son de LX. 5Vb.

esta declinacion non se puede saber que tanta es. 5Rb.

con esto podras saber . . . que tanta sera su altura sobrell orizon. 26Ra.

En la quantidad de la declinacion del çerco de los signos que tanta es del çerco dell yguador del dia. 5Rb (chapter title).

No examples of *qué tan* appear, unless one count *que tamanno*.[3] This perhaps deserves to be counted because of the fact that it maintained itself alongside of the synonymous *quamanno,* which bears the same relationship to *que tamanno* as *cuánto* bears to *qué tanto*. Examples from *Albateni* are:

[3] Not used adjectivally in modern Spanish.

de saber que tanta es la longura de las estrellas de la tierra, & que tamannos son sos diametros. 2Ra.

Quando quisieres saber que tamanno es ell annadimiento del dia mayor sobrel dia egual. 9Va.

There is a similarity between this medieval use of *qué tanto* and the puristic rule for *cuál* as opposed to *qué* in modern Spanish: it does not appear as an adjunct. The adjunct form is *quanto,* as witness:

la particion es saber quantas uezes es doble el mayor del menor. *Albateni* 3Rb.

(*Quanto* appears freely in other positions: "de saber quanta es" [*Astronomía* II 66 14.[) No such restrictions obtain in the modern usage of *qué tanto,* as Kany's examples show.

Qué tan and *qué tanto* are felt to be incorrect by most cultured Spanish Americans whom I have questioned. Amado Alonso rejected all the *qué tan* and *qué tanto* expressions in a questionnaire submitted to him except the obviously substantive "¿A qué tanto por ciento se presta el dinero?" One of the editors of the *Diario de Costa Rica* criticized a subordinate for translating a dispatch with "Ignórase qué tan fuerte resistencia hayan hecho los iraneses" (issue of 26 Aug. 1941, p. 3/4). The majority of the Spanish Americans who reject the phrases do so, however, with some hesitation; they are inclined to say "doubtful" rather than "wrong," and to be inconsistent. Thus one Central American writer of note rejected "¿Qué tantas personas hay en la sala?" but felt that "¿A qué tantos días del mes estamos?" was all right; a close acquaintance of his, likewise a writer, rejected both. The nonadjunct uses enjoy a wider acceptance, probably because they approach the substantive (in "¿Qué tanto es?," for example, we can construe *tanto* as a noun, in which category it is universal), as do also, I suspect, locutions where *qué tanto* is a shade more precise than *cuánto*—inquiring not merely 'how much,' but 'just how much.'

Writings of Dwight Bolinger

(1) "Spanish on the Air in Wisconsin," *Modern Language Journal*, 18 (1934), 217-221.

(2) "The Living Language," *Words* (Los Angeles), September 1937 to October 1940.

(3) "Verbal Rarities," *Words*, 3 (1937), 58-59, 163; 5 (1939), 77.

(4) "Victory for *Gadget*," *Words*, 3 (1937), 179.

(5) "Victorian Styles in Fertilizer," *Commonwealth*, 4 (1938), 19-20. Reprinted in *Magazine Digest*, January 1939.

(6) "Whence the *A* in 'Kind of A'," *Words*, 4 (1938), 32.

(7) "Our Migratory Adverbs," *Words*, 4 (1938), 62-63.

(8) "Distinguish Between *Infer* and *Imply*," *Words*, 4 (1938), 118.

(9) "Profanity and Social Sanction," *American Speech*, 13 (1938), 153-154.

(10) "Glass," *Fortnightly*, December 1938, 702-712.

(11) "Streamliner," *San Francisco Newsletter and Wasp*, March 31, 1939, 11.

(12) "In Defense of the Purists," *Correct English*, September 1939.

(13) "*Bozo*," *American Speech*, 14 (1939), 238-239.

(14) "A Reconsideration of *As* and *So*," *English Journal* (in College Edition only), 28 (1939), 56.

(15) "*Different* - Comparative Degree?" *English Journal* (in College Edition only), 28 (1939), 480.

(16) "Must We use Fewer Words?" *Better English*, October 1939, 39-41.

(17) "Profits in Flesh and Blood," *Commonwealth*, 5 (December 1939), 19-21.

(18) "A Leaf from Your Thesaurus," *The Amateur Writer*, December 1939, 15.

(19) "Word Affinities," *American Speech*, 15 (1940), 62-73.

(20) "*Trivia*," *American Speech*, 15 (1940), 332-333.

(21) "*Churchianity, Churchanity; Trojan Horse*," *American Speech*, 15 (1940), 452, 453-454.

(22) "The Great American Lottery," *The Writer's Forum*, March 1940, 27-29.

(23) "How Do You Use *Data*?" *Better English*, April 1940, 167.

(24) "The Unspoken Language," *The Writer's Forum*, May 1940, 14-15.

(25) "Press and Profundity," *The Writer's Forum*, September 1940, 14-15.

(26) "Ambrose Bierce and 'All of'," *College English*, 2 (1940), 69-70.

(27) "Apposite and Opposite," *The Writer's Forum*, January 1941, 18-19.

(28) "Among the New Words," *American Speech*, April 1941 to February 1944 (a continuing department).

(29) "Neologisms," *American Speech*, 16 (1941), 64-67.

(30) "Heroes and Hamlets: The Protagonists of Baroja's Novels," *Hispania*, 24 (1941), 91-94.

(31) "Plurals and Collectives," *Words*, 7 (1941), 15-16.

(32) *What is Freedom? For the Individual - for Society?* Norman, Oklahoma, Cooperative Books, 1941.

(33) "Whoming," *Words*, 7 (1941), 70.

(34) "Battle of the Matics," *Word Study*, 17, No. 2 (1941), 7.

(35) *The Symbolism of Music*, Yellow Springs, Ohio, Antioch Press, 1941.

(36) "Is Our Religion Spineless?" *Christian Century*, 58 (1941), 1614.

(37) "*Need*, Auxiliary," *College English*, 4 (1942), 62-65.

(38) "About Those Exchanges," *Journal of Higher Education*, 13 (1942), 438-440.

(39) "Toward a New Conception of Grammar," *Modern Language Journal*, 27 1943), 170-174.

(40) "Son of Something," *Hispania*, 26 (1943), 184.

(41) "The Position of the Adverb in English - A Convenient Analogy to the Position of the Adjective in Spanish," *Hispania*, 26 (1943), 191-192.

(42) "*Fifth Column* Marches On," *American Speech*, 19 (1944), 47-49.

(43) "Split Infinitive," *Word Study*, 19, No. 3 (1944), 4-5.

(44) "Purpose with *Por* and *Para*," *Modern Language Journal*, 28 (1944), 15-21.

(45) "More on *Ser* and *Estar*," *Modern Language Journal*, 28 (1944), 233-238.

(46) "The Case of the Disappearing Grammar," *Hispania*, 27 (1944), 372-381.

(47) "New Words and Meanings," *Britannica Book of the Year*, 1944, 769-770.

(48) "Corina Rodríguez: Impressions of Isthmian Politics," *New Mexico Quarterly Review*, 14 (1944), 389-402.

(49) "Neuter *Todo*, Substantive," *Hispania*, 28 (1945), 78-80.

(50) "Note on the Volitional Future," *Notes and Queries*, 188 (1945), 121-123.

(51) "Inhibited and Uninhibited Stress," *Quarterly Journal of Speech*, 31 (1945), 202-207.

(52) "Universal Military Training," *Bulletin of the American Association of University Professors* , 31 (1945), 97-102.

(53) "The Minimizing Downskip," *American Speech*, 20 (1945), 40-45.
(54) "Spanish Intonation," (review) *American Speech*, 20 (1945), 128-130.
(55) "Famous Coincidences of Science," *American Journal of Pharmacy*, 117 (1945), 431-435.
(56) "Spanish Inflection," (review) *Hispania*, 18 (1945), 582-583.
(57) "*Qué tanto - Qué tan*," *Hispanic Review*, 14 (1946), 167-169.
(58) "The Intonation of Quoted Questions," *Quarterly Journal of Speech*, 32 (1946), 197-202.
(59) "Thoughts on *Yep* and *Nope*," *American Speech*, 21 (1946), 90-95.
(60) "The Future and Conditional of Probability," *Hispania*, 29 (1946), 363-375.
(61) "Visual Morphemes," *Language*, 22 (1946) 333-340.
(62) "Spanish *Parece Que* Again," *Language*, 22 (1946), 359-360.
(63) "Analogical Correlatives of *Than*," *American Speech*, 21 (1946), 199-202.
(64) "Transformación inglesa de dos palabras españolas," *América Comercial*, 1 (1947), 16.
(65) "Still More on *Ser* and *Estar*," *Hispania*, 30 (1947), 361-367.
(66) "American English Intonation," *American Speech*, 22 (1947), 134-136.
(67) "Comments on *The Intonation of American English*," (review) *Studies in Linguistics* 5 (1947), 69-78.
(68) "Dictionaries Hate To Give Offense," *Correct English*, November 1947, 39-40.
(69) "More on the Present Tense in English," *Language*, 23 (1947), 434-436.
(70) "On Defining the Morpheme," *Word*, 4 (1948), 18-23.
(71) "The Intonation of Accosting Questions," *English Studies*, 29 (1948), 109-114.
(72) "1464 Identical Cognates in English and Spanish," *Hispania* 31 (1948), 271-279.
(73) *Intensive Spanish*, Philadelphia, Russell Press, 1948.
(74) "There's Gold in Them There Sewers," *Progressive*, 13 (1949), 27.
(75) "Discontinuity of the Spanish Conjunctive Pronoun," *Language*, 25 (1949), 253-260.
(76) "The Indivisibility of Tolerance," *Bulletin of the American Association of University Professors* 35 (1949), 661-664.
(77) "Intonation and Analysis," *Word* 5 (1949), 248-254.
(78) "The *What* and the *Way*," *Language Learning*, 2 (1949), 86-88.
(79) "The Sign Is Not Arbitrary," *Boletín del Instituto Caro y Cuervo* (= *Thesaurus*), 5 (1949), 52-62.
(80) "The Comparison of Inequality in Spanish," *Language*, 26 (1950), 28-62.
(81) "*Shivaree* and the Phonestheme," *American Speech*, 25 (1950), 134-135.
(82) "Complementation Should Complement," *Studies in Linguistics*, 8 (1950), 29-39).
(83) "Retained Objects in Spanish," *Hispania*, 33 (1950), 237-239.

(84) "Rime, Assonance, and Morpheme Analysis, *Word,* 6 (1950), 117-136.
(85) "*En efecto* Does not Mean *In Fact,*" *Hispania,* 33 (1950), 349-350.
(86) "Ricardo J. Alfaro, *Diccionario de Anglicismos*" (review), *Hispania,* 33 (1950), 284-286.
(87) "Are We Playing Fair with Our Students Linguistically? *Hispania,* 34 (1951), 131-136.
(88) "Intonation: Levels Versus Configurations," *Word,* 7 (1951), 199-210.
(89) "Evidence on X," *Hispania,* 35 (1952), 49-63.
(90) "The Pronunciation of X and Puristic Anti-Purism," *Hispania,* 35 (1952), 442-444.
(91) "Ser Bien," *Hispania,* 35 (1952), 474-475.
(92) "Linear Modification," *PMLA,* 67 (1952), 1117-1144.
(93) "Addenda to the Comparison of Inequality in Spanish," *Language,* 29 (1953), 62-66.
(94) "... And Should Thereby Be Judged," *Books Abroad,* 27 (1953), 129-132.
(95) "The Life and Death of Words," *American Scholar,* 22 (1953), 323-335.
(96) "Anna Granville Hatcher, *Modern English Word-formation and Neo-Latin*" (review), *Word,* 9 (1953), 83-85.
(97) "Verbs of Being," *Hispania,* 36 (1953), 343-345.
(98) "*Next* and *Last,*" *American Speech,* 28 (1953), 232-233.
(99) "Verbs of Emotion," *Hispania,* 36 (1953), 459-461.
(100) "Salvador Fernández Ramírez, *Gramática Española*" (review), *Romance Philology,* 7 (1953), 209-215.
(101) "Articles in Old Familiar Places," *Hispania,* 37 (1954), 79-82.
(102) "Retooling Retrospect," *Modern Language Journal,* 38 (1954), 113-117.
(103) "English Prosodic Stress and Spanish Sentence Order," *Hispania,* 37 (1954), 152-156.
(104) "Education Trend: A Spanish Boom," *Los Angeles Times,* May 30, 1954, Editorial page.
(105) "Identity, Similarity, and Difference," *Litera,* 1 (1954), 5-16.
(106) "Who Is Intellectually Free?" *Journal of Higher Education,* 25 (1954), 464-468. Reprinted in the *Bulletin of the American Association of University Professors,* 41 (1955), 13-18; abridged in *Education Digest,* November 1955, 9-11.
(107) "Meaningful Word Order in Spanish," *Boletín de Filología* (Universidad de Chile), 8 (1954-1955), 45-56.
(108) "James E. Iannucci, *Lexical Number in Spanish Nouns*" (review), *Romance Philology,* 8 (1954), 111-17.
(109) "Prescriptive Statements and Mallo's Anglicisms," *Hispania,* 38 (1955), 76-78.

(110) "The Melody of Language," *Modern Language Forum*, 40 (1955), 19-30.
(111) "The Relative Importance of Grammatical Items," *Hispania*, 38 (1955), 261-264.
(112) "More on Prescribers and Describers," *Hispania*, 38 (1955), 309-311.
(113) "Intersections of Stress and Intonation," *Word*, 11 (1955), 195-203.
(114) "Intonation as Stress-Carrier," *Litera*, 2 (1955), 35-40.
(115) *Spanish Review Grammar*, New York, Holt, 1956.
(116) "Stress on Normally Unstressed Elements" and "*Contestar* Versus *Contestar a*," *Hispania*, 39 (1956), 105-106.
(117) "Subjunctive *-ra* and *-se* - Free Variation?" *Hispania*, 39 (1956), 345-349.
(118) "Mary Reifer, *Dictionary of New Words*" (review), *Modern Language Forum*, 41 (1956), 53-55.
(119) "Daniel M. Crabb, *A Comparative Study of Word Order in Old Spanish and Old French Prose Works*," (review), *Word*, 12 (1956), 148-151.
(120) "Delinquent Parents," *Progressive*, 21 (1957), 10-13.
(121) "English Stress: The Interpenetration of Strata," *The Study of Sounds*, Tokyo, Phonetic Society of Japan, 1957, 295-315.
(122) "Prepositions in English and Spanish," *Hispania*, 40 (1957), 212-214.
(123) "Locus versus Class," in *Miscelánea Homenaje a André Martinet*, Tenerife, Universidad de La Laguna, 1957. Vol.1, 31-37.
(124) "Maneuvering for Stress and Intonation," *College Composition and Communication*, 8 (1957), 234-238.
(125) "M. M. Ramsey and Robert K. Spaulding, *A Textbook of Modern Spanish*" (review) *Romance Philology*, 11 (1957), 59-64.
(126) "Disjuncture as a Cue to Constructs," *Word* 13 (1957), 246-255 (With Louis J. Gerstman).
(127) "On Certain Functions of Accents A and B," *Litera*, 4 (1957), 80-89.
(128) *Interrogative Structures of American English, Publications of the American Dialect Society*, 28, University, Ala., University of Alabama Press, 1957.
(129) "Intonation and Grammar," *Language Learning*, 8 (1957-58), 31-38.
(130) "A Theory of Pitch Accent in English," *Word*, 14 (1958), 109-149.
(131) "Stress and Information," *American Speech*, 33 (1958), 5-20.
(132) "On Intensity as a Qualitative Improvement of Pitch Accent," *Lingua*, 7 (1958), 175-182.
(133) "Gleanings from CLM: Indicative versus Subjunctive in Exclamations," *Hispania*, 42 (1959), 372-373.
(134) "The Intonation of 'Received Pronunciation,'" (review) *American Speech*, 34 (1959), 197-201.
(135) *Modern Spanish*, New York, Harcourt, Brace & World, 1960 (with J. Donald Bowen, Agnes M. Brady, Ernest F. Haden, Lawrence Poston, Jr. and Norman P. Sacks).

(136) "Cool Fountain," (Translation of verse "Fonte Frida"), *La Voz* (New York), November, 1960, 3.
(137) "To the Father of the Bomb," *Fellowship*, November 1, 1960, 9.
(138) "The President's Corner," *Hispania*, 43 (1960); 85-86, 245-246, 425-426, 579.
(139) "Linguistic Science and Linguistic Engineering," *Word*, 16 (1960), 374-391.
(140) *Generality, Gradience, and the All-or-none*, The Hague, Mouton, 1961.
(141) "Algo más que entrenamiento," *Hispania*, 44 (1961), 16-20.
(142) "Three Analogies," *Hispania*, 44 (1961), 134-137.
(143) "More on Pitfalls in Modern Language Teaching," *School and Society*, 89 (1961), 279-280.
(144) "Contrastive Accent and Contrastive Stress," *Language*, 37 (1961), 83-96.
(145) "Ambiguities in Pitch Accent," *Word*, 17 (1961), 309-317.
(146) "Verbal Evocation," *Lingua*, 10 (1961), 113-127.
(147) "Ambassador without Portfolio," *Hispania*, 44 (1961), 692-693.
(148) "Syntactic Blends and Other Matters," *Language*, 37 (1961), 366-381.
(149) "Kenneth Croft, *A Practice Book on English Stress and Intonation*" (review), *Language Learning*, 11 (1961), 189-195.
(150) "Acento melódico, acento de intensidad," *Boletín de Filología*, (1961), 33-48 (with Marion Hodapp).
(151) "Unwelcome Allies," *German Quarterly*, 35 (1962), 98.
(152) " 'Secondary Stress' in Spanish," *Romance Philology*, 15 (1962), 273-279.
(153) "J. E. Jurgens Buning and C. H. van Schooneveld: *The Sentence Intonation of Contemporary Standard Russian as a Linguistic Structure*" (review), *Language*, 38 (1962), 79-84.
(154) "Binomials and Pitch Accent," *Lingua*, 11 (1962), 34-44.
(155) "The Tragedy Must Go On," *American Liberal*, November 1962, 26.
(156) "Reference and Inference: Inceptiveness in the Spanish Preterit," *Hispania*, 46 (1963), 128-135.
(157) "It's So Fun," *American Speech*, 38 (1963), 236-240.
(158) "Donald D. Walsh: *What's What: A List of Useful Terms for the Teacher of Modern Languages*" (review), *Hispania*, 46 (1963), 866.
(159) "Where's the Teacher?" *Denver Post, Contemporary*, October 20, 1963, 8-9.
(160) "Length, Vowel, Juncture," *Linguistics*, 1 (1963), 5-29.
(161) "Robert M. W. Dixon: *Linguistic Science and Logic*" (review), *Linguistics*, 1 (1963), 104-112.
(162) "The Uniqueness of the Word," *Lingua*, 12 (1963), 113-136.
(163) "Around the Edge of Language: Intonation," *Harvard Educational Review*, 34 (1964), 282-296. Reprinted in Bolinger, *Intonation: Selected Readings*, 1972, 19-29.

(164) "Intonation as a Universal," in Horace G. Lunt, ed., *Proceedings of the Ninth International Congress of Linguists,* The Hague, Mouton, 1964, 833-848.

(165) *Forms of English: Accent, Morpheme, Order.* Edited by Isamu Abe and Tetsuya Kanekiyo. Cambridge, Harvard University Press, Tokyo, Hokuou, 1965.

(166) "Language Is for Speaking," *Harvard Graduate Society for Advanced Study and Research Newsletter,* January 15, 1965, 2-5.

(167) "Charles C. Fries, *Linguistics and Reading*" (review), *Linguistics,* 11 (1965), 57-64.

(168) "Trabajar para," *Hispania,* 48 (1965), 884-886 (with Robert Jackson).

(169) "The Atomization of Meaning," *Language,* 41 (1965), 555-573.

(170) "Transformulation: Structural Translation," *Acta Linguistica Hafniensia,* 9 (1966), 130-144.

(171) "Demonocracy: The Perversion of Consensus," *Fellowship,* March 1966, 10-11.

(172) "Georges Faure: *Recherches sur les caractères et le rôle des éléments musicaux dans la prononciation anglaise*" (review), *Language,* 42 (1966), 670-690.

(173) *Modern Spanish,* Second Edition. New York, Harcourt Brace Jovanovich, 1966 (with Joan E. Ciruti and Hugo H. Montero).

(174) "Adjective Comparison: A Semantic Scale," *Journal of English Linguistics,* 1 (1967), 2-10.

(175) "Adjectives in English: Attribution and Predication," *Lingua,* 18 (1967), 1-34.

(176) "The Foreign Language Teacher and Linguistics," in Joseph Michel, ed., *Foreign Language Teaching, an Anthology,* New York, Macmillan, 1967, 285-296.

(177) "The Imperative in English," in *To Honor Roman Jakobson,* The Hague, Mouton, 1967, 335-362.

(178) "A Grammar for Grammars: the Contrastive Structures of English and Spanish" (review), *Romance Philology* 21 (1967), 186-212.

(179) "Damned Hyphen," *American Speech* 42 (1967), 297-299.

(180) "Apparent Constituents in Surface Structure," *Word* 23 (1967), 47-56.

(181) *Aspects of Language,* New York, Harcourt, Brace, and World, 1968.

(182) "Literature Yes, but When?" *Hispania* 51 (1968), 118-119.

(183) "Postposed Main Phrases: An English Rule for the Romance Subjunctive," *Canadian Journal of Linguistics* 14 (1968), 3-30.

(184) "The Theorist and the Language Teacher," *Foreign Language Annals* 2 (1968), 30-41.

(185) "Judgments of Grammaticality," *Lingua* 21 (1968), 34-40.

(186) "Entailment and the Meaning of Structures," *Glossa* 2 (1968), 119-127.

(187) "A New Functional Linguistic Theory" (review), *American Speech* 43 (1968), 145-147.

(188) "Categories, Features, Attributes," *Brno Studies in English* 8 (1969), 37-41.

(189) "Of Undetermined Nouns and Indeterminate Reflexives," *Romance Philology* 22 (1969), 484-489.

(190) "Genericness: A 'Linguistic' Universal?" *Linguistics* 53 (1969), 5-9.

(191) "The Sound of the Bell," *Kivung* 2, No. 3 (1969), 2-7.

(192) "Modes of Modality in Spanish and English" (review), *Romance Philology* 23 (1970), 572-580.

(193) "Getting the Words In," *American Speech*, 45 (1970), 78-84. Reprinted in Raven I. McDavid, Jr. and Audrey R. Duckert, eds., *Lexicography in English. Annals of the New York Academy of Sciences*, 1973. Vol. 211, 8-13.

(194) "The Meaning of *Do So*," *Linguistic Inquiry* 1 (1970), 140-144.

(195) "The Lexical Value of *It*," *Working Papers in Linguistics* (University of Hawaii), 2, No, 8 (1970), 57-76.

(196) "Relative Height," in Pierre Léon, ed., *Prosodic Feature Analysis*, Montreal, Marcel Didier, 1970, 109-127. Reprinted in Bolinger, *Intonation: Selected Readings* (1972), 137-153.

(197) "Let's Change Our Base of Operations," *Modern Language Journal* 55 (1971), 148-156.

(198) "Contrast in Depth of Embedding," *Journal of English Linguistics* 5 (1971), 29-30.

(199) "The Nominal in the Progressive," *Linguistic Inquiry* 11 (1971), 246-250.

(200) "Intensification in English," *Language Sciences* 16 (1971), 1-5.

(201) "Semantic Overloading: A Restudy of the Verb *Remind*," *Language* 47 (1971), 522-547.

(202) "A Further Note on the Nominal in the Progressive," *Linguistic Inquiry* 2 (1971), 584-586.

(203) *The Phrasal Verb in English*, Cambridge, Harvard University Press, 1971.

(204) "Hans H. Hartvigson, *On the Intonation and Position of the So-called Sentence Modifiers in Present-Day English*" (review), *Language*, 48 (1972), 454-463.

(205) "What Did John Keep the Car That Was In?" *Linguistic Inquiry* 3 (1972), 109-114.

(206) "Adjective Position Again," *Hispania* 55 (1972), 91-94.

(207) "The Influence of Linguistics: Plus and Minus," *TESOL Quarterly* 6 (1972), 107-120.

(208) *That's That*. The Hague, Mouton, 1972.
(209) "Corporate Linguistics," *LSA Bulletin*, No. 53, (June 1972), 12-14.
(210) "Accent Is Predictable (If You're a Mind-Reader)," *Language* 48 (1972), 633-644.
(211) *Degree Words*, The Hague, Mouton, 1972.
(212) *Intonation: Selected Readings*, Harmondsworth, Penguin Books, 1972.
(213) "Das Essenz-Akzidenz-Problem," in Gerhard Nickel (Hrsg.), *Reader zur kontrastiven Linguistik*, Frankfurt am Main, Athenäum Fischer Taschenbuch Verlag, 1972, 147-156.
(214) "The Syntax of *Parecer*," in Albert Valdman, ed., *Papers in Linguistics and Phonetics to the Memory of Pierre Delattre*, The Hague and Paris, Mouton, 1972, 65-76.
(215) "A Look at Equations and Cleft Sentences," in Evelyn Scherabon Firchow et al., eds., *Studies for Einar Haugen, Presented by Friends and Colleagues*, The Hague and Paris, Mouton, 1972, 96-114.
(216) "Objective and Subjective: Sentences Without Performatives," *Linguistic Inquiry* 4 (1973), 414-417.
(217) "Truth Is a Linguistic Question," *Language* 49 (1973), 539-550.
(218) "Ambient *It* Is Meaningful Too," *Journal of Linguistics*, 9 (1973), 261-270.
(219) "Essence and Accident: English Analogs of Hispanic *Ser-Estar*," in Braj B. Kachru et al., eds., *Issues in Linguistics: Papers in Honor of Henry and Renée Kahane*, Urbana, Illinois, University of Illinois Press, 1973, 58-69.
(220) "Meaning and Form," *Transactions of the New York Academy of Sciences*, 36 (Series II) (1974), 218-233.
(221) "El español para los angloparlantes," *Vórtice* (Stanford University) 1 (1974), 82-92.
(222) "*Do* Imperatives," *Journal of English Linguistics* 8 (1974), 1-5.
(223) "*Darn, Durn, Down, Doon, Damn*," *Verbatim* 1 (1974), No. 1, 1-2.
(224) "*John's Easiness to Please," in Gerhard Nickel, ed., *Special Issue of IRAL on the Occasion of Bertil Malmberg's 60th Birthday*, Heidelberg, Julius Groos Verlag, 1974, 17-28.
(225) "One Subjunctive or Two?" *Hispania* 57 (1974), 462-471.
(226) "Concept and Percept: Two Infinitive Constructions and Their Vicissitudes," in *World Papers in Phonetics: Festschrift for Dr. Onishi's Kiju*, Tokyo, Phonetic Society of Japan, 1974, 65-91.
(227) "Postscript to Poston on the Article," *Modern Language Journal*, 59 (1975), 181-185.
(228) *Aspects of Language*, Second Edition. New York, Harcourt Brace Jovanovich, 1975.

(229) "A Common-Sense Solution to the Canning-Lid Crisis," *Media and Consumer*, August 1975, 9.

(230) "George Steiner, *After Babel*" (review), *Verbatim*, 2 No. 2, (1975), 6-8. Expanded version in *Language Sciences*, 43 (1976), 28-32.

(231) "A Note on *Can* and *Be Able*," *Kritikon Litterarum*, 4 (1975), 71-73.

(232) "Are You a Sincere *H*-Dropper?" *American Speech*, 50 (1975), 313-15.

(233) "The In-Group: *One* and Its Compounds," in Peter A. Reich, ed., *The Second LACUS Forum*, 1975, Columbia, S.C., Hornbeam, 1976, 229-37.

(234) "Again--One or Two Subjunctives?" *Hispania*, 59 (1976), 41-49.

(235) "Adam Makkai, *Idiom Structure in English*" (review), *Language*, 52 (1976), 238-41.

(236) "Ralph Long--1906-1976," *TESOL Quarterly*, 10 (1976), 259-61.

(237) "Meaning and Memory," *Forum Linguisticum*, 1 (1976), 1-14.

(238) "Gradience in Entailment," *Language Sciences*, 41 (1976), 1-13.

(239) "The Price of Language," in Adam and Valerie Makkai, eds., *The Third LACUS Forum, 1976*, Columbia, S.C., Hornbeam, 1977, 3-11.

(240) "Pronouns and Repeated Nouns," Indiana University Linguistics Club, March 1977.

(241) *Meaning and Form*. London and New York, Longman, 1977. Japanese translation, Kobian, 1981.

(242) "Another Glance at Main Clause Phenomena," *Language* 53 (1977), 511-19.

(243) "Idioms Have Relations," *Forum Linguisticum*, 2 (1977), 157-69.

(244) "Transitivity and Spatiality: The Passive of Prepositional Verbs," in Adam Makkai, Valerie Becker Makkai, and Luigi Heilmann, eds., *Linguistics at the Crossroads*, Padova, Italy, Liviana Editrice, and Lake Bluff, Illinois, Jupiter Press, 1977, 57-78.

(245) "Neutrality, Norm, and Bias," Indiana University Linguistics Club, December 1977.

(246) "Susan F. Schmerling, *Aspects of English Sentence Stress*" *The Finite String: American Journal of Computational Linguistics*, 14 (1977), No. 5, AJCL Microfiche 68.

(247) "Yes-No Questions Are Not Alternative Questions," in Henry Hiz, ed., *Questions*. Dordrecht, Reidel, 1978, 87-105.

(248) "Asking More than One Thing at a Time," in Henry Hiz, ed., *Questions*. Dordrecht, Reidel, 1978, 107-150.

(249) "Intonation Across Languages," in Joseph H. Greenberg, ed., *Universals of Human Language*. Vol. 2, *Phonology*, Stanford, Stanford University Press, 1978, 471-524.

(250) "Free Will and Determinism in Language: Or, Who Does the Choosing, the Grammar or the Speaker?" in Margarita Suñer, ed.,

Contemporary Studies in Romance Linguistics. Washington, D.C.: Georgetown University Press, 1978, 1-17.

(251) "A Semantic View of Syntax: Some Verbs that Govern Infinitives," in Mohammed Ali Jazayeri, Edgar C. Polomé, and Werner Winter, eds., *Linguistic and Literary Studies in Honor of Archibald A. Hill*, Lisse, The Netherlands, Peter de Ridder Press, 1978. Vol. 2, 9-18.

(252) "Passive and Transitivity Again," *Forum Linguisticum*, 3 (1978), 25-28.

(253) "Pronouns in Discourse," in Talmy Givón, ed., *Syntax and Semantics, Vol. 12: Discourse and Syntax*, New York, Academic Press, 1979, 289-309.

(254) "The Jingle Theory of Double *-ing*," in D. J. Allerton, Edward Carney, and David Holdcroft, eds., *Function and Context in Linguistic Analysis: A Festschrift for William Haas*, Cambridge, Cambridge University Press, 1979, 41-56.

(255) "For Hugo Montero," *Modern Language Journal* 63 (1979), 243-250 (with Raquel Halty Ferguson, Lorraine Ledford and Barbara F. Weissberger).

(256) "To Catch a Metaphor: *You* as Norm," *American Speech*, 54 (1979), 194-209.

(257) "Metaphorical Aggression: Bluenoses and Coffin Nails," in James E. Alatis and G. Richard Tucker, eds., *Language in Public Life*, Washington, D. C., Georgetown University Press, 1979, 258-271.

(258) "The Socially-Minded Linguist," *Modern Language Journal*, 63 (1979), 404-407.

(259) Foreword to Talmy Givón, *On Understanding Grammar*, New York, Academic Press, 1979, xi-xii.

(260) "*Couple:* An English Dual," in Sidney Greenbaum, Geoffrey Leech, and Jan Svartvik, eds., *Studies in English Linguistics for Randolph Quirk*, London and New York, Longman, 1980, 30-41.

(261) "Syntactic Diffusion and the Indefinite Article," Indiana University Linguistics Club, June 1980.

(262) *Language: The Loaded Weapon*. London and New York, Longman, 1980. Japanese translation, Kobian, 1988.

(263) "Intonation and Nature," in Mary LeCron Foster and Stanley H. Brandes, eds., *Symbol as Sense*. New York, Academic Press, 1980, 9-23.

(264) "The Personhood of *Who*," *Studia Linguistica*, 34 (1980), 1-6.

(265) "Accents that Determine Stress," in Mary Key, ed., *The Relationship of Verbal and Nonverbal Communication*, The Hague, Mouton, 1980, 37-47.

(266) *Aspects of Language*, Third Edition, New York, Harcourt Brace Jovanovich, 1980 (with Donald A. Sears).

(267) Foreword to Roger W. Wescott, *Sound and Sense: Linguistic Essays on Phonosemic Subjects*, Lake Bluff, Illinois, Jupiter Press, 1980, xi-xii.
(268) "*Wanna* and the Gradience of Auxiliaries," in Gunter Brettschneider and Christian Lehmann, eds., *Wege zur Universalien Forschung*, Tübingen, Gunter Narr Verlag, 1980, 292-299.
(269) "Progress Report on *One of Those Who Is*," *American Speech*, 55 (1980), 288-294.
(270) "Fire in a Wooden Stove: On Being Aware in Language," in Leonard Michaels and Christopher Ricks, eds., *The State of the Language*, Berkeley, Los Angeles, London, University of California Press, 1980, 379-388.
(271) "A Not Impartial Review of a Not Unimpeachable Theory," in Roger W. Shuy and Anna Shnukal, eds., *Language Use and the Uses of Language*, Washington, D.C., Georgetown University Press, 1980, 53-67.
(272) "An Uncouth Preposition," *Boletin de Filología*, 31 (1980-81), 625-632.
(273) "The Deflation of *Several*," *Journal of English Linguistics*, 15 (1981) 1-4.
(274) "Voice Imprints," *New York Times Magazine*, 26 July 1981, 7-8.
(275) "Some Intonation Stereotypes in English," in Pierre Léon and Mario Rossi, eds., *Problèmes de Prosodie*: Vol. II, *Expérimentations, Modèles et Fonctions*, Ottawa, Didier, 1981, 97-101.
(276) "Two Kinds of Vowels, Two Kinds of Rhythm," Indiana University Linguistics Club, 1981.
(277) "To Bury the Hatchetmen," *Verbatim*, 8 (1981), 22-23.
(278) "Consonance, Dissonance, and Grammaticalilty: The Case of *Wanna*," *Language and Communication*, 1 (1981), 189-206.
(279) "Intonation and Its Parts," *Language*, 58 (1982), 505-533.
(280) "Usage and Acceptability in Language," *American Heritage Dictionary*, Second College Edition, 1982, Boston, Houghton Mifflin, 30-33.
(281) "The Network Tone of Voice," *Journal of Broadcasting*, 26 (1982), 725-28.
(282) "Nondeclaratives from an Intonational Standpoint," in Robinson Schneider, Kevin Tuite, and Robert Chametzky, eds., *Papers from the Parasession on Nondeclaratives*, Chicago, Chicago Linguistics Society, 1982, 1-22.
(283) "On Pre-Accentual Lengthening," *Journal of the International Phonetic Association*, 12 (1982), 58-71 (with Richard Dasher).
(284) "Intonation and Gesture," *American Speech*, 58 (1983), 156-174.
(285) "Where Does Intonation Belong?" *Journal of Semantics*, 2 (1983), 101-120.
(286) "Affirmation and Default," *Folia Linguistica*, 17 (1983), 99-116.

(287) "The *Go*-Progressive and Auxiliary Formation," in Frederick B. Agard et al., eds., *Essays in Honor of Charles F. Hockett*, Leiden, E. J. Brill, 1983, 153-67.

(288) "Intonational Signals of Subordination," in Claudia Brugman and Monica Macaulay, eds., Berkeley Linguistics Society, *Proceedings of the Tenth Annual Meeting*. Berkeley Linguistics Society, 1984, 401-414.

(289) "Surprise," in Lawrence J. Raphael, Carolyn B. Raphael, and Miriam R. Valdovinos, eds., *Language and Cognition: Essays in Honor of Arthur J. Bronstein*, New York and London, Plenum Press, 1984, 45-58.

(290) "Two Views of Accent," *Journal of Linguistics*, 21 (1985) 79-123.

(291) "Defining the Indefinable," in Robert Ilson, ed., *Dictionaries, Lexicography and Language Learning*, ELT Documents 120, Oxford, Pergamon Press, 1985, 69-73.

(292) "The Inherent Iconism of Intonation," in John Haiman, ed., *Iconicity in Syntax*, Amsterdam and Philadelphia, John Benjamins, 1985, 97-108.

(293) "Intonation and Emotion," *Quaderni di Semantica*, 7 (1986), 13-21.

(294) *Intonation and Its Parts: Melody in Spoken English*, Stanford, Stanford University Press, 1986.

(295) "The English Beat: Some Notes on Rhythm," in Gerhard Nickel and James C. Stalker (eds.), *Problems of Standardization and Linguistic Variation in Present-Day English*. Heidelberg, Groos, 1986, 36-49.

(296) "*As* Strikes Back," *American Speech* 61 (1986), 332-336.

(297) "Intonation," in Thomas A. Sebeok, ed., *Encyclopedic Dictionary of Semiotics*, Berlin, Mouton de Gruyter, 1986. Vol. 1, 389-391.

(298) "*Each Other* and its Friends," in *Another Indiana University Linguistics Club Twentieth Anniversary Volume*, Bloomington, 1987, 1-36.

(299) "Power to the Utterance," in Jon Aske, Natasha Beery, Laura Michaelis, and Hana Filip, eds., Berkeley Linguistics Society, *Proceedings of the 13th Annual Meeting*, Berkeley, Berkeley Linguistics Society, 1987, 15-25.

(300) "The Remarkable Double *Is*," *English Today*, 9 (1987), 39-40.

(301) "Echoes Reechoed," *American Speech*, 62 (1987), 261-79.

(302) *On Accent*. Indiana University Linguistics Club, 1987 (with Carlos Gussenhoven and Cornelia Keijsper).

(303) "El español para los angloparlantes," in Joaquim Mattoso Camara J. et al., eds., *Atas do II Congresso Internacional da Associação de Lingüistica e Filologia da America Latina (ALFAL)*, São Paulo (Brasil) Janeiro de 1969. São Paulo, Universidade de São Paulo, Faculdade de Filosofia, Letras e Ciências Humanas, 1987, 65-76.

(304) "*One Each* in English and Spanish," in Joseph V. Ricapito, ed., *Hispanic Studies in Honor of Joseph H. Silverman*, Newark, Delaware, Juan de la Cuesta, 1988, 361-369.

(305) "May Day," *English Today*, 13 = 4 (1988) 5.

(306) "The Infinitive as Complement of Nouns in Spanish and English," in J. Klegraf and D. Nehls, eds., *Essays on the English Languae and Applied Linguistics on the Occasion of Gerhard Nickel's 60th Birthday.* Heidelberg, Groos, 1988, 227-234.

(307) "Bengt Altenberg, *Prosodic Patterns in Spoken English: Studies in the Correlation between Prosody and Grammar for Text-to-Speech conversion* (Lund Studies in English 76, Lund University Press, 1987)" (review), *Lingua, 76 (1988), 348-358.*

(308) "Anticipatory Lengthening," *Journal of Phonetics*, 16 (1988), 339-347 (with Diana Van Lanckerand Jody Kreiman).

(309) "Ataxis," in Rokko Linguistic Society, ed., *Gendai no Gengo Kenkyu (Linguistics Today)*, Tokyo, Kinseido, 1988, 1-17.

(310) "Extrinsic Possibility and Intrinsic Potentiality: 7 on *May* and *Can* + 1," *Journal of Pragmatics*, 13 (1989), 1-23.

(311) *Intonation and Its Uses: Melody in Grammar and Discourse.* Stanford, Stanford University Press, 1989.

(312) "Flux," in Kira Hall, Michael Meacham and Richard Shapiro, eds., *Proceedings of the 15th Annual Meeting of the Berkeley Linguistics Society.* Berkeley, 1989, 15-23.